THE NEW TESTAMENT BACKGROUND: SELECTED DOCUMENTS

Edited, with introductions,

by

C. K. BARRETT

HARPER TORCHBOOKS / The Cloister Library

HARPER & ROW, PUBLISHERS

New York

THE NEW TESTAMENT BACKGROUND

Printed in the United States of America

First published by S.P.C.K., London, in 1956
and reprinted by arrangement.

First HARPER TORCHBOOK edition published 1961

CONTENTS

INDEXES

ACKNOWLEDGEMENTS

ACKNOWLEDGEMENTS are due to the following for permission to reproduce copyright translations:

The Clarendon Press: 1 (E. G. Hardy, *Monumentum Ancyranum*); 68, 69, 70, 79 (P. E. Matheson, *Epictetus: The Discourses and Manual*); 77 (Gilbert Murray, *Five Stages of Greek Religion*); 78 (C. Bailey, *Epicurus*); 97–105, 207–10, 212–23, 225 (R. H. Charles, ed., *The Apocrypha and Pseudepigrapha of the Old Testament*); 127–32, 134–8, 140, 142, 147–50, 152–7, 165, 168, 170–8 (H. Danby, *The Mishnah*).

T. and T. Clark and Charles Scribner's Sons: 13 (A. Roberts, *Sulpicius Severus*); 123, 124, 198 (A. C. McGiffert, *Eusebius: Ecclesiastical History*)—both in the series Nicene and Post-Nicene Christian Fathers.

J. M. Dent and Sons, Ltd, and the Beacon Press: 59–67 (E. Bevan, *Later Greek Religion*).

The Egypt Exploration Society: 36 (B. P. Grenfell and A. S. Hunt, *Oxyrhynchus Papyri*, Vol. I).

The Loeb Classical Library: 3 (C. E. Bennett, *Horace*); 6, 7 (J. Jackson, *Tacitus: Annals*); 8, 106–21, 125, 192–5, 199–205 (H. St J. Thackeray and R. Marcus, *Josephus*); 9, 12, 14, 16, 17 (J. C. Rolfe, *Suetonius*); 18 (W. Peterson, *Tacitus: Agricola*); 19 (H. Rackham, *Pliny*); 20–6, 30–4, 38–45 (A. S. Hunt and C. C. Edgar, *Papyri*); 71–6 (C. R. Haines, *Marcus Aurelius*); 80–2 (F. C. Conybeare, *Philostratus*); 83 (F. C. Conybeare, *Apollonius of Tyana*); 91 (F. C. Babbitt, *Plutarch*); 92 (E. H. Gifford, *Eusebius*); 94 (W. Adlington, rev. S. Gaselee, *Apuleius*); 122 (E. Cary, *Dio Cassius*); 126, 179–91, 206 (F. H. Colson and G. H. Whitaker, *Philo*).

Macmillan and Company, Ltd: 46 (F. J. Foakes-Jackson and K. Lake, *The Beginnings of Christianity*).

L. N. G. Montefiore, Esq: 141, 144, 145, 166 (C. G. Montefiore and H. Loewe, *A Rabbinic Anthology*).

John Murray (Publishers) Ltd: 15 (G. G. Ramsay, *The Histories of Tacitus*).

The Oxford University Press: 4 (J. Rhoades, *The Poems of Virgil*).

The Singer's Prayer-Book Publication Committee: 158–64 (S. Singer, *The Authorised Daily Prayer Book*).

The University of California: 28, 29, 35, 37 (B. P. Grenfell, A. S. Hunt, and E. S. Goodspeed, *Tebtunis Papyri*, Vol. II).

Other passages have been translated by the following: 10: F. de Zulueta (in *The Journal of Roman Studies*); 11: A. J. Church and W. J. Brodribb (*The Annals of Tacitus*); 27: A. Deissmann (*Light from the Ancient East*); 57, 58: B. Jowett (*The Dialogues of Plato*); 95: W. Whiston; 167: F. Gavin (*Jewish Antecedents of the Christian Sacraments*); 169: J. Jocz (*The Jewish People and Jesus Christ*); 2, 47–56, 84–90, 93, 96, 133, 139, 143, 146, 151, 196, 197: the Editor. 211 and 224 are taken from the Revised Version.

INTRODUCTION

SOME years ago I bought a copy of a small book by the late Paul Fiebig: *Die Umwelt des Neuen Testamentes: Religionsgeschichtliche und Geschichtliche Texte, in deutscher Übersetzung und mit Anmerkungen versehen, zum Verständnis des Neuen Testamentes* (Göttingen, 1926). It occurred to me at once that a similar work would be of great use to English students of the New Testament. There are not a few books which describe the history and thought of the world in which the Church was born, but none (so far as I know) which offers the reader a selection of those original documents which alone can make this past world live. The undergraduate reading Theology at a university hears constantly of papyri and inscriptions, of philosophers and emperors, of Rabbis and apocalyptists, of writers such as Philo and Josephus, of soldiers such as Judas Maccabaeus and Titus, without perhaps knowing any of them at first hand. Even if he has read Classics before turning to Theology, his knowledge may not extend far beyond the borders of the Roman Empire, and the more respectable Greek and Latin philosophical and historical writers. He has probably not read the *Hermetica*, and he has certainly not read the Talmud. Most men will never read such works, and even the best men will read little of them while they are undergraduates: all therefore might well be grateful for an opportunity of consulting a selection of ancient literature, all of it relevant to the New Testament, but some of it not readily accessible.

My first thought was to translate, or at least imitate, Fiebig's book; but it soon appeared that his method—of taking New Testament topics and illustrating them—would not suit my purpose, for though I hoped to assist New Testament studies I did not wish to reduplicate but rather to make more intelligible the material already available in many excellent commentaries. The world of the first century (or thereabouts) is worth studying for its own sake, and when studied for its own sake it becomes even more valuable as the setting in which the Christian faith appeared. I therefore drew up a plan of my own, intended to cover as far as possible the period under review. That many gaps remain, and must inevitably remain, is very clear to me, but I hope that the book as a whole gives an accurate and fair (and not unreadable) account of the ancient world; at least, I have tried hard to understand sympathetically every author I have quoted.

The selection, arrangement, and annotation of the passages quoted have occupied a good deal of my leisure during the last few years. Now that at length the work has been completed, I hope it may prove useful not only to undergraduates reading Theology, who were in my mind at the beginning, but to many other classes of reader also, and especially to those who, in Church or school, teach the New Testament.

My indebtedness to many translators is indicated in detail above; I have regularly checked their work, but it must not be assumed that I agree in every detail with all the versions I have quoted. As far as possible I have made consistent the capitalization, italicization, and spelling of transliterated words. I have also introduced consistency by indicating conjectural and explanatory supplements always by means of square brackets [ ]; mere grammatical supplements, which are often necessary in translation from ancient languages, are not indicated.

C. K. BARRETT

Durham

THE SOURCES[1]

Chapter 1

The story of the Roman Empire has long been familiar from well-known literary sources; in more recent times these have been supplemented by the use of evidence drawn from inscriptions, papyri, and coins.

The literary evidence is of different kinds, and of unequal value. Augustus's *Res Gestae*, though hardly an inspiring document, should not be missed; it is one of the few first-hand sources, drawn up by a leading actor in the story, and perhaps is none the worse for being as matter-of-fact as its author. The history of the whole period is told by Tacitus in the *Annals* and the *Histories*. It is not a perfect account, for it is tendentious, and parts of it have been lost; but even so it is a classical piece of historical writing, and on the whole Tacitus is faithful to his facts, though the interpretation he puts upon them is his own affair. Suetonius tells the same story in a different form and with less power in his books on the *Twelve Caesars*; and other historians, such as Appian and Dio Cassius, are of less importance for our purpose.

After reading Augustus himself and Tacitus, the student should look at the indirect literary evidence, the work of the literary men and philosophers of the period. Above all, Virgil claims attention, both in the *Aeneid*, which provides a religious and philosophical background for the achievements of Augustus and the greatness of Rome, and in the *Eclogues* and *Georgics*, which tell of the Italian's love for his native countryside. Other poets of the period take us for the most part into a different atmosphere; Horace, and still more Ovid, and satirists such as Martial and Juvenal, reflect the more sophisticated life of the city. Seneca may be read for practical Roman philosophy; interesting and often amusing glimpses of character and social custom under the Empire can be found in, for example, the works of Lucian, in *Trimalchio's Supper* (Petronius), and in the *Metamorphoses* (Apuleius).

For the use of papyri and inscriptions see below. The study of coins is a speciality which few can pursue at first hand; the student of early Christianity will find a striking example of its use in E. Stauffer's *Christ and the Caesars* (E. T., London, 1955).

---

[1] In this note, which, it is hoped, may be of service to those who wish to study in greater detail the matters dealt with in this book, I have kept in mind throughout the needs of the reader who knows no language but English.

Chapter 2.

The reader who wishes to see more of the daily life of the Empire revealed in the papyri cannot do better than use the volumes of A. S. Hunt and C. C. Edgar, referred to on p. 27. A smaller collection is that of G. Milligan, *Selections from the Greek Papyri* (Cambridge, 1927). He may see how a special problem is illuminated by papyri in *Jews and Christians in Egypt* (by H. I. Bell; London and Oxford, 1924). When he has exhausted collections such as these he must turn to the full-scale publications of papyri, such as *The Oxyrhynchus Papyri,* of which the first volume appeared in 1898, the twenty-second in 1954. Such a row of volumes may appear forbidding, but the contents are well tabulated and indexed, and it is easy to dip into them.

Chapter 3.

Inscriptions, unfortunately, are not so easily accessible; indeed, the reader who does not intend to use Latin and Greek can make very little headway with the subject. The most considerable collection of inscriptions provided with translations is perhaps that of the series *Monumenta Asiae Minoris Antiqua.* As its title implies, this series deals with only one part of the ancient world; but it serves as an excellent introduction. Further may be mentioned the very useful collections of W. Dittenberger (*Sylloge Inscriptionum Graecarum,* and *Orientis Graecae Inscriptiones Selectae*); and the three great *corpora*—*Corpus Inscriptionum Graecarum, Corpus Inscriptionum Latinarum,* and *Corpus Inscriptionum Semiticarum.*

Chapter 4.

The pre-Socratic philosophers are of doubtful importance for the student of early Christianity; the extant fragments of their works are translated in K. Freeman's *Ancilla to the Pre-Socratic Philosophers* (Blackwell, Oxford, 1948).

The story of Socrates is presumably still common knowledge. The essential parts of it can be conveniently read in the Penguin volume, *The Last Days of Socrates.* For Plato himself it is, perhaps, best to begin with the *Republic,* which provides an introduction to both his philosophical and his political thought. In Aristotle's *Nicomachean Ethics* the reader will find valuable discussions of a number of ethical and religious terms which reappear—though by no means always with the same meanings—in the New Testament.

The surviving works of Epicurus are not many; they are translated by C. Bailey in his book *Epicurus* (Oxford, 1926).

The earlier Stoics are difficult of access to the English reader. The fragments of their works are admirably collected in H. von Arnim, *Stoicorum Veterum Fragmenta* (four volumes, Leipzig, 1903–24), but no one has yet done for this volume what Miss Freeman (see above) has done for H. Diels, *Fragmente der Vorsokratiker* (three volumes, Berlin, 1951, 1952). There is, however, an excellent selection in E. Bevan's *Later Greek Religion* (London, 1927), an admirable collection of documents. Epictetus and Marcus Aurelius are available in several translations, and are well worth serious study.

Those commonly called "philosophers" were not the only Greek thinkers who pondered deeply the problems of human existence. The great tragic poets, Aeschylus, Sophocles, and Euripides, are among the most important representatives of the Greek power to observe and consider, and their work is a significant part of the New Testament background.

Finally, the student may be recommended to read through Philostratus's *Life of Apollonius of Tyana,* which provides a striking picture not only of this itinerant philosopher but also of the life of the Graeco-Roman world; and is a very entertaining story too.

Chapter 5.

It is no great task to read through the whole of the *Corpus Hermeticum*; in addition, however, to the first tractate (*Poimandres*), tractates 4, 10, and 13 may be picked out as specially rewarding. They can be read in English translation in the edition of W. Scott (Volume I, Oxford, 1924), but it should be noted that Scott treated the MS. text of the *Corpus* with considerable freedom. A more conservative text, together with a French translation, is given by A. D. Nock and A. J. Festugière (Collection Budé, Paris; Volumes I and II, 1945; Volumes III and IV, 1954).

Chapter 6.

For the reasons given below (p. 91), study of the Mystery Religions is very difficult, and there are few simple, straightforward texts that can be recommended for reading. The whole of Apuleius's *Metamorphoses* xi (part of which is quoted: **94**) may be read; and Euripides's *Bacchae.* Beyond these works, the reader may be referred to the exemplary treatment of one mystery religion by F. Cumont in *The Mysteries of Mithra*

(E. T., London and Chicago, 1910), or, better still, by the same author in *Textes et Monuments Figurés relatifs aux Mystères de Mithra* (two volumes, Brussels, 1896, 1899). See also M. J. Vermaseren, *Corpus Inscriptionum Religionis Mithriacae* (The Hague, 1956).

Chapter 7.

The story of the Jews in the Maccabean period is told in 1 and 2 Maccabees. The history is taken further by Josephus; see the *War* and *Antiquities* xii–xx. These are the main, and indispensable, sources. Parallel narratives, Jewish and non-Jewish, exist here and there; most of them are referred to in the notes in the edition of Josephus in the Loeb Classical Library, and need not be specified here.

Chapter 8.

An admirable introduction to reading in the Rabbinic literature is provided in *A Rabbinic Anthology,* edited by C. G. Montefiore and H. Loewe (London, 1938). It is of course true that, as the editors point out, their anthology *is* an anthology—that is, they were interested in collecting flowers, not weeds; and the weeds which undoubtedly exist in so wide a field are not found in the anthology. When this book of extracts has been used the reader should attempt a solid and continuous piece. There are two means to this end. One is the invaluable translation of the whole Mishnah by H. Danby (Oxford, 1933). The other is the series of Rabbinical texts (mostly Mishnah tractates) published by the S.P.C.K. Some of these contain text only, some text and translation, some translation only. The following Mishnah tractates are recommended for introductory study: Berakoth, Shabbath, Pesahim, Yoma, Sukkah, Megillah, Nedarim, Sanhedrin, Abodah Zarah, Aboth. Among the early midrashim, there is a very convenient edition of Mekilta (text and translation) by J. Z. Lauterbach (Philadelphia, 1933–1935). Valuable English translations of the later and longer Rabbinic texts are in course of publication by the Soncino Press.

Chapter 9.

For all but the philosopher, Philo is best approached by way of his historical writings, the book against Flaccus (*In Flaccum*), and the account of the Jewish mission from Alexandria to the Emperor Gaius (*Legatio ad Gaium*). These works show Philo as a loyal Jew, an aspect of his character which is of fundamental importance, though it is easy in his more philosophical writings to lose sight of it. From these straightforward narratives (which incidentally are historical documents of great importance) it is possible to work back to books like that *On Abraham,* where Philo retells the Biblical story, and draws from it on the whole moral rather than metaphysical lessons. Finally (though Philo himself might have reckoned it first in importance) may be read the detailed allegorical exposition of the Pentateuch. Much of Philo's most characteristic speculative thought is to be found in *On the Creation of the World* and *Allegories of the Laws,* both of which deal with the first few verses of Genesis and accordingly allow Philo to develop his cosmology.

Chapter 10.

Some of the works of Josephus were referred to above. There is much to be said for beginning the study of Josephus with the *Life* (in which he recapitulates a good deal of the story of the war with Rome) and the apologetic work *Against Apion.* The earlier books of the *Antiquities* may be left till last; for the most part Josephus rewrites in his own words the stories of the Old Testament, and rarely if ever improves them.

Chapter 11.

The Septuagint may be studied from two points of view. In the first place, it is most instructive (not least for the student of the New Testament) to set side by side and compare the Hebrew and Greek texts of the Old Testament. Through the Greek, Hebraic thought and speech came into the New Testament, but at the same time the Hebraic contents of the Old Testament suffered a measure of transposition. This kind of study of course requires knowledge of Hebrew and Greek. In the second place, the Septuagint presents the reader with a number of books not contained in the Hebrew Bible. These may be read in the Apocrypha published with or as supplementary to the ordinary English Bible; or, with commentaries, in *The Apocrypha and Pseudepigrapha of the Old Testament,* edited by R. H. Charles (Oxford, 1913; two volumes—the apocryphal books, with the exception of 4 Ezra (2 Esdras), are in the first). This edition is indispensable to the serious student of the subject. There are very useful volumes in the S.P.C.K. series (see above).

Of the apocryphal books, 1 and 2 Maccabees were referred to above; the Wisdom of Solomon, and Ecclesiasticus, belong to the Wisdom literature; Tobit and Judith are religious and moral romances; 4 Ezra is an apocalypse.

The whole of the Epistle of Aristeas, with its long (and legendary) account of the making of the Septuagint, can be read in the second volume of Charles's *Apocrypha and Pseudepigrapha*.

Chapter 12.

For the Apocalypses the second volume of Charles's work is indispensable, and the appropriate volumes in the S.P.C.K. series referred to above are very valuable. The apocalyptic material contained in the Old Testament itself (notably Daniel) should not be neglected. Out of the material contained in Charles's second volume, 4 Ezra, the Similitudes of Enoch (i.e. 1 Enoch 37–71), 2 Baruch, and the Testaments of the Twelve Patriarchs (though here Christian influence—and even Christian authorship—may be suspected) may be recommended for study.

I

THE ROMAN EMPIRE

A. *Augustus and the Imperial Settlement*

THE roots of that Empire in which the Christian faith was born ran deep and in many directions, not only into the Roman Republic but also into the Macedonian Empire of Alexander, and the Greek city states. Eventually, the Empire was able to seek philosophical justification in the cosmopolitanism of developed Stoicism (see pp. 71f., 74ff.); but at first it needed no justification beyond its own achievements. A world weary of civil war with its attendant social and economic disturbance and distress was prepared to welcome the victor of Actium as a saviour—after all, what more did the average man ask of his gods than the peace, security, and social welfare Augustus gave him? Of course, there were some malcontents. The senatorial families deplored changes which deprived them of the substance of power and placed it in the hands of one man, armed with an ultimate, if generally veiled, authority over life and property. But to the majority the Senate mattered little, and the provinces knew that they were far better governed than ever they had been under the Republic.

The character, motives, and intentions of Augustus; the political basis of the imperial constitution; the varying relations between the Emperors and the Senate—these all present historical problems of unusual depth and complexity. Here, at the risk of undue simplification, will be given only a few passages illustrating the work of Augustus and some of the succeeding Emperors.

1 *Res Gestae Divi Augusti* 12f., 24–7, 34f. Towards the close of his life, Augustus deposited with the Vestal Virgins four documents. One was his will, disposing of his personal property. Of the remaining three, one contained directions for the celebration of his funeral, another an account of the things he had done (*rerum a se gestarum*; Suetonius, *Augustus* 101), and the third a military and financial account of the state of the Empire. The brass tablets on which, pursuant to Augustus's

1

instructions, the *Res Gestae* were engraved have not been found; but the greater part of the document has been recovered from a bilingual (Greek-Latin) inscription in the temple of Rome and Augustus at Ancyra (the *Monumentum Ancyranum*), now supplemented by a Greek text found at Apollonia (in Pisidia) and a Latin found at Antioch (also in Pisidia). There can be little doubt that the *Res Gestae* were compiled partly for the purposes of propaganda; but the substantial accuracy of the facts contained in them seems to fail only through a few small lapses of memory.

At the same time, by decree of the Senate, a portion of the praetors and tribunes of the plebs, together with the consul, Q. Lucretius, and other men of note, were sent as far as Campania to meet my arrival, an honour which up to this day has been decreed
5 to none other but myself.

When in the consulship of Tiberius Nero and P. Quintilius I returned to Rome from Spain and Gaul after settling the affairs of those provinces with success, the Senate, to commemorate my return, ordered an altar to Pax Augusta to be consecrated in the
10 Campus Martius, at which it decreed that the magistrates, priests, and Vestal Virgins should celebrate an anniversary sacrifice.

Whereas our ancestors have willed that the gateway of Janus Quirinus should be shut, whenever victorious peace is secured by sea and by land throughout the empire of the Roman people, and
15 whereas before my birth twice only in all is it on record that the gateway has been shut, three times under my principate has the Senate decreed that it should be shut. . . .

After my victory I replaced in the temples of all the communities of the province of Asia the ornaments which my adversary in the
20 war had, after despoiling the temples, taken into his own possession.

Silver statues of myself, standing or on horseback or sitting in a chariot, were set up in the city to the number of about eighty, which I myself took down, and out of the money value I set up
25 gifts of gold in the temple of Apollo in my own name and in the names of those who had honoured me with the statues. I conquered the pirates and gave peace to the seas. In that war I handed over to their masters for punishment nearly 30,000 slaves who had run away from their owners, and taken up arms against the republic.
30 The whole of Italy of its own free will took the oath of fidelity to me, and demanded me as its leader in the war of which Actium was the crowning victory. An oath was also taken to the same effect by the provinces of Gaul, Spain, Africa, Sicily, and Sardinia.

Among those who at that time served under my standards were
35 more than seven hundred senators; out of that number, either
before that date or afterwards, up to the day on which these
records were written, eighty-three attained the consulship, and
about one hundred and seventy were elected to priesthoods.

I extended the frontiers of all the provinces of the Roman
40 people, which had as neighbours races not obedient to our empire.

I restored peace to all the provinces of Gaul and Spain and to
Germany, to all that region washed by the Ocean from Gades to
the mouth of the Elbe.

Peace too I caused to be established in the Alps from the region
45 nearest to the Hadriatic as far as the Tuscan sea, while no tribe was
wantonly attacked by war.

My fleet sailed along the Ocean from the mouth of the Rhine as
far towards the east as the borders of the Cimbri, whither no
Roman before that time had penetrated either by land or sea. The
50 Cimbri and the Charydes and the Semnones and other German
peoples of the same region through their envoys petitioned for
my friendship and that of the Roman people.

By my command and under my auspices two armies were led
almost at the same time, one into Ethiopia, the other into that part
55 of Arabia which is called Felix; and large forces of the enemy
belonging to both races were killed in battle, and many towns
captured. In Ethiopia the army advanced as far as Napata, the
nearest station to Meroe; in Arabia to the borders of the Sabaei to
the town of Mariba.

60 Egypt I added to the empire of the Roman people.

Greater Armenia, on the murder of its king Artaxes, I could
have made into a province, but I preferred, following the precedent
of our ancestors, and acting through Tiberius Nero, who was then
my stepson, to hand it over as a kingdom to Tigranes, son of Arta-
65 vasdes, and grandson of king Tigranes. Afterwards, when the same
race revolted and rebelled, I subdued it by means of my son,
Gaius, and handed it over to the rule of king Ariobarzanes, the son
of Artabazus, king of the Medes; and after his death, to his son,
Artavasdes. On the latter being killed, I sent out to the kingdom
70 Tigranes, a scion of the royal family of Armenia.

I regained possession of all the provinces on the farther side of
the Hadriatic towards the East and of all Cyrene, at a time when
they were for the most part in the occupation of foreign kings, as I
had already regained Sicily and Sardinia, when they were seized
75 in the servile war. . . .

In my sixth and seventh consulships, after I had extinguished the

civil wars, having been put in supreme possession of the whole empire by the universal consent of all, I transferred the republic from my own power into the free control of the Senate and Roman
80 people.

For the which service I received the appellation of Augustus by decree of the Senate, and the door-posts of my house were publicly decked with laurel leaves; the civic crown was fixed up above my gate, and a golden shield set up in the Julian senate-house, which,
85 as its inscription testifies, was granted to me by the Senate and Roman people to commemorate my virtue, clemency, justice, and piety.

After that time I stood before all others in dignity, but of actual power I possessed no more than my colleagues in each several
90 magistracy.

While I was holding my thirteenth consulship, the Senate and equestrian order and the whole Roman people gave me the title of father of my country, and decreed that the title should be inscribed in the vestibule of my house and in the senate-house and in
95 the forum of Augustus, under the chariot which was set up in my honour by decree of the Senate.

At the time when I wrote these records, I was in my seventy-sixth year.

l. 1   *At the same time.* On his return from Syria, October, 19 B.C.

l. 6   *In the consulship of Tiberius Nero and P. Quintilius,* 13 B.C. Tiberius Nero was subsequently the emperor Tiberius, the successor of Augustus. The Altar of the "Augustan Peace" stood on the Flaminian Road. Fragments of it have been preserved, and there are representations of it on the imperial coinage. Its erection, like the closing of the temple of Janus (below), emphasizes the blessing of peace and security bestowed on the world by Augustus.

l. 12   *The gateway of Janus Quirinus.* See the preceding note. According to Livy (i. 19) the gateway had been closed under king Numa and after the first Punic War (235 B.C.). Under Augustus it was closed in 29 B.C. (after the battle of Actium, in which Octavian (= Augustus) defeated Mark Antony and brought the civil war to an end), in 25 B.C. (after the war with the Cantabri), and again at a date that cannot be determined.

l. 18   *After my victory,* at Actium. "My adversary" (l. 19) is of course Antony, in contrast with whom Augustus shows his piety.

l. 26   *I conquered the pirates.* A reference to Octavian's victory over Sextus Pompeius in 36 B.C.

ll. 39, 41   *I extended the frontiers . . . I restored peace.* Augustus's military and administrative work in the provinces was far too extensive to be sketched here; but it is important to note that greatly improved conditions in the provinces were by no means the least achievement of the Augustan settlement. The provinces were divided into two classes; some remained (as under the Republic) under the direct control of the Senate, others (chiefly those where the danger of armed invasion or revolt was greatest) being reserved to the supervision of Augustus himself.

l. 60 *Egypt I added to the empire of the Roman people.* Egypt is not described as a province. It was too rich and valuable a territory to entrust to a governor who might become wealthy, strong, and rebellious, and was therefore kept under the direct authority of the Emperor.

l. 76 *In my sixth and seventh consulships,* 28 and 27 B.C.

l. 78 *I transferred the republic (rem publicam)* . . . This sentence is of crucial importance for the understanding of the position and authority of Augustus. The Triumvirate (Octavian, Antony, and Lepidus) had taken absolute power by law; when this association broke up, Octavian assumed (tacitly, it appears and without legal enactment; cf. however ll. 30ff.) universal authority, by means of which he settled once for all (by operations of which some have been briefly indicated above) the military problems of the dying republic. When this had been done he (a) expunged illegal acts of the Triumvirate, and (b) handed back to the Senate and people the trust he had enjoyed. How much sincerity, and how much craft, there were in this act cannot here be discussed. It was clear to all that if Octavian had become again no more than a private citizen all the conditions that had led to civil war would automatically have returned. Accordingly means were found within the republican constitution for Octavian to retain the substance of power without dictatorial or monarchical titles. The appearance of a senatorial republic was retained together with the practical advantages of a principate.

l. 81 *I received the appellation of Augustus.* This honorific title expressed the "unofficial" but sacred and dignified position of Octavian. *Rex,* and even *Romulus* (which Octavian would probably have liked), were titles too repugnant to Roman feeling. Octavian was *princeps senatus.*

l. 83 *Laurel leaves,* the sign of victory.
The civic crown of oak leaves was an award for saving the lives of citizens.

l. 88 *Before all others in dignity.* Read, probably, *authority (auctoritate).* *Auctoritas* is moral authority, almost "(power of) leadership". The *auctoritas* of Augustus, backed by his tribunician and proconsular rights, in fact gave him all the *potestas,* or actual power, he needed.

l. 93 *Father of my country* was another title which, like Augustus, expressed the authority of Octavian, and also the real esteem and affection in which he was held by most Romans.

l. 97 *In my seventy-sixth year.* Augustus was seventy-five on 23 September A.D. 13. He died on 19 August A.D. 14.

2 *Suetonius, Augustus* 31. After the death of Lepidus he assumed the office of high priest, which he had never presumed to do while Lepidus was alive. He brought in from all quarters and burnt the books of prophecy, both Latin and Greek (in number more than
5 two thousand), whose authors were unknown or little known, retaining only the Sibylline books, and of these he made a selection. He placed them in two gilt bookcases under the base of the statue of Apollo Palatinus. He brought back to its original regularity the

year which, set in order by the deified Julius, had subsequently
10 through neglect fallen into disorder and confusion. In this re-
ordering he called by his own name the month Sextilis, choosing
this rather than September, in which he was born, because in it he
had won his first consulate and most notable victories. He increased the number, dignity, and emoluments of the priests, and
15 especially of the Vestal Virgins. When it was necessary to choose
a new Vestal in place of one who had died, and many solicited not
to be required to submit their daughters for election, he swore that
if any of his granddaughters had been of the proper age he would
have offered her for the purpose. He restored several of the old
20 ceremonies which had gradually fallen into disuse, such as the
augury of Salus, the office of Flamen Dialis, the Lupercalian rite,
the Secular and Compitalitian Games. He forbad beardless boys to
run in the Lupercalia; and at the Secular Games he forbad young
persons of either sex to attend any of the shows at night unless
25 accompanied by some older relative. He ordered the Lares to be
decorated twice a year at the Compitalitia with spring flowers, and
autumn flowers. Next to the immortal gods he paid highest
honour to the memory of those generals who had extended the
empire of the Roman people from least to greatest. Accordingly
30 he restored their public works, retaining the original inscriptions,
and erected statues of them all, in triumphal dress, in both porches
of his forum. He declared by proclamation that his design was
that the citizens should require of him while he lived, and of
princes in succeeding ages, that they should copy their example.
35 He also removed from the senate-house where G. Caesar had been
killed, and placed under a marble arch over against the hall of his
theatre, the statue of Pompey.

l. 2 *The office of high priest*, which Lepidus could vacate only by death. Augustus
was glad to take the opportunity of becoming religious head of the state
and proceeded to restore the Roman system of religion, partly as a return to
what was old and good, partly to provide a cement for the newly established
principate. Augustus is here represented as reformer of both religion and
morals.

l. 22 *The Secular . . . Games.* See below, 3.

3 *Horace, Carmen Saeculare.* O Phoebus, and Diana, queen of forests,
radiant glory of the heavens, O ye ever cherished and ever to be
cherished, grant the blessings that we pray for at the holy season
when the verses of the Sibyl have commanded chosen maidens and
5 spotless youths to sing the hymn in honour of the gods who love
the Seven Hills.

O quickening Sun, that in thy shining car usherest in the day and hidest it, and art reborn another and yet the same, ne'er mayst thou be able to view aught greater than the city of Rome!

10 O Ilithyia, that, according to thy office, art gracious to bring issues in due season, protect our matrons, whether thou preferrest to be invoked as "Lucina" or as "Genitalis". Rear up our youth, O goddess, and bless the Fathers' edicts concerning wedlock and the marriage-law, destined, we pray, to be prolific in new offspring,

15 that the sure cycle of ten times eleven years may bring round again music and games thronged on three bright days and as many gladsome nights!

And ye, O Fates, truthful in your oracles, as has once been ordained, and may the unyielding order of events confirm it, link

20 happy destinies to those already past.

Bountiful in crops and cattle, may Mother Earth deck Ceres with a crown of corn; and may Jove's wholesome rains and breezes give increase to the harvest!

Do thou, Apollo, gracious and benign, put aside thy weapon and

25 give ear to thy suppliant sons! And do thou, O Luna, the constellations' crescent queen, to the maidens lend thine ear!

If Rome be your handiwork, and if from Ilium hailed the bands that gained the Tuscan shore (the remnant bidden to change their homes and city in auspicious course), they for whom righteous

30 Aeneas, survivor of his country, unscathed 'mid blazing Troy, prepared a way for liberty, destined to bestow more than had been left behind, then do ye, O gods, make teachable our youth and grant them virtuous ways; to the aged give tranquil peace; and to the race of Romulus, riches and offspring and every glory!

35 And what the glorious scion of Anchises and of Venus, with sacrifice of milk-white steers, entreats of you, that may he obtain, triumphant o'er the warring foe, but generous to the fallen! Already the Parthian fears the hosts mighty on land and sea, and fears the Alban axes. Already the Indians and Scythians, but

40 recently disdainful, are asking for our answer. Already Faith and Peace and Honour and ancient Modesty and neglected Virtue have courage to come back, and blessed Plenty with her full horn is seen.

May Phoebus, the prophet, who goes adorned with the shining bow, who is dear to the Muses nine, and with his healing art

45 relieves the body's wearied frame—may he, if he looks with favour on the altars of the Palatine, prolong the Roman power and Latium's prosperity to cycles ever new and ages ever better! And may Diana, who holds Aventine and Algidus, heed the entreaty of the Fifteen Men and incline her gracious ears to the children's

50 prayers! That such is the purpose of Jove and all the gods, we bear

home the good and steadfast hope, we the chorus trained to hymn the praises of Phoebus and Diana.

l. 4 *The verses of the Sibyl.* The Sibylline Books, carefully purged and preserved by Augustus (above, **2**), were the official prophetic literature of the Roman people. From them was derived the authority for holding the Secular Games (above, **2**), a celebration which took place only once in 110 years (or, according to other authorities, 100 years). The dates fell out conveniently for Augustus, who was able to celebrate his own achievements and the lasting vitality of Rome in a great festival held in 17 B.C. For this occasion the poet Horace was commissioned to write his *Carmen Saeculare*, which was sung by a choir of youths and maidens. It forms a poetic commentary on the work of Augustus, and represents many of his aims, and the general feeling of admiration for and gratitude to him.

l. 13 *The Fathers' edicts.* Childless marriages, and divorce, were at this period too common for the health of society. Augustus introduced into the Senate laws intended to deal with this situation.

l. 27 *From Ilium.* Horace shares with Virgil the legendary connection between Rome and Troy (Ilium) which is the foundation of the latter's *Aeneid*. See l. 35, below.

l. 35 *The glorious scion (sanguis) of Anchises and of Venus*; in the first instance Aeneas, the son of Anchises and Venus; but clearly Augustus is in mind.

l. 49 *The Fifteen Men*, the sacred body entrusted with the organization of the Games. Augustus (*Res Gestae* 22. 2) tells us that he acted on their behalf.

4 *Virgil, Eclogue IV.*

> Muses of Sicily, essay we now
> A somewhat loftier task! Not all men love
> Coppice or lowly tamarisk: sing we woods,
> Woods worthy of a Consul let them be.
> 5   Now the last age by Cumae's Sibyl sung
> Has come and gone, and the majestic roll
> Of circling centuries begins anew:
> Justice returns, returns old Saturn's reign,
> With a new breed of men sent down from heaven.
> 10 Only do thou, at the boy's birth in whom
> The iron shall cease, the golden age arise,
> Befriend him, chaste Lucina; 'tis thine own
> Apollo reigns. And in thy consulate,
> This glorious age, O Pollio, shall begin,
> 15 And the months enter on their mighty march.
> Under thy guidance, whatso tracks remain
> Of our old wickedness, once done away,
> Shall free the earth from never-ceasing fear
> He shall receive the life of gods, and see

20 Heroes with gods commingling, and himself
 Be seen of them, and with his father's worth
 Reign o'er a world at peace. For thee, O boy,
 First shall the earth, untilled, pour freely forth
 Her childish gifts, the gadding ivy-spray
25 With foxglove and Egyptian bean-flower mixed,
 And laughing-eyed acanthus. Of themselves,
 Untended, will the she-goats then bring home
 Their udders swollen with milk, while flocks afield
 Shall of the monstrous lion have no fear.
30 . . . . Nathless
 Yet shall there lurk within of ancient wrong
 Some traces, bidding tempt the deep with ships,
 Gird towns with walls, with furrows cleave the earth.
 Therewith a second Tiphys shall there be,
35 Her hero-freight a second Argo bear;
 New wars too shall arise, and once again
 Some great Achilles to some Troy be sent.
 Then, when the mellowing years have made thee man,
 No more shall mariner sail, nor pine-tree bark
40 Ply traffic on the sea, but every land
 Shall all things bear alike: the glebe no more
 Shall feel the harrow's grip, nor vine the hook;
 The sturdy ploughman shall loose yoke from steer,
 Nor wool with varying colours learn to lie;
45 But in the meadows shall the ram himself
 Now with soft flush of purple, now with tint
 Of yellow saffron, teach his fleece to shine.
 While clothed in natural scarlet graze the lambs.
 "Such still, such ages weave ye, as ye run,"
50 Sang to their spindles the consenting Fates
 By Destiny's unalterable decree.
 Assume thy greatness, for the time draws nigh,
 Dear child of gods, great progeny of Jove!
 See how it totters—the world's orbed might,
55 Earth, and wide ocean, and the vault profound,
 All, see, enraptured of the coming time!
 Ah! might such length of days to me be given,
 And breath suffice me to rehearse thy deeds,
 Nor Thracian Orpheus should out-sing me then,
60 Nor Linus, though his mother this, and that
 His sire should aid—Orpheus Calliope,
 And Linus fair Apollo. Nay, though Pan,

With Arcady for judge, my claim contest,
With Arcady for judge great Pan himself
65 Should own him foiled, and from the field retire.
   Begin to greet thy mother with a smile,
O baby-boy! ten months of weariness
For thee she bore: O baby-boy, begin!
For him, on whom his parents have not smiled,
70 Gods deem not worthy of their board or bed.

l. 10 *The boy's birth.* The identification of this "boy", and in general the interpretation of this "messianic eclogue", are endlessly debated. There can be little doubt that Virgil, who was later to write the epic of the Empire, was here celebrating it in another way; though simply to say this is to pass by problems of very great difficulty.

B. *Tiberius*

Tiberius succeeded his stepfather (and adoptive father) Augustus in A.D. 14. He was able, resolute, just, and (having regard to the fortunes of the Empire as a whole) successful; but he remained unpopular, and never stirred the public response that Augustus had won. A legend grew up about him which concealed his virtues and magnified his faults; the legend perverted the truth, but its very existence goes far to prove that all was not well. Yet for twenty-three years Tiberius maintained government (especially in the provinces) with undoubted efficiency.

5 *Suetonius, Tiberius* 36. Foreign religions, the Egyptian and Jewish religious rites, he suppressed, and compelled those who were engaged in that superstition to burn their religious vestments with all their apparatus. The Jewish youth he dispersed, under pretence of
5 military service, into provinces of unhealthy climate; the rest of that race, and those who adopted similar opinions, he expelled from the city, on pain of perpetual slavery if they did not obey. He also banished the astrologers; but when they petitioned him, and promised that they would forsake their art, he pardoned them.

6 *Tacitus, Annals* ii. 85. Another debate dealt with the proscription of the Egyptian and Jewish rites, and a senatorial edict directed that four thousand descendants of enfranchised slaves, tainted with that superstition and suitable in point of age, were to be shipped to
5 Sardinia and there employed in suppressing brigandage: "if they succumbed to the pestilential climate, it was a cheap loss." The

rest had orders to leave Italy, unless they had renounced their impious ceremonial by a given date.

7 *Tacitus, Annals* vi. 51. The son of Nero, on both sides he traced his origin to the Claudian house, though his mother, by successive acts of adoption, had passed into the Livian and, later, the Julian families. From earliest infancy he experienced the hazards of
5 fortune. At first the exiled attendant of a proscribed father, he entered the house of Augustus in the quality of stepson; only to struggle against numerous rivals during the heyday of Marcellus and Agrippa and, later, of Gaius and Lucius Caesar; while even his brother Drusus was happier in the love of his countrymen. But his
10 position was the most precarious after his preferment to the hand of Julia, when he had to tolerate, or to elude, the infidelities of his wife. Then came the return from Rhodes; and he was master of the heirless imperial house for twelve years, and later arbiter of the Roman world for virtually twenty-three. His character, again, has
15 its separate epochs. There was a noble season in his life and fame while he lived a private citizen or a great official under Augustus: an inscrutable and disingenuous period of hypocritical virtues while Germanicus and Drusus remained: with his mother alive, he was still an amalgam of good and evil; so long as he loved, or
20 feared, Sejanus, he was loathed for his cruelty, but his lust was veiled; finally, when the restraints of shame and fear were gone, and nothing remained but to follow his own bent, he plunged impartially into crime and into ignominy.

l. 1 *Nero*. Not to be confused with the Emperor Nero.
l. 2 *His mother*. Livia, the wife of Augustus (her second husband, not the father of Tiberius).
l. 22 *He plunged impartially into crime and into ignominy*. Tacitus is the chief exponent of the legend of Tiberius. He represents the point of view of the senatorial class, whom Tiberius ruthlessly repressed.

C. *Gaius (Caligula)*

Emperor from A.D. 37 to 41. Again, it is not easy to penetrate to Gaius's true character through the cloud of hatred with which he came to be surrounded. He seems to have suffered from megalomania, if from no other form of madness. The following incident illustrates the character of Gaius and his thoughtless policy, and at the same time the self-sacrificing public spirit of a Roman provincial governor of the best kind, whose first thought was for the good of those entrusted to his care.

8 *Josephus, War* ii, 184–7, 192–203. The insolence with which the emperor Gaius defied fortune surpassed all bounds: he wished to be considered a god and to be hailed as such, he cut off the flower of the nobility of his country, and his impiety extended even to
5 Judaea. In fact, he sent Petronius with an army to Jerusalem to instal in the sanctuary statues of himself; in the event of the Jews refusing to admit them, his orders were to put the recalcitrants to death and to reduce the whole nation to slavery. But these orders, as the sequel showed, were under God's care. Petronius accordingly
10 with three legions and a large contingent of Syrian auxiliaries, left Antioch on the march for Judaea. Among the Jews, some put no belief in the rumours of war, others believed, but saw no means of defence: alarm, however, soon became universal, the army having already reached Ptolemais. . . .
15 The Jews assembled with their wives and children in the plain of Ptolemais and implored Petronius to have regard first for the laws of their fathers, and next for themselves. Yielding so far to this vast multitude and their entreaties, he left the statues and his troops at Ptolemais and advanced into Galilee, where he summoned the
20 people, with all persons of distinction, to Tiberias. There he dwelt upon the power of the Romans and the emperor's menaces, and, moreover, pointed out the recklessness of their request; all the subject nations, he urged, had erected in each of their cities statues of Caesar, along with those of their other gods, and that
25 they alone should oppose this practice amounted almost to rebellion, aggravated by insult.

When the Jews appealed to their law and the custom of their ancestors, and pleaded that they were forbidden to place an image of God, much more of a man, not only in their sanctuary but even in
30 any unconsecrated spot throughout the country, Petronius replied, "But I too must obey the law of my master; if I transgress it and spare you, I shall be put to death, with justice. War will be made on you by him who sent me, not by me; for I too, like you, am under orders." At this the multitude cried out that they were ready to
35 endure everything for the law. Petronius, having checked their clamour, said, "Will you then go to war with Caesar?" The Jews replied that they offered sacrifice twice daily for Caesar and the Roman people, but that if he wished to set up these statues, he must first sacrifice the entire Jewish nation; and that they presented
40 themselves, their wives and their children, ready for the slaughter. These words filled Petronius with astonishment and pity at the spectacle of the incomparable devotion of this people to their religion and their unflinching resignation to death. So for the time he dismissed them, nothing being decided.

45   During the ensuing days he held crowded private conferences
with the aristocracy, and public meetings with the people; at these
he had recourse alternately to entreaty, to advice, most often,
however, to threats, holding over their heads the might of the
Romans, the fury of Gaius, and the necessity which circumstances
50 imposed upon himself. As, however, none of these efforts would
induce them to yield, and as he saw that the country was in danger
of remaining unsown—for it was seed-time and the people had
spent fifty days idly waiting upon him—he finally called them together and said: "It is better that I should take the risk. Either, God
55 aiding me, I shall prevail with Caesar and have the satisfaction of
saving myself as well as you, or, if his indignation is roused, I am
ready on behalf of the lives of so many to surrender my own."
With that he dismissed the multitude, who rained blessings on his
head, and collecting his troops left Ptolemais and returned to
60 Antioch. From that city he hastened to report to Caesar his expedi-
tion into Judaea and the entreaties of the nation, adding that, unless
he wished to destroy the country as well as its inhabitants, he
ought to respect their law and revoke the order. To this dispatch
Gaius replied in no measured terms, threatening to put Petronius
65 to death for his tardiness in executing his orders. However, it so
happened that the bearers of this message were weather-bound for
three months at sea, while others, who brought the news of the
death of Gaius, had a fortunate passage. So Petronius received this
last information twenty-seven days earlier than the letter convey-
70 ing his own death-warrant.

l. 5   *Petronius*, governor of the province of Syria.
l. 47 *Alternately*. I correct a small misprint in the translation used.

D. *Claudius*

Like Tiberius, Claudius (A.D. 41–54) has probably suffered from mis-
representation. Probably he was often wiser than his critics, and by no
means the half-wit they depict. He instituted not a few constitutional
and administrative reforms. For his treatment of the difficult situation
at Alexandria see pp. 44–7 (**45**). He touches the New Testament at
several points, one of which is treated in the first passage quoted.
Whether or not the second (on the violation of tombs) is directly
relevant to the New Testament is disputed. It is clear that those who did
not accept the Christian faith in the resurrection of Jesus might well

accuse his disciples of breaking the seal on his grave and stealing his body (cf. Matt. 27. 62–6; 28. 11–15). The name Nazareth is also suggestive. But it must be remembered that Jesus was not buried at Nazareth, that Nazareth did not, so far as we know, become a major centre of the Church, that the disciples were not prosecuted for violation, and that the date of the inscription is not certain—it may go back to the time of Augustus.

9 *Suetonius, Claudius* 25. . . . He forbade men of foreign birth to use the Roman names so far as those of the clans were concerned. Those who usurped the privileges of Roman citizenship he executed in the Esquiline field. He restored to the Senate the provinces
5 of Achaea and Macedonia, which Tiberius had taken into his own charge. He deprived the Lycians of their independence because of deadly intestine feuds, and restored theirs to the Rhodians, since they had given up their former faults. He allowed the people of Ilium perpetual exemption from tribute, on the ground that they
10 were the founders of the Roman race, reading an ancient letter of the Senate and people of Rome written in Greek to king Seleucus, in which they promised him their friendship and alliance only on condition that he should keep their kinsfolk of Ilium free from every burden. Since the Jews constantly made disturbances at the
15 instigation of Chrestus, he expelled them from Rome. He allowed the envoys of the Germans to sit in the orchestra, led by their naïve self-confidence; for when they had been taken to the seats occupied by the common people and saw the Parthian and Armenian envoys sitting with the Senate, they moved of their own accord to the same
20 part of the theatre, protesting that their merits and rank were no whit inferior. He utterly abolished the cruel and inhuman religion of the Druids among the Gauls, which under Augustus had merely been prohibited to Roman citizens; on the other hand he even attempted to transfer the Eleusinian rites from Attica to Rome,
25 and had the temple of Venus Erycina in Sicily, which had fallen to ruin through age, restored at the expense of the treasury of the Roman people. He struck his treaties with foreign princes in the Forum, sacrificing a pig and reciting the ancient formula of the fetial priests. But these and other acts, and indeed almost the whole
30 conduct of his reign, were dictated not so much by his own judgement as that of his wives and freedmen, since he nearly always acted in accordance with their interests and desires.

l.   4 *He restored to the Senate* . . . See above (pp. 4f. (1)) for the arrangement by which Augustus assumed responsibility for the government and defence of certain provinces, leaving others to the Senate.

l. 15 *At the instigation of Chrestus.* This is a not uncommon name, but it is possible that the disturbances were caused by Jewish-Christian controversy (*impulsore Christo*). Cf. Acts 18.2. The context in which this expulsion is described by Suetonius is illuminating.

l. 31 *His wives and freedmen.* Whether Claudius in fact lived in leading-strings is doubtful. Some of the regulations mentioned in this passage were not inspired by freedmen.

10 *Claudius, An Ordinance.* See *Journal of Roman Studies* xxii. (1932), 184–97 (F. de Zulueta): also *Documents illustrating the reigns of Claudius and Nero* (compiled by M. P. Charlesworth, 1939), 15. An inscription discovered at Nazareth.

> Ordinance of Caesar. It is my pleasure that graves and tombs remain undisturbed in perpetuity for those who have made them for the cult of their ancestors or children or members of their house.
> 5 If however any man lay information that another has either demolished them, or has in any other way extracted the buried, or has maliciously transferred them to other places in order to wrong them, or has displaced the sealing or other stones, against such a one I order that a trial be instituted, as in respect of the gods, so in regard to the cult of mortals. For it shall be much more obligatory
> 10 to honour the buried. Let it be absolutely forbidden for any one to disturb them. In case of contravention I desire that the offender be sentenced to capital punishment on charge of violation of sepulture.

l. 2 *For those,* reading τούτοις for τούτους.

E. *Nero*

After five years of good rule (the so-called *Quinquennium Neronis*), Nero (A.D. 54–68) lapsed into vicious ways and irresponsible government. His death led to a period of civil war in which Otho, Galba, Vitellius, and Vespasian (see below) successively seized power. The legal basis of Nero's persecution of Christians is obscure. The New Testament (Rev. 17. 12–17) as well as other sources attests the belief that Nero would after his death return to avenge himself upon his enemies.

11 *Tacitus, Annals* xv. 44. But all human efforts, all the lavish gifts of the emperor, and the propitiations of the gods did not banish the sinister belief that the conflagration was the result of an order. Consequently, to get rid of the report, Nero fastened the guilt and
5 inflicted the most exquisite tortures on a class hated for their abominations, called Christians by the populace. Christus, from

whom the name had its origin, suffered the extreme penalty during
the reign of Tiberius at the hands of one of our procurators,
Pontius Pilatus, and a most mischievous superstition thus checked
10 for the moment, again broke out not only in Judaea, the first
source of the evil, but even in Rome, where all things hideous and
shameful from every part of the world find their centre and become popular. Accordingly, an arrest was first made of all who
pleaded guilty; then, upon their information, an immense multi-
15 tude was convicted, not so much of the crime of firing the city, as
of hatred against mankind. Mockery of every sort was added to
their deaths. Covered with the skins of beasts, they were torn by
dogs and perished, or were nailed to crosses, or were doomed to
the flames and burnt, to serve as a nightly illumination when day-
20 light had expired. Nero offered his gardens for the spectacle, and
was exhibiting a show in the circus, while he mingled with the
people in the dress of a charioteer or stood aloft on a car. Hence,
even for criminals who deserve extreme and exemplary punishment, there arose a feeling of compassion; for it was not, as it
25 seemed, for the public good, but to glut one man's cruelty, that
they were being destroyed.

l. 5 *Hated for their abominations.* According to Tacitus, Nero, to divert attention
from himself, made scapegoats of an unpopular class. No legal machinery
beyond the absolute power of the emperor was involved.

12 *Suetonius, Nero* 16. He devised a new form for the buildings of the
city and in front of the houses and apartments he erected porches,
from the flat roofs of which fires could be fought; and these he put
up at his own cost. He had also planned to extend the walls as far as
5 Ostia and to bring the sea from there to Rome by a canal.
During his reign many abuses were severely punished and put
down, and no fewer new laws were made: a limit was set to ex-
penditures; the public banquets were confined to a distribution of
food; the sale of any kind of cooked viands in the taverns was
10 forbidden, with the exception of pulse and vegetables, whereas
before every sort of dainty was exposed for sale. Punishment was
inflicted on the Christians, a class of men given to a new and mischievous superstition. He put an end to the diversions of the chariot
drivers, who from immunity of long standing claimed the right of
15 ranging at large and amusing themselves by cheating and robbing
the people. The pantomimic actors and their partisans were
banished from the city.

l. 11 *Punishment was inflicted on the Christians.* This notice is included with a
number of other police measures, apparently intended to secure the good

order of the city. There is no reference to the great fire (though l. 3 probably indicates that it had at this time taken place).

13 *Sulpicius Severus, Chronicle* ii. 29. In the meantime, the number of the Christians being now very large, it happened that Rome was destroyed by fire, while Nero was stationed at Antium. But the opinion of all cast the odium of causing the fire upon the emperor,
5 and he was believed in this way to have sought for the glory of building a new city. And in fact Nero could not, by any means he tried, escape from the charge that the fire had been caused by his orders. He therefore turned the accusation against the Christians, and the most cruel tortures were accordingly inflicted upon the
10 innocent. Nay, even new kinds of deaths were invented, so that, being covered in the skins of wild beasts, they perished by being devoured by dogs, while many were crucified or slain by fire, and not a few were set apart for this purpose, that, when the day came to a close, they should be consumed to serve for light during the
15 night. In this way, cruelty first began to be manifested against the Christians. Afterwards, too, their religion was prohibited by laws which were enacted; and by edicts openly set forth it was proclaimed unlawful to be a Christian. At that time Paul and Peter were condemned to death, the former being beheaded with a
20 sword, while Peter suffered crucifixion.

l. 16 *Afterwards.* Sulpicius indicates that Nero's was the first exhibition of cruelty to the Christians, and also that from this time the new religion was legally proscribed.

14 *Suetonius, Nero* 57. He met his death in the thirty-second year of his age, on the anniversary of the murder of Octavia, and such was the public rejoicing that the people put on liberty-caps and ran about all over the city. Yet there were some who for a long time
5 decorated his tomb with spring and summer flowers, and now produced his statues on the rostra in the fringed toga, and now his edicts, as if he were still alive and would shortly return and deal destruction to his enemies. Nay more, Vologaesus, king of the Parthians, when he sent envoys to the Senate to renew his alliance,
10 earnestly begged this too, that honour be paid to the memory of Nero. In fact, twenty years later, when I was a young man, a person of obscure origin appeared, who gave out that he was Nero, and the name was still in such favour with the Parthians that they supported him vigorously and surrendered him with great
15 reluctance.

l. 2 *Octavia*, Nero's wife, whom he had put to death.

F. *Vespasian*

The death of Nero and the ensuing disturbances took place while Vespasian was engaged in the subjugation of Judaea (see pp. 130–3 (**119ff.**)); in due course he came to the purple, leaving his son Titus to continue military operations against Jerusalem. He was a wise, strong, sober ruler (A.D. 69–79), and Titus who succeeded him reproduced his good qualities, but unfortunately reigned only two years before being succeeded by his brother Domitian, who may have murdered him.

15 *Tacitus, Histories* ii. 4f. After inspecting the costly regal gifts and other objects which the Greek mind, with its love for antiquity, assigns to a dim and distant past, Titus inquired first about his own voyage. Assured of a prosperous course over a tranquil sea, he sacri-
5 ficed a number of victims, and then put some dark questions about himself. The priest, whose name was Sostratus, perceiving that the entrails were all alike favourable, and that the goddess looked approvingly upon some great enterprise, gave a brief and ordinary answer for the moment, and then, granting a private interview,
10 disclosed the future. Titus made his way back to his father in high spirits, bringing with him a great accession of confidence to the hesitating minds of the army and the provincials.

Vespasian had well nigh concluded the Judaean war. Nothing remained but the siege of Jerusalem, an undertaking formidable
15 rather from the mountainous character of the site, and the invincible superstition of the inhabitants, than because their forces were strong enough to endure the extremities of a siege. Vespasian himself, as above related, had three legions, inured to war, under his command; Mucianus had four. These last had seen no service;
20 but they had been saved from lethargy by an ambition to rival the glories of the neighbouring army, and they had gained as much in vigour from a period of unbroken rest, and by escaping the hardships of war, as the other army had acquired of hardihood by undergoing its toil and dangers. Each general had his auxiliaries of
25 horse and foot, his fleets and allied princes; each enjoyed an equal, though a different, reputation.

Vespasian was a keen soldier. He would march in front of his men, and choose the spots for encampment; he would work day and night over his plans, and himself take part in the fighting, if
30 need were; content with any food that came, scarce distinguishable in dress and bearing from any common soldier, had he only been free from avarice, he might have been ranked with the generals of olden days.

Mucianus, on the contrary, was a magnificent person. In wealth,
35 and in everything else, he lived on a scale above that of private life:
more ready of speech than Vespasian, he had more skill and foresight in the conduct of civil affairs: the virtues of the two men
without the faults of either would have formed an admirable
temper for an emperor.

40   As governors of adjoining provinces—Syria and Judaea—they
had been at variance, and jealous of each other; but on the death of
Nero they gave up their animosity and made common cause. In
the first instance friends had intervened; but it was Titus who became the chief bond of concord between them, putting an end to
45 unworthy rivalry in view of their common interests, being a man
specially fitted both by nature and by training to attract even such
a person as Mucianus.

The tribunes, centurions, and common soldiers were brought
over to the cause by their energy or their indolence, by the calls of
50 virtue or of pleasure, according to their several natures.

l. 3 *Titus inquired first*, at the temple of Paphian Venus, on Cyprus. This was in
    A.D. 69.
l. 18 *As above related*. In *Histories* i. 10.

G. *Domitian*

With Domitian (A.D. 81–96) the rule of "bad" emperors returned,
and a second reign of terror, more serious than Tiberius's, began. The
century closed hopefully, however, and the work of Domitian's successors, Nerva, Trajan, and Hadrian, saw the empire enter upon the
happiest and most prosperous period in its history.

16 *Suetonius, Domitian* 13. When he became emperor, he did not hesi-
tate to boast in the Senate that he had conferred their power on
both his father and his brother, and that they had but returned him
his own; nor on taking back his wife after their divorce, that he
5 had "recalled her to his divine couch". He delighted to hear the
people in the amphitheatre shout on his feast day: "Good Fortune
attend our Lord and Mistress." Even more, in the Capitoline
competition, when all the people begged him with great unanimity
to restore Palfurius Sura, who had been banished some time before
10 from the Senate, and on that occasion received the prize for oratory,
he deigned no reply, but merely had a crier bid them be silent.
With no less arrogance he began as follows in issuing a circular
letter in the name of his procurators, "Our Master and our God
bids that this be done." And so the custom arose of henceforth

15 addressing him in no other way even in writing or in conversation. He suffered no statues to be set up in his honour in the Capitol, except of gold and silver and of a fixed weight. He erected so many and such huge vaulted passage-ways and arches in the various regions of the city, adorned with chariots and triumphal
20 emblems, that on one of them someone wrote in Greek: "It is enough." He held the consulship seventeen times, more often than any of his predecessors. Of these the seven middle ones were in successive years, but all of them he filled in name only, continuing none beyond the first of May and few after the Ides of January.
25 Having assumed the surname after his two triumphs, he renamed the months of September and October from his own names, calling them "Germanicus" and "Domitianus", because in the former he had come to the throne and was born in the latter.

l. 13 *Our Master and our God.* Most of the earlier emperors had hesitated to claim divinity.
l. 20 *"It is enough.* "*Arci* in Latin suggests *arcus,* an arch, but could also be a transliteration of the Greek δοκεῖ, it is enough.

17 *Suetonius, Domitian* 12. Reduced to financial straits by the cost of his buildings and shows, as well as by the additions he had made to the pay of the soldiers, he tried to lighten the military expenses by diminishing the number of his troops; but perceiving that in
5 this way he exposed himself to the attacks of the barbarians, and nevertheless had difficulty in easing his burdens, he had no hesitation in resorting to every sort of robbery. The property of the living and the dead was seized everywhere on any charge brought by any accuser. It was enough to allege any action or word deroga-
10 tory to the majesty of the prince. Estates of those in any way connected with him were confiscated, if but one man came forward to declare that he had heard from the deceased during his lifetime that Caesar was his heir. Besides other taxes, that on the Jews was levied with the utmost rigour, and those were prosecuted who
15 without publicly acknowledging that faith yet lived as Jews, as well as those who concealed their origin and did not pay the tribute levied upon their people. I recall being present in my youth when the person of a man ninety years old was examined before the procurator and a very crowded court, to see whether he
20 was circumcised. . . .

l. 13 *That on the Jews.* See p. 133 (**121**). After the fall of Jerusalem in A.D. 70 the tax formerly paid to the Temple was required by the Romans.
l. 15 *Without publicly acknowledging that faith.* Possibly the persons known as "God-fearers" (see p. 164) are meant.

l. 16 *Who concealed their origin.* Christians, who were readily confounded with the Jews yet knew themselves to be distinct from them, may have been included here.

18 *Tacitus, Agricola* 2. It is recorded that when Rusticus Arulenus extolled Thrasea Paetus, when Herennius Senecio extolled Helvidius Priscus, their praise became a capital offence, so that persecution fell not merely on the authors themselves but on the very books:
5 to the public hangman, in fact, was given the task of burning in the courtyard of the forum the memorials of our noblest characters.

They imagined, no doubt, that in those flames disappeared the voice of the people, the liberty of the Senate, the conscience of mankind; especially as the votaries of philosophy also were
10 expelled, and all liberal culture exiled, in order that nowhere might anything of good report present itself to men's eyes.

THE PAPYRI

No single material substance has in recent years contributed to our knowledge of the world in which the New Testament was written, and indeed of the New Testament itself, more than papyrus. This writing material, the preparation and characteristics of which are described below, was in common use before, in, and after New Testament times. The oldest New Testament MSS. are papyri, and it is very probable that the autographs themselves of the New Testament books were written on papyrus. Even more important, however, than this, is the fact that during the last fifty or sixty years thousands of papyrus documents—the vast majority of them fleeting notes never intended for perpetuity—have been recovered and edited. Not only do they throw a flood of light upon the social and religious customs of the country of their origin (almost all have been found in Egypt where alone the climatic conditions favour the preservation of papyrus); they also illustrate in a most striking way the language, and sometimes the thought, of the New Testament and the early Church.

The bearing of the papyri upon social and religious history will be briefly illustrated in the following pages. Here it must be emphasized that they are essentially non-literary. It is true that numbers of papyri have been found containing literary texts, and some have contributed fresh material to the known corpus of Greek literature; but the great bulk of papyrus material represents the writing of everyday life. We read countless private letters, bills, contracts, agreements, schoolboys' exercises, magical spells, charms, prayers, public announcements, petitions, and so on. We see the officials and common folk of Egypt (in many ways a unique, yet in others a not unrepresentative, province of the eastern part of the Roman Empire) going about their daily tasks with no suspicion that they are being observed, governing and being governed, buying and selling, teaching and learning, marrying and being given in marriage, begetting children and either exposing them or rearing and educating them. Here then is a quantity of source material such as the historian dreams of but (in ancient history) rarely sees. On the basis of it not the political history only but the daily life of a people can be reconstructed.

The grammatical and lexicographical importance of the papyri cannot be treated here. The student should consult first the Introduction to the *Vocabulary of the Greek Testament* by J. H. Moulton and G. Milligan, where are given excellent examples of the way in which linguistic problems in the New Testament have been solved by means of the new texts. There is much further material in G. A. Deissmann's *Bible Studies* and *Light from the Ancient East*, and in J. H. Moulton's *Grammar of New Testament Greek*. The contribution made by papyrology to the understanding of New Testament Greek must not be underestimated; but it seems right to add here that it is perhaps not quite so great as its most enthusiastic advocates have suggested. The language of the New Testament is not identical with that of the papyri. Simple words with a commercial or legal background, such as ἀρραβών (*earnest*) and βεβαιοῦν (*guarantee*), are admirably illuminated by the commercial and legal papyri, but the central words of the New Testament, such as ἀγάπη (*love*) and δικαιοσύνη (*righteousness*), cannot be adequately explained on this basis; the background must be extended to take into account not only the LXX (see Chapter 11) but also the unique creative impulse which produced the New Testament and laid its stamp upon the language in which the New Testament was written.

A. *Preparation and Use of Papyrus*

The following account needs little explanation. It is given at some length not only because knowledge of the materials and make-up of papyrus is useful in palaeography but also because it affords interesting information about manufacturing processes and economic conditions in antiquity.

19 *Pliny, Natural History* xiii. 68–83. We have not yet touched on the marsh-plants nor the shrubs that grow by rivers. But before we leave Egypt we shall also describe the nature of papyrus, since our civilization or at all events our records depend very largely on the
5 employment of paper. According to Marcus Varro we owe even the discovery of paper to the victory of Alexander the Great, when he founded Alexandria in Egypt, before which time paper was not used. First of all people used to write on palm-leaves and then on the bark of certain trees, and afterwards folding sheets of lead be-
10 gan to be employed for official muniments, and then also sheets of

linen or tablets of wax for private documents; for we find in
Homer [*Iliad* vi. 168] that the use of writing tablets existed even
before the Trojan period, but when he was writing even the land
itself which is now thought of as Egypt did not exist as such, while
15 now paper grows in the Sebennytic and Saitic nomes of Egypt,
the land having been subsequently heaped up by the Nile, inasmuch
as Homer wrote that the island of Pharos, which is now joined to
Alexandria by a bridge, was twenty-four hours' distance by sailing-
ship from the land. Subsequently, also according to Varro, when
20 owing to the rivalry between King Ptolemy and King Eumenes
about their libraries Ptolemy suppressed the export of paper,
parchment was invented at Pergamum; and afterwards the employment of the material on which the immortality of human
beings depends spread indiscriminately.

25   Papyrus then grows in the swamps of Egypt or else in the
sluggish waters of the Nile where they have overflowed and lie
stagnant in pools not more than about three feet in depth; it has a
sloping root as thick as a man's arm, and tapers gracefully up with
triangular sides to a length of not more than about fifteen feet,
30 ending in a head like a thyrsus; it has no seed, and is of no use
except that the flowers are made into wreaths for statues of the
gods. The roots are employed by the natives for timber, and not
only to serve as firewood but also for making various utensils and
vessels; indeed the papyrus itself is plaited to make boats, and the
35 inner bark is woven into sail-cloth and matting, and also cloth, as
well as blankets and ropes. It is also used as chewing-gum, both in
the raw state and when boiled, though only the juice is swallowed.

Papyrus also grows in Syria on the borders of the lake round
which grows the scented reed already mentioned [xii. 104], and
40 King Antiochus would only allow ropes made from this Syrian
papyrus to be used in his navy, the employment of esparto not yet
having become general. It has recently been realized that papyrus
growing in the Euphrates near Babylon can also be used in the
same way for paper; nevertheless up to the present the Parthians
45 prefer to embroider letters upon cloths.

The process of making paper from papyrus is to split it with a
needle into very thin strips made as broad as possible, the best
quality being in the centre of the plant, and so on in the order of its
splitting up. The first quality used to be called "hieratic paper"
50 and was in early times devoted solely to books connected with
religion, but in a spirit of flattery it was given the name of Augustus, just as the second best was called "Livia paper" after his consort, and thus the name "hieratic" came down to the third class.

The next quality had been given the name of "amphitheatre
55 paper", from the place of its manufacture. This paper was taken
over by the clever workshop of Fannius at Rome, and its texture
was made finer by a careful process of insertion, so that it was
changed from common paper into one of first-class quality, and
received the name of the maker; but the paper of this kind that did
60 not have this additional treatment remained in its own class as
amphitheatre paper. Next to this is the Saitic paper named from
the town where it is produced in the greatest abundance, being
made from shavings of inferior quality, and the Taeneotic, from a
neighbouring place, made from material still nearer the outside
65 skin, in the case of which we reach a variety that is sold by mere
weight and not for its quality. As for what is called "emporitic"
paper, it is no good for writing but serves to provide covers for
documents and wrappers for merchandise, and consequently takes
its name from the Greek word for a merchant. After this comes the
70 actual papyrus, and its outermost layer, which resembles a rush and
is of no use even for making ropes except those used in water.

Paper of all kinds is "woven" on a board moistened with water
from the Nile, muddy liquid supplying the effect of glue. First an
upright layer is smeared on to the table, using the full length of
75 papyrus available after the trimmings have been cut off at both
ends, and afterwards cross strips complete the lattice-work. The
next step is to press it in presses, and the sheets are dried in the sun
and then joined together, the next strip used always diminishing in
quality down to the worst of all. There are never more than
80 twenty sheets to a roll.

There is a great difference in the breadth of the various kinds of
paper: the best is thirteen inches wide, the hieratic two inches less,
the Fannian measures ten inches and the amphitheatre paper one
less, while the Saitic is still fewer inches across and is not as wide
85 as the mallet used in making it, as the emporitic kind is so narrow
that it does not exceed six inches. Other points looked at in paper
are fineness, stoutness, whiteness and smoothness. The status of
best quality was altered by the Emperor Claudius. The reason was
that the thin paper of the period of Augustus was not strong
90 enough to stand the friction of the pen, and moreover as it let the
writing show through there was a fear of a smudge being caused
by what was written on the back, and the great transparency of the
paper had an unattractive look in other respects. Consequently the
foundation was made of leaves of second quality and the woof or
95 cross layer of leaves of the first quality. Claudius also increased the
width of the sheet, making it a foot across. There were also

eighteen-inch sheets called "*macrocola*", but examination detected a
defect in them, as tearing off a single strip damaged several pages.
On this account Claudius paper has come to be preferred to all
100 other kinds, although the Augustus kind still holds the field for
correspondence; but Livia paper, having no quality of a first-class
kind, but being entirely second class, has retained its position.

Roughness is smoothed out with a piece of ivory or a shell, but
this makes the lettering apt to fade, as owing to the polish so given
105 the paper does not take the ink so well, but has a shinier surface.
The damping process if carelessly applied often causes difficulty in
writing at first, and it can be detected by a blow with the mallet, or
even by the musty smell if the process has been rather carelessly
carried out. Spottiness also may be detected by the eye, but a bad
110 porous strip inserted in the middle of the pasted joins, owing to the
sponginess of the papyrus, sucks up the ink and so can scarcely be
detected except when the ink of a letter runs: so much opportunity
is there for cheating. The consequence is that another task is added
to the process of paper-weaving.

115   The common kind of paste for paper is made of fine flour of the
best quality mixed with boiling water, with a very small sprinkle of
vinegar; for carpenter's paste and gum make too brittle a com-
pound. But a more careful process is to strain the crumb of leavened
bread in boiling water; this method requires the smallest amount
120 of paste at the seams, and produces a paper softer than even linen.
But all the paste used ought to be exactly a day old—not more nor
yet less. Afterwards the paper is beaten thin with a mallet and run
over with a layer of paste, and then again has its creases removed
by pressure and is flattened out with the mallet. This process may
125 enable records to last a long time; at the house of the poet and most
distinguished citizen Pomponius Secundus I have seen documents
in the hands of Tiberius and Gaius Gracchus; while as for autographs of Cicero, of his late Majesty Augustus, and of Virgil, we
see them constantly.

l. 5 *Marcus Varro.* Varro of Reate (so called to distinguish him from Varro of
Atax); 116–27 B.C.

l. 15 *Nomes,* the ancient provinces into which Egypt was divided; they were
retained in Ptolemaic and Roman administration.

l. 20 *King Eumenes,* presumably Eumenes II (197–158 B.C.) is meant. The tale
finds some support in the name περγαμηνή, *pergamena* (parchment).

l. 30 *Thyrsus*: "A staff twined round with ivy and vine-shoots, borne by Bacchus
and the Bacchantes" (Lewis and Short, *s.v.*). *It has no seed.* This is not strictly
correct.

l. 73 *The effect of glue, vim glutinis.* The translation is perhaps not correct. *Glutinis*
is probably not the genitive of *gluten* but the dative plural of *glutinum,* the

form of the word used by Pliny (e.g. l. 117, below). Some kind of glue was used with the muddy Nile water.

l. 82 *Thirteen inches.* "Inch" here (and throughout this passage) renders the Latin *digitus*, which is approximately threequarters of an English inch.

l. 97 *Macrocola.* " 'Long-limbed', in long strips; Cicero, *ad Atticum* XVI. 3. 1 and XIII. 25. 3, and some MSS. here also give *macrocollum*, 'long-glued', made of strips pasted together" (H. Rackham, Loeb Classical Library, ad loc.).

l. 124 *This process may enable records to last a long time.* The best papyrus remains however much less durable than parchment. It follows that very early MSS. of the New Testament will always be few; and those that are found will almost all be of Egyptian origin. From the manufacturing process described by Pliny it will readily be understood that papyrus was usually (because most conveniently) formed into rolls, not codices. The fact that New Testament papyrus codices did exist is therefore significant; no more than one gospel could be written on a roll and the Christians evidently felt it necessary to keep their sacred books together since they formed a collection (or canon). This seems a probable conclusion, but a different view is taken by Dr C. H. Roberts (*J.T.S.* l. (1949), 155–68).

B. *Form and Style of Letter-writing in the Papyri*

Of the twenty-seven books of the New Testament twenty-one are (or appear to be) letters. In addition, Revelation contains the seven letters to the seven churches, and Acts the letter sent by the Council of Jerusalem to the churches of Asia Minor (15.23–9) and that sent by the tribune Claudius Lysias to the procurator Felix (23.26–30). It has already been noted that many of the papyri are letters, and it is not surprising that there are frequent similarities between the New Testament letters and letters roughly contemporary with them. A few illustrations of this resemblance will suffice.

20 *P. Lond.* 42 (H.E. 97).[1] 168 B.C.

Isias to her brother Hephaestion greeting. If you are well and other things are going right, it would accord with the prayer which I make continually to the gods. I myself and the child and all the household are in good health and think of you always. When I
5 received your letter from Horus, in which you announce that you are in detention in the Serapeum at Memphis, for the news that you are well I straightway thanked the gods, but about your not coming home, when all the others who had been secluded there have come, I am ill-pleased, because after having piloted myself
10 and your child through such bad times and been driven to every

---

[1] References are inserted where possible to the admirable collection of papyri edited by A. S. Hunt and C. C. Edgar (Loeb Classical Library, two volumes, 1932 and 1934).

extremity owing to the price of corn I thought that now at least, with you at home, I should enjoy some respite, whereas you have not even thought of coming home nor given any regard to our circumstances, remembering how I was in want of everything 15 while you were still here, not to mention this long lapse of time and these critical days, during which you have sent us nothing. As, moroever, Horus who delivered the letter has brought news of your having been released from detention, I am thoroughly ill-pleased. Notwithstanding, as your mother also is 20 annoyed, for her sake as well as for mine please return to the city, if nothing more pressing holds you back. You will do me a favour by taking care of your bodily health. Goodbye. Year 2, Epeiph 30. [Addressed] To Hephaestion.

l. 1   *Brother.* It is clear from the letter that Hephaestion and Isias are man and wife. "Brother" (ἀδελφός) may be a term of endearment, or may be intended literally. Marriage between brother and sister was not unusual in Egypt.
Greeting. In this papyrus the word "Greeting" (χαίρειν) is supplied by the editor in a small hiatus. The restoration is however certain, because the word is so common in the opening sentences of letters. As here, the form is usually "A to B, greeting". In the New Testament χαίρειν (as an epistolary formula) is used only at Acts 15.23; 23.26; James 1.1; in the Pauline epistles the similar but characteristically Christian word χάρις (*grace*) is used (together with εἰρήνη, which recalls the common Semitic greeting, שלום, *peace*).

l. 2   *The prayer which I make continually.* The Pauline epistles also regularly begin with thanksgiving and prayer.

l. 6   *In detention in the Serapeum.* Serapis, presumably, had, through his priests, ordered Hephaestion to remain in the temple.

l. 17 (cf. l. 5) *Horus.* In Paul's epistles we sometimes hear of a messenger who carries the letter and is also able to give supplementary information; e.g. Col. 4: 7ff. (All my affairs shall Tychicus make known unto you . . . whom I have sent unto you for this very purpose. . . . They shall make known unto you all things that are done here).

l. 22 *Goodbye,* ἔρρωσο. This word occurs in Acts 15. 29 (in the plural) and 23. 30 (according to some texts). Paul regularly uses Christian formulas.

l. 23 *To Hephaestion.* The letter is addressed, as usual, on the verso.

21 *P. Oxy.* 292 (H.E. 106). About A.D. 25.

Theon to the most honoured Tyrannus very many greetings. Heraclides, the bearer of this letter, is my brother, wherefore I entreat you with all my power to take him under your protection. I have also asked your brother Hermias by letter to inform 5 you about him. You will do me the greatest favour if you let him win your approval. Before all else I pray that you may have health and the best of success, unharmed by the evil eye. Goodbye. [Addressed] To Tyrannus the dioecetes.

l. 3   *I entreat you . . . to take him under your protection.* Letters of commendation
are naturally not rare among the papyri. In the New Testament cf. Rom.
16. 1 (συνίστημι δὲ ὑμῖν Φοίβην τὴν ἀδελφὴν ἡμῶν, I commend unto you
Phoebe our sister) and 2 Cor. 3. 1 (Are we beginning again to commend
(συνιστάνειν) ourselves? or need we, as do some, epistles of commendation
(συστατικῶν ἐπιστολῶν) to you or from you?) The word in this document translated "under your protection" is συνεσταμένον.
l. 8   *Dioecetes*: in Ptolemaic times a very important financial officer of the
crown; later a subordinate official.

22 B.G.U. 27 (H.E. 113). Second or third century A.D.

Irenaeus to Apollinarius his dearest brother many greetings. I pray
continually for your health, and I myself am well. I wish you to
know that I reached land on the sixth of the month Epeiph and we
unloaded our cargo on the eighteenth of the same month. I went
5 up to Rome, on the twenty-fifth of the same month and the place
welcomed us as the god willed, and we are daily expecting our
discharge, it so being that up till to-day nobody in the corn fleet
has been released. Many salutations to your wife and to Serenus
and to all who love you, each by name. Goodbye. Mesore 9.
10 [Addressed] To Apollinarius from his brother Irenaeus.

l. 7   *The corn fleet*, from Egypt to Rome.
l. 9   *Each by name*, κατ' ὄνομα. Cf. 3 John 15.

C. *Magical and Religious Papyri*

Jewish and Christian papyri are not included here, nor are MSS. of
literary texts. It is partly for this reason that the papyri quoted may give
the impression that the religion of Egypt in the Hellenistic and Roman
periods had little real religious feeling in it, but was on the one hand
commercial and official, on the other magical. One would not expect
the more personal and mystical aspects of religion to be treated in non-
literary documents of the kind commonly preserved among the papyri.

23 P. Oxy. 1211. (H.E. 403). Second century A.D. This note lists the
articles needed for a sacrifice at "the festival which is still held about the
summer solstice when the river begins to rise" (H.E. ii. 525). Evidently
the strategus was responsible for providing the sacrificial material, or
at least for paying for it.

To the strategus. Articles for the sacrifice to the most sacred Nile
on Pauni 30: 1 calf, 2 jars of sweet-smelling wine, 16 wafers, 16

garlands, 16 pine-cones, 16 cakes, 16 green palm-branches, 16 reeds likewise, oil, honey, milk, every spice except frankincense.

l. 1 *Strategus* (στρατηγός): not, as usually in Greek, a military title, but that of the local civil administrative official.

24 *P. Tebt.* 294 .(H.E. 353). A.D. 146. The religion of Egypt was maintained by the state, and its servants held official paid positions for which application, accompanied by a fee, had to be made to the local authorities. It will be seen that the duties of the "prophet" are very different from the activities of Old Testament and Christian prophets.

Copy. To Tiberius Claudius Justus, administrator of the private account, from Pakebkis son of Marsisouchus, exempted priest of the famous temple of Soknebtunis also called Cronus and the most great associated gods, which is situated in the village of Tebtunis
5 in the division of Polemon in the Arsinoite nome. I wish to purchase the office of prophet in the aforesaid temple, which has been offered for sale for a long time, on the understanding that I shall
. . . and carry the palm-branches and perform the other functions of the office of prophet and receive in accordance with the orders
10 the fifth part of all the revenue which falls to the temple, at the total price of 2,200 drachmae instead of the 640 drachmae offered long ago by Marsisouchus son of Pakebkis, which sum I will pay, if my appointment is ratified, into the local public bank at the customary dates; and I and my descendants and successors shall
15 have the permanent ownership and possession of this office for ever with all the same privileges and rights, on payment (by each one) of 200 drachmae for admission. If therefore it seem good to you, my lord, you will ratify my appointment here in the city upon these terms and write to the strategus of the nome about this
20 matter, in order that the due services of the gods who love you may be performed. The fifth share of the proceeds of the revenues which falls to me, as aforesaid, after deducting expenses is 50 artabae of wheat, 9⅜ artabae of lentils, 60 drachmae of silver. Farewell. The 10th year of the Emperor Caesar Titus Aelius
25 Hadrianus Antoninus Augustus Pius, Tubi 10.

l. 1   *The private account*, ἴδιος λόγος. The ancient kingdom of Egypt was regarded as the private property of its kings, and its revenues were their own income. This conception was continued by the Ptolemies and adopted by Augustus, who in this as in many other ways treated Egypt differently from other provinces.

l. 2   *Exempted*, that is, from the payment of certain taxes. This was one of the advantages of holding an official religious position.

l. 6 *The office of prophet*, ἡ προφητεία.

l. 10 *The revenue which falls to the temple*. The temples possessed estates of "sacred land" which were administered for their financial benefit.

l. 18 *The city*, Alexandria.

25 *P. Oxy.* 1148. (H.E. 193). First century A.D. A question addressed to an oracle.

O Lord Sarapis Helios, beneficent one. [Say] whether it is fitting that Phanias my son and his wife should not agree now with his father, but oppose him and not make a contract. Tell me this truly. Goodbye.

l. 4 *Goodbye*. The form of the request suggests a letter to the god; see above, p. 28 (**20**).

26 *P. Oxy.* 1478. (H.E. 198). About A.D. 300. A charm for victory.

Charm for victory for Sarapammon son of Apollonius . . . [Here follow ten or eleven magical symbols] . . . Give victory and safety in the racecourse and the crowd to the aforesaid Sarapammon in the name of Sulicusesus.

l. 4 *Sulicusesus*: a god, of whom nothing is known.

27 *Paris Magical Papyrus* (lines 3,007–3,085). Published by C. Wessely, *Griechische Zauberpapyri von Paris und London*, in *Denkschrift der kaiserlichen Akademie der Wissenschaften zu Wien*, Phil.-Hist. Klasse, xxxvi. (1888). See also G. A. Deissmann, *Light from the Ancient East* (250–60). About A.D. 300. Outside the official cults maintained by the state, religion in Egypt reflected the mixed population of the country, in which native Egyptians, Greek settlers, merchants, and administrators, and Roman soldiers and officials were joined by various orientals, including numerous Jews. Those in particular who practised magic were willing to adopt from any source names and formulas which sounded impressive and effective. Of the resulting amalgam the following passage is an excellent example. Its Jewish affiliations are unmistakable; but it was certainly not written by an orthodox Jew, and probably not by a Jew of any kind. Yet there were Jewish exorcists (cf. e.g. Matt. 12. 27=Luke 11. 19; Acts 19. 13), and it may be that some of them used methods akin to those described in this papyrus. The reality of the demon world, constantly assumed in the New Testament, is clearly presupposed.

For those possessed by daemons, an approved charm by Pibechis. Take oil made from unripe olives, together with the plant

mastigia and lotus pith, and boil it with marjoram
(very colourless), saying: "Joel, Ossarthiomi,
5 Emori, Theochipsoith, Sithemeoch, Sothe,
Joe, Mimipsothiooph, Phersothi, Aeeioyo,
Joe, Eochariphtha: come out of such an one (and the other usual
formulae)."
But write this phylactery upon a little sheet of
tin: "Jaeo, Abraothioch, Phtha, Mesen-
10 tiniao, Pheoch, Jaeo, Charsoc", and hang it
round the sufferer: it is of every demon a thing to be trembled at,
which
he fears. Standing opposite, adjure him. The adjuration is
this: "I adjure thee by the god of the Hebrews
Jesu, Jaba, Jae, Abraoth, Aia, Thoth, Ele,
15 Elo, Aeo, Eu, Jiibaech, Abarmas, Jaba-
rau, Abelbel, Lona, Abra, Maroia, arm,
thou that appearest in fire, thou that art in the midst of earth and
snow
and vapour, Tannetis: let thy angel descend,
the implacable one, and let him draw into captivity the
20 daemon as he flieth around this creature
which God formed in his holy paradise.
For I pray to the holy god, through the might of Ammon-
ipsentancho." Sentence. "I adjure thee with bold, rash words:
Jacuth,
Ablanathanalba, Acramm." Sentence. "Aoth, Jatha-
25 bathra, Chachthabratha, Chamynchel, Abro-
oth. Thou art Abrasiloth, Allelu, Jelosai,
Jael: I adjure thee by him who appeared unto
Osrael in the pillar of light and in the cloud by
day, and who delivered his word from the taskwork
30 of Pharaoh and brought upon Pharaoh the
ten plagues because he heard not. I adjure
thee, every daemonic spirit, say whatsoever
thou art. For I adjure thee by the seal
which Solomon laid upon the tongue
35 of Jeremiah and he spake. And say thou
whatsoever thou art, in heaven, or of the air,
or on earth, or under the earth or below the ground,
or an Ebusaean, or a Chersaean, or a Pharisee. Say
whatsoever thou art, for I adjure thee by God the light-
40 bringer, invincible, who knoweth what is in the heart
of all life, who of the dust hath formed the race

of men, who hath brought out of uncertain [places]
and maketh thick the clouds and causeth it to rain upon the earth
and blesseth the fruits thereof; who is
45 blessed by every power in heaven of angels,
of archangels. I adjure thee by the great God Sabaoth,
through whom the river Jordan returned
backward,—the Red Sea also,
which Israel journeyed over and it stood impassable.
50 For I adjure thee by him who revealed the hundred
and forty tongues and divided them
by his command. I adjure thee by him who
with his lightnings the [race?] of stiff-necked giants consumed, to whom the heaven of heavens sings praises,
55 to whom Cherubin his wings sing praises.
I adjure thee by him who hath set mountains about the sea,
a wall of sand, and hath charged it not to pass
over, and the deep hearkened. And do thou
hearken, every daemonic spirit, for I adjure thee
60 by him that moveth the four winds since
the holy aeons, him the heaven-like, sea-
like, cloud-like, the light-bringer, invincible.
I adjure thee by him that is in Jerosolymum the pure, to whom the
unquenchable fire through every aeon is
65 offered, through his holy name Jaeo-
baphrenemun (Sentence), before whom trembleth the Genna of
fire
and flames flame round about and iron
bursteth and every mountain feareth from its foundations.
I adjure thee, every daemonic spirit, by him that
70 looketh down on earth and maketh tremble the
foundations thereof and hath made all things
out of things which are not into Being." But I adjure thee,
thou that usest this adjuration: the flesh of swine
eat not, and there shall be subject unto thee every spirit
75 and daemon, whatsoever he be. But when thou adjurest,
blow, sending the breath from above [to the feet] and
from the feet to the face, and he [the daemon] will
be drawn into captivity. Be pure and keep it. For the sentence
is Hebrew and kept by men
80 that are pure.

---

l. 1 *Those possessed by daemons*, δαιμονιαζομένους. Cf. the New Testament word
δαιμονίζεσθαι.

An approved charm, δόκιμον. For this word and its meaning cf. 1 Pet. 1. 7. "Charm" is here, of course, supplied by the context.

l. 4 *Joel.* Some of the curious words in this and similar papyri have no discoverable meaning, and are probably mere mumbo-jumbo which doubtless sounded very impressive when uttered in the right way and in the right circles. Others were borrowed from various sources, some in this papyrus from the Old Testament.

l. 6 *Joe.* This may be a form of the Hebrew divine name יהוה (YHWH). Cf. Jaeo, Jaba, Jae, below.

Aeeioyo; not a word, but the vowels of the Greek alphabet.

l. 7 *Come out of*, ἔξελθε ἀπό. The same command is used in the New Testament (Luke 4. 35, cf. Mark 1. 25; 5. 8; 9. 25). It was probably a common formula with exorcists.

l. 9 *Phtha*, the name of an Egyptian god.

l. 11 *A thing to be trembled at*, φρικτόν. Cf. James 2. 19.

l. 12 *Adjure*, ὁρκίζειν. Cf. e.g. Acts 19. 13. This too was probably a common word with exorcists.

l. 14 *Jesu.* As Deissmann points out, neither a Jew nor a Christian would speak of Jesus as the god of the Hebrews. But a non-Christian gentile (or perhaps even a very unorthodox Jew) might well hear the name and, recognizing both its effectiveness in exorcism and its connection with Judaism, think it appropriate for his purpose. In the list of names which follows Jaba and Jae recall YHWH; Thoth is the name of an Egyptian god, and Ele, Elo suggest the Hebrew אל, אלהים (*'el*, *'elohim*; God).

l. 17 *Thou that appearest in fire.* There may be an allusion to the appearance of God to Moses in the burning bush (Ex. 3. 2); but fire is a common element in theophanies.

l. 21 *Which God formed* (ἔπλασεν—cf. Gen. 2. 7) *in his holy paradise*; a reference to the biblical narrative of the creation of man, but not necessarily at first hand; cf. *Corpus Hermeticum* i. and the notes on pp. 83–7 (85ff.).

l. 22 *Through the might of . . .* This renders ἐπί . . . Cf. the New Testament formula ἐπὶ τῷ ὀνόματι.

l. 28 *Osrael* may be simply a slip for Israel. If it is a genuine mistake the writer of the papyrus certainly had no first-hand acquaintance with the Old Testament; but the correct form occurs in l. 49.

In the pillar of light and in the cloud by day. Another biblical allusion (Ex. 13. 21f.), but again an imperfect one. In the Old Testament we have "pillar of fire" (πυρός), not "pillar of light" (στῦλος φωτινός).

l. 29 *Word*—a slip; λόγον was written instead of λαόν, *people*.

ll. 32f. (and 38f.) *Say whatsoever thou art.* The New Testament also illustrates the importance attached to knowing the name of a demon; cf. Mark 5. 9.

l. 34 *Solomon* enjoyed great repute as an exorcist and his seal was well known; but the connection with Jeremiah does not seem to be attested elsewhere.

l. 38 *Pharisee.* This is evidently the name of a demon or class of demons; the writer was probably not familiar with the Jewish party bearing this name. Deissmann explains the proper names in this line as follows (p. 257). "This remarkable trio of daemons obviously comes from the LXX, Gen. 15. 20; Ex. 3. 8, 17 etc., where we find Χετταῖοι (who have become Χερσαῖοι i.e.

'land daemons'), Φερεζαῖοι (who have become the more intelligible 'Pharisees'), and 'Ιεβουσαῖοι."

l. 39 (and 62) *Light-bringer*; possibly an allusion to Gen 1. 3, and other Old Testament passages; there are many such allusions in the following lines.

l. 50 *The hundred and forty tongues.* Some Jews believed that on Sinai the Law was delivered in seventy languages, corresponding to the seventy nations of the earth. This does not account for the number 140; it is quite possible that the exorcist was simply trying to improve on the traditional and orthodox number by doubling it; or he may have conceived the notion of a heavenly corresponding to each earthly language; or he may have had a different tradition.

l. 55 *Cherubin his wings.* Deissmann apparently so translates in order to bring out the fact that Cherubin is in the papyrus wrongly taken as a singular (τοῦ χερουβίν). The same mistake is made in the LXX (2 Sam. 22. 11; 2 Chron. 3.11), as well as in some later VSS. of the Old Testament.

l. 56 *Mountains*, ὄρη, is probably a corruption of "bounds", ὄρια.

l. 63 *Jerosolymum, sic.*

l. 66 *Genna, sic.*

l. 68 *Bursteth.* Deissmann's translation is not certain, but probably correct.

l. 73 *The flesh of swine eat not.* This Jewish prohibition could easily be accommodated in Egyptian religion, and in the partly ascetical practice of gnostic magic. It is to be noted that the Jewish law in its entirety is not enjoined.

l. 79 *Hebrew.* Clearly not in language, but in origin. Foreign origin, like the use of unintelligible names, was probably thought to add to the efficacy of a charm.

28 *P. Tebt.* 276. Late second or third century A.D. A special feature of gnostic-magical religion was astrology, which fascinated the Hellenistic world, and held with a paralysing grip the Hellenistic mind. The following is a fragment from a "technical" astrological work.

. . . If in addition Mercury is in conjunction, and Saturn is irregularly situated, . . . from an unfavourable position; if at the same time Mars is in opposition to Saturn, the aforesaid position being maintained [he will destroy?] profits of transactions. Saturn in
5 triangular relation to Mars signifies [bad] fortune. Jupiter in triangular relation to Mars or in conjunction makes great kingdoms and empires. Venus in conjunction with Mars causes fornications and adulteries; if in addition Mercury is in conjunction with them, they in consequence make scandals and lusts. If Mercury is in
10 conjunction with Jupiter or appears in triangular relation, this causes favourable actions or commerce, or a man will gain his living by . . . or by reason, and . . . If Mars appear in triangular relation to Jupiter and Saturn, this causes great happiness, and he will make great acquisitions and . . . If while Jupiter and Saturn
15 are in this position Mars comes into conjunction with either, . . . after obtaining [wealth] and collecting a fortune he will spend and

lose it. If Jupiter, Mercury, and Venus are in conjunction, they
cause glories and empires and great prosperity; and if the conjunction takes place at the morning rising [of Venus], they cause
20 prosperity from youth upwards.

D. *Papyri illustrating Social and Economic Conditions*

There is hardly one of the thousands of extant papyri which could not
be quoted with some degree of relevance under this head. In the following pages an attempt is made to illustrate some of the conditions of
private life—birth, employment, marriage, the family, death; to show
how the papyri afford data for economic history—goods, prices, taxes,
and the like; and to give some examples of legal documents. Finally
one very important political document is quoted. For the most part
these papyri (except when used by specialists for detailed study)
require little comment, but the reader who will pursue them—and the
many similar papyri—with attention and sympathetic imagination will
be rewarded with an insight into the world of primitive Christianity
which he could hardly obtain by any other means.

29 *P. Tebt.* 299. About A.D. 50. Notice of birth.

To Arius son of Lysimachus, comogrammateus of Tebtunis, from
Psoiphis son of Harpocras son of Pakebkis, his mother being Then-
marsisuchus daughter of Psoithis and Kellauthis, inhabitants of
the village, priest of the fifth tribe of the gods at the village,
5 Cronos, the most great god, and Isis and Sarapis, the great gods,
and one of the fifty exempted persons. I register Pakebkis, the son
born to me and Taasies daughter of ... and Taopis in the 10th
year of Tiberius Claudius Caesar Augustus Germanicus Imperator,
and request that the name of my aforesaid son Pakebkis be
10 entered on the list. . . .

This papyrus is mutilated in places, and the restorations are not
certain; but all are probable.

l. 1 *Comogrammateus*, an official of the village (κώμη).
l. 6 *Exempted*. See above, p. 30 (**24**).
l. 10 *Entered on the list*. It is probable that the boy was intended for the priesthood.

30 *P. Oxy.* 275 (H.E. 13). A.D. 66. Agreement of apprenticeship.

Tryphon son of Dionysius son of Tryphon and of Thamounis
daughter of Onnophris, and Ptolemaeus son of Pausirion son of
Ptolemaeus and of Ophelous daughter of Theon, weaver, both

being inhabitants of Oxyrhynchus, mutually acknowledge that
5 Tryphon has apprenticed to Ptolemaeus his son Thoonis, whose
mother is Saraeus daughter of Apion, and who is not yet of age, for
a period of one year from the present day, to serve and to follow all
the instructions given to him by Ptolemaeus in the art of weaving
as far as he himself knows it, the boy to be fed and clothed for the
10 whole period by his father Tryphon, who will also be responsible
for all the taxes on him, on the condition that Ptolemaeus will pay
to him monthly on account of food five drachmae and at the close
of the whole period on account of clothing twelve drachmae, nor
shall Tryphon have the right to remove the boy from Ptolemaeus
15 until the completion of the period, and for whatever days therein
the boy plays truant, he shall send him to work for the like number
at the end of it or else forfeit one drachma of silver for each day,,
and for removing him within the period he shall pay a penalty of
100 drachmae and the like sum to the Treasury. If Ptolemaeus fails
20 to instruct the boy fully, he shall be liable to the same penalties. This
contract of apprenticeship is valid. The 13th year of Nero Claudius
Caesar Augustus Germanicus Imperator, the 21st of the month
Sebastus. [Signed—in a different hand] I, Ptolemaeus son of
Pausirion son of Ptolemaeus and of Ophelous daughter of Theon,
25 will do everything in the one year. I, Zoilus son of Horus son of
Zoilus and of Dieus daughter of Sokeus have written for him, as he
is illiterate. The 13th year of Nero Claudius Caesar Augustus
Germanicus Imperator, Sebastus 21.

31 *B.G.U.* 1052. (H.E. 3). 13 B.C. A contract of marriage.

To Protarchus from Thermion daughter of Apion, with her
guardian Apollonius son of Chaereas, and from Apollonius son of
Ptolemaeus. Thermion and Apollonius son of Ptolemaeus agree
that they have come together to share a common life, and the said
5 Apollonius son of Ptolemaeus acknowledges that he has received
from Thermion by hand from the house a dowry of a pair of gold
earrings weighing three quarters and ... silver drachmae; and
from now Apollonius son of Ptolemaeus shall furnish to Thermion
as his wedded wife all necessaries and clothing in proportion to his
10 means and shall not ill-treat her nor cast her out nor bring in
another wife, or he shall straightway forfeit the dowry increased
by half, with right of execution upon both the person of Apollonius
son of Ptolemaeus and all his property as if by legal decision, and
Thermion shall fulfil her duties towards her husband and their
15 common life and shall not absent herself from the house for a
night or a day without the consent of Apollonius son of Ptolemaeus

nor dishonour nor injure their common home nor consort with another man, or she again if guilty of any of these actions shall, after trial, be deprived of the dowry, and in addition the transgress-
20 ing party shall be liable to the prescribed fine. The 17th year of Caesar, Pharmouthi 20.

l. 21 *Caesar.* The emperor Augustus is meant.

32 *P. Oxy.* 744. (H.E. 105). 1 B.C. A letter from husband to wife.

Hilarion to his sister Alis very many greetings, likewise to my lady Berous and Apollonarion. Know that we are still in Alexandria. Do not be anxious; if they really go home, I will remain in Alexandria. I beg and entreat you, take care of the little one, and
5 as soon as we receive our pay I will send it up to you. If by chance you bear a child, if it is a boy, let it be, if it is a girl, cast it out. You have said to Aphrodisias "Do not forget me." How can I forget you? I beg you then not to be anxious. The 29th year of Caesar, Pauni 23. [Addressed, on the verso] Deliver to Alis from Hilarion.

l. 1 *Sister.* See the note on *brother*, p. 28 (**20**).
l. 6 *Cast it out.* The exposure of children was apparently not uncommon; the author of the Epistle to Diognetus thinks it worth while to point out that though Christians marry and beget as do other men they do not cast out their children (5. 6).
l. 7 *Aphrodisias,* who brought the message to Hilarion, possibly with a letter.
l. 8 *Caesar.* See above, **31**.

33 *Rev. Ég.* 1919, p. 201. (H.E. 133). Early third century A.D. A letter from son to father.

To my lord and father Arion from Thonis greeting. Before all else I make supplication for you every day, praying also before the ancestral gods of my present abode that I may find you and all our folk thriving. Look you, this is my fifth letter to you, and you
5 have not written to me except only once, not even a word about your welfare, nor come to see me; though you promised me saying "I am coming," you have not come to find out whether the teacher is looking after me or not. He himself is inquiring about you almost every day, saying, "Is he not coming yet?" And I just say "Yes."
10 Endeavour then to come to me quickly in order that he may teach me as he is eager to do. If you had come up with me, I should have been taught long ago. And when you come, remember what I have often written to you about. Come to us quickly then before he goes up country. I send my salutations to all our folk, each by
15 name, together with those who love us. Salutations also to my

teachers. Goodbye, my lord and father, and may you prosper, as I
pray, for many years along with my brothers whom may the evil
eye harm not. [Postscript] Remember our pigeons. [Addressed] To
Arion my father from . . .

34 *B.G.U.* 1103. (H.E. 6). 13 B.C. Deed of divorce.

To Protarchus from Zois daughter of Heraclides, with her guardian
her brother Irenaeus son of Heraclides, and from Antipater son of
Zenon. Zois and Antipater agree that they have separated from
each other, severing the union which they had formed on the basis
5 of an agreement made through the same tribunal in Hathur of the
current 17th year of Caesar, and Zois acknowledges that she has
received from Antipater by hand from his house the material which
he received for dowry, clothes to the value of 120 drachmae and a
pair of gold earrings. The agreement of marriage shall henceforth
10 be null, and neither Zois nor other person acting for her shall take
proceedings against Antipater for restitution of the dowry, nor
shall either party take proceedings against the other about co-
habitation or any other matter whatsoever up to the present day,
and hereafter it shall be lawful both for Zois to marry another
15 man and for Antipater to marry another woman without either of
them being answerable. In addition to this agreement being valid,
the one who transgresses it shall moreover be liable both to
damages and to the prescribed fine. The 17th year of Caesar,
Pharmouthi 2.

35 *P. Tebt.* 381. A.D. 123. A will.

The 8th year of the Emperor Caesar Trajanus Hadrianus Augustus,
Choiak 22, at Tebtunis in the division of Polemon of the Arsinoite
nome. Thaesis daughter of Orsenouphis son of Onnophris, her
mother being Thenobastis, of the aforesaid village of Tebtunis,
5 aged about seventy-eight years, having a scar on the right forearm,
acting with her guardian, her kinsman Cronion son of Ameis, aged
about twenty-seven, having a scar between his eyebrows, acknowledges that she, the acknowledging party, Thaesis, has consented
that after her death there shall belong to Thenpetesuchus, her
10 daughter by her late departed husband Pansais, and also to Sansneus
son of Tephersos, the son of her other daughter Taorseus, now
dead, to the two of them, property as follows: to Thenpetesuchus
alone, the house, yard and all effects belonging to Thaesis in the
said village of Tebtunis by right of purchase from Thenpetesuchus
15 daughter of Petesuchus, and the furniture, utensils, household stock
and apparel left by Thaesis. and the sums due to her and other

property of any kind whatsoever, while to Sansneus she has bequeathed eight drachmae of silver, which Sansneus shall receive
from Thenpetesuchus after the death of Thaesis ; on condition that
20 the daughter Thenpetesuchus shall properly perform the obsequies
and laying out of her mother, and shall discharge such private
debts as Thaesis shall prove to owe, but as long as her mother
Thaesis lives she shall have power to . . .

l. 6 *Guardian.* As a woman, though an elderly one, Thaesis has a male guardian,
though he is fifty years younger than she.

l. 18 *Eight drachmae of silver.* There is some evidence that this sum was a conventional amount bequeathed where only a courtesy legacy was intended.

l. 23 The will probably continued with the assertion that during her life Thaesis
should have full right of disposal of her own property; this provision is
fairly common in wills.

36 *P. Oxy.* 39. A.D. 52. Release on medical grounds from military
service.

Copy of a release dated and signed in the 12th year of Tiberius
Claudius Caesar Augustus Germanicus Imperator, Pharmouthi 29.
Release from service was granted by Gn. Vergilius Capito, praefect
of Upper and Lower Egypt, to Tryphon, son of Dionysius, weaver,
5 suffering from cataract and shortness of sight, of the metropolis of
Oxyrhynchus. Examination was made in Alexandria.

l. 4 *Of Upper and Lower Egypt*: literally, "of both" (ἀμφοτέρων). It is clear that
the two districts are intended.

37 *P. Tebt.* 300. A.D. 151. Notice of death.

To Melanas, comogrammateus of Tebtunis, from Paopis son of
Psoiphis son of Paopis, exempted priest of the famous temple at
Tebtunis. My father Psoiphis son of Paopis and Asis, of the said
village, exempted priest of the said temple, died in the month Tubi
5 of the present 14th year of Antoninus Caesar the lord. Wherefore I
present this notice, that this name may be struck off and may be
inscribed in the list of such persons, and I swear by the Fortune of
Antoninus Caesar the lord that the information above given is
true. I, Paopis son of Psoiphis, have presented the notice. The 14th
10 year of the Emperor Caesar Titus Aelius Hadrianus Antoninus
Augustus Pius, Mecheir 15.
[On the verso is written the title of the document (ὑπόμ(νημα)
τελευτ(ῆς) Ψύφις Παῶπις), with the signature of Melanas.]

l. 5 *The lord,* τοῦ κυρίου.

l. 7 *The Fortune,* τὴν . . . τύχην.

l. 9 *I, Paopis . . . the notice.* This sentence is in different handwriting from the rest, presumably that of Paopis himself. The rest was no doubt written by a professional writer or official.

38 *P. Cairo Zen.* 59092. (H.E. 182). About 257 B.C. A list of clothes.

Zenon's trunk in which are contained: 1 linen wrap, washed; 1 clay-coloured cloak, for winter, washed, and 1 worn, 1 for summer, half-worn, 1 natural-coloured, for winter, washed, and 1 worn, 1 vetch-coloured, for summer, new; 1 white tunic for winter, with
5 sleeves, washed, 1 natural-coloured, for winter, with sleeves, worn, 1 natural-coloured, for winter, worn, 2 white, for winter, washed, and 1 half-worn, 3 for summer, white, new, 1 unbleached, 1 half-worn; 1 outer garment, white, for winter, washed; 1 coarse mantle; 1 summer garment, white, washed, and 1 half-worn; 1
10 pair of Sardian pillow-cases; 2 pairs of socks, clay-coloured, new, 2 pairs of white, new; 2 girdles, white, new. [On the verso] From Pisicles, a list of Zenon's clothes.

39 *P. Tebt.* 35. (H.E. 223). 111 B.C. Official regulation of the price of myrrh (a government monopoly).

Apollonius to the epistatae in the division of Polemon and to the other officials greeting. For the myrrh distributed in the villages no one shall exact more than 40 drachmae of silver for a mina-weight or in copper 3 talents 2,000 drachmae with a charge of 200
5 drachmae on the talent for carriage; which sum shall be paid not later than the 3rd of Pharmouthi to the collector sent for the purpose. Let the subjoined notice be posted up with the concurrence of the village secretary, who shall sign his name below the order along with you. Whoever contravenes these instructions will
10 render himself liable to accusation. We have therefore also sent the sword-bearers. Goodbye. Year 6, Pharmouthi 2.

. 1 *Epistatae.* Village overseers.
l. 5 *For carriage,* because the quantities of copper involved would be so heavy.
l. 7 *Subjoined notice.* The notice is still subjoined. It is not printed here because it repeats the earlier notice addressed to the epistatae almost word for word.
l. 11 *Sword-bearers.* Apollonius's action in sending armed police suggests that he expected the proclamation to be unpopular.

40 *P. Oxy.* 1439. (H.E. 381). A.D. 75. A toll receipt.

Sarapion has paid the one per cent tax for toll dues of the Oasis upon one ass-load of barley and one ass-load of garlic. The 2nd year of Vespasianus the lord, seventh (7th) day of Mecheir.

41 *P. Amh.* 51. (H.E. 28). 88 B.C. Deed of sale of a house.

[Column 1, summary] The 26th year, Mesore 28. Peteesis son of
Pates has sold to Pelaeas son of Eunous the house belonging to him
in the eastern part of Pathyris, built raftered and furnished with
doors, the boundaries of which are given in the deed of sale.
5 [Column 2, text of deed] In the 26th year of the reign of Ptolemy
surnamed Alexander and of Cleopatra the sister, gods Philometores
Soteres, the priests and priestesses and the canephorus being those
now in office, the 28th of the month Mesore, at Pathyris, before
Hermias, agoranomus of the upper toparchy of the Pathyrite nome.
10 Peteesis son of Pates, Persian, aged about forty years, of medium
height, fair-skinned, smooth-haired, long-faced, straight-nosed,
with a scar under the left eyebrow, has sold the house belonging
to him, built and raftered and furnished with doors, at the so-called
fountain in the eastern part of Pathyris, of which the boundaries
15 are, to the south the house of Pelaeas the purchaser, on the north
the house of Taenoutis daughter of Psenpoeris, of which Totoes son
of Panechates has possession, on the east and west a royal street,
or whatever the boundaries may be all round. Pelaeas son of
Eunous has bought it for one talent of copper. Negotiator and
20 guarantor of all the terms of this deed of sale: Peteesis the vendor,
who has been accepted by Pelaeas the purchaser. [Subscribed]
Registered by me, Hermias.

l. 7 *Canephorus.* A priestess at Alexandria.
l. 9 *Agoranomus.* A public official through whom contracts were drawn up.

42 *P. Ryl.* 175 (H.E. 278). A.D. 28–9. A householder complains to the
police that he has been robbed.

To Serapion, chief of police, from Orsenouphis son of Harpaesis,
notable of the village of Euhemeria in the division of Themistes.
In the month Mesore of the past 14th year of Tiberius Caesar Augustus I was having some old walls on my premises demolished by
5 the mason Petesouchus son of Petesouchus, and while I was absent
from home to gain my living, Petesouchus in the process of demoli-
tion discovered a hoard which had been secreted by my mother in a
little box as long ago as the 16th year of Caesar, consisting of a pair
of gold earrings weighing 4 quarters, a gold crescent weighing 3
10 quarters, a pair of silver armlets of the weight of 12 drachmae of
uncoined metal, a necklace with silver ornaments worth 80 drachmae, and 60 silver drachmae. Diverting the attention of his
assistants and my people he had them conveyed to his own home by
his maiden daughter, and after emptying out the aforesaid objects

15 he threw away the box empty in my house, and he even admitted
finding the box, though he pretends that it was empty. Wherefore
I request, if you approve, that the accused be brought before you
for the consequent punishment. Farewell.

Orsenouphis, aged fifty, scar on left forearm.

43 *P. Hamb. i.* 4. (H.E. 249). A.D. 87. Engagement to appear in court.

Copy of bond. To Nemesion, royal scribe of the division of Heraclides, from Lucius Vettius Epaphroditus. I swear by the Emperor
Caesar Domitianus Augustus Germanicus that I will present myself
in Alexandria not later than the 23rd of the month Pharmouthi of
5 the current 6th year of the Emperor Caesar Domitianus Augustus
Germanicus and will attend the most sacred court of his excellency
the praefect Gaius Septimius Vegetus until I have contested the case
which Marcus Antonius Tituleius, soldier, is bringing against me,
in conformity with the order delivered to Claudius Chares, late
10 strategus, otherwise may I incur the consequences of the oath.
Isidorus, public scribe, has written for him, as he professes to be
illiterate. Epaphroditus, aged thirty-five years, with a scar on the
small finger of the right hand, described by Tebulus, assistant. The
6th year of the Emperor Caesar Domitianus Augustus Germani-
15 cus, Pharmouthi 3.

l. 13 *Tebulus*, who adds this sentence, was apparently instructed to note down a
description of Epaphroditus, for later use, if necessary, in identification.

44 *P. Oxy.* 37 (H.E. 257). A.D. 49. Minutes of legal proceedings before
a strategus.

From the minutes of Tiberius Claudius Pasion, strategus. The 9th
year of Tiberius Claudius Caesar Augustus Germanicus Imperator,
Pharmouthi 3, at the court. Pesouris *versus* Saraeus. Aristocles,
advocate for Pesouris, said: "Pesouris, for whom I appear, in the
5 7th year of Tiberius Claudius Caesar the lord picked up from a
rubbish-heap a male foundling called Heraclas. This he entrusted
to the defendant, and the nurse's contract which was made here
referred to it as a son of Pesouris. She received her wages for the
first year. The pay-day for the second year came round and again
10 she received them. To show that these statements are true, we have
her receipts in which she acknowledges payment. As the foundling
was being starved, Pesouris took it away. Subsequently, seizing an
opportunity, she burst into the house of my client and carried the
foundling off; and she seeks to obtain the foundling as being her
15 free-born child. I have here, first, the written contract for nursing,

I have, secondly, the receipt for the wages. I demand that these be recognized." Saraeus: "I weaned my own child and the foundling of these persons was entrusted to me. I have received from them the whole eight staters. Subsequently the foundling died, [.]
20 staters being still unearned. Now they seek to take away my own child." Theon: "We have the papers relating to the foundling." The strategus: "Since from its looks the child appears to be the son of Saraeus, if she and her husband will sign a sworn declaration that the foundling entrusted to her by Pesouris has died, I give
2 5 judgement in accordance with the decision of our lord the praefect that on paying back the money which she has received she shall have her own child."

l. 5 . . . *picked up from a rubbish-heap* . . .—perhaps not a very uncommon occurrence; cf. Hilarion's letter above, p. 38 (**32**).

l. 19 [.] *staters being still unearned*—that paid in advance for the latter part of the second year, after the child's death.

l. 21 *Theon*. Perhaps the advocate of Saraeus.

l. 25 *The praefect*. The strategus could act only under the direction of the praefect. Apparently he has already received an instruction from his superior.

45 *P. Lond.* 1912. (H.E. 212). A.D. 41. A letter of the Emperor Claudius to the Alexandrians. This letter is of great historical and constitutional importance. See pp. 13, 136ff. (**125f.**).

Proclamation by Lucius Aemilius Rectus. Seeing that all the populace, owing to its numbers, was unable to be present at the reading of the most sacred and most beneficent letter to the city, I have deemed it necessary to display the letter publicly in order
5 that reading it one by one you may admire the majesty of our god Caesar and feel gratitude for his goodwill towards the city. Year 2 of Tiberius Claudius Caesar Augustus Germanicus Imperator, the 14th of Neus Sebastus.

Tiberius Claudius Caesar Augustus Germanicus Imperator,
10 Pontifex Maximus, holder of the tribunician power, consul designate, to the city of Alexandria greeting. Tiberius Claudius Barbillus, Apollonius son of Artemidorus, Chaeremon son of Leonidas, Marcus Julius Asclepiades, Gaius Julius Dionysius, Tiberius Claudius Phanias, Pasion son of Potamon, Dionysius son of
15 Sabbion, Tiberius Claudius Archibius, Apollonius son of Ariston, Gaius Julius Apollonius, Hermaiscus son of Apollonius, your ambassadors, having delivered to me the decree, discoursed at length concerning the city, directing my attention to your goodwill towards us, which from long ago, you may be sure, had been
20 stored up to your advantage in my memory; for you are by nature

reverent towards the Augusti, as I know from many proofs, and
in particular have taken a warm interest in my house, warmly
reciprocated, of which fact (to mention the last instance, passing
over the others) the supreme witness is my brother Germanicus
25 addressing you in words more clearly stamped as his own. Wherefore I gladly accepted the honours given to me by you, though I
have no weakness for such things. And first I permit you to keep
my birthday as a *dies Augustus* as you have yourselves proposed,
and I agree to the erection in their several places of the statues of
30 myself and my family; for I see that you were anxious to establish
on every side memorials of your reverence for my house. Of the
two golden statues the one made to represent the Pax Augusta
Claudiana, as my most honoured Barbillus suggested and entreated when I wished to refuse for fear of being thought too
35 offensive, shall be erected at Rome, and the other according to your
request shall be carried in procession on name-days in your city;
and it shall be accompanied by a throne, adorned with whatever
trappings you choose. It would perhaps be foolish, while accepting
such great honours, to refuse the institution of a Claudian tribe and
40 the establishment of groves after the manner of Egypt; wherefore
I grant you these requests as well, and if you wish you may also
erect the equestrian statues given by Vitrasius Pollio my procurator.
As for the erection of those in four-horse chariots which you wish
to set up to me at the entrances into the country, I consent to let
45 one be placed at Taposiris, the Lybian town of that name, another
at Pharos in Alexandria, and a third at Pelusium in Egypt. But I
deprecate the appointment of a high priest to me and the building
of temples, for I do not wish to be offensive to my contemporaries,
and my opinion is that temples and such forms of honour have by
50 all ages been granted as a prerogative to the gods alone.

Concerning the requests which you have been anxious to obtain
from me, I decide as follows. All those who have become *ephebi* up
to the time of my principate I confirm and maintain in possession
of the Alexandrian citizenship with all the privileges and indul-
55 gences enjoyed by the city, excepting such as by beguiling you have
contrived to become *ephebi* though born of servile mothers; and it
is equally my will that all the other favours shall be confirmed
which were granted to you by former princes and kings and prae-
fects, as the deified Augustus also confirmed them. It is my will that
60 the *neocori* of the temple of the deified Augustus in Alexandria
shall be chosen by lot in the same way as those of the said deified
Augustus in Canopus are chosen by lot. With regard to the civic
magistracies being made triennial your proposal seems to me to be

very good; for through fear of being called to account for any
65 abuse of power your magistrates will behave with greater circum-
spection during their term of office. Concerning the senate, what
your custom may have been under the ancient kings I have no
means of saying, but that you had no senate under the former
Augusti you are well aware. As this is the first broaching of a novel
70 project, whose utility to the city and to my government is not
evident, I have written to Aemilius Rectus to hold an inquiry and
inform me whether in the first place it is right that a senate should
be constituted and, if it should be right to create one, in what
manner this is to be done.

75   As for the question which party was responsible for the riots and
feud (or rather, if the truth must be told, the war) with the Jews,
although in confrontation with their opponents your ambassadors,
and particularly Dionysius son of Theon, contended with great
zeal, nevertheless I was unwilling to make a strict inquiry, though
80 guarding within me a store of immutable indignation against
whichever party renews the conflict; and I tell you once for all
that unless you put a stop to this ruinous and obstinate enmity
against each other, I shall be driven to show what a benevolent
prince can be when turned to righteous indignation. Wherefore
85 once again I conjure you that on the one hand the Alexandrians
show themselves forbearing and kindly towards the Jews who for
many years have dwelt in the same city, and dishonour none of the
rites observed by them in the worship of their god, but allow them
to observe their customs as in the time of the deified Augustus,
90 which customs I also, after hearing both sides, have sanctioned;
and on the other hand I explicitly order the Jews not to agitate for
more privileges than they formerly possessed, and not in future to
send out a separate embassy as if they lived in a separate city, a
thing unprecedented, and not to force their way into gymnasi-
95 archic or cosmetic games, while enjoying their own privileges and
sharing a great abundance of advantages in a city not their own,
and not to bring in or admit Jews who come down the river from
Syria or Egypt, a proceeding which will compel me to conceive
serious suspicions; otherwise I will by all means take vengeance on
100 them as fomenters of what is a general plague infecting the whole
world. If desisting from these courses you consent to live with
mutual forbearance and kindliness, I on my side will exercise a
solicitude of very long standing for the city, as one which is bound
to us by traditional friendship. I bear witness to my friend Bar-
105 billus of the solicitude which he has always shown for you in my
presence and of the extreme zeal with which he has now advocated

your cause, and likewise to my friend Tiberius Claudius Archibius. Farewell.

l. 1 *Lucius Aemilius Rectus*, the praefect.
l. 25 ... *in words more clearly stamped as his own*—because they were spoken in Greek, not written in Latin.
l. 39 *A Claudian tribe*, in the city of Alexandria.
l. 52 *Ephebi* : youths born in families possessing the citizenship.
l. 60 *Neocori* : official temple guardians.

3

INSCRIPTIONS

An immense number of inscribed stones and metals, written in Latin, Greek, and Semitic languages, has been preserved, in various degrees of mutilation, from the world in which primitive Christianity arose. Taken together they furnish a very great deal of valuable material for the reconstruction of the military, political, social, and religious history of the ancient world. A complete account, or even an adequate sketch, of this material would clearly be out of place in this book, as would also be a description of the methods by which inscriptions may be, and have been, sought, excavated, deciphered, and interpreted. The following non-Christian inscriptions all bear directly, though in different ways, upon the history of early Christianity; it must be remembered that other inscriptions, which have no such direct reference, are nevertheless of great importance to the historian who would study the New Testament and other early Christian documents in their original setting.

A. *The Gallio Inscription at Delphi*

46 [See F. J. F. Jackson and K. Lake, *The Beginnings of Christianity*, V, pp. 460–4]. Four fragments of a stone bearing a rescript of the emperor Claudius (see pp. 13ff.) were discovered in the present century at Delphi, in Greece (Achaea), which refer to Gallio as proconsul of the province; cf. Acts 18. 12. The stone is dated, and consequently makes possible greater precision in the dating of Paul's visit to Corinth. Parts of the inscription have perished, and conjectural supplements (most of which are very probable) are indicated by square brackets, so far as this is possible in translation.

> Tiberius [Claudius] Caesar Augustus Germanicus, [Pontifex Maximus, in his tribunician] power
>
> [year 12, acclaimed Emperor for] the 26th time, father of the country, [consul for the 5th time, censor, sends greeting to the city of Delphi.]

I have for long been zealous for the city of Delphi [and favourable to it from the]

beginning, and I have always observed the cult of the [Pythian] Apollo, [but with regard to]

5 the present stories, and those quarrels of the citizens of which [a report has been made by Lucius]

Junius Gallio my friend, and [pro]consul [of Achaea] . . .

[Several lines follow which can be read with only partial certainty, and are not significant for the present purpose.]

l. 1 *Claudius* . . . The extent of the supplements in this and other lines is less striking than may appear at first sight. Most official inscriptions are stereotyped in form, and a knowledge of the usual formulae and of the space which must once have been filled often suffices for confident reconstruction.

l. 2 *Year 12, acclaimed Emperor for the 26th time.* The number 26 is extant in the inscription; 12 is a supplement. The figures are of great importance, since it is by means of them that the inscription is dated. It is to be noted that the emperors assumed the tribunician power at their accession and retained it continuously, the years being reckoned from the date of accession (for Claudius, 25 January 41); the acclamations were irregular, and (often) more frequent. The exact date of Claudius's 26th acclamation is not known. In his 11th year (of reign and tribunician power) he was acclaimed for the 22nd, 23rd and 24th times; in his 12th (and not later than 1 August) he was acclaimed for the 27th time. (These facts are all drawn from other inscriptions.) The 26th acclamation must therefore have taken place at the close of the 11th year (which would require five acclamations in that year), or, as is perhaps more probable, in the first half of the 12th year (i.e. between 25 January and 1 August A.D. 52); consequently the inscription itself falls within this period.

l. 4 *The Pythian Apollo.* The god who granted the famous oracles of Delphi.

l. 5 *The present stories.* We can only conjecture what disturbances had taken place at Delphi.

l. 6 *Gallio . . . proconsul of Achaea.* Achaea was a senatorial province, governed by a proconsul appointed by the Senate (see pp. 4f. (1)). It was customary for such provincial governors to remain in office for one year, or, less frequently, for two. They took up their duties in early summer, perhaps June. It thus appears that the latest date for Gallio's entry upon his office is June 52; this however is not likely, since it would mean that between June and the end of July Claudius had dealt with the trouble at Delphi, his rescript had been recorded and he had been acclaimed the 27th time. This is of course not impossible, but it seems on the whole more likely that Gallio became proconsul of Achaea in 51, or in 50, if he held office two years. This is an important datum for New Testament chronology, though it is to be noted that we do not know at what point in his proconsulship Paul was brought before Gallio.

B. *A Temple Inscription*

47 [See J. A. Robinson, *St Paul's Epistle to the Ephesians*, pp. 160f.] The inscription translated below explains itself. Gentiles were allowed in the outer but not the inner areas of the temple at Jerusalem, and Josephus (*War* v. 193f.; cf. *War* vi. 125; *Ant.* xv. 417; Philo, *Leg. ad Gaium* 212) says: "Proceeding across this [the open court] towards the second court of the temple, one found it surrounded by a stone balustrade, three cubits high and of exquisite workmanship; in this at regular intervals stood slabs giving warning, some in Greek, others in Latin characters, of the law of purification, to wit that no foreigner was permitted to enter the holy place, for so the second enclosure of the temple was called." One of these warning notices was discovered in 1871 by Clermont-Ganneau. It runs:

> No man of another nation to enter within the fence and enclosure round the temple. And whoever is caught will have himself to blame that his death ensues.

We may compare Acts 21. 26–30; and only add the comment that the notice of the warnings receives a special addition in the Slavonic Josephus; see p. 207 (**205**).

C. *Synagogue Inscriptions*

[See A. Deissmann, *Light from the Ancient East* (1927), p. 16; E. Schürer, *The Jewish People in the time of Jesus Christ*, II. ii. 248; F. J. F. Jackson and K. Lake, *Beginnings of Christianity*, IV, p. 67; V, p. 64.] Jewish communities, many of them equipped with synagogues, were to be found in many towns of the Roman Empire. The following inscriptions attest the existence of synagogues at Corinth, Rome, and Jerusalem.

48 *A Synagogue at Corinth.* [Deissmann, loc. cit.]

[Syn]agogue of the Hebr[ews].

49 *A Synagogue at Rome.* [*C.I.G.* 9909.]

Here lies
Salo(me)
daughter of Ga-
dia, father

5 of the synagogue
of the Hebrews. She
lived forty-one years.
In peace
be her
10 sleep.

l. 5   *Synagogue of the Hebrews.* On the synagogue in general see pp. 162f. The
exact meaning of the expression in these inscriptions, and particularly in that
found at Rome, turns upon the meaning of "Hebrews"; does this mean
Hebrews by race, or Hebrew (or Aramaic) speaking Jews? Perhaps the best
suggestion is that this synagogue (and at Rome there were, as inscriptions attest, synagogues of the Augusteans, the Volumnians, the Herodians,
the Campesians, the Syburesians, the Vernaculi, the Calcaremians, the Tri-
politans, the Elaians, the Sekeni, and (?) the Calabrians) was that of the
original small group of Jews resident in Rome (as early as the time of
Pompey), and that when other synagogues were added fresh and more
particular names were found for them; but it must be understood that this,
like all other suggestions on the matter, is hypothetical.

50 *A Synagogue at Jerusalem.* [Jackson and Lake, op. cit., IV, p. 67.]

Theodotus, son of Vettenus, priest and
archisynagogue, son of an archisynagogue, grandson of an archisynagogue, built
the synagogue for the read-
5 ing of the Law and the teaching of the commandments, and
the guest-house and the rooms and the wa-
ter supplies as an inn for those
who have need when they come from abroad; which [synagogue]
his fathers founded and the eld-
10 ers and Simonides.

l. 1   *Theodotus, Son of Vettenus.* It is very improbable that a Jewish inscription
would be made in Jerusalem after A.D. 70 (see pp. 132f. (120)), and the appearance of the inscribed letters confirms a date not far from the middle of the
first century A.D. The combination of the Greek name Theodotus with the
Latin Vettenus (in a Greek inscription) suggests the possibility that
Theodotus was a freedman, since freedmen often took the names of their
former owners, and the inscription may therefore throw light upon Acts
6. 9 (the synagogue called that of the Libertines, or freedmen); but it must
be remembered that the inscription does not say that either Theodotus or
Vettenus was a freedman.
    Priest and archisynagogue. For the office of archisynagogue cf. Mark 5. 22.
Theodotus was also a priest; temple and synagogue were not in opposition
to one another, even though the former was to some extent the stronghold
of the Sadducees, the latter of the Pharisees.

l. 6 *The guest-house.* Jews of the dispersion attended the Pilgrim Feasts as far as they were able (see pp. 155–9 (**150ff.**)), and did so in such numbers that it became extremely difficult to find accommodation in Jerusalem. The advantage of a synagogue building equipped as a hostel is evident.

l. 9 *His fathers founded,* i.e. probably, the father and grandfather referred to above. The probable meaning is that they founded the establishment, and that Theodotus rebuilt and perhaps increased it. Simonides is unknown.

D. *Sacral Manumission*

In the ancient world slavery was a common and hardly questioned institution. Consequently the states of freedom and bondage, and the transition between the two, were more familiar to the New Testament writers than to ourselves. As there were many ways by which a person might become a slave, so also there were several methods of emancipation. For example, a god and his priests might assist the process; this method suggests the possibility of parallels with various New Testament metaphors, and may be illustrated by the following inscriptions.

51 *W. Dittenberger, Sylloge Inscriptionum Graecarum, 2nd edition, 845.* An inscription of 200–199 B.C., found (with others) on a wall of the temple of Apollo at Delphi.

> The Pythian Apollo
> bought from Sosibius
> of Amphissa for freedom
> a female slave, whose name
> 5 is Nicaea, by race a Roman, at a price
> of three silver minas and
> a half-mina. Former seller according to
> the law was Eumnastus
> of Amphissa. He has received
> 10 the price. The deed of sale
> Nicaea has entrusted to
> Apollo for freedom.

l. 1 *The Pythian Apollo bought.* On Apollo at Delphi see p. 49 (**46**). The god is said to have bought the slave from her former owner, but it is clear, from this and other inscriptions, that the slave had first paid the price into the temple treasury; as a slave she could not herself negotiate the sale.

l. 3 *For freedom* (cf. l. 12). The god has purchased the slave not with a view to her serving him as a slave, but with a view to her freedom; the contract is therefore a form of manumission.

l. 8 *Eumnastus,* who sold Nicaea to Sosibius, is named as guaranteeing Sosibius's right to sell.

l. 10 *The deed of sale* is in fact the inscription, given publicity and permanence in the temple. An alternative translation of the word (ὠνά—written for ὠνή) is "price"; Nicaea entrusted the purchase money to Apollo who then effected the transaction.

52 *C.I.G.* 2114 *bb.* This inscription was found at Panticapaeum, in the Crimea. It is plainly of Jewish origin, and shows both the wide extent of the Diaspora (see pp. 136 ff.), and that the Jews also practised manumission at their sacred places.

> In the reign of king Tibe-
> rius Julius Rhescuporis, friend of
> Caesar and friend of Rome, the pi-
> ous; in the year 377, in the month Peniti-
> 5 us, the 20th [or 23rd], I, Chreste, formerly wife
> of Nicias, son of Sotas, release at the house of
> prayer my slave Heraclas
> to be completely free according to my vow.
> He is not to be retained or dis-
> 10 turbed by any heir of mine,
> but to go wherever he wish-
> es, without let or hindrance according to
> my vow, except for the house of prayer
> which is for worship and meet-
> 15 ing. Assent is given to this
> also by my heirs, Peri-
> cleides and Heliconias.
> Joint oversight will be taken also by the
> synagogue of the Jews.

l. 4 *In the year 377. . . .* The date is January A.D. 81.

l. 6 *The house of prayer.* This word (προσευχή, not συναγωγή) is frequently used of the building (or place) used for Jewish worship. It can also be quoted in heathen use (e.g. *C.I.G.* 2079), but there is no question of the Jewish origin of the present inscription (see l. 19). It may be noted also that this inscription, unlike the last, makes no reference to a fictitious sale to a god.

l. 8 *My vow.* The owner had evidently vowed the freedom of Heraclas in circumstances of which we are not informed. It is the vow, not a sale, which is here operative in manumission.

l. 13 *Except for the house of prayer.* The meaning of the phrase is obscure. Probably Heraclas was to continue under certain obligations as far as the house of prayer was concerned. This recalls, though distantly, pagan forms of sacral manumission.

l. 19 *The synagogue of the Jews.* Synagogue here means not a place of meeting but the local Jewish community, which met in the house of prayer.

4

THE PHILOSOPHERS

PHILOSOPHY, in the strict sense in which the term is now understood, plays only a small part in the background of the New Testament. In the early Christian period the age of the great philosophers was past. The "failure of nerve" (to use Dr Gilbert Murray's vivid phrase) had long set in. The fearless freedom of thought which had marked Periclean Athens had disappeared; men had lost confidence in the power of their own intelligence to solve by abstract ratiocination the problems of mind and matter, man and the universe. Dogmatism, revelation, religion, and even superstition replaced independent thought; interest in metaphysics was replaced by interest in practical ethics—how was a virtuous man to live in evil surroundings? When the problems of cosmology were envisaged they were seen as divine secrets revealed only to the elect.

To write thus is to paint perhaps too dark a picture. A preoccupation with ethics is after all no discredit to any age, and Christianity (like the Judaism from which it emerged) entered the ancient world as a revelation. But even a slight sketch of Platonism and Aristotelianism as metaphysical systems would be out of place in this book. Plato's work as the virtual founder of idealism was even in the first century important enough; but what the first century made of it was Gnosticism, or something much like Gnosticism (see Chapter 5), and the "philosophy" condemned by Paul (Col. 2. 8) was a worship of angels rather than a pursuit of truth and the Ideal Good. The first century was in philosophy an eclectic age, and no attempt will be made here to delineate the views of the several philosophical "schools" (though certain venerable labels will be retained). The following extracts may, however, help to suggest the atmosphere in which the Christian faith was propagated.

A. *Heraclitus and the Logos*

It is very improbable that those fragments of the philosopher Heraclitus (who flourished in Ephesus in the fifth century B.C.) that contain the word λόγος have anything to do with John's Logos-doctrine, or indeed with any New Testament doctrine. It has, however been maintained that Heraclitus's extremely obscure remarks are important for the study of the New Testament, and they are printed here for the convenience of the reader, who may consider the question for himself.

53 *Fragment* 1 *(Walzer).*[1] Though the word always exists men are without understanding, both before they hear it, and after they have heard it the first time. For though all things happen in accordance with this word men seem as if they had no acquaint-
5 ance with them, making trial of both words and deeds such as I set forth, distinguishing each thing according to its nature and showing how it is. But other men know not what they do even when they are awake, as they forget what they do when they are asleep.

l. 1 *Though the word always exists*; perhaps, though the word is always true. It seems clear that both here and in l. 4 λόγος means the speech, almost the prophetic oracle, of Heraclitus.

54 *Fragment* 2 *(Walzer).* It is necessary therefore to follow the common. But though the word is common most men live as if they had a wisdom of their own.

l. 2 *The word* again seems to refer to Heraclitus's message.

55 *Fragment* 31 *(Walzer).* Transformations of fire: first, sea, and half of sea is earth, and half is waterspout. . . . The sea liquefies and is measured by the same measure as before it became earth.

l. 3 *Measure*, λόγος. The word has no special sense here. There is a similar use in Fragments 45, 115.

56 *Fragment* 50 *(Walzer).* It is wise to listen not to me but to the word, and to confess that all things are one.

l. 1 It would be accurate to render, "to my word"; Heraclitus means that his message is true, whatever may be thought of the messenger.

B. *Plato: the Philosopher's Mission and the Doctrine of Ideas*

A discussion of the relation between Socrates and the Sophists would take us far beyond the limits of this book. That Socrates himself was able to distinguish sharply between his own work and that of the

---

[1] R. Walzer, *Eraclito: raccolta dei Frammenti* (Firenze, 1939).

common run of sophists is clear; but it is equally clear that there was no small superficial resemblance between them. He sometimes appeared, like them, to make "the worse appear the better reason"; this was because he questioned every conventional, unexamined motive, bade men examine themselves and their presuppositions, and dared to give a fresh opinion—or at least ask fresh questions—on such matters as the religion and established order of the state. He made powerful enemies by the devastating *elenchus* with which he exposed the hollow shams especially of those who were reputed to be wise and influential. The sophists were teachers of rhetoric; Socrates taught men to know themselves, and in that knowledge to discover their own ignorance. This was his mission to Athens, and in the faithful execution of it he became the prototype of the philosophic missionary (see below, pp. 75–9), and indeed of the philosophic martyr.

57 *Plato, Apology of Socrates* 28D–30C. In this work Socrates answers the charge, on which he was convicted and put to death, that "he had corrupted the young men of the city, and did not believe in the gods believed in by the city but had introduced other new divinities". In reply Socrates describes the origin of his "mission". The Delphic oracle had pronounced him the wisest of men. This he found incredible, and to prove it false, he proceeded to interrogate those who had a reputation for wisdom. He was amazed to find that, notwithstanding their reputation, they were ignorant men, and came to believe that he might after all be the wisest of men since, though he too was ignorant, he at least knew that he was ignorant (cf. l. 19 below). The theme of his mission is developed further.

Strange, indeed, would be my conduct, O men of Athens, if I who, when I was ordered by the generals whom you chose to command me at Potidaea and Amphipolis and Delium, remained where they placed me, like any other man, facing death—if now, when,
5 as I conceive and imagine, God orders me to fulfil the philosopher's mission of searching into myself and other men, I were to desert my post through fear of death, or any other fear; that would indeed be strange, and I might justly be arraigned in court for denying the existence of the gods, if I disobeyed the oracle because I was
10 afraid of death, fancying that I was wise when I was not wise. For the fear of death is indeed the pretence of wisdom, and not real wisdom, being a pretence of knowing the unknown; and no one knows whether death, which men in their fear apprehend to be the greatest evil, may not be the greatest good. Is not this ignor-

15 ance of a disgraceful sort, the ignorance which is the conceit that a
man knows what he does not know? And in this respect only I
believe myself to differ from men in general, and may perhaps
claim to be wiser than they are :—that whereas I know but little of
the world below, I do not suppose that I know : but I do know that
20 injustice and disobedience to a better, whether God or man, is
evil and dishonourable, and I will never fear or avoid a possible
good rather than a certain evil. And therefore if you let me go now,
and are not convinced by Anytus, who said that since I had been
prosecuted I must be put to death; (or if not that I ought never to
25 have been prosecuted at all); and that if I escape now, your sons
will all be utterly ruined by listening to my words—if you say to
me, Socrates, this time we will not mind Anytus, and you shall be
let off, but upon one condition, that you are not to inquire and
speculate in this way any more, and that if you are caught doing so
30 again you shall die;—if this was the condition on which you let
me go, I should reply : Men of Athens, I honour and love you ; but
I shall obey God rather than you, and while I have life and strength
I shall never cease from the practice and teaching of philosophy,
exhorting any one whom I meet and saying to him after my
35 manner : You, my friend,—a citizen of the great and mighty and
wise city of Athens,—are you not ashamed of heaping up the
greatest amount of money and honour and reputation, and caring
so little about wisdom and truth and the greatest improvement of
the soul, which you never regard or heed at all? And if the person
40 with whom I am arguing, says : Yes, but I do care; then I do not
leave him or let him go at once; but I proceed to interrogate and
examine and cross-examine him, and if I think that he has no virtue
in him, but only says that he has, I reproach him with undervalu-
ing the greater, and overvaluing the less. And I shall repeat the
45 same words to every one whom I meet, young and old, citizen
and alien, but especially to the citizens, inasmuch as they are my
brethren. For know that this is the command of God; and I
believe that no greater good has ever happened in the state than
my service to the God. For I do nothing but go about persuading
50 you all, old and young alike, not to take thought for your persons
or your properties, but first and chiefly to care about the greatest
improvement of the soul. I tell you that virtue is not given by
money, but that from virtue comes money and every other good
of man, public as well as private. This is my teaching, and if this is
55 the doctrine which corrupts the youth, I am a mischievous person.
But if any one says that this is not my teaching, he is speaking an
untruth. Wherefore, O men of Athens, I say to you, do as Anytus

bids or not as Anytus bids, and either acquit me or not: but
whichever you do, understand that I shall never alter my ways, not
60 even if I have to die many times.

l. 1 *Strange, indeed, would be my conduct* ... Socrates explains why he has not
abandoned the task of philosophizing and "examination".

l. 3 *At Potidaea and Amphipolis and Delium.* At the battles fought in these places, in
432, 422 and 424 B.C. respectively. In at least two of these Socrates was
distinguished by his bravery.

l. 5 *God orders me*; by the Delphic oracle; perhaps there is a reference also to the
"daemon" or guiding spirit by which Socrates believed himself to be
directed. Cf. l. 47.

58 *Plato, Republic* vii. 514A–517A. This famous Allegory of the Cave
sets forth in outline Plato's doctrine of ideas. It is significant that the
allegory is given a practical, moral, setting and application.

And now, I said, let me show in a figure how far our nature is
enlightened or unenlightened:—Behold! human beings living in
an underground den, which has a mouth open towards the light and
reaching all along the den; here they have been from their child-
5 hood, and have their legs and necks chained so that they cannot
move, and can only see before them, being prevented by the chains
from turning round their heads. Above and behind them a fire is
blazing at a distance, and between the fire and the prisoners there is
a raised way; and you will see, if you look, a low wall built along
10 the way, like the screen which marionette players have in front of
them, over which they show the puppets.
I see.
And do you see, I said, men passing all along the wall carrying
all sorts of vessels, and statues and figures of animals made of wood
15 and stone and various materials, which appear over the wall?
Some of them are talking, others silent.
You have shown me a strange image, and they are strange
prisoners.
Like ourselves, I replied; and they see only their own shadows,
20 or the shadows of one another, which the fire throws on the
opposite wall of the cave?
True, he said; how could they see anything but the shadows if
they were never allowed to move their heads?
And of the objects which are being carried in like manner they
25 would only see the shadows?
Yes, he said.
And if they were able to converse with one another, would they
not suppose that they were naming what was actually before them?

Very true.

30 And suppose further that the prison had an echo which came from the other side, would they not be sure to fancy when one of the passers-by spoke that the voice which they heard came from the passing shadow?

No question, he replied.

35 To them, I said, the truth would be literally nothing but the shadows of the images.

That is certain.

And now look again, and see what will naturally follow if the prisoners are released and disabused of their error. At first, when
40 any of them is liberated and compelled suddenly to stand up and turn his neck round and walk and look towards the light, he will suffer sharp pains; the glare will distress him, and he will be unable to see the realities of which in his former state he had seen the shadows; and then conceive someone saying to him, that what he
45 saw before was an illusion, but that now, when he is approaching nearer to being and his eye is turned towards more real existence, he has a clearer vision,—what will be his reply? And you may further imagine that his instructor is pointing to the objects as they pass and requiring him to name them,—will he not be perplexed?
50 Will he not fancy that the shadows which he formerly saw are truer than the objects which are now shown to him?

Far truer.

And if he is compelled to look straight at the light, will he not have a pain in his eyes which will make him turn away to take
55 refuge in the objects of vision which he can see, and which he will conceive to be in reality clearer than the things which are now being shown to him?

True, he said.

And suppose once more, that he is reluctantly dragged up a steep
60 and rugged ascent, and held fast until he is forced into the presence of the sun himself, is he not likely to be pained and irritated? When he approaches the light his eyes will be dazzled, and he will not be able to see anything at all of what are now called realities.

Not all in a moment, he said.

65 He will require to grow accustomed to the sight of the upper world.   And first he will see the shadows best, next the reflections of men and other objects in the water, and then the objects themselves; then he will gaze upon the light of the moon and the stars and the spangled heaven; and he will see the sky and the stars by
70 night better than the sun or the light of the sun by day?

Certainly.

Last of all he will be able to see the sun, and not mere reflections of him in the water, but he will see him in his own proper place, and not in another; and he will contemplate him as he is.

75   Certainly.

He will then proceed to argue that this is he who gives the seasons and the years, and is the guardian of all that is in the visible world, and in a certain way the cause of all things which he and his fellows have been accustomed to behold?

80   Clearly, he said, he would first see the sun and then reason about him.

And when he remembered his old habitation, and the wisdom of the den and his fellow-prisoners, do you not suppose that he would felicitate himself on the change, and pity them?

85   Certainly, he would.

And if they were in the habit of conferring honours among themselves on those who were quickest to observe the passing shadows and to remark which of them went before, and which followed after, and which were together; and who were therefore

90   best able to draw conclusions as to the future, do you think that he would care for such honours and glories, or envy the possessors of them? Would he not say with Homer,

"Better to be the poor servant of a poor master,"

and to endure anything, rather than think as they do and live

95   after their manner?

Yes, he said, I think that he would rather suffer anything than entertain these false notions and live in this miserable manner.

Imagine once more, I said, such an one coming suddenly out of the sun to be replaced in his old situation; would he not be certain

100   to have his eyes full of darkness?

To be sure, he said.

And if there were a contest, and he had to compete in measuring the shadows with the prisoners who had never moved out of the den, while his sight was still weak, and before his eyes had become

105   steady (and the time which would be needed to acquire this new habit of sight might be very considerable), would he not be ridiculous? Men would say of him that up he went and down he came without his eyes; and that it was better not even to think of ascending; and if any one tried to loose another and lead him up to

110   the light, let them only catch the offender, and they would put him to death.

No question, he said.

C. *The Earlier Stoics*

As a philosophical system, Stoicism was materialist; much more important than this, however, is the fact that in spirit it was deeply religious and thoroughly moral. The universe, the Stoics held, was not a meaningless place, nor was man's place in it fortuitous. Pervading the whole of the material order was Reason and Purpose, λόγος, itself divine and indeed the only god the Stoics recognized (see however **61** for their readiness to make some acknowledgement of the gods popularly believed in). It was this divine Reason that ordered the regular motions of the heavenly bodies, the rotation of the seasons and the exact performance by natural objects of their appointed functions. Man's duty was to live in accordance with this Reason or Natural Law (κατὰ λόγον); indeed a spark or seed of the universal Reason (a λόγος σπερματικός) resided within men, or at least within the best and wisest of them. Like Socrates, the Stoic must obey the divine spark at all costs, even at the cost of life itself. It might even in certain circumstances be the most appropriate course for the wise and dutiful man to take his own life—life that had lost its dignity and worth was not to be preferred to death. This sounds a cold and cheerless creed, and so perhaps it was; yet beyond question it nerved many a man to face the battle of life with a clear head and a brave heart, and it inculcated humanity and forbearance in a world in which these virtues were not common.

The works of none of the earlier Stoics have come down to us in their entirety, and the authors themselves are imperfectly known to us. The founder of the school was Zeno (*c.* 336–263 B.C.) who taught in the Painted Porch (*Stoa*) at Athens—whence the name of the school. Almost contemporary with him was Cleanthes (*c.* 331–232 B.C.). In a later generation Chrysippus (*c.* 280–205 B.C.) was perhaps the most voluminous of all Stoic writers. Posidonius, who is also quoted in this section, belongs to a later period (*c.* 135–51 B.C.), and is particularly important because he did much to fuse Stoic and Platonic thought.

59 *Zeno, Fragments*[1] 175, 176. Destiny is the concatenated causality of things, or the scheme according to which the kosmos is directed.
    Zeno defined Destiny as "a power which moves Stuff". "Providence" and "Nature" are other names which he gave to the same
5 thing.

---

[1] In J. von Arnim, *Stoicorum Veterum Fragmenta*, I (1938).

ll. 1, 2 *Destiny* (εἱμαρμένη) . . . *the scheme* (λόγος). Already in Zeno appears the
characteristic Stoic doctrine that the universe is informed by Logos, which
is at once the scheme according to which things move, and the power that
makes them move. Through the notion of Destiny it is linked with the
regular movements of the celestial bodies, which in their turn controlled the
affairs of men.

60 *Zeno, Fragment* 98. The element of all the things which exist is Fire,
and the origins of this Fire are Stuff and God. Both of these are
bodily substances: God the active substance, and Stuff the passive
substance. At certain destined periods of time the whole universe
5 is turned to fire; then again it is once more constituted an ordered
manifold world. But the primal fire subsists in it like a kind of
seminal fluid, containing in itself the formulas and causes of all
the things which have been and are and shall be; the concatenation
and sequence of these things is Destiny or Understanding or Truth,
10 an inevitable and ineluctable Law of things. Thus the whole universe is governed excellently well, like a city-state in which Law
reigns supreme.

l. 2 *The origins of this Fire are Stuff* (ὕλη) *and God.* This is a scarcely accurate
representation (by Eusebius) of Stoic thought. God *was* fire; and when the
cosmos was constituted some fire was turned into stuff.

l. 4 *The whole universe is turned to fire.* This, the Stoics believed, happened
periodically. The process was called ἐκπύρωσις.

l. 5 *It is once more constituted.* This also was a recurring event. Fire became matter;
see above.

l. 7 *Formulas* (λόγοι). The Logos, or reason of the whole universe, could be
distinguished (though hardly separated) from the logoi which controlled
every single being.

61 *Zeno, Fragments* 162, 152. The General Law, which is Right
Reason, pervading everything, is the same as Zeus, the Supreme
Head of the government of the universe.
Zeno used to propound the following argument:
5 "It is reasonable to honour the gods:
but it is not reasonable to honour beings which do not exist:
therefore gods exist."

l. 1 *Right Reason* (ὀρθὸς λόγος) . . . *is the same as Zeus.* In this way Stoicism
came to terms with theism; though, as appears from this passage, its theism
was pantheism.

l. 5 *It is reasonable to honour the gods.* It is astonishing that Zeno failed to see the
petitio principii involved in this premise.

62 *Cleanthes, Fragment*[1] 537.

Thou, O Zeus, art praised above all gods: many are thy names and thine is all power for ever.

The beginning of the world was from thee: and with law thou rulest over all things.

5   Unto thee may all flesh speak: for we are thy offspring.

Therefore will I raise a hymn unto thee: and will ever sing of thy power.

The whole order of the heavens obeyeth thy word: as it moveth around the earth:

10   With little and great lights mixed together: how great art thou, King above all for ever!

Nor is anything done upon earth apart from thee: nor in the firmament, nor in the seas:

Save that which the wicked do: by their own folly.

15   But thine is the skill to set even the crooked straight: what is without fashion is fashioned and the alien akin before thee.

Thus hast thou fitted together all things in one: the good with the evil:

That thy word should be one in all things: abiding for ever.

20   Let folly be dispersed from our souls: that we may repay thee the honour, wherewith thou hast honoured us:

Singing praise of thy works for ever: as becometh the sons of men.

l. 1 *O Zeus.* For Stoic readiness to countenance the accepted gods, see above; but Zeus in this hymn (as it may rightly be called) differs much from the Zeus of popular belief.

l. 3 *Law* (νόμος), the right reason which governs the universe (above, **61**), here represented as the instrument of a personal god.

l. 5 *We are thy offspring*; perhaps rather, *They* are thy offspring (see von Arnim, ad loc.). A similar statement was made by Aratus of Soli (*Phaenomena* 5), and quoted by Paul at Athens (Acts 17. 28).

l. 14 *Save that which the wicked do.* Evil is the revolt of men against the divine Logos, or law; God cannot be held responsible for it.

63 *Chrysippus, Fragment*[2] 625. The Stoics say that when the planets return, at certain fixed periods of time, to the same relative positions, in length and breadth, which they had at the beginning, when the cosmos was first constituted, this produces the conflagration and 5 destruction of everything which exists. Then again the cosmos is restored anew in a precisely similar arrangement as before. The stars again move in their orbits, each performing its revolution in

---

[1] J. von Arnim, op. cit.
[2] J. von Arnim, op. cit., II (1923).

the former period, without any variation. Socrates and Plato and
each individual man will live again, with the same friends and
10 fellow-citizens. They will go through the same experiences and the
same activities. Every city and village and field will be restored,
just as it was. And this restoration of the universe takes place,
not once, but over and over again—indeed to all eternity without
end. Those of the gods who are not subject to destruction, having
15 observed the course of one period, know from this everything
which is going to happen in all subsequent periods. For there will
never be any new thing other than that which has been before, but
everything is repeated down to the minutest detail.

l. 1 *The planets.* The fatalistic belief in destiny (above, **59**) was closely bound up
with astrology; there is no doubt that the regular unalterable movement of
the stars was a most impressive and influential phenomenon.

l. 4 *The conflagration and destruction.* See above, **60**. History was a succession of
cycles, each exactly the same as the last.

64 *Chrysippus, Fragment* 1169. On the problem of evil.

There can be nothing more inept than the people who suppose
that good could have existed without the existence of evil. Good
and evil being antithetical, both must needs subsist in opposition,
each serving, as it were, by its contrary pressure as a prop to the
5 other. No contrary, in fact can exist, without its correlative
contrary. How could there be any meaning in "justice", unless
there were such things as wrongs? What *is* justice but the preven-
tion of injustice? What could anyone understand by "courage",
but for the antithesis of cowardice? Or by "continence", but for
10 that of self-indulgence? What room for prudence, unless there was
imprudence? Why do not such men in their folly go on to ask
that there should be such a thing as truth, and not such a thing as
falsehood? The same may be said of good and evil, felicity and
inconvenience, pleasure and pain. These things are tied, as Plato
15 puts it, each to the other, by their heads: if you take away one,
you take away the other.

65 *Chrysippus, Fragment* 1192. If there are gods and they do not declare to men beforehand future events, either (1) they do not love
men, or (2) they are themselves ignorant of the future, or (3) they
do not consider that it is to man's interest to have knowledge of the
5 future, or (4) they do not think that it sorts with their dignity to
foreshow the future to men, or (5) the gods themselves have not
the power to do it. But (1) it is not the case that they do not love
us, being beneficent and friends of mankind; (2) they cannot be

ignorant of things which they themselves have instituted and
10 ordained; (3) it *is* to our interest to know what is going to happen,
for we shall act more prudently, if we know; (4) the gods cannot
think such disclosure beneath their dignity, for nothing is of higher
worth than to do good; and lastly (5) divination regarding the
future cannot lie outside their power. To suppose, then, that there
15 are gods and that they do not give signs of the future, is impossible.
But there are gods. Therefore they must give signs of the future.
Further, if they give signs, it cannot be that they give us no means
of reading those signs; for in that case they would give signs to no
purpose. If they give us the means, we cannot deny the existence of
20 divination. Therefore divination is a reality.

l. 9 *They themselves have instituted and ordained.* That all things have been pre-
destined by the "gods" is a popular way of saying that all things happen in
accordance with universal reason. The Stoics were thus able to defend the
popular belief in divination.

66 *Posidonius, apud Sextus Empiricus, adv. Math.* vii. 93. Just as light,
Posidonius says, explaining Plato's *Timaeus*, is apprehended by
the vision, which is itself of luminous quality, just as a voice is
apprehended by the hearing, which is itself of airy quality, so
5 the Nature of the Universe ought to be apprehended by the
Reason, which is akin to it.

l. 2 *Explaining Plato's Timaeus.* Platonism now (with Posidonius) began strongly
to influence Stoicism. The *Timaeus* in particular came to be looked on almost
as Holy Writ, an inspired revelation of the nature of things.

67 *Posidonius* [Cf. Galen, *De Hippocratis et Platonis Decretis* iv. 7.]

The cause of the passions—the cause, that is, of disharmony and
of the unhappy life—is that men do not follow absolutely the
daemon that is in them, which is akin to, and has a like nature with,
the Power governing the whole cosmos, but turn aside after the
5 lower animal principle, and let it run away with them. Those
who fail to see this neither thereby set the cause of the passions
in any better light, nor hold the right belief regarding happiness
and concord. They do not perceive that the very first point in
happiness is to be led in nothing by the irrational, unhappy,
10 godless element in the soul.

l. 3 *The daemon that is in them,* or seminal reason (λόγος σπερματικός; see above,
p. 61); but this force leading to right thought and conduct was now thought
of in more personal terms, and the view of human nature involved becomes
more dualistic. Cf. the "daemon" of Socrates, by which he was guided.
l. 7 *Happiness and concord, sc.* "with self and Nature" (Bevan).

D. *Stoic Ethics*

It has already been stated that Stoicism was from the beginning a moral philosophy; but the earlier Stoics engaged in a speculative physics which, though it was by no means abandoned by their successors in the Roman period, retreated into the background, ethical interests becoming more and more predominant as Stoicism became the prevailing philosophy of the ever practical Romans. Epictetus was a lame slave belonging to Epaphroditus, himself a freedman of Nero's. He was allowed to study philosophy, and eventually emancipated. He was born in Asia Minor, came to Rome, and later settled at Nicopolis in Epirus. The exact dates of his life cannot be determined, but he was already active as a philosopher in A.D. 89, and survived till towards the middle of the second century. Marcus Aurelius Antoninus was emperor of Rome from A.D. 161 to 180. From an early age he was marked for high distinction, and enjoyed all that wealth and position could afford. These things, however, meant nothing to him in comparison with the virtuous life of a moral philosopher, and he was perhaps history's nearest approach to the ideal of the philosopher-king. "It is a striking testimony to the wide range of Stoic influence that it should have found its highest expression in a Roman Emperor and a Greek slave, both finding common ground in the Stoic doctrine and the language of the later Greek world" (P. E. Matheson, *Epictetus, The Discourses and Manual* (Oxford, 1916) i. 13).

68 *Epictetus, Discourses* I, xvi. 1–8, 15–21. On Providence.

Marvel not that the other creatures have their bodily needs supplied—not only meat and drink, but a bed to lie on—and that they want no shoes nor rugs nor clothes, while we want all these things. For it would not have been a good thing that these
5 creatures, born not for themselves but for service, should have been created liable to wants. Consider what it would be for us to have to take thought not only for ourselves but for sheep and asses, how they were to dress and what shoes they were to put on, and how they should find meat and drink. But just as soldiers when
10 they appear before their general are ready shod, and clothed and armed, and it would be a strange thing indeed if the tribune had to go round and shoe or clothe his regiment, so also nature has made the creatures that are born for service ready and prepared and able

to dispense with any attention. So one small child can drive sheep
15 with a rod.

Yet we forbear to give thanks that we have not to pay the same
attention to them as to ourselves, and proceed to complain against
God on our own account. I declare, by Zeus and all the gods, one
single fact of nature would suffice to make him that is reverent
20 and grateful realize the providence of God: no great matter, I
mean; take the mere fact that milk is produced from grass and
cheese from milk and wool from skin. Who is it that has created
or contrived these things?

"No one", he says.
25 Oh, the depth of man's stupidity and shamelessness! . . .

If we had sense we ought to do nothing else, in public and in
private, than praise and bless God and pay him due thanks. Ought
we not, as we dig and plough and eat, to sing the hymn to God?
"Great is God that he gave us these instruments wherewith we
30 shall till the earth. Great is God that he has given us hands, and
power to swallow, and a belly, and the power to grow without
knowing it, and to draw our breath in sleep." At every moment we
ought to sing these praises and above all the greatest and divinest
praise, that God gave us the faculty to comprehend these gifts and
35 to use the way of reason.

More than that: since most of you are walking in blindness,
should there not be some one to discharge this duty and sing
praises to God for all? What else can a lame old man as I am do but
chant the praise of God? If, indeed, I were a nightingale I should
40 sing as a nightingale, if a swan, as a swan: but as I am a rational
creature I must praise God. This is my task, and I do it: and I will
not abandon this duty, so long as it is given me; and I invite you all
to join in this same song.

l. 40 *A rational creature*, λογικός, endowed with λόγος and therefore corresponding to the divine nature of things.

69 *Epictetus, Discourses* II, viii. 9–14. Will you not then seek the true
nature of the good in that, the want of which makes you refuse to
predicate good in other things?

"What do you mean? Are not they too God's works?"
5 They are, but not his principal works, nor parts of the Divine.
But you are a principal work, a fragment of God himself, you have
in yourself a part of him. Why then are you ignorant of your high
birth? Why do you not know whence you have come? Will you
not remember, when you eat, who you are that eat, and whom you
10 are feeding, and the same in your relations with women? When

you take part in society, or training, or conversation, do you not know that it is God you are nourishing and training? You bear God about with you, poor wretch, and know it not. Do you think I speak of some external god of silver or gold? No, you bear
15 him about within you and are unaware that you are defiling him with unclean thoughts and foul actions. If an image of God were present, you would not dare to do any of the things you do; yet when God himself is present within you and sees and hears all things, you are not ashamed of thinking and acting thus: O slow
20 to understand your nature, and estranged from God!

l. 4 *They too,* secondary objects, which show God's providence in that they are equipped with properties that make them serviceable to us; see **68** above.
l. 6 *A fragment of God himself,* in that there is within you a spark or seed of that universal λόγος which is God.

70 *Epictetus, Discourses* IV, i. 1–23, 128–31. That man is free, who lives as he wishes, who is proof against compulsion and hindrance and violence, whose impulses are untrammelled, who gets what he wills to get and avoids what he wills to avoid.
5   Who then would live in error?
No one.
Who would live deceived, reckless, unjust, intemperate, querulous, abject?
No one.
10   No bad man then lives as he would, and so no bad man is free.
Who would live in a state of distress, fear, envy, pity, failing in the will to get and in the will to avoid?
No one.
Do we then find any bad man without distress or fear, above
15 circumstance, free from failure?
None. Then we find none free.
If a man who has been twice consul hear this, he will forgive you if you add, "But *you* are wise, this does not concern you." But if you tell him the truth, saying, "You are just as much a slave your-
20 self as those who have been thrice sold", what can you expect but a flogging?
"How can I be a slave?" he says; "my father is free, my mother is free, no one has bought me; nay, I am a senator, and a friend of Caesar, I have been consul and have many slaves."
25   In the first place, most excellent senator, perhaps your father too was a slave of the same kind as you, yes and your mother and your grandfather and the whole line of your ancestors. And if really they were ever so free, how does that affect you? What does it

matter if they had a fine spirit, when you have none, if they were
30 fearless and you are a coward, if they were self-controlled and you
are intemperate?

"Nay, what has this to do with being a slave?" he replies.

Does it seem to you slavery to act against your will, under
compulsion and without groaning?

35 "I grant you that," he says, "but who can compel me except
Caesar, who is lord of all?"

Why, then, your own lips confess that you have one master: you
must not comfort yourself with the thought that he is, as you say,
the common master of all, but realize that you are a slave in a
40 large household. You are just like the people of Nicopolis, who are
wont to cry aloud, "By Caesar's fortune, we are free."

However, let us leave Caesar for the moment if you please, but
tell me this: Did you never fall in love with any one, with a girl,
or a boy, or a slave, or a free man?

45 "What has that to do with slavery or freedom?"

Were you never commanded by her you loved to do anything
you did not wish? Did you never flatter your precious slave-boy?
Did you never kiss his feet? Yet if any one compel you to kiss
Caesar's, you count it an outrage, the very extravagance of
50 tyranny. What is this if not slavery? Did you never go out at
night where you did not wish, and spend more than you wished
and utter words of lamentation and groaning? Did you put up
with being reviled and shut out? If you are ashamed to confess
your own story, see what Thrasonides says and does: he had
55 served in as many campaigns or more perhaps than you and yet,
first of all, he has gone out at night, at an hour when Getas does
not dare to go, nay, if he were forced by his master to go, he
would have made a loud outcry and have gone with lamentations
over his cruel slavery, and then, what does he say?

60   A worthless girl has made a slave of me,
       Whom never foe subdued.

Poor wretch, to be slave to a paltry girl and a worthless one
too! Why do you call yourself free then any more? Why do you
boast of your campaigns? Then he asks for a sword, and is angry
65 with the friend who refuses it out of goodwill, and sends gifts to
the girl who hates him, and falls to praying and weeping, and then
again when he has a little luck he is exultant. How can we call him
free when he has not learnt to give up desire and fear? . . .

Come now and let us review the conclusions we have agreed to.
70 He is free, whom none can hinder, the man who can deal with
things as he wishes. But the man who can be hindered or compelled

or fettered or driven into anything against his will, is a slave. And
who is he whom none can hinder? The man who fixes his aim on
nothing that is not his own. And what does "not his own" mean?
75 All that it does not lie in our power to have or not to have, or to
have of a particular quality or under particular conditions. The
body then does not belong to us, its parts do not belong to us, our
property does not belong to us. If then you set your heart on one
of these as though it were your own, you will pay the penalty
80 deserved by him who desires what does not belong to him. The
road that leads to freedom, the only release from slavery is this, to
be able to say with your whole soul:

> Lead me, O Zeus, and lead me, Destiny,
> Whither ordainéd is by your decree.

71 *Marcus Aurelius, To Himself* ii. 1. Say to thyself at daybreak: I
shall come across the busybody, the thankless, the bully, the
treacherous, the envious, the unneighbourly. All this has befallen
them because they know not good from evil. But I, in that I have
5 comprehended the nature of the Good that it is beautiful, and
the nature of Evil that it is ugly, and the nature of the wrong-
doer himself that it is akin to me, not as partaker of the same
blood and seed but of intelligence and a morsel of the Divine, can
neither be injured by any of them—for no one can involve me in
10 what is debasing—nor can I be wroth with my kinsman and hate
him. For we have come into being for co-operation, as have the
feet, the hands, the eyelids, the rows of upper and lower teeth.
Therefore to thwart one another is against Nature; and we do
thwart one another by shewing resentment and aversion.

l. 1 *Say to thyself at daybreak.* Marcus's meditations (addressed to himself) are
characteristically full of counsels for the discipline and culture of the moral
life.
l. 9.   *No one can involve me in what is debasing*: that is, against my will. Others
may injure my body, but I only can debase myself.

72 *Marcus Aurelius, To Himself* iii. 7. Prize not anything as being to
thine interest that shall ever force thee to break thy troth, to surrender thine honour, to hate, suspect, or curse any one, to play the
hypocrite, to lust after anything that needs walls and curtains.
5 For he that has chosen before all else his own intelligence and
good "genius", and to be a devotee of its supreme worth, does
not strike a tragic attitude or whine, nor will he ask for either a
wilderness or a concourse of men; above all he will live neither
chasing anything nor shunning it. And he recks not at all whether
10 he is to have his soul imprisoned in his body for a longer or a

shorter span of time, for even if he must take his departure at once, he will go as willingly as if he were to discharge any other function that can be discharged with decency and orderliness, making sure through life of this one thing, that his thoughts
15 should not in any case assume a character out of keeping with a rational and civic creature.

l. 16 *A rational and civic creature*, νοερὸν καὶ πολιτικὸν ζῷον. That man is, or should be, a creature of intelligence (νοῦς) is of course common to all the Stoics; that Marcus insists upon his social obligations is not indeed peculiar to but is characteristic of him. Cf. 74f. below.

73 *Marcus Aurelius, To Himself* iv. 7. Efface the opinion, *I am harmed*, and at once the feeling of being harmed disappears; efface the feeling, and the harm disappears at once.

74 *Marcus Aurelius, To Himself* vi. 54. That which is not in the interests of the hive cannot be in the interests of the bee.

75 *Marcus Aurelius, To Himself* viii. 34. Thou hast seen a hand cut off or a foot, or a head severed from the trunk, and lying at some distance from the rest of the body. Just so does the man treat himself, as far as he may, who wills not what befalls and severs himself
5 from mankind or acts unsocially. Say thou hast been torn away in some sort from the unity of Nature; for by the law of thy birth thou wast a part; but now thou hast cut thyself off. Yet here comes in that exquisite provision, that thou canst return again to thy unity. To no other part has God granted this, to come together
10 again, when once separated and cleft asunder. Aye, behold his goodness, wherewith he hath glorified man! For he hath let it rest with a man that he be never rent away from the Whole, and if he do rend himself away, to return again and grow onto the rest and take up his position again as part.

76 *Marcus Aurelius, To Himself* xii. 35f. Not even death can bring terror to him who regards that alone as good which comes in due season, and to whom it is all one whether his acts in obedience to right reason are few or many, and a matter of in-
5 difference whether he look upon the world for a longer or a shorter time.
    Man, thou hast been a citizen in this World-City, what matters it to thee if for five years or a hundred? For under its laws equal treatment is meted out to all. What hardship then is there in being
10 banished from the city, not by a tyrant or an unjust judge but by

Nature who settled thee in it? So might a praetor who commissions a comic actor, dismiss him from the stage. *But I have not played my five acts, but only three.* Very possibly, but in life three acts count as a full play. For he, that is responsible for thy composition
15 originally and thy dissolution now, decides when it is complete. But thou art responsible for neither. Depart then with a good grace, for he that dismisses thee is gracious.

l. 1 *Not even death . . .* These are the last words of Marcus's book.
l. 7 *A citizen in this World-City.* Since all men were related by their common participation in logos it was more reasonable (according to the Stoics) to think of oneself as a citizen of the world than of any single state. The relationship especially between the wise and good cuts across all frontiers.

E. *Epicurus*

Stoics and Epicureans resembled one another more closely than either party would allow. Both saw that in a chaotic world the only way to peace was the disciplining of desire. Epicurus (*c.* 342–270 B.C.), though often called an atheist, did not deny the existence of gods, but taught that as they are beings who themselves enjoy continual bliss they will never cause harm or suffering to men; there is nothing to fear from them, but neither can they be placated or cajoled—if they listened to all the prayers men offer the whole race would come to an end, so foolish and contradictory are the petitions they would hear. Suffering does come to men, but it can be endured, as Epicurus himself had proved, not merely with "Stoicism" but with happiness. Severe pains are short; lasting pains are rarely severe. Moreover, pains can never hurt us if our minds are abstracted from them. Pleasure (Epicurus does not mean sensual or individualist pleasure) is the chief good; and it can be attained by those who seek it wisely. In Physics, Epicurus taught an atomic system. Lucretius, who is quoted here, was a Roman Epicurean (*c.* 99–55 B.C.) who found, as many did, in the teaching of Epicurus so great a relief from fear and distress that he could express it only in the language of religion; Epicurus was a Saviour—from religion.

77 *Lucretius, On the Nature of Things* i. 62–79.

When Man's life upon earth in base dismay,
Crushed by the burthen of Religion, lay,
Whose face, from all the regions of the sky,
Hung, glaring hate upon mortality,
5 First one Greek man against her dared to raise

His eyes, against her strive through all his days;
Him noise of gods nor lightnings nor the roar
Of raging heaven subdued, but pricked the more
His spirit's valiance, till he longed the Gate
10 To burst of this low prison of man's fate.
And thus the living ardour of his mind
Conquered, and clove its way; he passed behind
The world's last flaming wall, and through the whole
Of space uncharted ranged his mind and soul.
15 Whence, conquering, he returned to make Man see
At last what can, what cannot, come to be;
By what law to each Thing its power hath been
Assigned, and what deep boundary set between;
Till underfoot is tamed religion trod,
20 And, by his victory, Man ascends to God.

l. 2 *The burthen of Religion*. Religion consisted in the multifarious rites, prayers,
    and sacrifices necessary to propitiate the gods and ensure their favour.

78 *Epicurus, Epistle to Menoeceus* 123ff., 127*b*–132. The things which
I used unceasingly to commend to you, these do and practise,
considering them to be the first principles of the good life. First
of all believe that god is a being immortal and blessed, even
5 as the common idea of a god is engraved on men's minds, and
do not assign to him anything alien to his immortality or ill-suited
to his blessedness: but believe about him everything that can uphold his blessedness and immortality. For gods there are, since
the knowledge of them is by clear vision. But they are not such as
10 the many believe them to be: for indeed they do not consistently
represent them as they believe them to be. And the impious man
is not he who denies the gods of the many, but he who attaches to
the gods the beliefs of the many. For the statements of the many
about the gods are not conceptions derived from sensation, but
15 false suppositions, according to which the greatest misfortunes
befall the wicked and the greatest blessings [the good] by the gift
of the gods. For men being accustomed always to their own
virtues welcome those like themselves, but regard all that is not
of their nature as alien.
20   Become accustomed to the belief that death is nothing to us. For
all good and evil consists in sensation, but death is deprivation of
sensation. And therefore a right understanding that death is nothing
to us makes the mortality of life enjoyable, not because it adds to it
an infinite span of time, but because it takes away the craving for
25 immortality. For there is nothing terrible in life for the man who

has truly comprehended that there is nothing terrible in not living. So that the man speaks but idly who says that he fears death not because it will be painful when it comes, but because it is painful in anticipation. For that which gives no trouble when it comes, is
30 but an empty pain in anticipation. So death, the most terrifying of ills, is nothing to us, since so long as we exist, death is not with us; but when death comes, then we do not exist. It does not then concern either the living or the dead, since for the former it is not, and the latter are no more. . . .

35   We must consider that of desires some are natural, others vain, and of the natural some are necessary and others merely natural; and of the necessary some are necessary for happiness, others for the repose of the body, and others for very life. The right understanding of these facts enables us to refer all choice and avoidance to the
40 health of the body and [the soul's] freedom from disturbance, since this is the aim of the life of blessedness. For it is to obtain this end that we always act, namely, to avoid pain and fear. And when this is once secured for us, all the tempest of the soul is dispersed, since the living creature has not to wander as though in search of
45 something that is missing, and to look for some other thing by which he can fulfil the good of the soul and the good of the body. For it is then that we have need of pleasure, when we feel pain owing to the absence of pleasure; [but when we do not feel pain], we no longer need pleasure. And for this cause we call pleasure the
50 beginning and end of the blessed life. For we recognize pleasure as the first good innate in us, and from pleasure we begin every act of choice and avoidance, and to pleasure we return again, using the feeling as the standard by which we judge every good.

    And since pleasure is the first good and natural to us, for this
55 reason we do not choose every pleasure, but sometimes we pass over many pleasures, when greater discomfort accrues to us as the result of them: and similarly we think many pains better than pleasures, since a greater pleasure comes to us when we have endured pains for a long time. Every pleasure then because of its natural
60 kinship to us is good, yet not every pleasure is to be chosen: even as every pain also is an evil, yet not all are always of a nature to be avoided. Yet by a scale of comparison and by the consideration of advantages and disadvantages we must form our judgement on all these matters. For the good on certain occasions we treat as bad,
65 and conversely the bad as good.

    And again independence of desire we think a great good—not that we may at all times enjoy but a few things, but that, if we do not possess many, we may enjoy the few in the genuine persuasion

that those have the sweetest pleasure in luxury who least need it,
70 and that all that is natural is easy to be obtained, but that which is
superfluous is hard. And so plain savours bring us a pleasure equal
to a luxurious diet, when all the pain due to want is removed; and
bread and water produce the highest pleasure, when one who
needs them puts them to his lips. To grow accustomed therefore to
75 simple and not luxurious diet gives us health to the full, and makes
a man alert for the needful employments of life, and when after
long intervals we approach luxuries disposes us better towards
them, and fits us to be fearless of fortune.

When, therefore, we maintain that pleasure is the end, we do not
80 mean the pleasures of profligates and those that consist in sensu-
ality, as is supposed by some who are either ignorant or disagree
with us or do not understand, but freedom from pain in the body
and from trouble in the mind. For it is not continuous drinkings
and revellings, nor the satisfaction of lusts, nor the enjoyment of
85 fish and other luxuries of the wealthy table, which produce a
pleasant life, but sober reasoning, searching out the motives for
all choice and avoidance, and banishing mere opinions, to which
are due the greatest disturbance of the spirit.

l. 15 *The greatest misfortunes . . . the greatest blessings.* On the contrary, there is
nothing either to hope or to fear from the gods. By recognizing what is
necessary and what is not man is delivered from the chains of destiny (cf.
pp. 61f. (59)).
40 *Freedom from disturbance,* ἀταραξία, the Epicurean goal.
l. 83 *For it is not . . .* The common modern use of the adjective "Epicurean"
is a slander upon Epicurus.

F. *The Philosophic Missionary*

In the age of the New Testament philosophy was not exclusively
the affair of the study and university. It was (see above, pp. 54, 66–72)
essentially practical, and was intended to be practised. The teachers of
philosophy saw their own beliefs as the needed cure for men's ills and
proceeded to offer them to the public (cf. *Corpus Hermeticum* i. 27,
pp. 88f. (89)). The philosopher became a street-corner orator, and the
Cynics in particular preached their "gospel" to all who would listen,
and it was often delivered—and received—less as a reasoned system of
beliefs about the universe than as a divine revelation.

79 *Epictetus, Discourses* III, xxii. 19–26. First then you must make
your Governing Principle pure, and hold fast this rule of life,

"Henceforth my mind is the material I have to work on, as the carpenter has his timber and the shoemaker his leather: my busi-
5 ness is to deal with my impressions aright. My wretched body is nothing to me, its parts are nothing to me. Death? Let it come when it will, whether to my whole body or to a part of it. Exile? Can one be sent into exile beyond the Universe? One cannot. Wherever I go, there is the sun, there is the moon, there are the
10 stars, dreams, auguries, conversation with the gods."

The true Cynic when he has ordered himself thus cannot be satisfied with this: he must know that he is sent as a messenger from God to men concerning things good and evil, to show them that they have gone astray and are seeking the true nature of good and
15 evil where it is not to be found, and take no thought where it really is: he must realize, in the words of Diogenes when brought before Philip after the battle of Chaeronea, that he is sent "to reconnoitre". For indeed the Cynic has to discover what things are friendly to men and what are hostile: and when he has accurately
20 made his observations he must return and report the truth, not driven by fear to point out enemies where there are none, nor in any other way disturbed or confounded by his impressions.

He must then be able, if chance so offer, to come forward on the tragic stage, and with a loud voice utter the words of Socrates:
25 "Oh race of men, whither are ye hurrying? What are you doing, miserable creatures? You wander up and down like blind folk: you have left the true path and go away on a vain errand, you seek peace and happiness elsewhere, where it is not to be found, and believe not when another shows the way."

l. 17 *To reconnoitre*, as a spy (κατάσκοπος). The philosopher discovers, for example, that there is nothing to fear in death, and then communicates his knowledge to the main army of men.

80 *Philostratus, Life of Apollonius* i. 17. When a certain quibbler asked him, why he asked no questions of him, he replied: "Because I asked questions when I was a stripling; and it is not my business to ask questions now, but to teach people what I have
5 discovered." "How then," the other asked him afresh, "O Apollonius, should the sage converse?" "Like a law-giver," he replied, "for it is the duty of the law-giver to deliver to the many the instructions of whose truth he has persuaded himself." This was the line he pursued during his stay in Antioch, and
10 he converted to himself the most unrefined people.

l. 1 *A certain quibbler asked him*, that is, Apollonius. Apollonius of Tyana lived through most of the first Christian century. The *Life* by Philostratus, published some time after A.D. 217, contains legendary material but probably conveys a not altogether false impression of this very impressive Pythagorean philosopher, who travelled extensively, worked miracles, and taught everywhere.

81 *Philostratus, Life of Apollonius* iv. 20. Now while he was discussing the question of libations, there chanced to be present in his audience a young dandy who bore so evil a reputation for licentiousness, that his conduct had once been the subject of coarse
5 street-corner songs. His home was Corcyra, and he traced his pedigree to Alcinous the Phaeacian who entertained Odysseus. Apollonius then was talking about libations, and was urging them not to drink out of a particular cup, but to reserve it for the gods, without ever touching it or drinking out of it. But when he also
10 urged them to have handles on the cup, and to pour the libation over the handle, because that is the part of the cup at which men are least likely to drink, the youth burst out into loud and coarse laughter, and quite drowned his voice. Then Apollonius looked up at him and said: "It is not yourself that perpetrates this insult, but
15 the demon, who drives you on without your knowing it." And in fact the youth was, without knowing it, possessed by a devil; for he would laugh at things that no one else laughed at, and then he would fall to weeping for no reason at all, and he would talk and sing to himself. Now most people thought that it was the
20 boisterous humour of youth which led him into such excesses; but he was really the mouthpiece of a devil, though it only seemed a drunken frolic in which on that occasion he was indulging. Now when Apollonius gazed on him, the ghost in him began to utter cries of fear and rage, such as one hears from people who are being
25 branded or racked; and the ghost swore that he would leave the young man alone and never take possession of any man again. But Apollonius addressed him with anger, as a master might a shifty, rascally, and shameless slave and so on, and he ordered him to quit the young man and show by a visible sign that he had done so. "I
30 will throw down yonder statue," said the devil, and pointed to one of the images which was in the king's portico, for there it was that the scene took place. But when the statue began by moving gently, and then fell down, it would defy anyone to describe the hubbub which arose thereat and the way they clapped their hands
35 with wonder. But the young man rubbed his eyes as though he had just woke up, and he looked towards the rays of the sun, and won the consideration of all who now had turned their attention to him; for he no longer showed himself licentious, nor did he stare madly about, but he had returned to his own self, as thoroughly as if he

40 had been treated with drugs; and he gave up his dainty dress and
summery garments and the rest of his sybaritic way of life, and he
fell in love with the austerity of philosophers, and donned their
cloak, and stripping off his old self modelled his life in future upon
that of Apollonius.

l. 41 *He fell in love with the austerity of philosophers.* The similarity between this
narrative of exorcism and conversion and some of the New Testament
stories appears in several places.

82 *Philostratus, Life of Apollonius* v. 24. Such were his experiences in
Rhodes, and others ensued in Alexandria, as soon as his voyage
ended there. Even before he arrived Alexandria was in love with
him, and its inhabitants longed to see Apollonius as one friend
5 longs for another; and as the people of Upper Egypt are in-
tensely religious they too prayed him to visit their several
societies. For owing to the fact that so many come hither and
mix with us from Egypt, while an equal number pass hence to
visit Egypt, Apollonius was already celebrated among them and
10 the ears of the Egyptians were literally pricked up to hear him. It is
no exaggeration to say that, as he advanced from the ship into the
city, they gazed upon him as if he was a god, and made way for
him in the alleys, as they would for priests carrying the sacraments. As he was being thus escorted with more pomp than if he
15 had been a governor of the country, he met twelve men who were
being led to execution on the charge of being bandits; he looked at
them and said: "They are not all guilty, for this one," and he gave
his name, "has been falsely accused or he would not be going with
you." And to the executioners by whom they were being led, he
20 said: "I order you to relax your pace and bring them to the ditch a
little more leisurely, and to put this one to death last of all, for he is
guiltless of the charge; but you would anyhow act with more
piety, if you spared them for a brief portion of the day, since it
were better not to slay them at all." And withal he dwelt upon this
25 theme at what was for him unusual length. And the reason for his
doing so was immediately shown; for when eight of them had had
their heads cut off, a man on horseback rode up to the ditch, and
shouted: "Spare Pharion; for", he added, "he is no robber, but he
gave false evidence against himself from fear of being racked, and
30 others of them in their examination under torture have acknow-
ledged that he is guiltless." I need not describe the exultation of
Egypt, nor how the people, who were anyhow ready to admire
him, applauded him for this action.

83 *Apollonius of Tyana, Epistle* iii. You have visited the countries
that lie between me and Italy, beginning from Syria, parading
yourself in the so-called royal cities. And you had a philosopher's
doublet all the time, and a long white beard, but besides that
5 nothing. And now how comes it that you are returning by sea
with a full cargo of silver, of gold, of vases of all sorts, of em-
broidered raiment, of every other sort of ornament, not to mention overweening pride, and boasting and unhappiness? What
cargo is this, and what the purport of these strange purchases?
10 Zeno never purchased but dried fruits.

1 *You*, one Euphrates, who for the sake of gain had acted as a travelling
philosopher.

THE HERMETIC LITERATURE

THERE have been transmitted from antiquity, mainly through Christian channels, a considerable number of tractates more or less closely connected with the divine person Hermes Trismegistus. Of these, many are simply astrological or magical, and may be discounted. The rest contain a body of teaching which might with equal justice be called religious or philosophical. This teaching, which here and there shows contact with the Greek Old Testament, is an important element in the background of the New Testament.

Hermes Trismegistus (Thrice-Greatest Hermes) is the Greek title of the Egyptian god Thoth. Trismegistus probably represents an Egyptian expression meaning "very great", and served to distinguish the foreign god from the native Greek Hermes. In most of the tractates Hermes himself, or a similar divine figure, communicates secret knowledge (*gnosis*) about God, about creation, or about salvation, to a disciple, who is sometimes but not always named. The revelation is generally given in the form of a dialogue in which the disciple's share is limited to asking questions and expressing admiration. Prayers and praise addressed to God are also found.

The date of the Hermetic writings cannot be established with certainty, but it seems probable that most of them were composed between A.D. 100 and 200, though it is by no means impossible that some fall within the first century A.D. What is more important is that these literary remains give the impression of being the deposit of many years of oral teaching, as well as of reflection and mystical meditation. It seems very probable, though the matter is not capable of proof, that ideas similar to those contained in the written *Hermetica* were entertained and discussed, in Egypt and perhaps elsewhere, at the time when the New Testament documents were written and when Christianity was spreading westwards from Palestine into the Greek world.

This westward movement of Christianity is to be noted here because the *Hermetica* also represent, in part, the transition of Jewish and

Egyptian, that is of Oriental, thoughts into Greek shape and expression. In order to understand the *Hermetica* it is above all necessary to grasp that their authors were men who believed that there had been revealed to them a Gospel which it was their mission to preach to mankind. This is made perhaps clearest of all in the tractate quoted below. Man is a double-natured creature; he is of the earth earthy, but he has also celestial elements in him. It rests with man himself whether he will succumb to his earthy nature, or, by subduing and eventually relinquishing it, rise to the true home of his proper being in God. The primary means of this escape, or salvation, is the knowledge of God. To know the truth sets man free. To God's disclosure of himself, however, he must respond in a suitable way. He must learn to hate his body, which belongs to the material order, and to train his soul by abstraction and meditation. It is his business both to praise God, not with bloody sacrifices and material gifts but with offerings of heart and mind, and also to reveal to others what has been communicated to him; hence the mission of the Hermetic preachers.

Some of the "saving truths" of the Hermetic religion will be brought out in the passages quoted below. These are all drawn from the first Hermetic tractate, often called the *Poimandres*, from the name of the revealer god who appears in it. It would have been possible to illustrate a wider range of the thought of the Hermetic corpus by taking passages from more than one tractate; but by using one only it is possible to show not only its content but also its form, and the form of the tractates is not without significance for the student of the New Testament. The *Poimandres* is moreover fairly representative of the corpus as a whole. "It tells how the God revealed to his prophet in ecstasy the divine origin of the universe and of man, and commissioned him to preach the way of salvation to mankind in general. It makes use of various forms of religious appeal familiar to us from the literature of Judaism and Christianity—the inspired myth of the beginning of things, the doctrine of immortality, the divine promises and threats of judgement, eschatology, and the call to repentance, concluding with a hymn of praise and aspiration. Its actual teaching is of a type common to most of the *Hermetica*, but this teaching is presented in a more imaginative way than is usual, with more appeal to the emotions, and its address to all who will hear contrasts with the esotericism of some of the other Hermetic writings" (C. H. Dodd, *The Bible and the Greeks* (1935), p. 99). The tractate opens with the appearance of Poimandres, and the disciple's request for knowledge. Thereupon is manifested a vision which teaches the origin of the universe, and, in mythical form, the origin, and hence the nature, of man is revealed. His story is traced from original archetypal man to the present state of empirical fallen humanity. In this way both the cause and character of man's ills are indicated, and with them the way of escape. Leaving behind everything mortal and corruptible the soul must rise through the seven spheres until it enters into God himself and so becomes divine. That this may take place is the Gospel of Poimandres. Having received it the disciple becomes an apostle and preaches to mankind the way of salvation; some refuse it, others accept, and seek instruction. These last the prophet gathers about him and bids them give thanks to God. When they have departed he himself blesses God in a short psalm.

84 *Poimandres* 1ff. Introduction.

It happened once that, when I had begun to reflect upon the things that are, and my thoughts had been caught up on high, and when my bodily senses had been put under restraint, like those who are weighed down by sleep resulting from overeating or bodily
5 fatigue, I seemed to see an immense figure of boundless size who was calling me by name and saying to me, "What do you wish to hear and to behold, and, by your thought, to learn and know?" "Who are you?" I said. "I am Poimandres," said he, "the Mind of the Sovereignty. I know what you wish, and I am with you
10 everywhere." "I wish", I said, "to learn the things that are, and to understand their nature, and to know God; how I wish to hear this!" He replied, "Keep in your mind the things you wish to learn, and I will teach you."

l. 3 *When my bodily senses had been put under restraint.* It is a consequence of the dualism which plays so large a part in the *Hermetica* (as in much mystical literature) that spiritual vision is believed to become most acute when bodily perception ceases. This thought is common (for example) in Philo; thus *Leg. Alleg.* iii. 42 : It is not possible that he whose abode is in the body should attain to being with God; this is possible only for him whom God rescues out of the prison. Cf. *Corpus Hermeticum* xiii. 7.

l. 8 *Poimandres, the Mind* (νοῦς) *of the Sovereignty.* This designation is not very different from what a Christian might have understood by the Word (λόγος) or Spirit (πνεῦμα) of the supreme God. It is probably incorrect to derive the name Poimandres from the Greek ποιμήν (shepherd), ἀνήρ (man). It is rather a Greek form of the Coptic *p-eimi-n-re,* "the knowledge of the [sun-] God". For such a name cf. Manda de Ḥayye, "the knowledge of life" (or salvation), the name given by the Mandaeans to the saviour and revealer.

l. 10 *To learn the things that are, and to understand their nature, and to know God.* It would be difficult to sum up more comprehensively and clearly the goal at which the Hermetists aimed and which they believed they had in some measure attained. Knowledge of God was everything; "this alone brings salvation to man, the knowledge of God (ἡ γνῶσις τοῦ θεοῦ)" (*Corpus Hermeticum* x. 15). Cf. *Poimandres* 26 (pp. 87f. (88)).

85 *Poimandres* 4ff., 9. Cosmogony.

When he had said this his aspect changed. Everything was opened to me in a moment, and I beheld a boundless vision; all became light, a calm and joyous light, and when I saw it I was captivated by it. And after a little there came in its turn a downward-
5 bearing darkness, terrible and grim, twisted in crooked spirals, like (it seemed to me) a snake. Then the darkness changed into a wet nature, unspeakably agitated and giving forth smoke, as from a fire, and producing an unutterable mournful sound. Then was sent out from it an inarticulate cry, like (it seemed) the noise of a
10 fire, and coming from the light ... a holy Word assailed the nature, and fire unmixed leapt up from the wet nature towards the height. It was light and swift, and at the same time active, and the air, being light, followed the [fiery] breath, ascending from the earth and water as far as the fire, so that it seemed to be suspended
15 from it; but the earth and water remained in their place mingled together, so that the earth could not be distinguished from the water. Earth and water were kept in motion by the breath-like word which was rushing audibly over them. Then said Poimandres to me, "Have you understood what this
20 vision means?" "I shall know it," I said. "That light", said he, "am I, Mind, thy God, who was before the wet nature which appeared out of darkness; the luminous Word which came forth from Mind is son of God." "What then?" "You must understand it thus. That which sees and hears in you is the word of the Lord,
25 and your mind is God the Father. These are not separated one from another, for the union of them is life." "Thank you," I said. "But now", he went on, "consider the light and understand that." ... Then Mind (or God), being bisexual, existing as life and light, generated by a word another Mind, as Demiurge. The latter, being
30 god of fire and breath, created seven administrators, who in their orbits envelop the world of sense perception. Their administration is called Destiny.

ll. 2, 4 *All became light ... a downward-bearing darkness.* Dualism is naturally expressed in terms of light and darkness. The myth of Gen. 1 is recalled, but here light, not darkness, is mentioned first, because, as will be stated below, the light *is* God. Darkness and light are in the beginning distinct. The origin of the empirical universe, and of empirical humanity, lies in the mingling of the two.

l. 10 *A holy word assailed the nature.* It is, as in the biblical narrative, the divine word that produces coherent activity in the wet nature (or chaos).

l. 17 *Earth and water were kept in motion by the breath-like word which was rushing audibly over them.* Here the dependence of the Hermetist upon Genesis (1. 2) is particularly clear, both in language and in the substance of the thought. In Genesis the Spirit of God (πνεῦμα θεοῦ) is said to have been rushing over (ἐπεφέρετο) the water. In the *Hermetica* πνεῦμα has not the same meaning as in the Bible; it is warm gas or breath. Accordingly, to make the matter clear, we have the breath-like word (πνευματικὸς λόγος) rushing over (ἐπιφερόμενον) and keeping in motion earth and water, which are not yet distinguished. Here, as in Genesis, it is the all-powerful Word of God that creates; but, as will appear, the Word is not simply the biblical word of command ("Let there be . . ."). Jewish thinkers, however, conceived of the activity of Wisdom or Torah in the process of creation.

l. 20 *That light am I, Mind* (νοῦς), *thy God.* There is some confusion here; earlier it seemed that Poimandres was the Mind of the supreme God; now Mind *is* the supreme God.

l. 22 *The luminous word which came forth from Mind is son of God.* The meaning is made clear by analogy. In man the mind corresponds to God the Father, the process of seeing and hearing to the Word (λόγος). In the divine, as in human, life, the one is prior to the other, but the two are inseparable.

l. 28 *Then.* In *Poimandres* 7f., which are not printed here, it is said that the Light, being the divine mind and archetypal world, resolved itself into innumerable divine powers. The lower world, animated by the divine Word, imitated the archetypal world, and thus came into being the infinite number of souls.

Bisexual . . . life and light. The idea of the bisexuality of God, and the use of the terms life and light, are both very widespread in the literature of the gnostic piety of which the *Hermetica* are an example. Life and light are also biblical terms (e.g. John 1. 3f.), and in some Jewish speculation the first man was said (in dependence on Gen. 1. 27) to be bisexual.

l. 29 *Another Mind as Demiurge.* The primal God, being above all contact with matter and time, must produce a second Mind to set in motion the process of creation.

l. 30 *Seven administrators . . . destiny.* The seven administrators closely correspond to the seven planets ruling in their seven spheres, which lie between man and God. Genesis also (1. 14-18) records the creation of heavenly bodies designed both to give light and to rule. Destiny (εἱμαρμένη) is a Stoic word and concept; it is here (as often) bound up with astrological ideas. In 10f. the emergence of animal life is described.

86 *Poimandres* 12-15. Archetypal Man and his Fall.

Mind, the Father of all, being life and light, generated a Man equal to himself, whom he loved as being his own offspring, for he was very beautiful since he bore the image of his father. Truly

therefore did God love his own form, and delivered over to him
5 all his own creations. And when the Man had considered the
creation which the Demiurge had made in the fire, he himself also
wished to create, and was permitted to do so by his father. He
came into the sphere of the Demiurge, where he was to have all
authority, and considered the creations of his brother. They loved
10 him, and each one gave him a share in his own rank. Having
perceived their essence and partaken of their nature, he wished
to break out of the bounding circle of the orbits and to know the
might of him who is set over the fire.

And he that had all authority over the world of mortal beings
15 and the irrational creatures looked down through the framework
of the orbits, having broken through the vault of heaven, and he
showed the fair form of God to the downward-bearing Nature.
When Nature saw him who had in himself the unfailing beauty and
all the power of the administrators, and the form of God, she
20 smiled in love because she saw the image of the Man's most
beautiful form reflected in the water and his shadow upon the
earth. When he saw this form like himself in her, reflected, that is,
in the water, he loved it, and desired to dwell there. With the will
came the act, and he inhabited the irrational form; but Nature,
25 when she had received him whom she loved, enfolded him altogether and they were united; for they were in love.

And for this reason, alone among all the living creatures upon
earth, man is twofold. He is mortal by reason of the body, immortal by reason of the essential Man. For although he is immortal
30 and has authority over all things, yet he endures mortal conditions
since he is subjected to Destiny. Although therefore he is above
the framework of the orbits he has yet become a slave to it; and
although he is bisexual, since he came from a bisexual father, and
not subject to sleep since he came from one not subject to sleep,
35 yet is he held fast. . . .

l. 1 *A Man equal to himself.* We have not yet reached the creation of empirical
   man. The supreme God can make only perfect creatures, Mind and archetypal Man. The latter was (cf. Gen. 1. 26f.) the image of God and so might
   properly be loved by the gnostic God, since in loving him God loved his
   own perfection.

l. 9 *The creations of his brother,* that is, the things made by the second Mind, the
   first creation of the supreme God as the Man was his second.

l. 14 *He that had all authority;* that is, the archetypal Man. We now reach the
   climax of the Poimandres myth. The crux of every gnostic system was the
   explanation of the appearance in the world of evil; since a perfect God
   could create only good, how comes the evil which is manifest in creation?
   Some unfortunate accident must have occurred. So it is here.

l. 26 *They were united.* A mythical marriage between Nature and the archetypal Man, the perfect creation of the supreme God, accounts for the mixed nature of man. It is to be observed that whereas Nature fell in love with Man, who showed her the fair image of God, Man fell in love with the image of himself reflected in the primeval water; like God, he could love only himself.

l. 28 *Man is twofold*, for the reason already given. He is mortal because he is composed partly of corruptible nature; he is subject to Destiny, because Man descended through the seven spheres of the administrators. Yet, equally with Nature, the essential, real, Man was a partner in the union, and man does not altogether lose his immortality.

l. 35 *He is held fast* . . . Something is wanting in the text; perhaps "by love and sleep". In the following paragraphs (16f.), which are not printed here, we learn that the issue of the marriage is seven men, bisexual, and similar to the seven administrators.

87 *Poimandres* 18f. Man as he is.

Hear now this point which you so long to hear. When the period was completed, the bond by which all things were held together was loosed by the will of God. For all living creatures, which up to that time had been bisexual, were differentiated (man among
5 them) into male and female. At the same time God spoke with a holy word, "Increase greatly, and greatly multiply, all ye creatures that have been created and made; and let him that has mind know that he is immortal, and that love is the cause of death, and let him know all things that are."

10   When God had said this, Providence working by Destiny and the framework of the orbits effected the unions of male and female, and set up the processes of birth, and all things multiplied according to their species. He that has come to know himself has passed into the abounding good; he who loves the body which
15 springs from the error of passion abides in darkness, erring still, suffering in his senses the experiences of death.

l. 4 *Were differentiated.* Up to this point, all creatures, like God himself, were bisexual. This differentiation marks the beginning of life as lived in the present world. Many Jews thought of Adam as originally a bisexual creature.

l. 5 *God spoke with a holy word.* This command has certainly been taken from Gen. 1. 22, 28. It is much more appropriate in the context of Judaism than in the present context, where sexual union is discouraged.

l. 8 *Love is the cause of death.* It was love that brought the essential Man into the sphere of matter and creation; and the gnostic who is to rise into the supernatural world must eschew the pleasures of sense.

l. 13 *He that has come to know himself.* Men may be divided into two groups. The good and fortunate are those who have achieved self-knowledge; but self-knowledge here does not mean what it meant to earlier and more critical philosophers. It means knowledge of man's place in some such cosmological myth as that which the Hermetist has now unfolded, and the consequent knowledge of the mystical way of salvation.

l. 14 *He who loves the body.* Those on the other hand who are wedded to the material world are without hope. They abide in darkness (μένει ἐν τῷ σκότει—a striking Johannine phrase). Since they have chosen darkness rather than light there is no hope of their attaining the truth.

88 *Poimandres* 24ff. Man as he shall be.

"You have taught me all things well, O Mind, as I wished. But tell me further of the ascent by which men mount." Poimandres replied, "First, then, at the dissolution of the material body, you give up your body to be changed, and the form you had disappears.
5 Your former character, now become inactive, you hand over to the demon, and your bodily senses return to their respective sources, becoming parts of them and absorbed once more into their energies. Feeling and passion depart into irrational nature. And thus man speeds upward through the framework of the orbits. To
10 the first zone he gives up the power which effects increase and decrease; to the second, evil devices, as guile now inactive; to the third, the lust by which men are deceived, now no longer active; to the fourth, ostentatious authority, no longer greedy of power; to the fifth, unholy audacity and presumptuous temerity; to the
15 sixth, the evil resources, now no longer active, of wealth, and to the seventh zone, the falsehood that ever lies in wait. Then, stripped of those qualities which the spheres have wrought in him, man reaches the ogdoatic nature, having simply his own proper power (*or*, meaning, δύναμιν); with the beings that are he hymns
20 the Father, and all who are present rejoice together at his presence. Having become like his companions, he hears also certain Powers above the ogdoatic nature singing with sweet voice to God; and then, in order, they ascend to the Father, give themselves up to the Powers, and having become Powers enter into God. This is the
25 happy end of those who have acquired knowledge, namely, to become God. And now, why do you delay? Will not you, as one who has received the whole truth (πάντα), become guide to those who are worthy, that through you the human race may be saved by God?"

l. 2 *The ascent by which men mount.* The Hermetic scheme of salvation as a whole is a means of ascent. Man, mixed creature as he is and domiciled below the spheres and thus subject to Destiny, must leave behind his material nature and ascend through the spheres if he is to attain to God. Already in the mortal life it is possible, by asceticism and abstract meditation (the Herme- tists, unlike the exponents of the mystery religions, have nothing to say

about sacraments), to make some progress; but only at death is the soul
fully liberated from the body and so enabled to mount to God.

l. 5 *You hand over to the demon.* The demon is your personal demon, or genius;
character has too much to do with feeling and passion to be retained.

l. 9 *Upward through the framework of the orbits;* through the seven heavens or
spheres governed by the seven administrators (planets). The soul escapes
from Destiny.

l. 18 *The ogdoatic nature,* that is, the space (though this word is too material to be
used by the Hermetist) outside the seven spheres, where the soul joins all
other purely spiritual and essential beings in the immediate presence of God.

l. 25 *This is the happy end of those who have acquired knowledge* (γνῶσις), *namely, to
become God.* To know oneself is to know God; to know God is to become
God. Apotheosis is the essence of the Hermetic Gospel. The purified soul
loses its identity in God. As soon as this final truth is enunciated the disciple
is called to his prophetic mission.

89 *Poimandres* 27ff. The Prophet's Mission.

When he had said these things Poimandres before my eyes
mingled with the Powers. And I, having given thanks and blessed
the Father of all things was dismissed by him [Poimandres], filled
with power and instructed regarding the nature of the universe and
5 the supreme vision. And I began to preach to men the beauty of
piety and knowledge: "O peoples, earth-born men, who have
given yourselves up to drunkenness and sleep and to ignorance of
God, be sober, cease your orgies, bewitched as you are by irrational sleep."

10   When they heard, they joined me with one accord. I said,
"Why, O earth-born men, have you given yourselves up to death,
when you have the right to partake of immortality? Repent, you
who have journeyed with error and kept company with ignorance.
Rid yourselves of the light which is darkness. Abandon corrup-
15 tion, partake of immortality."

And some of them mocked me and went away, having given
themselves up to the way of death; others begged me to teach
them, throwing themselves at my feet. I raised them up and became the guide of the human race, teaching them the doctrine
20 which showed how and in what way they should be saved. I
sowed in them the words of wisdom, and they were nourished
upon the water of immortality. And when evening was come and
the sun's light had begun to disappear completely, I bade them give
thanks to God, and when they had completed the thanksgiving
25 each one turned to his own bed.

l. 5 *I began to preach to men the beauty of piety and knowledge.* The tractate is not
indulging in fiction; we need not doubt that Hermetic philosophers did

preach their Gospel, and found both converts and opponents. Ammonius Saccas, for example, must have taught a doctrine very similar to that of the *Hermetica*, and in his teaching Plotinus, after a long search, found that which satisfied his longings.

l. 12 *The right to partake of immortality.* Cf. John 1. 12.
  Repent. Cf. Mark 1. 15; and the New Testament *passim.*
l. 16 *Some of them . . . others.* The same mixed reception was accorded to the Christian preachers; cf. e.g. 1 Cor. 1. 18.
l. 21 *I sowed in them.* For the metaphor cf. Mark 4. 14; 1 John 3. 9. It is not uncommon elsewhere.
l. 22 *The water of immortality.* Cf. John 4. 10.

90 *Poimandres* 30ff. The Sacrifice of Praise and Thanksgiving.

But for my part I wrote down for myself (*or,* inscribed in memory) the benefaction of Poimandres, and, being filled with those things I had desired, I rejoiced greatly. For the sleep of my body had become watchfulness of soul, and the closing of my eyes true vision, and my silence pregnant with good, and the utterance of my speech a brood of good things. This befell me because I received them from my mind, that is, from Poimandres, the word of the Sovereignty. So I came, inspired with the spirit of truth. Wherefore with all my soul and with all my strength I offer blessing to God the Father.

Holy is God, the Father of all things.

Holy is God, whose will is accomplished by his own Powers.

Holy is God, who wills to be known and who is known to his own.

Holy art thou, who by the Word hast constituted all things that are.

Holy art thou, of whom all Nature is the image.

Holy art thou, whom Nature did not form.

Holy art thou, who art stronger than every Power.

Holy art thou, who art greater than all excellence.

Holy art thou, who art above praises.

Accept pure rational sacrifices from a soul and a heart stretched upward toward thee, O thou ineffable, unspeakable, named in silence. Grant me my prayer that I may not fall from the knowledge which befits our essence, and empower me. Then will I enlighten with this grace those of the human race who are in ignorance, my brothers, thy sons. Wherefore I believe and I bear witness; I move into life and light. Blessed art thou, O Father. Thy man wishes to share in thy holiness, as thou hast delivered to him all authority.

l. 13 *Who wills to be known and who is known to his own* (τοῖς ἰδίοις; cf. John 1. 11). It is the nature of the supreme God to communicate knowledge of himself; he takes the initiative in salvation. But not all men receive knowledge.

l. 15 *Who by the Word hast constituted all things that are.* For Word should perhaps be substituted speech. God spoke and it was done. Gen. 1 is in the writer's mind.

l. 17 *Of whom all Nature is the image,* since Nature received the Man who bears the image of God.

l. 22 *Pure rational sacrifices.* In the New Testament cf. Rom. 12. 1; 1 Peter 2. 2, 5; Heb. 13. 15. Like other philosophers, and like some Jewish and Christian propagandists, the Hermetists would have nothing to do with material sacrifices; and logically enough, for a God who must not be defiled by matter cannot be honoured by the offering of animals.

l. 27 *I believe and I bear witness; I move into life and light.* The Christian (and, more specifically, Johannine) words are striking; but there is no ground for suspecting Christian influence. God is life and light; the mystic moves into God, and therefore moves into life and light. The insistence upon his witness-bearing is important.

l. 29 *Thy man wishes to share in thy holiness.* The translation is difficult (συναγιάζειν σοι βούλεται); perhaps, "wishes to share with thee in the work of sanctification."

l. 30 *As thou hast delivered to him all authority* (τὴν πᾶσαν ἐξουσίαν). Cf. Matt. 11. 27 (=Luke 10. 22); Matt. 28. 18; John 5. 20, 27, *et passim.* The supreme God earlier gave authority to the archetypal Man (13), together with power over all creatures, and leave to create. Apparently the mystic has reached the position of the archetypal Man, made in the image of God.

6

MYSTERY RELIGIONS

THE evidence upon which our knowledge of the so-called mystery religions rests is for the most part fragmentary and by no means easy to interpret. Very much of it consists of single lines and passing allusions in ancient authors (many of whom were either bound to secrecy or inspired with loathing with regard to the subject of which they were treating), inscriptions (many of them incomplete), and artistic and other objects discovered by archaeologists. If a small selection of such evidence were given it would be meaningless, or perhaps misleading; if it were given in bulk it would swell this chapter into several volumes. It is impossible therefore to present here a serious account of even one mystery cult; instead, some of the longest and clearest passages available have been selected and arranged so as to illustrate features which were (in various forms and degrees) common to most of the cults.

The object of the mystery cults was to secure salvation for men who were subject to moral and physical evil, dominated by Destiny, and unable by themselves to escape from the corruption that beset the material side of their nature (cf. pp. 81, 86ff.). Salvation accordingly meant escape from Destiny, release from corruption and a renewed moral life. It was effected by what may broadly be called sacramental means. By taking part in prescribed rites the worshipper became united with God, was enabled in this life to enjoy mystical communion with him, and further was assured of immortality beyond death. This process rested upon the experiences (generally including the death and resurrection) of a Saviour-God, the Lord (κύριος) of his devotees. The myth, which seems often to have been cultically represented, rested in many of these religions upon the fundamental annual cycle of agricultural fertility; but rites which probably were in earlier days intended to secure productiveness in field and flock were now given an individual application and effect.

The following are among the most important features of the mystery religions.

A. *The Myth*

The saving cycle of events in the experience of the god were recounted in a tale conveniently described as a myth. Examples taken from two of the cults, that of Isis, which originated in the religion of ancient Egypt but became hellenized and came to have points of resemblance to the religion of Dionysus; and that of Cybele, the Great Mother, which was brought from Pessinus and installed in Rome in 205 B.C. during the second Punic War (Livy xxix. 10), are given here.

91 *Plutarch, Isis and Osiris* 12–19. They say that the Sun, when he became aware of Rhea's intercourse with Cronus, invoked a curse upon her that she should not give birth to a child in any month or any year; but Hermes, being enamoured of the goddess, consorted
5 with her. Later, playing at draughts with the moon, he won from her the seventieth part of each of her periods of illumination, and from all the winnings he composed five days, and intercalated them as an addition to the three hundred and sixty days. The Egyptians even now call these five days intercalated and celebrate them as the
10 birthdays of the gods. They relate that on the first of these days Osiris was born, and at the hour of his birth a voice issued forth saying, "The Lord of All advances to the light." . . . On the second of these days Arueris was born whom they call Apollo, and some call him also the elder Horus. On the third day Typhon was born,
15 but not in due season or manner, but with a blow he broke through his mother's side and leapt forth. On the fourth day Isis was born in the regions that are ever moist; and on the fifth Nephthys, to whom they give the name of Finality and the name of Aphrodite, and some also the name of Victory. There is also a tradition that Osiris
20 and Arueris were sprung from the Sun, Isis from Hermes, and Typhon and Nephthys from Cronus. . . . They relate, moreover, that Nephthys became the wife of Typhon; but Isis and Osiris were enamoured of each other and consorted together in the darkness of the womb before their birth. Some say that Arueris came from this
25 union and was called the elder Horus by the Egyptians, but Apollo by the Greeks.
    One of the first acts related of Osiris in his reign was to deliver the Egyptians from their destitute and brutish manner of living. This he did by showing them the fruits of cultivation, by giving
30 them laws, and by teaching them to honour the gods. Later he travelled over the whole earth civilizing it without the slightest need of arms, but most of the peoples he won over to his way by

the charm of his persuasive discourse combined with song and all manner of music. Hence the Greeks came to identify him with
35 Dionysus.

During his absence the tradition is that Typhon attempted nothing revolutionary because Isis, who was in control, was vigilant and alert; but when he returned home Typhon contrived a treacherous plot against him and formed a group of conspirators
40 seventy-two in number. He had also the co-operation of a queen from Ethiopia who was there at the time and whose name they report as Aso. Typhon, having secretly measured Osiris's body and having made ready a beautiful chest of corresponding size artistically ornamented, caused it to be brought into the room where the
45 festivity was in progress. The company was much pleased at the sight of it and admired it greatly, whereupon Typhon jestingly promised to present it to the man who should find the chest to be exactly his length when he lay down in it. They all tried it in turn, but no one fitted it; then Osiris got into it and lay down, and those
50 who were in the plot ran to it and slammed down the lid, which they fastened by nails from the outside and also by using molten lead. Then they carried the chest to the river and sent it on its way to the sea through the Tanitic Mouth. . . .

. . . Isis, when the tidings reached her, at once cut off one of her
55 tresses and put on a garment of mourning in a place where the city still bears the name of Kopto. Others think that the name means deprivation, for they also express "deprive" by means of "koptein". But Isis wandered everywhere at her wits' end; no one whom she approached did she fail to address, and even when she met some
60 little children she asked them about the chest. As it happened, they had seen it, and they told her the mouth of the river through which the friends of Typhon had launched the coffin into the sea. . . .

Thereafter Isis, as they relate, learned that the chest had been cast up by the sea near the land of Byblus and that the waves had
65 gently set it down in the midst of a clump of heather. The heather in a short time ran up into a very beautiful and massive stock and enfolded and embraced the chest with its growth and concealed it within its trunk. The king of the country admired the great size of the plant, and cut off the portion that enfolded the chest (which
70 was now hidden from sight), and used it as a pillar to support the roof of his house. These facts, they say, Isis ascertained by the divine inspiration of Rumour, and came to Byblus and sat down by a spring, all dejection and tears; she exchanged no word with anybody, save only that she welcomed the queen's maidservants
75 and treated them with great amiability. . . .

... Then the goddess disclosed herself and asked for the pillar which served to support the roof. She removed it with the greatest ease and cut away the wood of the heather which surrounded the chest; then, when she had wrapped up the wood in a linen cloth 80 and had poured perfume upon it, she entrusted it to the care of the kings; and even to this day the people of Byblus venerate this wood which is preserved in the shrine of Isis. Then the goddess threw herself down upon the coffin with such a dreadful wailing that the younger of the king's sons expired on the spot. The 85 elder son she kept with her, and, having placed the coffin on board a boat, she put out from land. ...

In the first place where she found seclusion, when she was quite by herself, they relate that she opened the chest and laid her face upon the face within and caressed it and wept. The child came 90 quietly up behind her and saw what was there, and when the goddess became aware of his presence, she turned about and gave him one awful look of anger. The child could not endure the fright, and died. ...

As they relate, Isis proceeded to her son Horus, who was being 95 reared in Buto, and bestowed the chest in a place well out of the way; but Typhon, who was hunting by night in the light of the moon, happened upon it. Recognizing the body he divided it into fourteen parts and scattered them, each in a different place. Isis learned of this and sought for them again, sailing through the 100 swamps in a boat of papyrus. ...

The traditional result of Osiris's dismemberment is that there are many so-called tombs of Osiris in Egypt; for Isis held a funeral for each part when she had found it. ...

Later, as they relate, Osiris came to Horus from the other world 105 and exercised and trained him for the battle. After a time Osiris asked Horus what he held to be the most noble of all things. When Horus replied, "To avenge one's father and mother for evil done to them". Osiris then asked him what animal he considered the most useful for them who go forth to battle; and when Horus 110 said, "A horse", Osiris was surprised and raised the question why it was that he had not rather said a lion than a horse. Horus answered that a lion was a useful thing for a man in need of assistance, but that a horse served best for cutting off the flight of an enemy and annihilating him. When Osiris heard this he was 115 much pleased, since he felt that Horus had now an adequate preparation. It is said that, as many were continually transferring their allegiance to Horus, Typhon's concubine, Thueris, also came over to him; and a serpent which pursued her was cut to pieces by

120 Horus's men, and now, in memory of this, the people throw down a rope in their midst and chop it up.

Now the battle, as they relate, lasted many days and Horus prevailed. Isis, however, to whom Typhon was delivered in chains, did not cause him to be put to death, but released him and let him go. Horus could not endure this with equanimity, but laid hands 125 upon his mother and wrested the royal diadem from her head; but Hermes put upon her a helmet like unto the head of a cow.

Typhon formally accused Horus of being an illegitimate child, but with the help of Hermes to plead his cause it was decided by the gods that he also was legitimate. Typhon was then overcome in 130 two other battles. Osiris consorted with Isis after his death, and she became the mother of Harpocrates, untimely born and weak in his lower limbs.

l. 17 *Ever moist.* Isis was goddess of the Nile, and of the sea; but it is not certain that this is the allusion.

l. 35 *Dionysus.* This mythological connection corresponds to a practical connection between the cult of Isis and Osiris, and that of Dionysus.

l. 52 *The river*—the river Nile.

l. 57 *Koptein.* The Greek verb κόπτειν means in the active "to smite", "to smite with a cutting edge", hence "to cut off"; and in the middle "to smite oneself", hence "to smite one's head or breast", "to lament".

l. 104 *Osiris came to Horus from the other world.* In Osiris's return to life lay the hope of his worshippers.

92 *Eusebius, Praeparatio Evangelica* II, ii. 22ff. The Phrygians say that Maeon was king of Phrygia and begat a daughter named Cybele, who first invented a pipe, and was called the Mountain Mother. And Marsyas the Phrygian, who was friendly with her, was the 5 first to join flutes together, and he lived in chastity to the end of his life.

But Cybele became pregnant by intercourse with Attis, and when this was known, her father killed Attis and the nurses; and Cybele became mad and rushed out into the country, and there 10 continued howling and beating a drum.

She was accompanied by Marsyas, who entered into a musical contest with Apollo, and was defeated, and flayed alive by Apollo.

And Apollo became enamoured of Cybele and accompanied her in her wanderings as far as the Hyperboreans, and ordered the body 15 of Attis to be buried, and Cybele to be honoured as a goddess.

Wherefore the Phrygians keep this custom even to the present day, lamenting the death of the youth, and erecting altars, and honouring Attis and Cybele with sacrifices.

And afterwards, at Pessinus in Phrygia, they built a costly temple,
20 and instituted most magnificent worship and sacrificial rites.

l. 10 *Howling and beating a drum.* This behaviour was recalled in the rites of the
Great Mother. The myth and the ritual alike could be, and were, understood
in the most diverse ways, as magical aids to fertility or as an allegory of the
soul's search for God.
l. 19 *Pessinus.* See above, p. 92.

B. *Initiation*

Rites of initiation opened the way into membership of the cults, and
generally seem to have consisted primarily of some ceremonial by
means of which the initiand was incorporated into the divine action of
the myth, and so achieved life by virtue of the resurrection of the god.
Of the following passages the former describes the rite of the *taurobolium*, in which the worshipper was drenched with the blood of a bull.
It will be noted that the *taurobolium* described by Prudentius was carried
out not as a means of initiation but for the purpose of consecrating a
priest (of the Great Mother). It was to this cult that the rite originally
belonged, but it may also have become an institution of Mithraism.
The latter passage recounts Apuleius's initiation into the religion of
Isis; it is less explicit in details, but it is impossible to doubt the reality
and sincerity of Apuleius's conversion.

93 *Prudentius, Peristephanon* x. 1011-50. The high priest who is to be
consecrated is brought down under ground in a pit dug deep,
marvellously adorned with a fillet, binding his festive temples with
chaplets, his hair combed back under a golden crown, and wearing
5 a silken toga caught up with Gabine girding.
   Over this they make a wooden floor with wide spaces, woven of
planks with an open mesh; they then divide or bore the area and
repeatedly pierce the wood with a pointed tool that it may appear
full of small holes.
10 Hither a huge bull, fierce and shaggy in appearance, is led, bound
with flowery garlands about its flanks, and with its horns sheathed;
yea, the forehead of the victim sparkles with gold, and the flash of
metal plates colours its hair.
   Here, as is ordained, the beast is to be slain, and they pierce its
15 breast with a sacred spear; the gaping wound emits a wave of hot
blood, and the smoking river flows into the woven structure beneath it and surges wide.
   Then by the many paths of the thousand openings in the lattice
the falling shower rains down a foul dew, which the priest buried

20 within catches, putting his shameful head under all the drops, defiled both in his clothing and in all his body.

Yea, he throws back his face, he puts his cheeks in the way of the blood, he puts under it his ears and lips, he interposes his nostrils, he washes his very eyes with the fluid, nor does he even spare his
25 throat but moistens his tongue, until he actually drinks the dark gore.

Afterwards, the flamens draw the corpse, stiffening now that the blood has gone forth, off the lattice, and the pontiff, horrible in appearance, comes forth, and shows his wet head, his beard heavy
30 with blood, his dripping fillets and sodden garments.

This man, defiled with such contagions and foul with the gore of the recent sacrifice, all hail and worship at a distance, because profane blood and a dead ox have washed him while concealed in a filthy cave.

l. 5 *With Gabine girding*, "a manner of girding, in which the toga was tucked up; its corner being thrown over the left shoulder, was brought under the right arm round to the breast (this manner was customarily employed in religious festivals)" (Lewis and Short, *s.v. cinctus*).

l. 11 *Sheathed*, restrained from doing damage (*impeditis*).

l. 32 *All hail and worship*. The consecrated priest, emerging from the blood bath with the gift of divine life (drawn from the sacred bull) himself becomes divine and is therefore worshipped. Those who received the *taurobolium* could be described as "born again for eternity" (*renatus in aeternum*, *C.I.L.* vi. 510; many other inscriptions refer to the *taurobolium* and prove the rite to have been in use early in the second century A.D.).

l. 33 *Profane blood*. It must be remembered that Prudentius was a Christian and that to him the blood was profane (*vilis*) and the whole rite not only repulsive but blasphemous.

94 *Apuleius, The Golden Ass* (*Metamorphoses*) xi. 22–6. In a dark night she appeared to me in a vision, declaring in words not dark that the day was come which I had wished for so long; she told me what provision and charges I should be at for the supplications, and how
5 that she had appointed her principal priest Mithras, that was joined unto my destiny (as she said) by the ordering of the planets, to be a minister with me in my sacrifices. When I had heard these and the other divine commandments of the high goddess, I greatly rejoiced, and arose before day to speak with the great priest, whom I for-
10 tuned to espy coming out of his chamber. Then I saluted him, and thought with myself to ask and demand with a bold courage that I should be initiate, as a thing now due; but as soon as he perceived me, he began first to say: "O Lucius, now know I well that thou

art most happy and blessed, whom the divine goddess doth so
15 greatly accept with mercy. Why dost thou stand idle and delay?
Behold the day which thou didst desire with prayer, when as thou
shalt receive at my hands the order of most secret and holy religion,
according to the divine commandment of this goddess of many
names." Thereupon the old man took me by the hand, and led me
20 courteously to the gate of the great temple, where, after that it was
religiously opened, he made a solemn celebration, and after the
morning sacrifice was ended, he brought out of the secret place of
the temple cértain books written with unknown characters . . .
thence he interpreted to me such things as were necessary to the use
25 and preparation of mine order. This done, I diligently gave in
charge to certain of my companions to buy liberally whatsoever
was needful and convenient; but part thereof I bought myself. Then
he brought me, when he found that the time was at hand, to the
next baths, accompanied with all the religious sort, and demanding
30 pardon of the gods, washed me and purified my body according to
the custom: after this, when two parts of the day was gone, he
brought me back again to the temple and presented me before the
feet of the goddess, giving me a charge of certain secret things
unlawful to be uttered, and commanding me generally before all
35 the rest to fast by the space of ten continual days, without eating of
any beast or drinking of any wine: which things I observed with a
marvellous continency. Then behold the day approached when as
the sacrifice of dedication should be done; and when the sun de-
clined and evening came, there arrived on every coast a great
40 multitude of priests, who according to their ancient order offered
me many presents and gifts. Then was all the laity and profane people
commanded to depart, and when they had put on my back a new
linen robe, the priest took my hand and brought me to the most
secret and sacred place of the temple. Thou wouldest peradventure
45 demand, thou studious reader, what was said and done there:
verily I would tell thee if it were lawful for me to tell, thou
wouldest know if it were convenient for thee to hear; but both thy
ears and my tongue should incur the like pain of rash curiosity.
Howbeit I will not long torment thy mind, which peradventure is
50 somewhat religious and given to some devotion; listen therefore,
and believe it to be true. Thou shalt understand that I approached
near unto hell, even to the gates of Proserpine, and after that I was
ravished throughout all the elements, I returned to my proper
place: about midnight I saw the sun brightly shine, I saw likewise
55 the gods celestial and the gods infernal, before whom I presented
myself and worshipped them. Behold now have I told thee, which

although thou hast heard, yet it is necessary that thou conceal it; wherefore this only will I tell, which may be declared without offence for the understanding of the profane.

60   When morning came and that the solemnities were finished, I came forth sanctified with twelve stoles and in a religious habit, whereof I am not forbidden to speak, considering that many persons saw me at that time . . . In my right hand I carried a lighted torch, and a garland of flowers was upon my head, with white palm-
65 leaves sprouting out on every side like rays; thus I was adorned like unto the sun, and made in fashion of an image, when the curtains were drawn aside and all the people compassed about to behold me. Then they began to solemnize the feast, the nativity of my holy order . . . I began to say in this sort: "O holy and blessed dame, the
70 perpetual comfort of human kind, who by thy bounty and grace nourishest all the world, and bearest a great affection to the adversities of the miserable as a loving mother, thou takest no rest night or day, neither art thou idle at any time in giving benefits and succouring all men as well on land as sea; thou art she that
75 puttest away all storms and dangers from men's life by stretching forth thy right hand, whereby likewise thou dost unweave even the inextricable and tangled web of fate, and appeasest the great tempests of fortune, and keepest back the harmful course of the stars. The gods supernal do honour thee; the gods infernal have
80 thee in reverence; thou dost make all the earth to turn, thou givest light to the sun, thou governest the world, thou treadest down the power of hell. By thy mean the stars give answer, the seasons return, the gods rejoice, the elements serve: at thy commandment the winds do blow, the clouds nourish the earth, the seeds prosper,
85 and the fruits do grow. The birds of the air, the beasts of the hill, the serpents of the den, and the fishes of the sea do tremble at thy majesty: but my spirit is not able to give thee sufficient praise, my patrimony is unable to satisfy thy sacrifices; my voice hath no power to utter that which I think of thy majesty, no, not if I had a
90 thousand mouths and so many tongues and were able to continue for ever. Howbeit as a good religious person, and according to my poor estate, I will do what I may: I will always keep thy divine appearance in remembrance, and close the imagination of thy most holy god-head within my breast."

95   When I ended my oration to the great goddess, I went to embrace the great priest Mithras, now my spiritual father, clinging upon his neck and kissing him oft, and demanding his pardon, considering I was unable to recompense the good which he had done me: and after much talk and great greetings and thanks I departed

100 from him straight to visit my parents and friends, after that I had
been so long absent. And so within a short while after, by the
exhortation of the goddess I made up my packet and took shipping
towards the city of Rome, and I voyaged very safely and swiftly
with a prosperous wind to the port of Augustus, and thence
105 travelling by chariot, I arrived at that holy city about the twelfth
day of December in the evening. And the greatest desire which I
had there was daily to make my prayers to the sovereign goddess
Isis, who, by reason of the place where her temple was builded,
was called Campensis, and continually is adored of the people of
110 Rome: her minister and worshipper was I, a stranger to her church,
but not unknown to her religion.

l. 2 *She*, Isis. Apuleius had for some time been seeking initiation.

l. 18 *Of many names.* See below on l. 70.

l. 37 *A marvellous continency.* It cannot be said that Apuleius had shown this in the
early part of his story. It seems clear that his conversion to the religion of
Isis was not without moral accompaniments and consequences.

l. 44 *Thou wouldest peradventure demand.* Apuleius was of course under bond of
secrecy not to divulge the mystery of the cult.

l. 52 *The gates of Proserpine.* Proserpine (in Greek, Persephone) was the daughter
of Demeter, who sought her when Pluto had carried her off to Hades. The
two goddesses were celebrated in the Eleusinian mysteries. Apuleius means
that he was brought down to (and up again from) the threshold of the underworld.

l. 70 *The perpetual comfort* . . . Such aretalogies, listing the names (cf. l. 18),
virtues, and powers of the goddess, are characteristic of the worship of Isis.

l. 96 *My spiritual father.* For this relation of the initiating minister to the neophyte,
cf. in the New Testament 1 Cor. 4. 15; Gal. 4. 19.

l. 104 *The port of Augustus*, Ostia.

l. 105 *That holy city.* To more religions than one Rome was the Holy City. Cf.
W. L. Knox, *J.T.S.* old series xlvii. 180–4.

l. 109 *Campensis.* The temple was in the Campus Martius.

C. Worship

Some rites of the mystery cults have already been described. They
were almost infinitely various, ranging from the licentious to the truly
spiritual.

95 *Josephus, Antiquities* xviii. 66–80. There was at Rome a woman
whose name was Paulina: one who on account of the dignity of
her ancestors, and by the regular conduct of a virtuous life, had a
great reputation. She was also very rich. And although she were of
5 a beautiful countenance, and in that flower of age wherein women

are the most gay, yet did she lead a life of great modesty. She was
married to Saturninus; one that was every way answerable to her
in an excellent character. Decius Mundus, a man very high in the
equestrian order, fell in love with this woman: and as she was of
10 too great dignity to be seduced by presents, and had always
rejected them, though they had been sent in great abundance, he
was still more inflamed with love to her: insomuch that he
promised to give her two hundred thousand Attic drachmae for
one night's lodging. And when this would not prevail upon her,
15 and he was not able to bear this misfortune in his amours, he resolved to famish himself to death, for want of food, on account of
Paulina's refusal: and he went on with his purpose accordingly.
Now Mundus had a freedwoman, who had been made free by his
father, whose name was Ide; one skilful in all sorts of mischief.
20 This woman was much grieved at the young man's resolution to
kill himself (for he did not conceal his intentions to destroy himself from others); and came to him, and encouraged him by her
discourse, and made him to hope, by some promises she gave him,
that he might obtain a night's lodging with Paulina. And when he
25 joyfully hearkened to her, she said, she wanted no more than
fifty thousand drachmae for entrapping of the woman. So when
she had encouraged the young man, and gotten as much money as
she required, she did not take the same methods as had been taken
before; because she perceived that the woman was by no means to
30 be tempted by money. But as she knew that she was much devoted
to the worship of the goddess Isis, she devised the following stratagem: She went to some of Isis's priests, and upon the strongest
assurances of concealment, she persuaded them by words, but
chiefly by the offer of twenty-five thousand drachmae in hand, and
35 as much more when the thing had taken effect; and told them the
passion of the young man; and persuaded them to use all possible
means to beguile the woman. So they were drawn in to promise so
to do, by the large sum of gold they were to have. Accordingly the
oldest of them went immediately to Paulina; and upon his admit-
40 tance, he desired to speak with her by herself. When that was
granted him, he told her, that he was sent by the god Anubis, who
was fallen in love with her, and enjoined her to come to him. Upon
this she took the message very kindly: and valued herself greatly
upon this condescension of the deity: and told her husband, that she
45 had a message sent her, and was to sup and to lie with Anubis. So
he agreed to her acceptance of the offer, as fully satisfied with the
chastity of his wife. Accordingly she went to the temple: and after
she had supped there, and it was the hour to go to sleep, the priest

shut the doors of the temple; when in the holy part of it the lights
50 were also put out. Then did Mundus leap out; and she was at his
service all the night, as supposing he was the god. And when he
was gone away, which was before those priests who knew nothing
of this stratagem were stirring, Paulina came early to her husband,
and told him how Anubis had appeared to her. Among her friends
55 also she declared how great a value she put upon this favour. They
partly disbelieved the thing, when they reflected on its nature; and
partly were amazed at it, as having no pretence for not believing
it, when they considered the modesty, and the dignity of the person. But on the third day after what had been done, Mundus met
60 Paulina, and said, "Nay, Paulina, thou hast saved me two hundred
thousand drachmae; which sum thou mightest have added to thine
own family. Yet hast thou not failed to be at my service in the
manner I invited thee. As for the reproaches thou hast laid upon
Mundus, I value not the business of names; but I rejoice in the
65 pleasure I reaped by what I did, while I assumed the name of
Anubis." When he had said this, he went his way. But now she
began to come to the sense of the grossness of what she had done;
and rent her garments, and told her husband of the horrid nature of
this contrivance, and prayed him not to neglect to assist her in this
70 case. So he discovered the fact to the emperor. Whereupon
Tiberius inquired into the matter thoroughly, by examining the
priests about it; and ordered them to be crucified; as well as Ide,
who was the occasion of their perdition, and who had contrived
the whole matter, which was so injurious to the woman. He also
75 demolished the temple of Isis; and gave order that her statue should
be thrown into the river Tiber. But he only banished Mundus; because he supposed that what crime he had committed was done out
of the passion of love.

l. 41 *Anubis* was the son of Osiris and Nephthys (the sister of Isis). It should be
noted that the whole sordid story narrated by Josephus presupposes the fact
that intelligent and respectable people like Paulina and Saturninus believed
in the gods, and that a "divine marriage" could take place.

96 *A Mithras Liturgy* (Paris Papyrus 574). See A. Dieterich, *Eine
Mithrasliturgie* (third edition, Leipzig and Berlin, 1923), 2–15.

Be gracious unto me, Providence and Fate, as I write down these
first traditional mysteries, [granting] immortality to my only
child, a worthy initiate into this our power, which the great god
Helios Mithras commanded to be imparted to me by his archangel,
5 in order that I alone, an eagle, might tread heaven and behold all
things.

This is the invocation of the prayer:

"First origin of my origin, first beginning of my beginning, spirit of spirit, firstfruit of the spirit within me, fire which art god-given to my mixing, the mixing of the mixings within me, first-fruit of the fire within me, water of water, firstfruit of the water within me, earthy substance, firstfruit of the earthy substance with-in me, whole body of me, A, son of my mother B, framed by the honourable arm and incorruptible right hand in a world un-illuminated yet bright, with no living soul, yet with a living soul: if it seem good to you to give me, held as I am by my underlying nature, to immortal birth, in order that, after the present need which presses sore upon me, I may behold by deathless spirit the deathless Beginning, by deathless water, by solid earth and air, that I may be born anew by Thought, that I may be initiated and that the sacred spirit may breathe in me, that I may marvel at the holy fire, that I may behold the terrible great deep of the Day-spring, that the life-giving and surrounding Aether may hear me; for to-day I am to gaze with deathless eyes, I who was born mortal from a mortal womb, but transformed by mighty power and an incorruptible right hand. . . ."

. . . But you shall see how the gods gaze upon you, and influence you. Lay at once your right [fore-]finger upon your mouth and say, "Silence! Silence! Silence!" (a symbol of the living, in-corruptible god). "Guard me, Silence!" Then whistle long, then sneeze, and say . . . and then you will see the gods looking graciously upon you, and no longer influencing you but going upon their own course of business. . . .

"O Lord, hail, great in power, king great in sovereignty, greatest of gods, Helios, Lord of heaven and earth, god of gods, mighty is thy breath, mighty is thy power. Lord, if it please thee, announce me to the greatest god, who hath begotten and made thee; for I am a man, A, the son of my mother B, born of the mortal womb of B and of lifegiving seed, and this day by thee who hast been re-generated, who out of so many thousands have been brought into immortality in this hour by the counsel of god, who is good be-yond measure—a man who wills and prays to worship thee according to his human power." When you have said this, he will come into the vault of heaven and you will see him walking as on a road.

. . . Gaze on the god, groan long, and greet him thus: "O Lord, hail, ruler of water, hail, founder of earth, hail, sovereign of spirit. Lord, having been born again I depart; increasing and having been increased I die; born of a life-giving birth I am set free for death

50 and go on my way, as thou didst ordain, as thou didst enact and
didst make the mystery."

l. 1 *I write down*. The writer of the papyrus is an official in the Mithraic cult
providing instructions for his "child", who is to be born again as a disciple
of the god.

l. 8 *First origin of my origin* . . . The prayers in this liturgy are marked by "vain
repetition" and there are places where the original, and with it the translation, does not make sense. It also contains many meaningless, magical, words,
which are not represented in the translation. The many parallels with New
Testament language are very striking, and will be apparent to the English
reader; they are even more evident in Greek.

l. 27 *Influence you*, in a harmful way; cf. l. 32.

l. 51 *Make the mystery*. Dieterich translates "*geschaffen hast das Sakrament*", with
direct reference to the cult act in which regeneration takes place.

JEWISH HISTORY

THE history of the Jews in the New Testament period is a long story of which fortunately many details are known. To provide it here with even half complete documentation is neither possible nor necessary; instead, a few salient points receive brief illustration.

A. *The Maccabean Period*

The Jewish nation emerged from a period of obscurity in the first half of the second century B.C. Alexander the Great's decade of vigorous campaigning had changed the shape of the Near East more radically than many preceding centuries; Alexandria and Antioch (to go no farther) became the centres of powerful Hellenistic monarchies, and Palestine suffered as a buffer state between the Ptolemies in the one and the Seleucids in the other. The Jews found themselves in a potent and persuasive atmosphere of Hellenistic life and culture, which undoubtedly began to influence their own civilization, and might well have long continued to do so had not Antiochus IV Epiphanes (of Syria; 176–164 B.C.), by seeking to accelerate the process, aroused the Jewish conscience, thereby provoking a fierce and resolute resistance which gave direction and impetus to the history of the next 300 years. Of the period dominated by the Maccabean family, 1 Maccabees is a more or less contemporary, sober, and on the whole trustworthy record; but not all its sources are of equal value.

97 1 *Macc.* 1. 5–15. And after these things he took to his bed, and perceived that he was about to die. Then he called his chief ministers, men who had been brought up with him from his youth, and divided his kingdom among them while he was yet alive. And Alex-
5 ander had reigned twelve years when he died. And his ministers ruled, each in his particular domain. And after he was dead they all assumed the diadem, and their sons after them did likewise; and this continued for many years. And these wrought much evil on the earth.

10   And a sinful shoot came forth from them, Antiochus Epiphanes,
the son of Antiochus the king, who had been a hostage in Rome, and
had become king in the one hundred and   forty-third   year of the
Greek kingdom. In those days there came forth out of Israel lawless
men, and persuaded many, saying: "Let us go and make a cove-
15 nant with the nations that are round about us; for since we separated
ourselves from them many evils have come upon us." And the
saying appeared good in their eyes; and as certain of the people
were eager to carry this out, they went to the king, and he gave
them authority to introduce the customs of the Gentiles. And they
20 built a gymnasium in Jerusalem according to the manner of the
Gentiles. They also submitted themselves to uncircumcision, and
repudiated the holy covenant; yea, they joined themselves to the
Gentiles, and sold themselves to do evil.

l. 1 *He took to his bed*—Alexander the Great, who was taken ill in the night of
31 May 323 B.C., and died eleven days later. The author of 1 Maccabees is
here less accurate than usual—not unnaturally, since he is describing events
which took place long before his own time. Not all of Alexander's generals
became kings, nor is it probable that he divided his kingdom among them.

l. 10 *Antiochus Epiphanes.* His father, Antiochus III, was defeated by the Romans
at Magnesia in 190 B.C., and the son lived twelve years in Rome as a hostage.
No doubt these experiences gave him a clear sense of the growing power
of Rome, and this probably lay behind the provocative actions which the
author of 1 Maccabees sees rather as the fruit of unbridled wickedness and
folly. For the payment of tribute to Rome, and for the accumulation of
treasure, Antiochus found it necessary to rob temples; that at Jerusalem was
not the only one that suffered. Further, he may well have come to believe
that the eastern states could only stand against Rome on the basis of a
"united Hellenistic front", to which Jews no less than others were required
to conform.

l. 12 *The one hundred and thirty-seventh year of the Greek kingdom,* that is, of the
Seleucid kingdom, which was founded in 312 B.C.

l. 13 *There came forth out of Israel lawless men.* The spontaneous movement towards
Hellenization (above, p. 105) received a new impulse. There are more details
in 2 Maccabees 4, where Jason the high priest is mentioned as one of the
Hellenizers.

98 1 *Macc.* 1. 20–4. And Antiochus, after he had smitten Egypt, returned in the one hundred and fifty-third year, and went up against
Israel and Jerusalem with a great army. And in his arrogance he
entered into the sanctuary, and took the golden altar, and the
5 candlestick for the light, and all its accessories, and the table of the
shew-bread, and the cups, and the bowls, and the golden censers,
and the veil, and the crowns, and the golden adornment on the
façade of the Temple, and he scaled it all off. Moreover, he took

the silver, and the gold, and the choice vessels; he also took the
10 hidden treasures which he found. And having taken everything, he
returned to his own land.

l. 1 *After he had smitten Egypt.* Antiochus's depradations began after his first
Egyptian campaign. They were continued after his second (1 Macc. 1. 29f.).
Certainly on the latter occasion, probably on the former (see Josephus,
Ant. xii. 244, 246), Antiochus had been repelled from Egypt not by local
resistance but by Roman threats; these would doubtless intensify the fears
mentioned above.

99 1 *Macc.* 1. 54–64. And on the fifteenth day of Chislev in the one
hundred and forty-fifth year they set up upon the altar an "abomination of desolation", and in the cities of Judah on every side they
established high-places; and they offered sacrifices at the doors of
5 the houses and in the streets. And the books of the Law which they
found they rent in pieces, and burned them in the fire. And with
whomsoever was found a book of the covenant, and if he was
found consenting unto the Law, such an one was, according to the
king's sentence, condemned to death. Thus did they in their
10 might to the Israelites who were found month by month in their
cities. And on the twenty-fifth day of the month they sacrificed
upon the altar which was upon the altar of burnt-offering. And,
according to the decree, they put to death the women who had
circumcised their children, hanging their babes round their
15 mothers' necks, and they put to death their entire families, together with those who had circumcised them. Nevertheless many
in Israel stood firm and determined in their hearts that they would
not eat unclean things, and chose rather to die so that they might
not be defiled with meats, thereby profaning the holy covenant:
20 and they did die. And exceeding great wrath came upon Israel.

l. 2 *"Abomination of desolation".* Cf. Dan. 11. 31; 12. 11. This phrase refers to
the heathen altar set up on the great altar of the Temple (see l. 12).
l. 11 *On the twenty-fifth day of the month.* On this day, three years later, the Temple
was reconsecrated. See pp. 109ff. (102).
l. 20 *And they did die,* perhaps the first martyrs for religion. See pp. 223–6 (210).

100 1 *Macc.* 2. 15–28. And the king's officers who were enforcing the
apostasy came to the city of Modin to make them sacrifice. And
many from Israel went unto them; but Mattathias and his sons
gathered themselves together. Then the king's officers answered
5 and spake to Mattathias, saying: "A ruler art thou, and illustrious
and great in this city, and upheld by sons and brothers. Do thou,
therefore, come first, and carry out the king's command, as all the

nations have done, and all the people of Judah, and they that have
remained in Jerusalem; then shalt thou and thy house be numbered
10 among the friends of the king, and thou and thy sons shall be
honoured with silver and gold, and with many gifts." Thereupon
Mattathias answered and said with a loud voice: "If all the nations
that are within the king's dominions obey him by forsaking, every
one of them, the worship of their fathers, and have chosen for
15 themselves to follow his commands, yet will I and my sons and my
brethren walk in the covenant of our fathers. Heaven forbid that
we should forsake the Law and the ordinances; but the law of the
king we will not obey by departing from our worship either to the
right hand or to the left." And as he ceased speaking these words, a
20 Jew came forward in the sight of all to sacrifice upon the altar
in Modin in accordance with the king's command. And when
Mattathias saw it, his zeal was kindled, and his heart quivered with
wrath; and his indignation burst forth for judgement, so that he
ran and slew him on the altar; and at the same time he also killed
25 the king's officer who had come to enforce the sacrificing, pulled
down the altar, and thus showed forth his zeal for the Law, just as
Phinehas had done in the case of Zimri the son of Salom. And
Mattathias cried out with a loud voice in the city, saying, "Let
every one that is zealous for the Law and that would maintain the
30 covenant come forth after me!" And he and his sons fled into the
mountains, and left all that they possessed in the city.

l. 3 *Mattathias and his sons.* Mattathias was a priest living at Modin; his sons were
John, Simon, Judas (called Maccabaeus), Eleazar, and Jonathan.
l. 7 *As all the nations have done.* Antiochus's desire for conformity was probably
due not so much to anti-Semitism as to his plan to unite the Hellenistic
states (above, p. 106).
l. 10 *The friends of the king,* apparently an official title.

101 1 *Macc.* 3. 10–26. And Apollonius gathered the Gentiles together,
and a great host from Samaria, to fight against Israel. And Judas
perceived it, and went forth to meet him, and smote him, and slew
him; and many fell wounded to death, and the rest fled. And they
5 took their spoils; and Judas took the sword of Apollonius, and
therewith fought he all his days.
And Seron, the commander of the host of Syria, heard that Judas
had gathered a gathering and a congregation of faithful men with
him, and of such as went out to war; and he said: "I will make a
10 name for myself, and get me glory in the kingdom; and I will fight
against Judas and them that are with him, that set at nought the
word of the king." And he went up again; and there went up with

him a mighty army of the ungodly to help him, to take vengeance
on the children of Israel. And he came near to the ascent of Beth-
15 horon; and Judas went forth to meet him with a small company.
But when they saw the army coming to meet them, they said unto
Judas: "What? shall we be able, being a small company, to fight
against so great and strong a multitude? And we, for our part, are
faint, having tasted no food this day." And Judas said: "It is an
20 easy thing for many to be shut up in the hands of a few, and there is
no difference in the sight of Heaven to save by many or by few; for
victory in battle standeth not in the multitude of an host, but
strength is from Heaven. They come unto us in fullness of insolence
and lawlessness, to destroy us and our wives and our children, for
25 to spoil us; but we fight for our lives and our laws. And he himself
will discomfit them before our face; but as for you, be ye not afraid
of them." Now when he had left off speaking he leapt suddenly
upon them, and Seron and his army were discomfited before him.
And they pursued them at the descent of Bethhoron unto the
30 plain; and there fell of them about eight hundred men; and the
rest fled into the land of the Philistines.

Then began the fear of Judas and of his brethren, and the dread
of them fell upon the nations round about them. And his name
came near even unto the king; and every nation told of the battles
35 of Judas.

.1 *Apollonius.* The name is introduced without explanation. Comparison of
1 Macc. 1. 29 with 2 Macc. 5. 24 suggests that Apollonius had previously
been entrusted with the spoliation of Jerusalem.

l. 2 *Judas.* His father Mattathias was now dead (1 Macc. 2. 70). He had recommended Judas among his sons as fittest for military leadership.

l. 14 *The ascent of Bethhoron*; cf. l. 29, *descent of Bethhoron.* This place evidently
commanded the road down from Jerusalem to the coastal plain and was
more than once the scene of bitter fighting.

102 1 *Macc.* 4. 36–61. But Judas and his brethren said: "Behold, our
enemies are discomfited: let us go up to cleanse the Holy Place, and
re-dedicate it." And all the army was gathered together, and they
went unto mount Sion, and they saw our sanctuary laid desolate,
5 and the altar profaned, and the gates burned up, and shrubs growing in the courts as in a forest or upon one of the mountains, and the
chambers of the priests pulled down; and they rent their garments,
and made great lamentation, and put ashes on their heads; and they
fell on their faces to the ground, and they blew the solemn blasts
10 upon the trumpets, and cried unto heaven. Then Judas appointed
a certain number of men to fight against those that were in the
citadel, until he should have cleansed the Holy Place. And he chose

blameless priests, such as had delight in the Law; and they cleansed
the Holy Place, and bare out the stones of defilement into an un-
15 clean place. And they took counsel concerning the altar of burnt-
offerings, which had been profaned, what they should do with it.
And a good idea occurred to them namely to pull it down, lest it
should be a reproach unto them, because the Gentiles had defiled it;
so they pulled down the altar, and laid down the stones in the
20 mountain of the House, in a convenient place, until a prophet
should come and decide as to what should be done concerning
them. And they took whole stones according to the Law, and built
a new altar after the fashion of the former one; and they built
the Holy Place, and the inner parts of the house, and hallowed
25 the courts. And they made the holy vessels new, and they brought
the candlestick, and the altar of burnt-offerings and of incense, and
the table, into the Temple. And they burned incense upon the altar,
and they lighted the lamps that were upon the candlestick in order to
give light in the Temple. And they set loaves upon the table, and hung
30 up the veils, and finished all the works which they had undertaken.
And they rose up early in the morning on the twenty-fifth day of
the ninth month, which is the month Chislev, in the one hundred
and forty-eighth year, and offered sacrifice, according to the Law,
upon the new altar of burnt-offerings which they had made. At the
35 corresponding time of the month and on the corresponding day
on which the Gentiles had profaned it, on that day was it dedicated
afresh, with songs and harps and lutes, and with cymbals. And all
the people fell upon their faces, and worshipped, and gave praise,
looking up unto heaven, to him who had prospered them. And
40 they celebrated the dedication of the altar for eight days, and
offered burnt-offerings with gladness, and sacrificed a sacrifice of
deliverance and praise. And they decked the forefront of the Temple
with crowns of gold and small shields, and dedicated afresh the
gates and the chambers of the priests, and furnished them with
45 doors. And there was exceeding great gladness among the people,
and the reproach of the Gentiles was turned away. And Judas and
his brethren and the whole congregation of Israel ordained, that
the days of the dedication of the altar should be kept in their
seasons year by year for eight days, from the twenty-fifth day of
50 the month Chislev, with gladness and joy. And at that season they
built high walls and strong towers around mount Sion, lest haply
the Gentiles should come and tread them down, as they had done
aforetime. And he set there a force to keep it, and they fortified
Bethsura to keep it, that the people might have a stronghold over
55 against Idumaea.

l. 2 *Our enemies are discomfited.* Since the rout of Seron (above, p. 108f. (**101**)) the Jews had defeated Gorgias and Lysias.

l. 12 *In the citadel.* Very early in his proceedings against the Jews Antiochus had fortified "the city of David", that is the southern, and lower, part of the Temple mount. This "became a sore menace, for it was a place to lie in wait in against the sanctuary, and an evil adversary to Israel continually" (1 Macc. 1. 36). It remained in the possession of the Syrians until the time of Simon (1 Macc. 13. 50).

l. 14 *The stones of defilement,* the stones of which the heathen altar (the "abomination of desolation", p. 107 (**99**)) had been made.

l. 15 *The altar of burnt-offerings,* the Jewish altar which had been profaned by the heathen altar erected upon it.

l. 46 *Judas and his brethren . . . ordained.* This was the origin of the feast of *Hanukkah* (חנכה; in Greek, ἐγκαίνια, John 10. 22), also called the feast of Lights. (For a different theory of its origin and meaning see O. S. Rankin, *The Origins of the Festival of Hanukkah* (Edinburgh, 1930).) It was celebrated in a way similar to the feast of Tabernacles (see pp. 157ff. (**152**)), and was sometimes called "the feast of Tabernacles in the month Chislev".

103 1 *Macc.* 8. 17–32. And Judas chose Eupolemus, the son of John, the son of Accos, and Jason, the son of Eleazar, and sent them to Rome, to make a league of amity and confederacy with them, and that they should take the yoke from them, when they saw that the king-
5 dom of the Greeks did keep Israel in bondage. And they went to Rome, and the way was exceeding long; and they entered into the senate house, and answered and said: "Judas, who is also called Maccabaeus, and his brethren and the whole people of the Jews, have sent us unto you, to make a confederacy and peace with you,
10 and that we might be registered as your confederates and friends." And the thing was well-pleasing in their sight. And this is the copy of the writing which they wrote back again on tablets of brass, and sent to Jerusalem, that it might be with them there for a memorial of peace and confederacy:
15   "Good success be to the Romans, and to the nation of the Jews, by sea and by land for ever; the sword also and the enemy be far from them. But if war arise for Rome first, or for any of their confederates in all their dominion, the nation of the Jews shall help them as confederates as the occasion shall prescribe to them, with
20 all their heart; and unto them that make war they [i.e. the Jews] shall not give, neither supply, food, arms, money, or ships, as it hath seemed good unto Rome; and they [i.e. the Jews] shall observe their obligations, receiving nothing [in the way of a bribe]. In the same manner, moreover, if war come first upon the nation of the
25 Jews, the Romans shall help them as confederates with all their soul, as the occasion shall prescribe to them; and to them that are

confederates there shall not be given corn, arms, money, or ships, as it hath seemed good unto Rome; and they shall observe these obligations, and that without deceit. According to these words 30 have the Romans made a treaty with the people of the Jews. But if hereafter the one party or the other shall determine to add or diminish anything, they shall do it at their pleasure, and whatsoever they shall add or take away shall be established. And as touching the evils which king Demetrius doeth unto you, we have 35 written to him saying: 'Wherefore hast thou made thy yoke heavy upon our friends and confederates the Jews? If, therefore, they plead any more against thee, we will do them justice, and fight thee by sea and by land.'"

l. 1 *Judas . . . sent them to Rome.* Here may be noted on the one hand the astuteness of the Jewish rulers throughout this period in picking the winning side in foreign quarrels, and on the other the Roman principle of *divide et impera*—the Jews might first be used against the Syrian kingdom, and then themselves subjugated at leisure.

l. 22 *As it hath seemed good unto Rome*; cf. l. 28. The advantage given by the treaty to Rome is manifest.

l. 34 *Demetrius.* Demetrius I, now king in Antioch.

104 1 *Macc.* 11. 54–62. Now after this Tryphon returned, and with him the young child Antiochus; and he reigned, and put on a diadem. And there were gathered unto him all the forces which Demetrius had sent away in disgrace; and they fought against him, and he 5 fled, and was put to rout. And Tryphon took the elephants, and became master of Antioch. And the young Antiochus wrote unto Jonathan, saying: "I confirm unto thee the high-priesthood, and appoint thee over the four governments, and to be one of the king's friends." And he sent unto him golden vessels and furniture 10 for the table, and gave him leave to drink in golden vessels, and to be clothed in purple, and to have a golden buckle. And his brother Simon he made governor over the district from the Ladder of Tyre unto the borders of Egypt. And Jonathan went forth, and took his journey beyond the river, and through the cities; and all 15 the forces of Syria gathered themselves unto him for to be his confederates. And he came to Askalon, and they of the city met him honourably. And he departed thence to Gaza, and they of Gaza shut him out; and he laid siege unto it, and burned the suburbs thereof with fire, and spoiled them. And they of Gaza made re-20 quest unto Jonathan, and he gave them his right hand, and took the sons of their princes for hostages, and sent them away to Jerusalem. And he passed through the country as far as Damascus.

l. 1 *Tryphon* played a powerful part in the complicated politics of this period. He opposed king Demetrius II, and was responsible for putting forward Antiochus VI in his place.

l. 2 *The young child Antiochus*, the son of Alexander Balas, who had been living in the care of Imalcue the Arabian. Tryphon doubtless hoped to be able to use the youthful king as a puppet while he himself retained the substance of power.

l. 3 *Demetrius.* Demetrius II, son of the Demetrius mentioned above (p. 112 (103)).

l. 7 *I confirm unto thee the high-priesthood.* Jonathan (his brother Judas being now dead) had been appointed high priest by Alexander Balas (1 Macc. 10. 20). The family of Mattathias was a priestly family and therefore eligible for the office, which was regularly held by the later rulers of the Jews (see pp. 113-18).

l. 8 *The four governments*, the prefectures of Aphaerema, Lydda and Ramathaim; together with Judaea (which however is probably to be taken for granted, the other four governments being additional), or Ptolemais or Ekron.

l. 9 *Golden vessels, etc.* These are marks of royal dignity. This passage marks one of the peaks of Jewish good fortune in this period.

B. *The High Priests*

The rule of Jonathan may serve as a transition to the period in which a succession of high priests exercised both religious and civil power in Jerusalem. At first they continued to be of the Maccabean, or Hasmonean, family. The political history of the period is very complicated, and over-simplified conclusions must not be drawn from the few documents quoted here.

105 1 *Macc.* 14. 25-49. But when the people heard these things, they said: "What thanks shall we give to Simon and his sons? For he, and his brethren, and his father's house have made themselves strong, and have chased away in fight the enemies of Israel from
5 them, and established liberty for it." And they wrote on tablets of brass, and set them upon a pillar in mount Sion. And this is the copy of the writing: "On the eighteenth day of Elul, in the one hundred and seventy-second year—that is the third year of Simon the high priest, and the prince of the people of God—in a great congrega-
10 tion of priests and people and princes of the nation, and of the elders of the country, the following was promulgated by us: Forasmuch as oftentimes there have been wars in the country, Simon the son of Mattathias, the son of the children of Joarib, and his brethren, put themselves in jeopardy, and withstood the enemies of their
15 nation, that their sanctuary and the Law might be upheld; and they glorified their nation with great glory. And Jonathan assembled their nation together, and became high priest to them; and he was

gathered to his people. Then their enemies determined to invade
their country, that they might destroy their country utterly, and
20 stretch forth their hands against their sanctuary. Then rose up
Simon and fought for his nation; and he spent much of his own
substance, and armed the valiant men of his nation, and gave them
wages. And he fortified the cities of Judaea, and Bethsura that lieth
upon the borders of Judaea, where the arms of the enemies were
25 aforetime, and set there a garrison of Jews. And he fortified Joppa
which is by the sea, and Gazara which is upon the borders of
Azotus, wherein the enemies dwelt aforetime; and he placed Jews
there, and whatsoever things were needful for the sustenance of
these he put in them. And when the people saw the faith of Simon,
30 and the glory which he sought to bring unto his nation, they made
him their leader and high priest, because he had done all these
things, and because of the justice and the faith which he kept to his
nation, and because he sought by all means to exalt his people. And
in his days things prospered in his hands, so that the Gentiles were
35 taken away out of their [the Jews'] country; and they also that
were in the city of David, they that were in Jerusalem, who had
made themselves a citadel, out of which they issued, and polluted
all things round about the sanctuary, and did great hurt unto its
purity, these did he expel; and he made Jews to dwell therein, and
40 fortified it for the safety of the country and of the city; and he
made high the walls of Jerusalem. And king Demetrius confirmed
him in the high-priesthood in consequence of these things, and
made him one of his friends, and honoured him with great honour.
For he had heard that the Jews had been proclaimed by the Romans
45 friends, and confederates, and brethren, and that they had met the
ambassadors of Simon honourably. And the Jews and the priests
were well pleased that Simon should be their leader and high
priest for ever, until a faithful prophet should arise; and that he
should be a captain over them, to set them over their works, and
50 over the country, and over the arms, and over the strongholds,
and that he should take charge of the sanctuary, and that he
should be obeyed by all, and that all instruments in the country
should be written in his name, and that he should be clothed in
purple, and wear gold; and that it should not be lawful for anyone
55 among the people or among the priests to set at nought any of these
things, or to gainsay the things spoken by him, or to gather an
assembly in the country without him, or that any other should be
clothed in purple, or wear a buckle of gold; but that whosoever
should do otherwise, or set at nought any of these things, should
60 be liable to punishment. And all the people consented to ordain

for Simon that it should be done according to these words. And Simon accepted hereof, and consented to fill the office of high priest, and to be captain and governor of the Jews and of the priests, and to preside over all matters."

65 And they commanded to put this writing on tablets of brass, and to set them up within the precinct of the sanctuary in a conspicuous place; and copies of this they caused to be placed in the treasury, to the end that Simon and his sons might have them.

l. 2 *What thanks shall we give to Simon?* Tryphon, no longer content to be the power behind Antiochus's throne, resolved upon seizing the monarchy for himself; fearing that Jonathan would prove faithful to Antiochus he had him captured and killed by treachery. Simon succeeded his brother, defeated Tryphon, made a treaty with Demetrius II, captured Gazara and the citadel of Jerusalem (above, p. 109 (**102**)), and renewed the treaty with Rome. His son John became his general.

l. 9 *The high priest, and prince of the people of God.* The Greek reads "the high priest in Asaramel" (or Saramel). This is probably due to corruption of an original Hebrew שַׂר עַם אֵל (*sar 'am 'el*) "prince of the people of God", or perhaps of שַׂר יִשְׂרָאֵל (*sar yisra'el*) "prince of Israel". In any case it is clear (ll. 62ff.) that Simon was the military and political head of his people as well as high priest.

l. 48 *For ever*; that is, the office was to be hereditary in his family. The Hasmoneans were in effect both kings and high priests

106 *Josephus, Ant.* xiii. 372–6. As for Alexander, his own people revolted against him—for the nation was aroused against him—at the celebration of the festival, and as he stood beside the altar and was about to sacrifice, they pelted him with citrons, it being a custom
5 among the Jews that at the festival of Tabernacles everyone holds wands made of palm branches and citrons—these we have described elsewhere; and they added insult to injury by saying that he was descended from captives and was unfit to hold office and to sacrifice; and being enraged at this, he killed some six thousand of
10 them, and also placed a wooden barrier about the altar and the Temple as far as the coping [of the court] which the priests alone were permitted to enter, and by this means blocked the people's way to him. He also maintained foreign troops of Pisidians and Cilicians, for he could not use Syrians, being at war with them.
15 And after subduing the Arabs of Moab and Galaaditis, whom he forced to pay tribute, he demolished Amathūs, as Theodorus did not venture to meet him in the field. Then he engaged in battle with Obedas, the king of the Arabs, and falling into an ambush in a rough and difficult region, he was pushed by a multitude of
20 camels into a deep ravine near Garada, a village of Gaulanis, and

barely escaped with his own life, and fleeing from there, came to Jerusalem. But when the nation attacked him upon this misfortune, he made war on it and within six years slew no fewer than fifty thousand Jews. And so when he urged them to make an end of
25 their hostility toward him, they only hated him the more on account of what had happened. And when he asked what he ought to do and what they wanted of him, they all cried out, "To die"; and they sent to Demetrius Akairos, asking him to come to their assistance.

l. 1 *Alexander*, Alexander Jannaeus, who ruled from 104 to 78 B.C. His coins, bearing the bilingual inscription יהונתן המלך (King Jonathan), ΒΑΣΙΛΕΩΣ ΑΛΕΞΑΝΔΡΟΥ (King Alexander), show that he claimed the royal title. He was unpopular with the people, among whom the Pharisees (see p. 126 (115)) were gaining favour, but a vigorous and not unsuccessful soldier.

l. 8 *He was descended from captives*. This slander was brought against John Hyrcanus, father of Alexander (*Ant*. xiii. 292; cf. Lev. 21. 14).

l. 16 *Theodorus*. Amathus was in Arab territory (east of Jordan), and Theodorus therefore probably an Arab chief. He had massacred 10,000 Jews and plundered Alexander's baggage (*Ant*. xiii. 356).

l. 20 *Gaulanis*. Read, against the MSS., on the ground of the parallel in *War* i. 90.

l. 28 *Demetrius Akairos*, Demetrius III, king of Syria. He defeated Alexander, but this reversal of fortune brought round many Jews to Alexander's side and he was able to recover his position.

107 *Josephus, Ant.* xiv. 69–79. Now when the siege-engine was brought up, the largest of the towers was shaken and fell, making a breach through which the enemy poured in . . . And there was slaughter everywhere. For some of the Jews were slain by the Romans, and
5 others by their fellows; and there were some who hurled themselves down the precipices, and setting fire to their houses, burned themselves within them, for they could not bear to accept their fate. And so of the Jews there fell some twelve thousand, but of the Romans only a very few. One of those taken captive was Absalom,
10 the uncle and at the same time father-in-law of Aristobulus. And not light was the sin committed against the sanctuary, which before that time had never been entered or seen. For Pompey and not a few of his men went into it and saw what it was unlawful for any but the high priests to see. But though the golden table was there
15 and the sacred lampstand and the libation vessels and a great quantity of spices, and beside these, in the treasury, the sacred moneys amounting to two thousand talents, he touched none of these because of piety, and in this respect also he acted in a manner worthy of his virtuous character. And on the morrow he instructed

20 the Temple servants to cleanse the Temple and to offer the customary
sacrifice to God, and he restored the high-priesthood to Hyrcanus
because in various ways he had been useful to him and particularly
because he had prevented the Jews throughout the country from
fighting on Aristobulus's side; and those responsible for the war he
25 executed by beheading. . . . And he made Jerusalem tributary to
the Romans, and took from its inhabitants the cities of Coele-Syria
which they had formerly subdued, and placed them under his own
governor; and the entire nation, which before had raised itself so
high, he confined within its own borders. He also rebuilt Gadara,
30 which had been demolished a little while before, to please Demetrius the Gadarene, his freedman; and the other cities, Hippus,
Scythopolis, Pella, Dium, Samaria, as well as Marisa, Azotus,
Jamneia, and Arethusa, he restored to their own inhabitants. And
not only these cities in the interior, in addition to those that had
35 been demolished, but also the coast cities of Gaza, Joppa, Dora, and
Straton's Tower—this last city, which Herod refounded magnificently and adorned with harbours and temples, was later renamed
Caesarea—all these Pompey set free and annexed them to the
province.
40   For this misfortune which befell Jerusalem Hyrcanus and Aristobulus were responsible, because of their dissension. For we lost our
freedom and became subject to the Romans, and the territory
which we had gained by our arms and taken from the Syrians we
were compelled to give back to them, and in addition the Romans
45 exacted of us in a short space of time more than ten thousand
talents; and the royal power which had formerly been bestowed
on those who were high priests by birth became the privilege of
commoners. But of this we shall speak in the proper place. Now
Pompey gave over to Scaurus Coele-Syria and the rest of Syria as
50 far as the Euphrates river and Egypt, and two Roman legions, and
then went off to Cilicia, making haste to reach Rome. And with
him he took Aristobulus in chains, together with his family; for he
had two daughters and as many sons; but one of them, Alexander,
got away, while the younger son, Antigonus, was carried off to
55 Rome together with his sisters.

l. 1 *Now*, in 63 B.C. As at later times (see pp. 127–33 (**116–21**)), faction proved the
downfall of the Jewish State. Alexander Jannaeus was succeeded by his
widow Alexandra, who made her eldest son Hyrcanus high priest, and
would have had him for her successor; but on her death his brother Aristobulus seized power. Civil war ensued. Pompey the Great was now active
in the East and both parties solicited his aid. After complicated political
manœuvres he found himself besieging the adherents of Aristobulus in
Jerusalem.

l. 5 *By their fellows.* Within Jerusalem there were also adherents of Hyrcanus, who
    wished to open the gates to Pompey.

l. 12 *Had never been entered or seen,* except by the high priests.

l. 27 *His own governor,* the legate of the province of Syria, Scaurus; see l. 49.

l. 33 *He restored to their own inhabitants.* The cities had earlier been taken by the
    Jews from Gentile inhabitants. Josephus's list is incomplete; other cities in
    the same area reckoned their dates from their liberation by Pompey.

l. 39 *To the province,* of Syria.

l. 48 *In the proper place;* in the next book, *Ant.* xv.

l. 51 *Making haste.* Nevertheless, he wintered in Asia Minor.

C. Herod the Great

We are brought to the threshold of the New Testament period by
one of the most curious epochs in Jewish history. The Idumaean ad-
venturer Antipater, and his son Herod the Great, both of them
audacious, cunning, capable, and fortunate, became rulers of a Jewish
kingdom, and founded a dynasty which lasted a century and a half—a
long time in such turbulent days. Antipater had already been active
before Pompey's intervention, as our first passage shows.

108 *Josephus, War* i. 123–6. The unexpected triumph of Aristobulus
alarmed his adversaries, and, in particular, Antipater, an old and
bitterly hated foe. An Idumaean by race, his ancestry, wealth, and
other advantages put him in the front rank of his nation. It was he
5 who now persuaded Hyrcanus to seek refuge with Aretas, king of
Arabia, with a view to recovering his kingdom, and at the same
time urged Aretas to receive him and to reinstate him on the
throne. Heaping aspersions on the character of Aristobulus and
encomiums on Hyrcanus, he represented how becoming it would
10 be in the sovereign of so brilliant a realm to extend a protecting
hand to the oppressed; and such, he said, was Hyrcanus, robbed of
the throne which by right of primogeniture belonged to him.
    Having thus prepared both parties for action, Antipater one
night fled with Hyrcanus from the city, and, pushing on at full
15 speed, safely reached the capital of the Arabian kingdom, called
Petra. There he committed Hyrcanus into the hands of Aretas, and,
by dint of conciliatory speeches and cajoling presents, induced the
king to furnish an army, fifty thousand strong, both cavalry and
infantry, to reinstate his ward. This force Aristobulus was unable to
20 resist. Defeated in the first encounter he was driven into Jerusalem.

ll. 1, 5 *Aristobulus . . . Hyrcanus.* See above, pp. 116f. (**107**).

l. 13 *Having thus prepared both parties for action.* The methods here described are
    characteristic of Antipater and his son.

109 *Josephus, War* i. 199–207. After hearing both speakers, Caesar pronounced Hyrcanus to be the more deserving claimant to the high-priesthood, and left Antipater free choice of office. The latter, replying that it rested with him who conferred the honour to fix
5 the measure of the honour, was then appointed viceroy of all Judaea. He was further authorized to rebuild the ruined walls of the metropolis. Orders were sent by Caesar to Rome for these honours to be graven in the Capitol, as a memorial of his own justice and of Antipater's valour.

10   After escorting Caesar across Syria, Antipater returned to Judaea. There his first act was to rebuild the wall of the capital which had been overthrown by Pompey. He then proceeded to traverse the country, quelling the local disturbances, and everywhere combining menaces with advice. Their support of Hyrcanus, he told them,
15 would ensure them a prosperous and tranquil existence, in the enjoyment of their own possessions and of the peace of the realm. If, on the contrary, they put faith in the vain expectations raised by persons who for personal profit desired revolution, they would find in himself a master instead of a protector, in Hyrcanus a tyrant
20 instead of a king, in the Romans and Caesar enemies instead of rulers and friends; for they would never suffer their own nominee to be ousted from his office. But, while he spoke in this strain, he took the organization of the country into his own hands, finding Hyrcanus indolent and without the energy necessary to a king. He
25 further appointed his eldest son, Phasael, governor of Jerusalem and the environs; the second, Herod, he sent with equal authority to Galilee, though a mere lad.

    Herod, energetic by nature, at once found material to test his metal. Discovering that Ezekias, a brigand-chief, at the head of a
30 large horde, was ravaging the district on the Syrian frontier, he caught him and put him and many of the brigands to death. This welcome achievement was immensely admired by the Syrians. Up and down the villages and in the towns the praises of Herod were sung, as the restorer of their peace and possessions. This exploit,
35 moreover, brought him to the notice of Sextus Caesar, a kinsman of the great Caesar and governor of Syria. Phasael, on his side, with a generous emulation, vied with his brother's reputation; he increased his popularity with the inhabitants of Jerusalem, and kept the city under control without any tactless abuse of authority.
40 Antipater, in consequence, was courted by the nation as if he were king and universally honoured as lord of the realm. Notwithstanding this, his affection for Hyrcanus and his loyalty to him underwent no change.

l. 1 *Both speakers.* Antigonus, son of Aristobulus, and Antipater, who had accused each other.

Caesar, Julius Caesar. Pompey was now dead, and Antipater had promptly transferred his allegiance to the new master of the Roman world.

l. 5 *Viceroy,* or procurator.

l. 27 *A mere lad.* According to *Ant.* xiv. 158, Herod was fifteen years old.

110 *Josephus, War* i. 386f., 392*b*, 393*a*, 394, 396, 400. But, this peril surmounted, Herod was instantly plunged into anxiety about the
security of his position. He was Antony's friend, and Antony had
been defeated by Caesar at Actium. (In reality, he inspired more
5 fear than he felt himself; for Caesar considered his victory to be incomplete so long as Herod remained Antony's ally.) The king,
nevertheless, resolved to confront the danger and, having sailed to
Rhodes, where Caesar was sojourning, presented himself before
him without a diadem, a commoner in dress and demeanour, but
10 with the proud spirit of a king. His speech was direct; he told the
truth without reserve. . . .

". . . I therefore now confirm your kingdom to you by decree;
and hereafter I shall endeavour to confer upon you some further
benefit, that you may not feel the loss of Antony."

15 Having thus graciously addressed the king, he placed the diadem
on his head, and publicly notified this award by a decree, in which
he expressed his commendation of the honoured man in ample and
generous terms. . . .

Subsequently, when Caesar passed through Syria on his way to
20 Egypt, Herod entertained him for the first time with all the resources of his realm; he accompanied the emperor on horseback
when he reviewed his troops at Ptolemais; he entertained him and
all his friends at a banquet; and he followed this up by making
ample provision for the good cheer of the rest of the army. . . .

25 Accordingly, when Caesar reached Egypt, after the death of
Cleopatra and Antony, he not only conferred new honours upon
him, but also annexed to his kingdom the territory which Cleopatra had appropriated, with the addition of Gadara, Hippos, and
Samaria and the maritime towns of Gaza, Anthedon, Joppa, and
30 Strato's Tower. . . .

Finally, on the death of Zenodorus, he further assigned to him all
the territory between Trachonitis and Galilee. But what Herod
valued more than all these privileges was that in Caesar's affection
he stood next after Agrippa, in Agrippa's next after Caesar.
35 Thenceforth he advanced to the utmost prosperity; his noble spirit
rose to greater heights, and his lofty ambition was mainly directed
to works of piety.

l. 1 *This peril surmounted,* an attack by the Arabs.

l. 4 *Caesar,* Octavius (subsequently Augustus).

l. 10 *His speech was direct.* In i. 388–90 Herod argues that his service to Antony proves him a faithful friend to those who are his friends; Antony's downfall was caused by his infatuation for Cleopatra. Caesar praises him for his fidelity.

l. 30 *Strato's Tower.* See below, III.

l. 31 *Zenodorus,* who had ruled in the region of Trachonitis.

l. 34 *Agrippa* was Augustus's chief helper and confidant until his death in 12 B.C.

III *Josephus, War* i. 401ff., 408, 417, 422. Thus, in the fifteenth year of his reign, he restored the Temple and, by erecting new foundation-walls, enlarged the surrounding area to double its former extent. The expenditure devoted to this work was incalculable, its magni-
5 ficence never surpassed; as evidence one would have pointed to the great colonnades around the Temple courts and to the fortress which dominated it on the north. The colonnades Herod recon-structed from the foundations; the fortress he restored at a lavish cost in a style no way inferior to that of a palace, and called it
10 Antonia in honour of Antony. His own palace, which he erected in the upper city, comprised two most spacious and beautiful buildings, with which the Temple itself bore no comparison; these he named after his friends, the one Caesareum, the other Agrippeum.
15 He was not content, however, to commemorate his patrons' names by palaces only; his munificence extended to the creation of whole cities. In the district of Samaria he built a town enclosed within magnificent walls twenty furlongs in length, introduced into it six thousand colonists, and gave them allotments of highly productive
20 land. In the centre of this settlement he erected a massive temple, enclosed in ground, a furlong and a half in length, consecrated to Caesar; while he named the town itself Sebaste. The inhabitants were given a privileged constitution. . . .

His notice was attracted by a town on the coast, called Strato's
25 Tower, which, though then dilapidated, was, from its advantageous situation, suited for the exercise of his liberality. This he entirely rebuilt with white stone, and adorned with the most magnificent palaces, displaying here, as nowhere else, the innate grandeur of his character. . . .
30 No man ever showed greater filial affection. As a memorial to his father he founded a city in the fairest plain of his realm rich in rivers and trees, and named it Antipatris. Above Jericho he built the walls of a fortress, remarkable alike for solidity and beauty, which he dedicated to his mother under the name of Cypros. . . .
35 After founding all these places, he proceeded to display his

generosity to numerous cities outside his realm. Thus, he provided gymnasia for Tripolis, Damascus, and Ptolemais, a wall for Byblus, halls, porticoes, temples, and market-places for Berytus and Tyre, theatres for Sidon and Damascus, an aqueduct for Laodicea-on-sea,
40 baths, sumptuous fountains and colonnades, admirable alike for their architecture and proportions, for Ascalon; to other communities he dedicated groves and meadow-land.

l. 22 *Sebaste* is Greek for Augustus.
l. 24 *Strato's Tower*. The new town was called Caesarea.
l. 36 *Numerous cities*. Notably, in addition to those mentioned in this paragraph, Athens and Antioch.

II2 *Josephus, War* i. 429–33. Herod's genius was matched by his physical constitution. Always foremost in the chase, in which he distinguished himself above all by his skill in horsemanship, he on one occasion brought down forty wild beasts in a single day; for
5 the country breeds boars and, in greater abundance, stags and wild asses. As a fighter he was irresistible; and at practice spectators were often struck with astonishment at the precision with which he threw the javelin, the unerring aim with which he bent the bow. But besides these pre-eminent gifts of soul and body, he was blessed by
10 good fortune; he rarely met with a reverse in war, and, when he did, this was due not to his own fault, but either to treachery or to the recklessness of his troops.

But, in revenge for his public prosperity, fortune visited Herod with troubles at home; his ill-fated career originated with a
15 woman to whom he was passionately attached. For, on ascending the throne, he had dismissed the wife whom he had taken when he was still a commoner, a native of Jerusalem named Doris, and married Mariamme, daughter of Alexander, the son of Aristobulus. It was she who brought into his house the discord, which, beginning
20 at an early date, was greatly aggravated after his return from Rome. For, in the first place, in the interests of his children by Mariamme, he banished from the capital the son whom he had had by Doris, namely Antipater, allowing him to visit it on the festivals only. Next he put to death, on suspicion of conspiracy,
25 Hyrcanus, Mariamme's grandfather, who had come back from Parthia to Herod's court.

l. 18 *Alexander . . . Aristobulus*. See above, p.118.
l. 24 *He put to death . . . Hyrcanus*. Other executions and murders followed in a melancholy succession. His wives and his sons were not spared, so that it was said that it was safer to be Herod's pig (in view of his conformity to Jewish law) than Herod's son.

D. *The Procurators*

After Herod's death (4 B.C.) his kingdom was divided among his surviving sons, but the arrangement did not last long, and the kingdom was not again united until the time of his grandson, Herod Agrippa I (A.D. 41–4). Judaea, after a short period of unsatisfactory rule by Archelaus, a son of Herod the Great, became a subordinate Roman province under a procurator.

113 *Josephus, War* ii. 111ff., 117. Archelaus, on taking possession of his ethnarchy, did not forget old feuds, but treated not only the Jews but even the Samaritans with great brutality. Both parties sent deputies to Caesar to denounce him, and in the ninth year of
5 his rule he was banished to Vienna, a town in Gaul, and his property confiscated to the imperial treasury. It is said that, before he received his summons from Caesar, he had this dream: he thought he saw nine tall and full-grown ears of corn on which oxen were browsing. He sent for the soothsayers and some
10 Chaldeans and asked them their opinion of its meaning. Various interpretations being given, a certain Simon, of the sect of the Essenes, said that in his view the ears of corn denoted years and the oxen a revolution, because in ploughing they turn over the soil; he would therefore reign for as many years as there were ears of corn
15 and would die after a chequered experience of revolutionary changes. Five days later Archelaus was summoned to his trial. . . .
The territory of Archelaus was now reduced to a province, and Coponius, a Roman of the equestrian order, was sent out as procurator entrusted by Augustus with full powers, including the
20 infliction of capital punishment.

l. 4 *The ninth year of his rule.* According to *Ant.* xvii. 342, the tenth. The year was
  A.D. 6.
l. 12 *The Essenes.* See pp. 125f. **(115)**.

114 *Josephus, War* ii. 169–77. Pilate, being sent by Tiberius as procurator to Judaea, introduced into Jerusalem by night and under cover the effigies of Caesar which are called standards. This proceeding, when day broke, aroused immense excitement among the Jews;
5 those on the spot were in consternation, considering their laws to have been trampled under foot, as those laws permit no image to be erected in the city; while the indignation of the townspeople stirred the countryfolk, who flocked together in crowds. Hastening after Pilate to Caesarea, the Jews implored him to remove the

10 standards from Jerusalem and to uphold the laws of their ancestors. When Pilate refused, they fell prostrate around his house and for five whole days and nights remained motionless in that position.

On the ensuing day Pilate took his seat on his tribunal in the great stadium and summoning the multitude, with the apparent 15 intention of answering them, gave the arranged signal to his armed soldiers to surround the Jews. Finding themselves in a ring of troops, three deep, the Jews were struck dumb at this unexpected sight. Pilate, after threatening to cut them down if they refused to admit Caesar's images, signalled to the soldiers to draw their 20 swords. Thereupon the Jews, as by concerted action, flung themselves in a body on the ground, extended their necks, and exclaimed that they were ready rather to die than to transgress the Law. Overcome with astonishment at such religious zeal, Pilate gave orders for the immediate removal of the standards from Jeru-25 salem.

On a later occasion he provoked a fresh uproar by expending upon the construction of an aqueduct the sacred treasure known as *Corbonas*: the water was brought from a distance of 400 furlongs. Indignant at this proceeding, the populace formed a ring round the 30 tribunal of Pilate, then on a visit to Jerusalem, and besieged him with angry clamour. He, foreseeing the tumult, had interspersed among the crowd a troop of his soldiers, armed but disguised in civilian dress, with orders not to use their swords, but to beat any rioters with cudgels. He now from his tribunal gave the agreed 35 signal. Large numbers of the Jews perished, some from the blows which they received, others trodden to death by their companions in the ensuing flight. Cowed by the fate of the victims, the multitude was reduced to silence.

l. 1 *Pilate*. Pontius Pilate, procurator from A.D. 26 to 36, was not the worst of the governors of Judaea. When he saw how seriously the Jews took the affair of the standards he withdrew; his aqueduct he probably regarded as a benefit conferred on Jerusalem. Certainly he had successors whose little finger was thicker than his loins. See pp. 127–30 (116ff.).

l. 3 *Standards*. Josephus writes more accurately in *Ant*. xviii. 55 when he speaks of the effigies (busts) attached to the standards.

E. *Pharisees, Sadducees, and Essenes*

Two of these Jewish parties occupy prominent places in the New Testament. The Sadducees were too closely bound up with the political life of their nation to survive the disaster of A.D. 70, and the Rabbinic literature, which was written down after that date, presents a con-

sistently Pharisaic point of view. The Essenes, though not mentioned
in the New Testament, were certainly a not unimportant sect; cf. p. 123
(113), and Philo's account of the Therapeutae in Egypt in his *De Vita
Contemplativa*. Josephus gives more than one account of the three
parties.

115 *Josephus, War* ii. 119f., 122, 137–42, 152f., 162–6. Jewish philosophy,
in fact, takes three forms. The followers of the first school are
called Pharisees, of the second Sadducees, of the third Essenes.

The Essenes have a reputation for cultivating peculiar sanctity.
5 Of Jewish birth, they show a greater attachment to each other
than do the other sects. They shun pleasures as a vice and regard
temperance and the control of the passions as a special virtue.
Marriage they disdain, but they adopt other men's children, while
yet pliable and docile, and regard them as their kin and mould
10 them in accordance with their own principles. . . .

Riches they despise, and their community of goods is truly admirable; you will not find one among them distinguished by
greater opulence than another. They have a law that new members
on admission to the sect shall confiscate their property to the order,
15 with the result that you will nowhere see either abject poverty or
inordinate wealth; the individual's possessions join the common
stock and all, like brothers, enjoy a single patrimony. . . .

A candidate anxious to join their sect is not immediately admitted. For one year, during which he remains outside the
20 fraternity, they prescribe for him their own rule of life, presenting
him with a small hatchet, the loin-cloth already mentioned, and
white raiment. Having given proof of his temperance during this
probationary period, he is brought into closer touch with the rule
and is allowed to share the purer kind of holy water, but is not yet
25 received into the meetings of the community. For after this
exhibition of endurance, his character is tested for two years more,
and only then, if found worthy, is he enrolled in the society. But,
before he may touch the common food, he is made to swear tre-
mendous oaths: first that he will practise piety towards the Deity,
30 next that he will observe justice towards men: that he will wrong
none whether of his own mind or under another's orders; that he
will for ever hate the unjust and fight the battle of the just; that he
will for ever keep faith with all men, especially with the powers
that be, since no ruler attains his office save by the will of God; that,
35 should he himself bear rule, he will never abuse his authority nor,
either in dress or by other outward marks of superiority, outshine
his subjects; to be for ever a lover of truth and to expose liars; to

keep his hands from stealing and his soul pure from unholy gain; to conceal nothing from the members of the sect and to report
40 none of their secrets to others, even though tortured to death. He swears, moreover, to transmit their rules exactly as he himself received them; to abstain from robbery; and in like manner carefully to preserve the books of the sect and the names of the angels. Such are the oaths by which they secure their proselytes. . . .
45 The war with the Romans tried their souls through and through by every variety of test. Racked and twisted, burnt and broken, and made to pass through every instrument of torture, in order to induce them to blaspheme their lawgiver or to eat some forbidden thing, they refused to yield to either demand, nor ever once did
50 they cringe to their persecutors or shed a tear. Smiling in their agonies and mildly deriding their tormentors, they cheerfully resigned their souls, confident that they would receive them back again. . . .

Of the two first-named schools, the Pharisees, who are considered
55 the most accurate interpreters of the laws, and hold the position of the leading sect, attribute everything to Fate and to God; they hold that to act rightly or otherwise rests, indeed, for the most part with men, but that in each action Fate co-operates. Every soul, they maintain, is imperishable, but the soul of the good alone passes into
60 another body, while the souls of the wicked suffer eternal punishment.

The Sadducees, the second of the orders, do away with Fate altogether, and remove God beyond, not merely the commission, but the very sight, of evil. They maintain that man has the free
65 choice of good or evil, and that it rests with each man's will whether he follows the one or the other. As for the persistence of the soul after death, penalties in the underworld, and rewards, they will have none of them.

The Pharisees are affectionate to each other and cultivate har-
70 monious relations with the community. The Sadducees, on the contrary, are, even among themselves, rather boorish in their behaviour, and in their intercourse with their peers are as rude as to aliens. Such is what I have to say on the Jewish philosophical schools.

l. 1 *Jewish philosophy* is a most inappropriate term for what Josephus proceeds to describe. He is trying to make his account easy for his Hellenistic readers.

l. 4 *The Essenes.* The origin of this name is unknown. No suggested explanation is entirely convincing.

l. 8 *Marriage they disdain.* In 160f. Josephus describes a group of Essenes who accepted marriage.

l. 21 *A small hatchet.* For the burial of excrement. Cf. Deut. 23. 12ff.

The loin-cloth already mentioned, in ii. 129. It was worn while bathing to avoid complete nakedness.

l. 24 *Holy water*, for lustrations. Frequent ceremonial baths were an important feature of Essene ritual.

l. 28 *Common food*. The Essenes took their two daily meals in silence in a refectory.

l. 43 *The books of the sect*. What books the Essenes used in addition to those of the Old Testament is not known. They held Moses in special veneration, but Josephus says (ii. 136): "They display an extraordinary interest in the writings of the ancients . . . with the help of these . . . they make investigations into medicinal roots and the properties of stones." Apparently holy books were also used in predicting the future (ii. 159). It is possible that the MSS. found in Palestine in and since 1947 were in some way connected with Essene (or similar) communities. See Appendix.

The names of the angels. Here again we can only conjecture what is meant.

l. 52 *Receive them back again*. Josephus goes on to explain the Essene belief that the body is corruptible but the soul immortal and imperishable. They shared , he says, in the "belief of the sons of Greece" that there is for virtuous souls an "abode beyond the ocean".

l. 56 *Attribute everything to Fate and to God*. Cf. p. 143 (**131**). Josephus "hellenizes".

F. *The Jewish War of* A.D. 66–70

The rigour and corruption of the procurators, together with the folly and excesses of the revolutionary minority of Jews, drove the country with ever-increasing swiftness to war. The story cannot be told here, but a few salient points will be mentioned. For some other events in the early course of the war see pp. 192–5 (**193f.**).

116 *Josephus, War* ii. 254–6a, 258ff. But while the country was thus cleared of these pests, a new species of banditti was springing up in Jerusalem, the so-called *sicarii*, who committed murders in broad daylight in the heart of the city. The festivals were their special
5 seasons, when they would mingle with the crowd, carrying short daggers concealed under their clothing, with which they stabbed their enemies. Then, when they fell, the murderers joined in the cries of indignation and, through this plausible behaviour, were never discovered. The first to be assassinated by them was Jona-
10 than the high priest; after his death there were numerous daily murders. . . .
      Besides these there arose another body of villains, with purer hands but more impious intentions, who no less than the assassins ruined the peace of the city. Deceivers and impostors, under the
15 pretence of divine inspiration fostering revolutionary changes, they

persuaded the multitude to act like madmen, and led them out into
the desert in the belief that God would there give them tokens of
deliverance. Against them Felix, regarding this as but the preliminary to insurrection, sent a body of cavalry and heavy-armed
20 infantry, and put a large number to the sword.

l. 2 *These pests*, brigands put down by the procurator Felix.
l. 6 *Daggers.* The *sicarii* probably drew their name from the Latin *sica*, a dagger.

117 *Josephus, War* ii. 271–8*a*. Festus, who succeeded Felix as procurator,
proceeded to attack the principal plague of the country; he captured large numbers of the brigands and put not a few to death.
    The administration of Albinus, who followed Festus, was of an-
5 other order; there was no form of villainy which he omitted to
practise. Not only did he, in his official capacity, steal and plunder
private property and burden the whole nation with extraordinary
taxes, but he accepted ransoms from their relatives on behalf of
those who had been imprisoned for robbery by the local councils or
10 by former procurators; and the only persons left in gaol as malefactors were those who failed to pay the price. Now, too, the
audacity of the revolutionary party in Jerusalem was stimulated;
the influential men among their number secured from Albinus, by
means of bribes, immunity for their seditious practices; while of
15 the populace all who were dissatisfied with peace joined hands with
the governor's accomplices. Each ruffian, with his own band of
followers grouped around him, towered above his company like a
brigand chief or tyrant, employing his bodyguard to plunder
peaceable citizens. The result was that the victims of robbery kept
20 their grievances, of which they had every reason to complain, to
themselves, while those who escaped injury cringed to wretches
deserving of punishment, through fear of suffering the same fate. In
short, none could now speak his mind, with tyrants on every side;
and from this date were sown in the city the seeds of its impending
25 fall.
    Such was the character of Albinus, but his successor, Gessius
Florus, made him appear by comparison a paragon of virtue. The
crimes of Albinus were, for the most part, perpetrated in secret and
with dissimulation; Gessius, on the contrary, ostentatiously
30 paraded his outrages upon the nation, and, as though he had been
sent as a hangman of condemned criminals, abstained from no
form of robbery or violence. Was there a call for compassion, he
was the most cruel of men; for shame, none more shameless than
he. No man ever poured greater contempt on truth; none invented
35 more crafty methods of crime.

l. 1 *Procurator.* After the reign of Herod Agrippa I the government of Judaea reverted to Roman procurators. Felix governed A.D. 52–55, Festus 55(6)–62, Albinus 62–4, Gessius Florus 64–6.

118 *Josephus, War* ii. 285–96. The ostensible pretext for war was out of proportion to the magnitude of the disasters to which it led. The Jews in Caesarea had a synagogue adjoining a plot of ground owned by a Greek of that city; this site they had frequently endeavoured
5 to purchase, offering a price far exceeding its true value. The proprietor, disdaining their solicitations, by way of insult further proceeded to build upon the site and erect workshops, leaving the Jews only a narrow and extremely awkward passage. Thereupon, some of the hot-headed youths proceeded to set upon the builders and
10 attempted to interrupt operations. Florus having put a stop to their violence, the Jewish notables, with John the tax-collector, having no other expedient, offered Florus eight talents of silver to procure the cessation of the work. Florus, with his eye only on the money, promised them every assistance, but, having secured his pay, at
15 once quitted Caesarea for Sebaste, leaving a free field to sedition, as though he had sold the Jews a licence to fight the matter out.

On the following day, which was a Sabbath, when the Jews assembled at the synagogue, they found that one of the Caesarean mischief-makers had placed beside the entrance a pot, turned
20 bottom upwards, upon which he was sacrificing birds. This spectacle of what they considered an outrage upon their laws and a desecration of the spot enraged the Jews beyond endurance. The steady-going and peaceable members of the congregation were in favour of immediate recourse to the authorities; but the factious
25 folk and the passionate youth were burning for a fight. The Caesarean party, on their side, stood prepared for action, for they had, by a concerted plan, sent the man on to the mock sacrifice; and so they soon came to blows. Jucundus, the cavalry commander commissioned to intervene, came up, removed the pot and endeavoured to
30 quell the riot, but was unable to cope with the violence of the Caesareans. The Jews, thereupon, snatched up their copy of the Law and withdrew to Narbata, a Jewish district sixty furlongs distant from Caesarea. Their leading men, twelve in number, with John at their head, waited upon Florus at Sebaste, bitterly com-
35 plained of these proceedings and besought his assistance, delicately reminding him of the matter of the eight talents. Florus actually had them arrested and put in irons on the charge of having carried off the copy of the Law from Caesarea.

This news roused indignation at Jerusalem, though the citizens

40 still restrained their feelings. But Florus, as if he had contracted
to fan the flames of war, sent to the temple treasury and extracted
seventeen talents, making the requirements of the imperial service
his pretext. Instantly fired by this outrage, the people rushed in a
body to the Temple and with piercing cries invoked the name of
45 Caesar, imploring him to liberate them from the tyranny of Florus.
Some of the malcontents railed on the procurator in the most
opprobrious terms and carrying round a basket begged coppers for
him as for an unfortunate destitute. These proceedings, however,
far from checking his avarice, only provoked him to further
50 peculation. Accordingly, instead of betaking himself, as he should
have done, to Caesarea, to extinguish the flames of war, there
already breaking out, and to root out the cause of these disorders—
a task for which he had been paid—he marched with an army of
cavalry and infantry upon Jerusalem, in order to attain his object
55 with the aid of Roman arms, and by means of intimidation and
menaces to fleece the city.

The war thus provoked opened favourably for the Jews, and dragged
on indecisively. At length, Vespasian, entrusted (with his son Titus; on
both see pp. 18f. (15)) with the conduct of the campaign, slowly but
methodically penned the Jewish forces in Jerusalem, where they were
eventually destroyed as much by starvation and internecine conflict as
by the Roman arms. Josephus was taken prisoner (see pp. 193ff. (194)),
but not even his eloquence could move his compatriots to surrender.

119 *Josephus, War* v. 362-74. Josephus, accordingly, went round the
wall, and, endeavouring to keep out of range of missiles and yet
within earshot, repeatedly implored them to save themselves and
the people, to spare their country and their Temple, and not to dis-
5 play towards them greater indifference than was shown by aliens.
The Romans, he urged, though without a share in them, yet
reverenced the holy places of their enemies, and had thus far
restrained their hands from them; whereas men who had been
brought up in them and, were they preserved, would alone enjoy
10 them, were bent on their destruction. Indeed, they beheld their
stoutest walls prostrate and but one remaining, weaker than those
which had fallen; they knew that the might of the Romans was
irresistible and that to serve them was no new experience for
themselves. Be it granted that it was noble to fight for freedom,
15 they should have done so at first; but, after having once succumbed
and submitted for so long, to seek then to shake off the yoke was
the part of men madly courting death, not of lovers of liberty. To

scorn meaner masters might, indeed, be legitimate, but not those to
whom the universe was subject. For what was there that had
20 escaped the Romans, save maybe some spot useless through heat or
cold? Fortune, indeed, had from all quarters passed over them, and
God who went the round of the nations, bringing to each in turn the
rod of empire, now rested over Italy. There was, in fact, an established law, as supreme among brutes as among men, "Yield to the
25 stronger" and "The mastery is for those pre-eminent in arms".
That was why their forefathers, men who in soul and body, aye
and in resources to boot, were by far their superiors, had yielded to
the Romans—a thing intolerable to them, had they not known that
God was on the Roman side. As for them, on what did they rely
30 in thus holding out, when the main part of the city was already
captured, and when those within it, though their walls still stood,
were in a plight even worse than capture? Assuredly, the Romans
were not ignorant of the famine raging in the city, which was now
consuming the populace, and would ere long consume the com-
35 batants as well. For, even were the Romans to desist from the siege
and not fall upon the city with drawn swords, yet they had at their
doors a war with which none could contend, gaining strength
every hour, unless indeed they could take arms and fight against
famine itself and, alone of all men, master even its pangs. They
40 would do well, he added, to repent ere irretrievable disaster befell
them and to incline to salutary counsels while they had the
opportunity; for the Romans would bear them no malice for the
past, unless they persisted in their contumacy to the end: they were
naturally lenient in victory, and would put above vindictiveness
45 considerations of expediency, which did not consist in having on
their hands either a depopulated city or a devastated country. That
was why, even at this late hour, Caesar desired to grant them
terms; whereas, if he took the city by storm, he would not spare a
man of them, especially after the rejection of offers made to them
50 when in extremities. That the third wall would be quickly carried
was vouched for by the fall of those already captured; and even
were that defence impregnable, the famine would fight for the
Romans against them.

l. 7 *Reverenced the holy places.* According to Josephus, Titus even in the end tried
  unsuccessfully to save the Temple.
l. 44 *Lenient in victory.* Cf. Horace, *Carmen Saeculare* 51f. (p. 7 (3)), and Virgil,
  Aeneid vi. 851ff.:
              ". . . Remember, Roman, thou,
              To rule the nations as their master: these
              Thine arts shall be, to engraft the law of peace,
              Forbear the conquered, and war down the proud."

l. 47 *Caesar*. The Emperor Vespasian.

At length, in September A.D. 70, the city fell amid appalling scenes of famine and bloodshed.

120 *Josephus, War* vi. 392ff., 399–403*a*, 404–8. The earthworks having now been completed after eighteen days' labour, on the seventh of the month Gorpiaeus the Romans brought up the engines. Of the rebels, some already despairing of the city retired from the ram-
5 parts to the Acra, others slunk down into the mines; many, however, posting themselves along the wall, attempted to repel those who were bringing up the siege-engines. But these too the Romans overpowered by numbers and force, but, above all, by the high spirits in which they faced men already dispirited and un-
10 nerved. And when a portion of the wall broke down and some of the towers succumbed to the battering of the rams, the defenders at once took flight, and even the tyrants were seized with a needlessly serious alarm. . . . Here may we signally discern at once the power of God over unholy men and the fortune of the Romans.
15 For the tyrants stripped themselves of their security and descended of their own accord from those towers, whereon they could never have been overcome by force, and famine alone could have subdued them; while the Romans, after all the toil expended over weaker walls, mastered by the gift of fortune those that were im-
20 pregnable to their artillery. For the three towers, which we have described above, would have defied every engine of war.

Having then abandoned these, or rather been driven down from them by God, they found immediate refuge in the ravine below Siloam; but afterwards, having recovered a little from their panic,
25 they rushed upon the adjoining section of the barrier. Their courage, however, proving unequal to the occasion (for their strength was now broken alike by terror and misfortune), they were repulsed by the guards and dispersing hither and thither slunk down into the mines.
30 The Romans, now masters of the walls, planted their standards on the towers, and with clapping of hands and jubilation raised a paean in honour of their victory. . . . Pouring into the alleys, sword in hand, they massacred indiscriminately all whom they met, and burnt the houses with all who had taken refuge within. Often in
35 the course of their raids, on entering the houses for loot, they would find whole families dead and the rooms filled with the victims of the famine, and then, shuddering at the sight, retire empty-handed. Yet, while they pitied those who had thus perished, they had no similar feelings for the living, but, running everyone through who

40 fell in their way, they choked the alleys with corpses and deluged
the whole city with blood, insomuch that many of the fires were
extinguished by the gory stream. Towards evening they ceased
slaughtering, but when night fell the fire gained the mastery, and
the dawn of the eighth day of the month Gorpiaeus broke upon

45 Jerusalem in flames—a city which had suffered such calamities
during the siege, that, had she from her foundation enjoyed an
equal share of blessings she would have been thought unquestion-
ably enviable; a city undeserving, moreover, of these great misfortunes on any other ground, save that she produced a generation

50 such as that which caused her overthrow.

l. 2 *The seventh of the month Gorpiaeus.* About 25 September A.D. 70.

121 *Josephus, War* vii. 216ff. About the same time Caesar sent instructions to Bassus and Laberius Maximus, the procurator, to
farm out all Jewish territory. For he founded no city there, reserving the country as his private property, except that he did assign to

5 eight hundred veterans discharged from the army a place for
habitation called Emmaus, distant thirty furlongs from Jerusalem.
On all Jews, wheresoever resident, he imposed a poll-tax of two
drachmae, to be paid annually into the Capitol as formerly contributed by them to the Temple at Jerusalem. Such was the

10 position of Jewish affairs at this date.

l. 2 *Bassus,* legate in Judaea.
l. 6 *Emmaus.* Perhaps the Emmaus of Luke 24. 13, though the distances given by
Josephus and Luke do not agree.
l. 7 *Two drachmae.* Cf. Matt. 17. 24, where the temple tax is referred to as the
"didrachma".

G. *The Revolt of* A.D. 132–5

After the terrible events of A.D. 70 Palestine remained on the whole
quiet, though there were Jewish and anti-Jewish disturbances in other
parts of the Empire. Further revolt in the Holy Land itself seems to have
been provoked by a law forbidding circumcision and by Hadrian's
decision to build a heathen temple on the site of the former Jewish
Temple in Jerusalem (for the former see Spartian, *Hadrian* 4; for the
latter, Dio Cassius, quoted below, **122**). Our knowledge of the course
of the rebellion and the ensuing war is unfortunately far from complete.
The Jewish leader, hailed by R. Akiba (see pp. 142f. (**131**)) as Messiah,
was one Bar Coseba, or Bar Cocheba (also called, as is suggested by the
coins, Simon; see also p. 256). There can be no doubt that the war was

serious and protracted, and that Palestinian Christians (as well as others) suffered considerably as a result of it.

122 *Dio Cassius, Roman History* lxix. 12ff. At Jerusalem he [Hadrian] founded a city in place of the one which had been razed to the ground, naming it Aelia Capitolina, and on the site of the temple of the god he raised a new temple to Jupiter. This brought on a war
5 of no slight importance nor of brief duration, for the Jews deemed it intolerable that foreign races should be settled in their city and foreign religious rites planted there. So long, indeed, as Hadrian was close by in Egypt and again in Syria, they remained quiet, save in so far as they purposely made of poor quality such weapons as
10 they were called upon to furnish, in order that the Romans might reject them and they themselves might thus have the use of them; but when he went farther away, they openly revolted. To be sure, they did not dare try conclusions with the Romans in the open field, but they occupied the advantageous positions in the country
15 and strengthened them with mines and walls, in order that they might have places of refuge whenever they should be hard pressed, and might meet together unobserved underground; and they pierced these subterranean passages from above at intervals to let in air and light.
20   At first the Romans took no account of them. Soon, however, all Judaea had been stirred up, and the Jews everywhere were showing signs of disturbance, were gathering together, and were giving evidence of great hostility to the Romans, partly by secret and partly by overt acts; many outside nations, too, were joining them
25 through eagerness for gain, and the whole earth, one might almost say, was being stirred up over the matter. Then, indeed, Hadrian sent against them his best generals. First of these was Julius Severus, who was dispatched from Britain, where he was governor, against the Jews. Severus did not venture to attack his opponents in the
30 open at any one point, in view of their numbers and their desperation, but by intercepting small groups, thanks to the number of his soldiers and his under-officers, and by depriving them of food and shutting them up, he was able, rather slowly, to be sure, but with comparatively little danger, to crush, exhaust and exterminate
35 them. Very few of them in fact survived. Fifty of their most important outposts and 985 of their most famous villages were razed to the ground. 580,000 men were slain in the various raids and battles, and the number of those that perished by famine, disease and fire was past finding out. Thus nearly the whole of
40 Judaea was made desolate, a result of which the people had had forewarning before the war. For the tomb of Solomon, which the

Jews regard as an object of veneration, fell to pieces of itself and
collapsed, and many wolves and hyenas rushed howling into their
cities. Many Romans, moreover, perished in this war. Therefore
45 Hadrian in writing to the Senate did not employ the opening phrase
commonly affected by the emperors, "If you and your children
are in health, it is well; I and the legions are in health."

123 *Eusebius, Church History* IV, vi. 1–4. As the rebellion of the Jews at
this time grew much more serious, Rufus, governor of Judaea,
after an auxiliary force had been sent him by the emperor, using
their madness as a pretext, proceeded against them without mercy,
5 and destroyed indiscriminately thousands of men and women and
children, and in accordance with the laws of war reduced their
country to a state of complete subjection. The leader of the Jews at
this time was a man by the name of Bar Cocheba (which signifies a
star), who possessed the character of a robber and a murderer, but
10 nevertheless, relying upon his name, boasted to them, as if they
were slaves, that he possessed wonderful powers; and he pretended
that he was a star that had come down to them out of heaven to
bring them light in the midst of their misfortunes. The war raged
most fiercely in the eighteenth year of Hadrian, at the city of
15 Bithara, which was a very secure fortress, situated not far from
Jerusalem. When the siege had lasted a long time, and the rebels
had been driven to the last extremity by hunger and thirst, and the
instigator of the rebellion had suffered his just punishment, the
whole nation was prohibited from this time on by a decree, and by
20 the commands of Hadrian, from ever going up to the country
about Jerusalem. For the emperor gave orders that they should not
even see from a distance the land of their fathers. Such is the account
of Aristo of Pella. And thus, when the city had been emptied of the
Jewish nation and had suffered the total destruction of its ancient
25 inhabitants, it was colonized by a different race, and the Roman
city which subsequently arose changed its name and was called
Aelia, in honour of the emperor Aelius Hadrian.

l. 10 *Relying upon his name.* Its significance was probably (or was probably taken
to be) messianic. Cf. Num. 24. 17, and R. Akiba's recognition of Bar
Cocheba as Messiah.

l. 23 *Aristo of Pella.* We know practically nothing of this author, nor how much of
Eusebius's narrative of the revolt is drawn from him.

124 *Eusebius, Church History* IV, viii. 4. The same writer, speaking of
the Jewish war which took place at that time, adds the following:
"For in the late Jewish war Bar Cocheba, the leader of the Jewish

rebellion, commanded that Christians alone should be visited with
5 terrible punishments unless they would deny and blaspheme Jesus
Christ."

l. 1 *The same writer.* Justin Martyr, who died in Rome *c.* A.D. 165.

l. 4 *Christians.* It is clear that even Jewish Christians could not recognize Bar
Cocheba as Messiah; in consequence they would be unable to join in the
rebellion and must have seemed traitors to their race.

H. *The Dispersion*

From an early date Jews began to find their way to various parts of
the Mediterranean world, and to the lands east of it. Their presence in
many places can be proved not only by literary references but also by
inscriptions and (in Egypt) by papyri (see pp. 31–5, 44–7 (**27, 45**)).
They founded synagogues (for synagogues at Corinth, Rome, and
Panticapaeum see pp. 5off. (**48ff.**)), and there are many traces of their
community life, and of their relations with Jerusalem. The dispersed
Jews did not always find it easy to live on good terms with their
neighbours.

We are particularly well informed about the Jews in Alexandria, and
their disputes with the Alexandrians. The letter of Claudius (pp. 44–7
(**45**)) regulated these disputes; previously embassies had been sent from
both Jews and Alexandrian citizens to Claudius and to Gaius before him.
Parts of the proceedings are described in great detail by Philo in the
Flaccus and *Embassy to Gaius*. The same author describes the curious
sect of the Therapeutae (who resembled the Essenes) in *On the Contem-
plative Life*. Josephus also provides interesting material.

125 *Josephus, Ant.* xiv.110–18. But no one need wonder that there was
so much wealth in our Temple, for all the Jews throughout the
habitable world, and those who worshipped God, even those from
Asia and Europe, had been contributing to it for a very long time.
5 And there is no lack of witnesses to the great amount of the sums
mentioned, nor have they been raised to so great a figure through
boastfulness or exaggeration on our part, but there are many
historians who bear us out, in particular Strabo of Cappadocia, who
writes as follows. "Mithridates sent to Cos and took the money
10 which Queen Cleopatra had deposited there, and eight hundred
talents of the Jews." Now there is no public money among us
except that which is God's, and it is therefore evident that this
money was transferred to Cos by the Jews of Asia because of their

fear of Mithridates. For it is not likely that those in Judaea, who
15 possessed a fortified city and the Temple, would have sent money to
Cos, nor is it probable that the Jews living in Alexandria would
have done this either, since they had no fear of Mithridates. And
this same Strabo in another passage testifies that at the time
when Sulla crossed over to Greece to make war on Mithridates,
20 and sent Lucullus to put down the revolt of our nation in Cyrene,
the habitable world was filled with Jews, for he writes as follows.
"There were four classes in the state of Cyrene; the first consisted of
citizens, the second of farmers, the third of resident aliens (metics),
and the fourth of Jews. This people has already made its way into
25 every city, and it is not easy to find any place in the habitable
world which has not received this nation and in which it has not
made its power felt. And it has come about that Cyrene, which had
the same rulers as Egypt, has imitated it in many respects, particularly in notably encouraging and aiding the expansion of the
30 organized groups of Jews, which observe the national Jewish laws.
In Egypt, for example, territory has been set apart for a Jewish
settlement, and in Alexandria a great part of the city has been
allocated to this nation. And an ethnarch of their own has been
installed, who governs the people and adjudicates suits and super-
35 vises contracts and ordinances, just as if he were the head of a
sovereign state. And so this nation has flourished in Egypt because
the Jews were originally Egyptians and because those who left that
country made their homes near by; and they migrated to Cyrene
because this country bordered on the kingdom of Egypt, as did
40 Judaea—or rather, it formerly belonged to that kingdom." These
are Strabo's own words.

l. 3 *Those who worshipped God,* οἱ σεβόμενοι τὸν θεόν. The same expression is used
in the New Testament to describe Gentiles who, though attracted to the
theology, morals, and worship of the Synagogue, had not become full
proselytes. Cf. p. 164.

l. 8 *Strabo of Cappadocia*; known to us primarily as a geographer who wrote in
the time of Augustus, but he also wrote a large history.

l. 9 *Mithridates,* king of Pontus, who defeated the Romans in 88 B.C.

l. 23 *Metics,* μέτοικοι, a technical term for this class, frequent in the papyri and
elsewhere.

l. 33 *An ethnarch.* Cf. Philo, *In Flaccum* 74 (below, 126); Augustus apparently
replaced the ethnarch by a senate.

l. 37 *The Jews were originally Egyptians.* A common opinion, rebutted elsewhere
by Josephus himself.

126 *Philo, In Flaccum* 73ff. Having broken into everything like a
burglar and left no side of Jewish life untouched by a hostility

carried to the highest pitch, Flaccus devised another monstrous and unparalleled line of attack worthy of this perpetrator of enormities
5 and inventor of novel iniquities. Our Senate had been appointed to take charge of Jewish affairs by our saviour and benefactor Augustus, after the death of the ethnarch, orders to that effect having been given to Magius Maximus when he was about to take office for the second time as Governor of Alexandria and the
10 country. Of this Senate the members who were found in their houses, thirty-eight in number, were arrested by Flaccus, who having ordered them to be straightway put in bonds marshalled a fine procession through the middle of the market of these elderly men trussed and pinioned, some with thongs and others with iron
15 chains, and then taken into the theatre, a spectacle most pitiable and incongruous with the occasion. Then as they stood with their enemies seated in front to signalize their disgrace he ordered them all to be stripped and lacerated with scourges which are commonly used for the degradation of the vilest malefactors, so that in conse-
20 quence of the flogging some had to be carried out on stretchers and died at once, while others lay sick for a long time despairing of recovery.

l. 3 *Flaccus*, governor of the province of Egypt. After years of good government under the emperor Tiberius, he began to persecute the Jews, apparently in order to gain favour with Gaius, when he became emperor. The incident narrated here is by no means the most horrible in the record narrated by Philo.

8

RABBINIC LITERATURE AND RABBINIC JUDAISM

A. *The Rabbis*

RABBINIC JUDAISM, though it claimed to have sprung directly from Moses, may be said to have begun with Ezra and his contemporaries, and to have been handed down from them as the staple and official form of religion in Palestine in the time of our Lord. The following passages are intended (*a*) to bring out the strongly traditional character of Rabbinic Judaism, and (*b*) to introduce the names of a number of important Rabbis.

127 *Aboth* 1. 1ff. Moses received the Law from Sinai and committed it to Joshua, and Joshua to the elders, and the elders to the Prophets; and the Prophets committed it to the men of the Great Synagogue. They said three things: Be deliberate in judgement, raise up many 5 disciples, and make a fence around the Law.

Simeon the Just was of the remnants of the Great Synagogue. He used to say: By three things is the world sustained; by the Law, by the Temple-service, and by deeds of loving-kindness.

Antigonus of Soko received the Law from Simeon the Just. He 10 used to say: Be not like slaves that minister to the master for the sake of receiving a bounty, but be like slaves that minister to the master not for the sake of receiving a bounty; and let the fear of Heaven be upon you.

l. 1 *The Law* (תורה, *Torah*). Here the oral Law is meant. This was a body of material which in fact grew up as explanation and expansion of the written Law of the Old Testament. The Rabbis however regarded it as equally ancient and equally important with the written Law. Both were received by Moses from (God on) Sinai, but the latter was committed to writing at once.

l. 2 *The elders*. Cf. Josh. 24. 31.

l. 3 *The Great Synagogue*. This was popularly interpreted as a body, 120 strong, of prophets and teachers in the time of Ezra; but the reference to Simeon suggests that the Mishnah referred to a succession of teachers of whom he was one of the latest. That this account of what did not happen should be vague is of course not surprising.

l. 5 *Make a fence around the Law.* Make additional commandments in order to safeguard the original commandments; for example, certain acts should be avoided towards the approach of evening on Friday lest one should forget and inadvertently continue to do them on the Sabbath.

l. 6 *Simeon the Just.* See Josephus, *Ant.* xii. 43, 157, 224. It is impossible to determine with certainty whether this Simeon, who was high priest, lived at the beginning or at the end of the third century B.C. The saying attributed to him is characteristic of Rabbinic religion. The three pillars on which the world rests are God's revelation of himself and his will in the Law, written and unwritten, and man's study of and obedience to this revelation (for this is included in the word *torah*); the cultic worship carried out in the Temple (*'abodah*), and deeds of loving-kindness (*gemilluth hasadim*)—acts not specifically commanded in the Law but performed out of compassion and goodness. Truth, worship, and love sustain the universe.

l. 9 *Antigonus of Soko.* There is no reliable evidence about Antigonus. His Greek name should be noted; tradition made him one of the founders of the Sadducees. The saying attributed to him is important; the attitude of Judaism to rewards is not as simple as is all too often assumed.

128 *Aboth* 1. 12–15. Hillel and Shammai received the Law from them. Hillel said: Be of the disciples of Aaron, loving peace and pursuing peace, loving mankind and bringing them nigh to the Law.

He used to say: A name made great is a name destroyed, and he
5 that increases not decreases, and he that learns not is worthy of death, and he that makes worldly use of the crown shall perish.

He used to say: If I am not for myself who is for me? and being for mine own self what am I? and if not now, when?

Shammai said: Make thy study of the Law a fixed habit; say
10 little and do much, and receive all men with a cheerful countenance.

l. 1 *Hillel and Shammai* stand here in a series of "pairs" (*zugoth*) of names which were sometimes supposed to be those of Presidents and Vice-Presidents of the Sanhedrin. This however they cannot have been since (before the destruction of the Temple) the President was always the high priest. Hillel and Shammai would moreover have been very uneasy colleagues in the presidency, since many divergent and even contradictory interpretations and rulings were traced back to them, and they became the heads of two rival schools or factions (Beth Hillel, Beth Shammai). Both were active about the beginning of the Christian era; in general the former took the gentler and more lenient, the latter the stricter, view of any subject under debate. This general rule is "proved" in *Eduyoth* 4f. by a number of exceptions, in which "the School of Shammai adopted the more lenient, and the School of Hillel the more stringent ruling"; for example, "If an egg was laid on a Festival-day the School of Shammai say: It may be eaten. The School of Hillel say: It may not be eaten" (*Eduyoth* 4. 1); and is itself illustrated in *Gittin* 9. 10 ("The School of Shammai say: A man may not divorce his wife unless he has found unchastity in her. . . . And the School of Hillel say: He may divorce her even if she spoiled a dish for him. . . .")

l. 1 *From them, sc.* from Shemaiah and Abtalion.

l. 3 *Mankind*, literally, "the creatures", is used here, as the next sentence shows, of the Gentiles. Hillel advocates the making of proselytes (see below, pp. 164ff (**166f.**)).

l. 4 *A name made great* . . . He that exalts himself shall be abased.

l. 5 *He that increases not decreases.* This saying is probably to be interpreted in the light of the next. He who does not add to the common store of knowledge and learning is as if he diminished it.

l. 6 *The crown* is the crown of the Law, the privilege of knowing, teaching, and practising it. The saying is explained in *Aboth* 4. 5 ("Thus thou mayest learn that he that makes profit out of the words of the Law removes his life from the world"), and there are parallel sayings (e.g. *Nedarim* 62a, "He who makes use of the crown of the Law is rooted out of the world. Do the words of the Law for the doing's sake, and speak of them for their own sake. Make them not a crown with which to exalt thyself, or a spud with which to weed").

l. 7 *If I am not for myself* . . . Of this very obscure saying there are three possible interpretations. (*a*) Hillel speaks of a representative man. If a man does not shoulder his own responsibilities and do his own duty, who will do it for him? Yet if he does so by himself alone (without the help of God) what can he effect? And if he does not give obedience and service to God *now* in this life, when will he have another opportunity for doing so? (*b*) Instead of this individualist interpretation we may suppose that "I" is used for "Israel". (*c*) The "I" (אֲנִי, *'ani*) may be taken as a cryptic reference to God (אֲדֹנָי, *'adonai*), who is alone and eternal. This last interpretation seems far-fetched, but cf. *Sukkah* 53a; *Lev. R.* 35. 1.

129 *Aboth* 2. 1. Rabbi said: Which is the straight way that a man should choose? That which is an honour to him and gets him honour from men. And be heedful of a light precept as of a weighty one, for thou knowest not the recompense of reward of each precept; and
5 reckon the loss through the fulfilling of a precept against its reward, and the reward that comes from transgression against its loss. Consider three things and thou wilt not fall into the hands of transgression: know what is above thee—a seeing eye and a hearing ear and all thy deeds written in a book.

l. 1 *Rabbi* refers to R. Judah the Prince (or Patriarch; נָשִׂיא *nasi'*) who on the basis of earlier collections compiled the Mishnah (see below, p. 145). He was born A.D. 135, and probably lived till after the end of the century. It is worth noting that in addition to the customary Rabbinic studies he learned and liked Greek; and was said (though this must be regarded as quite uncertain) to have been a friend of a Roman Emperor.

l. 3 *Be heedful of a light precept* . . . This is a characteristic injunction. It was regarded as dangerous, and therefore undesirable, to arrange precepts in order of importance; to do so might lead to the neglect of those deemed to be less important.

130 *Aboth* 2. 8f. Rabban Johanan b. Zakkai received the Law from
Hillel and from Shammai. He used to say: If thou hast wrought
much in the Law claim not merit for thyself, for to this end wast
thou created. Five disciples had Rabban Johanan b. Zakkai, and
5 these are they: R. Eliezer b. Hyrcanus, and R. Joshua b. Hananiah,
and R. Jose the Priest, and R. Simeon b. Nathaniel, and R.
Eleazar b. Arak. Thus used he to recount their praise: Eliezer b.
Hyrcanus is a plastered cistern which loses not a drop; Joshua b.
Hananiah—happy is she that bare him; Jose the Priest is a saintly
10 man; Simeon b. Nathaniel is fearful of sin; Eleazar b. Arak is an
ever-flowing spring. He used to say: If all the Sages of Israel were
in the one scale of the balance and Eliezer b. Hyrcanus in the other,
he would outweigh them all. Abba Saul said in his name: If all the
Sages of Israel were in the one scale of the balance and with them
15 Eliezer b. Hyrcanus, and Eleazar b. Arak was in the other, he would
outweigh them all.

He said to them: Go forth and see which is the good way to
which a man should cleave. R. Eliezer said, A good eye. R.
Joshua said, A good companion. R. Jose said, A good neighbour.
20 R. Simeon said, One that sees what will be. R. Eleazar said, A
good heart. He said to them: I approve the words of Eleazar b.
Arak more than your words, for in his words are your words
included. He said to them: Go forth and see which is the evil way
which a man should shun. R. Eliezer said, An evil eye. R. Joshua
25 said, An evil companion. R. Jose said, an evil neighbour. R.
Simeon said, He that borrows and does not repay. He that borrows
from man is as one that borrows from God, for it is written, *The
wicked borroweth and payeth not again but the righteous dealeth
graciously and giveth* (Ps. 37. 21). R. Eleazar said, An evil heart. He
30 said to them: I approve the words of Eleazar b. Arak more than
your words for in his words are your words included.

l. 1 *Rabban Johanan b. Zakkai* was one of the most important of all the Rabbis.
After the destruction of the Temple in A.D. 70 he reconstituted the Sanhedrin
at Jabneh, and thereby helped to preserve Judaism for the future. He died
about A.D. 80, having made a number of important modifications necessi-
tated by the removal of the Temple; e.g. *Sukkah* 3. 12 "Beforetime the
Lulab (see below, pp. 157f. (**152**)) was carried seven days in the Temple, but
in the provinces one day only. After the Temple was destroyed, Rabban
Johanan b. Zakkai ordained that in the provinces it should be carried seven
days in memory of the Temple".

131 *Aboth* 3. 14–17. R. Akiba said: Jesting and levity accustom a man
to lewdness. The tradition is a fence around the Law: Tithes are a

fence around riches; vows are a fence around abstinence; a fence around wisdom is silence.

5   He used to say: Beloved is man for he was created in the image [of God]; still greater was the love in that it was made known to him that he was created in the image of God, as it is written, *For in the image of God made he man* (Gen. 9. 6). Beloved are Israel for they were called children of God; still greater was the love in that

10 it was made known to them that they were called children of God, as it is written, *Ye are the children of the Lord your God* (Deut. 14. 1). Beloved are Israel, for to them was given the precious instrument; still greater was the love, in that it was made known to them that to them was given the precious instrument by which the

15 world was created, as it is written, *For I give you good doctrine; forsake ye not my Law* (Prov. 4. 2).

All is foreseen, but freedom of choice is given; and the world is judged by grace, yet all is according to the excess of works [that be good or evil].

20 He used to say: All is given against a pledge, and the net is cast over all living; the shop stands open and the shopkeeper gives credit and the account-book lies open and the hand writes and every one that wishes to borrow let him come and borrow; but the collectors go their round continually every day and exact

25 payment of men with their consent or without their consent, for they have that on which they can rely; and the judgement is a judgement of truth; and all is made ready for the banquet.

l. 1 *R. Akiba* b. Joseph was born *c.* A.D. 50 and died a martyr in the revolt of Bar Cocheba (see pp. 133–6 (**122ff.**)) in A.D. 135. He did not enter Rabbinic circles naturally but was born an '*am ha-'aretz* (see pp. 163f. (**165**)), and became a Rabbi in later life (see *Pesahim* 49*b*: Akiba recalled his days as an '*am ha-'aretz* and declared that then he would wish to bite a scholar "like an ass". "Like a dog", his disciples corrected him. But he replied, "An ass's bite breaks the bone; a dog's does not"). He taught in B^ene Baraq; also in Lydda and Jabneh. When the revolt made head he proved himself a man of affairs as well as a scholar, and recognized Bar Cocheba as the Messiah. His great literary achievement was the first redaction of the oral Law in systematic written form. His "Mishnah" was developed by R. Meir, and finally used by R. Judah himself (see above, p. 141 (**129**)).

l. 2 *A fence.* See above (pp. 139f. (**127**)) on *Aboth* 1. 1.

l. 6 *Still greater* . . . Some texts omit this sentence. It (like later similar sentences) stresses the supreme value of the revelation granted to Israel, and the graciousness of God in giving it.

l. 12 *The precious instrument.* The Law is meant. In Prov. 8 Wisdom (חכמה, *ḥokmah*) is represented as having been active in co-operation with God in the work of creation. Wisdom was equated with Law, and so to the Law also cosmological functions were assigned.

l. 17 *All is foreseen, but freedom of choice is given.* According to Josephus (*War* ii.
162f.) "the Pharisees . . . attribute everything to Fate (εἱμαρμένη) and to
God; they hold that to act rightly or otherwise rests, indeed, for the most
part with man, but that in each action Fate co-operates." This resolute
assertion of the paradox of determinism and free will, with no attempt to
explain it, is characteristic of the unphilosophical style of Rabbinic thought.

l. 20 *All is given against a pledge.* This long and apparently complicated metaphor
is in fact straightforward. God is a creditor, to whom men are indebted;
they owe him obedience and good works.

l. 26 *That on which they can rely*; the record of men's debts kept in heaven.

l. 27 *The banquet*—the feast of the Age to Come, or kingdom of God.

132 *Aboth* 4. 1. Ben Zoma said: Who is wise? He that learns from all
men, as it is written, *From all my teachers have I got understanding* (Ps.
119. 99). Who is mighty? He that subdues his [evil] nature, as it is
written, *He that is slow to anger is better than the mighty, and he that*
5 *ruleth his spirit than he that taketh a city* (Prov. 16. 32). Who is rich?
He that rejoiceth in his portion, as it is written, *When thou eatest*
the labour of thy hands happy shalt thou be, and it shall be well with
thee (Ps. 128. 2). *Happy shalt thou be*—in this world; *and it shall be*
well with thee—in the world to come. Who is honoured? He that
10 honours mankind, as it is written, *For them that honour me I will*
honour, and they that despise me shall be lightly esteemed (1 Sam. 2. 30).

l. 1 *Ben Zoma*, a younger contemporary of R. Akiba, was in high repute as an
expositor: "When Ben Zoma died there were no more expounders"
(*Sotah* 9. 15). But he "entered into Paradise" (engaged in mystical exegesis
and theosophical speculation) and incurred suspicion. It should be noted that
he is not styled "Rabbi".

l. 2 *From all my teachers*, a common Rabbinic rendering of this verse; cf. R.V., I
have more understanding than all my teachers.

l. 3 *His evil nature*, his *yetzer* (יצר). This word (cf. in the Bible Gen. 6. 5; 8. 21;
Deut. 31. 21; Isa. 26. 3; 1 Chron. 28. 9; 29. 18) is used to describe the
inclination within man which gives him a tendency to sin, an innate source
of temptation. It was not in itself altogether bad since it was created by
God and could be used for good purposes (e.g. it is very frequently linked
by the Rabbis with sexual passion and temptation; but they also point out
that without it "no man would build a house, marry a wife, beget children,
or engage in trade" (*Gen. R.* 9. 7)). The inclination may be restrained by
repentance and the study of the Law. The earlier sources seem to have spoken
of only one (bad) inclination, the later of two, good and bad, acting in
conflict; see e.g. *Berakoth* 9. 5, where "with *all* thy heart" (Deut. 6. 5) is
said to mean "with both thine impulses, thy good impulse and thine evil
impulse".

ll. 8f. *In this world . . . in the world to come.* For this contrast see pp. 239–42 (**218f.**).

B. The Literature

The foundation of orthodox Judaism was the biblical Law. This was however supplemented by a tradition (in the New Testament, and Josephus, παράδοσις), at first oral but later written down. This oral Law (תורה שבעל פה) was believed equally with the written to have originated with Moses (see on *Aboth* I. I (**127**) above), and was consequently of equal authority. The process of writing down the oral Law, at first frowned upon, passed through several stages in the second century A.D., until at the end of the century the Mishnah as we know it was compiled, on the basis of earlier documents (notably the Mishnah of R. Meir), by R. Judah (see above p. 141 (**129**)). The Mishnah is on the whole a systematization and application of the Old Testament regulations for ceremonial and civil procedure (the tractate *Aboth* quoted in the preceding section and consisting mainly of religious and ethical maxims is exceptional), and is divided into six Orders, or Books, containing in all sixty-three tractates. The whole body of oral legal tradition was not used in R. Judah's Mishnah; a quantity that was left over forms the *Tosephta*, a body of material parallel in form and content to the Mishnah itself but lacking its authority. In turn the Mishnah was expounded and expanded, and in due course the whole body of Mishnah and comment was edited as the *Talmud*. The comment was known as *Gemara* and exists in two forms, which (with the Mishnah, which is common to both) make up the two Talmuds, the Babylonian and the Jerusalem, edited in the two main centres of Rabbinic activity, Babylonia and Palestine, c. A.D. 500. Most of the Talmudic material is *Halakah*; that is, it contains specific and authoritative direction for the life of Jewish obedience. (In addition to authorized *halakoth* it contains also many juridical opinions which were finally rejected by the majority of scholars.) Though the final date of recension is, as has been said, fairly late, the Talmuds contain a good deal that is early enough to be relevant to New Testament studies; in particular, the Gemara contains sayings described by the word *Baraita*; these are sayings of *Tannaim* (Rabbis of the pre-mishnaic period) which were not included in the Mishnah.

Halakah represents only one kind of Rabbinic literary activity. The other main direction of Rabbinic work was *Haggadah*—practical, homiletic, and often imaginative and even fanciful interpretation of Scripture. This kind of exposition is to be found principally in the *Midrashim*, among which may be noted *Mekilta* (a commentary on

Exodus), *Siphra* (on Leviticus), *Siphre* (on Numbers), *Siphre* (on Deuteronomy), and the *Midrash Rabbah* (or *Large Midrash*, on the Pentateuch and the five *Megilloth*). One other kind of literature may be noted—the liturgical. Here the most important sources for our purpose are the Book of Daily Prayers, still in use in various forms in the synagogue today, and the *Passover Haggadah*, or service for use in the home on Passover night. Parts of the Prayer Book are medieval and parts are modern; but others are very ancient (see for example pp. 162f. (**158–64**)). Comparison of the Passover service with the Mishnaic instructions regarding the feast proves that much of it also is primitive.

An exhaustive analysis of the literature cannot be attempted here, but the following forms are of interest to the student of the New Testament.

(1) *Exegesis*. Much of the Rabbinic literature consists of the exegesis of Scripture. Though this may often appear to the modern reader arbitrary it was in fact generally conducted in accordance with certain established principles (*Middoth*). Several sets of such principles exist: the seven *middoth* of Hillel (quoted below); the thirteen *middoth* of R. Ishmael (died *c.* A.D. 135); the thirty-two *middoth* of R. Eliezer ben R. Jose the Galilean (end of the second century A.D.).

133 *Tosephta Sanhedrin* 7. 11 (p. 427). Hillel the Elder expounded seven principles (*middoth*) before the elders of Petherah: *a minori ad maius*, analogy, a standard conclusion based on one passage (of scripture), a standard conclusion based on two passages, general and particu-
5 lar—particular and general, analogy with another passage, proof from the context. These seven things did Hillel the Elder expound before the men of Petherah.

l. 2 *A minori ad maius*, literally, "light and heavy", covering arguments from the less to the greater and from the greater to the less. This is a very common argument in Rabbinic usage.

l. 3 *Analogy*; an argument from one passage of Scripture to another, similar one. The validity of the analogy might be disputed, as for example in *Betzah* 1. 6: The School of Shammai say: They may not take Dough-offering or [Priests'] Dues to the priest on a Festival-day whether they were set apart on the day before or on the same day. And the School of Hillel permit it. The School of Shammai replied with an analogy (*gᵉzerah shawah*—the second *middah*): Dough-offering and [Priests'] Dues are a gift to the priest, and the Heave-Offering is a gift to the priest; as they may not bring Heave-offering, neither may they bring [Priests'] Dues. The School of Hillel replied: No! as ye argue of Heave-offering (which a man has not the right to set apart [on a Festival-day]) would ye also argue of [Priests'] Dues (which a man has the right to set apart [on a Festival-day])?

l. 4 *General and particular—particular and general.* This rule was expanded by R. Ishmael (see above) into eight.

(2) *Maxims.* Much of the moral teaching of the Rabbis resembles that of the older Wisdom literature in that it is delivered in the form of maxims, brief, sententious utterances, often epigrammatic in form. Some examples have already been given (see **127-32**); hundreds more could be quoted.

134 *Aboth* 2. 7. Moreover he saw a skull floating on the face of the water
and he said unto it, Because thou drownedst they drowned thee
and at the last they that drowned thee shall be drowned. He used to
say: The more flesh the more worms; the more possessions the
5   more care; the more women the more witchcrafts; the more bond-
women the more lewdness; the more bondmen the more
thieving; the more study of the Law the more life; the more
schooling the more wisdom; the more counsel the more understanding; the more righteousness the more peace. If a man has
10   gained a good name he has gained somewhat for himself; if he has
gained for himself words of the Law he has gained for himself life
in the world to come.

l. 1 *He.* Hillel.
l. 7 *The more life.* The Law is the means of (eternal) life—a very characteristic affirmation; cf. l. 11.

135 *Aboth* 3. 5. R. Nehunya b. Ha-Kanah [*c.* A.D. 70–130] said: He that
takes upon himself the yoke of the Law, from him shall be taken
away the yoke of the kingdom and the yoke of worldly care; but
he that throws off the yoke of the Law, upon him shall be laid the
5   yoke of the kingdom and the yoke of worldly care.

l. 3 *The kingdom.* When "the kingdom" is used absolutely in Rabbinic writings its meaning is usually "the earthly kingdom", the present authorities; often of course the Roman Empire. R. Nehunya means that the pious student of the Law will be delivered from trouble with the authorities.

Naturally, legal as well as moral pronouncements were cast in the form of maxims, for example the pronouncement of R. Meir in a question of what might or might not be permitted on the Sabbath.

136 *Shabbath* 15. 1. These are knots for which they [that tie them on
the Sabbath] are accounted culpable: camel-drivers' knots and
sailors' knots; and as a man is culpable through the tying of them

so is he culpable through the untying of them. R. Meir says: None
5 is accounted culpable because of any knot which can be untied
with one hand.

(3) *Parables* constitute another very common rabbinic form. There
is rarely any difficulty in their interpretation. Their most common
logical basis is that of the "light and heavy" argument (above, p. 146
(**133**)), but details are sometimes allegorized.

137 *Aboth* 3. 18. R. Eleazar b. Azariah [*c.* A.D. 50–120] said: If there is
no study of the Law there is no seemly behaviour, if there is no
seemly behaviour there is no study of the Law; if there is no
wisdom there is no fear [of God], if there is no fear [of God] there
5 is no wisdom; if there is no knowledge there is no discernment, if
there is no discernment there is no knowledge; if there is no meal
there is no study of the Law, if there is no study of the Law there is
no meal. He used to say: He whose wisdom is more abundant than
his works, to what is he like? To a tree whose branches are abun-
10 dant but whose roots are few; and the wind comes and uproots it
and overturns it, as it is written, *He shall be like a tamarisk in the
desert and shall not see when good cometh; but shall inhabit the parched
places in the wilderness* (Jer. 17. 6). But he whose works are more
abundant than his wisdom, to what is he like? To a tree whose
15 branches are few but whose roots are many; so that even if all the
winds in the world come and blow against it, it cannot be stirred
from its place, as it is written, *He shall be as a tree planted by the
waters, and that spreadeth out his roots by the river, and shall not fear
when heat cometh, and his leaf shall be green; and shall not be careful in
20 the year of drought, neither shall cease from yielding fruit* (Jer. 17. 8).

138 *Sukkah* 2. 9. Throughout the seven [days of the Feast] a man must
make his *Sukkah* a regular abode and his house a chance abode. If
rain fell, when may he empty out [*the Sukkah*]? When the por-
ridge would spoil. They propounded a parable: To what can it be
5 compared?—to a slave who came to fill the cup for his master and
he poured the pitcher over his face.

l. 2 *Sukkah*, the booth in which he was required to dwell during the Feast of
   Booths (below, pp. 157ff. (**152**)).
l. 6 *His face*. "The slave's. At the Feast of Tabernacles rain is a sign of God's
   anger (*Taanith* 1. 1). The slave (Israel) would perform his duties (the observance of the divinely ordained Feasts and living in booths), but his master
   (God) only shows his displeasure" (Danby, ad loc.).

139 *Shabbath* 153*a*. R. Eliezer said: Repent one day before your death. His disciples asked R. Eliezer: But does a man know on what day he will die? He said: So much the more must he repent today; perhaps he will die tomorrow. It follows that a man should repent
5 every day. Even so said Solomon in his wisdom, *Let thy garments be always white; and let not thy head lack ointment* (Eccles. 9. 8). R. Johanan b. Zakkai spoke a parable: [It is like] a king who invited his servants to a feast and did not appoint them a time. The wise among them adorned themselves and sat down by the door of the
10 palace, for they said: Is anything lacking in a palace? The foolish among them went to their work, for they said: Is a feast ever given without preparation? Suddenly the king summoned his servants. The wise among them went in before him adorned as they were, and the foolish went in before him in their working clothes. The
15 king rejoiced to see the wise and was angry to see the foolish, and said: These who adorned themselves for the feast shall sit down and eat and drink; but those who did not adorn themselves for the feast shall stand and look on. The son-in-law of R. Meir said in the name of R. Meir: If so, the latter would look on as waiters; but
20 rather both shall sit down; the former shall eat but the latter be hungry, the former shall drink but the latter be thirsty, as it is said, *Behold, my servants shall eat, but ye shall be hungry. . . .* (Isa. 65. 13, 14).

(4) The Rabbinic books often use *narrative* as a means of expressing or suggesting truth. Sometimes the narratives are straightforward stories of ordinary events leading to a legal question and decision; sometimes they are used for other purposes, for example, to reflect credit upon Israel or upon individual Jews. Miracles also are found, some of which form interesting parallels to the New Testament miracles.

140 *Nedarim* 9. 5. This narrative raises a question, and leads to a decision, about the validity and alterability of a vow.

They may open the way for a man by reason of his wife's *Ketubah*. It once happened that a man vowed to have no benefit from his wife, whose *Ketubah* was 400 *denars*. She came before R. Akiba and he declared him liable to pay her her *Ketubah*. He said, "Rabbi, my
5 father left about 800 *denars*, and my brother took 400 *denars* and I took 400; is it not enough that she should take 200 *denars* and I 200?" R. Akiba said to him, "Even if thou must sell the hair of thy head thou shalt pay her her *Ketubah*". The husband answered, "Had I known that this was so, I had not made my vow", and
10 R. Akiba released him from his vow.

l. 1 *Ketubah.* "Literally, 'a written document'; a wife's 'jointure'. The word is used (*a*) for the document (cf. *Ketuboth* 4. 7–12) in which the bridegroom pledges himself to assign a certain sum of money to the bride in the event of his death or of his divorcing her; and (*b*) for the sum of money so assigned (cf. *Ketuboth* 5. 1)" (Danby, p. 794).

l. 7 *Even if thou must sell* . . . The obligation of the *ketubah* is absolutely binding; the divorced woman may have no other resource at all.

l. 10 *Released him from his vow,* "opened the way for him" (l. 1). This example of the annulment of a vow occurs among others in which it is held that a man may be released because when he made his vow he failed to understand its implications.

141 *Y. Baba Metzia* ii. 5. 8*c.* Simeon b. Shetah [*fl. c.* 80 B.C.] was occupied with preparing flax. His disciples said to him, "Rabbi, desist; we will buy you an ass, and you will not have to work so hard." They went and bought an ass from an Arab, and a pearl was
5 found on it. They came to him and said, "From now on you need not work any more." He said, "Why?" They said, "We bought you an ass from an Arab, and a pearl was found on it." He said to them, "Does its owner know of it?" They said, "No." He said to them, "Go and give it back to him." They said, "But did not R.
10 Huna, in the name of Rab, report that, even according to him who said that no profit may be made [by a third party] from that which is *stolen* from a heathen, yet all the world agrees that, if you *find* something which belonged to a heathen, you may keep it?" He said, "Do you think that Simeon b. Shetah is a barbarian? No, he
15 would prefer to hear the Arab say, 'Blessed be the God of the Jews', than to possess all the riches of the world."

It is also proved, from the story of R. Hanina, that lost property should be restored for the sake of the sanctification of the Name. For once, some aged Rabbis bought a heap of corn from some
20 soldiers, and they found in it a bundle of *denarii*, and they returned it to the soldiers, who said, "Blessed be the God of the Jews."

142 *Taanith* 3. 8. Once they said to Onias the Circle-maker, "Pray that rain may fall." He answered, "Go out and bring in the Passover ovens that they be not softened." He prayed, but the rain did not fall. What did he do? He drew a circle and stood within it and said
5 before God, "O Lord of the world, thy children have turned their faces to me, for that I am like a son of the house before thee. I swear by thy great name that I will not stir hence until thou have pity on thy children." Rain began falling drop by drop. He said, "Not for such rain have I prayed, but for rain that will fill the
10 cisterns, pits, and caverns." It began to rain with violence. He said, "Not for such rain have I prayed, but for rain of goodwill, blessing,

and graciousness." Then it rained in moderation [and continued] until the Israelites went up from Jerusalem to the Temple Mount because of the rain. They went to him and said, "Like as thou
15 didst pray for the rain to come, so pray that it may go away!" He replied, "Go and see if the Stone of the Strayers has disappeared!" Simeon b. Shetah sent to him saying, "Hadst thou not been Onias I had pronounced a ban against thee! But what shall I do to thee?— thou importunest God and he performeth thy will, like a son that
20 importuneth his father and he performeth his will; and of thee Scripture saith, *Let thy father and thy mother be glad, and let her that bare thee rejoice* (Prov. 23. 25)".

l. 1 *Onias the Circle-maker* lived early in the first century B.C. It is difficult not to think (especially in view of Simeon's complaint (l. 18)) that his circle-drawing was related to magic. In the Midrash on Ps. 77. 1, with reference to Hab. 2. 1 (I will stand upon my watch), circle-drawing is a mark of impatience: Habakkuk will not move from his circle until God answers his question. But this may be a re-interpretation of an action whose origins lie further back.

l. 2 *Passover ovens*, specially made for roasting the Paschal sacrifices. They were made of clay.

l. 6 *A son of the house*, and thus specially intimate with God, able to make importunate petitions and obtain what he asked.

l. 16 *The Stone of the Strayers*, "Explained as a high stone from which lost articles were proclaimed (cf. *Baba Metzia* 2. 1–6), the 'Strayers' being those in search of their missing property" (Danby, ad loc.).

l. 17 *Simeon b. Shetah.* See above, **141**. Evidently he felt the proceedings to be unorthodox, but Onias's evident power with God placed him above punishment.

C. The Law

The Law was not only the basis of Rabbinic scholarship and writing (above, pp. 145f.) but the foundation of both religious and social life. It came from God, it afforded a divine revelation of all needful truth, and provided a practical way of salvation.

143 *Exodus Rabbah* 33. 1. A parable. It is like a king who had one only daughter. There came a certain king and took her to wife; and he sought to go to his own land and take his wife with him. The king said: My daughter, whom I have given you, is my only
5 daughter; I cannot be parted from her, but neither can I say to you, Do not take her, for she is your wife. But do me this kindness. Where you go, make a bedroom for me that I may dwell with

you, for I cannot let my daughter go. In the same way said the Holy One (blessed be he) to Israel: I have given you the Law, but
10 I cannot be separated from it; nor can I say to you, Do not take it. But wherever you go make me a house in which I may dwell, as it is said, *Let them make me a sanctuary that I may dwell among them* (Ex. 25. 8).

l. 9 *I have given you the Law*. It must not be thought that the father-daughter relationship in the parable assigns any metaphysical status to the Law. Such thoughts are foreign to this kind of exposition. The expositor wishes to emphasize that the Law is a gracious gift from God to Israel, a signal mark of his favour; and that the possession of it carries with it God's presence in a unique manner and degree.

144 *Siphre Numbers, Shelah,* §115, 35*a*. The Law is a precious gift, and presupposes God's redemption of his people.

Why is the Exodus from Egypt mentioned in connection with every single commandment? The matter can be compared to a king, the son of whose friend was taken prisoner. The king ransomed him, not as son, but as slave, so that, if at any time he should
5 disobey the king, the latter could say, "You are my slave." So, when he came back, the king said, "Put on my sandals for me, take my clothes to the bath house." Then the man protested. The king took out the bill of sale, and said, "You are my slave." So when God redeemed the children of Abraham his friend, he redeemed
10 them, not as children, but as slaves, so that if he imposed upon them decrees, and they obeyed not, he could say, "Ye are my slaves." When they went into the desert, he began to order them some light and some heavy commands, e.g. Sabbath and incest commands, and fringes and phylacteries. They began to protest.
15 Then God said, "You are my slaves. On this condition I redeemed you, that I should decree, and you should fulfil." [Nevertheless, God's slaves are unlike man's slaves. God's ways are not like those of "flesh and blood". For a man acquires slaves that they may look after and sustain *him*, but God acquires slaves that He may look
20 after and sustain *them*].

145 *Kiddushin* 30*b*. The words of the Law are likened to a medicine of life. Like a king who inflicted a big wound upon his son, and he put a plaster upon his wound. He said, "My son, so long as this plaster is on your wound, eat and drink what you like, and wash
5 in cold or warm water, and you will suffer no harm. But if you remove it, you will get a bad boil." So God says to the Israelites,

"I created within you the evil *yetzer*, but I created the Law as a drug. As long as you occupy yourselves with the Law, the *yetzer* will not rule over you. But if you do not occupy yourselves with
10 the Torah, then you will be delivered into the power of the *yetzer*, and all its activity will be against you."

l. 3 *Put a plaster;* derived from Deut. 11. 18 by a pun in Hebrew.
l. 7 *Yetzer.* See p. 144 (**132**).

D. *Feasts and Festivals*

After the Law itself, nothing did more to preserve the unity and uniqueness of Israel than the due celebration of the festivals prescribed in the Law. They were noted in Palestine and the Dispersion alike, but the three great pilgrim feasts (Passover, Pentecost and Booths) could only be fully observed in the Holy Land. This added so much more importance to the Sabbath, which everywhere distinguished Jews from their neighbours; nevertheless, Jews flocked to Jerusalem in great numbers to take part in the pilgrim feasts.

(1) *Sabbath.* Like all other commandments, the Sabbath was regarded as a gracious gift of God, and was to the pious Israelite no burden but an occasion of rejoicing. The best clothes were worn, the best food eaten. Worship was held in the synagogue.

146 *Mekilta on Ex.* 31. 13 (109*b*). The Sabbath is given over to you, not you to the Sabbath.

147 *Tamid* 7. 4. This was the singing which the Levites used to sing in the Temple. On the first day they sang *The earth is the Lord's and all that therein is, the round world and they that dwell therein* (Ps. 24);
on the second day they sang *Great is the Lord and highly to be*
5 *praised in the city of our God, even upon his holy hill* (Ps. 48); on the third day they sang *God standeth in the congregation of God, he is a judge among the gods* (Ps. 82); on the fourth day they sang *O Lord God to whom vengeance belongeth, thou God to whom vengeance belongeth, show thyself* (Ps. 94); on the fifth day they sang *Sing we*
10 *merrily unto God our strength, make a cheerful noise unto the God of Jacob* (Ps. 81); on the sixth day they sang *The Lord is king, and hath put on glorious apparel* (Ps. 93). On the Sabbath they sang *A Psalm: a Song for the Sabbath Day* (Ps. 92); a Psalm, a song for the time that is to come, for the day that shall be all Sabbath and rest in the
15 life everlasting.

l. 14 *The day that shall be all Sabbath.* The Sabbath was so great a delight that it was used as a type of the Age to Come.

148 *Shabbath* 7. 1f. A great general rule have they laid down concerning the Sabbath: whosoever, forgetful of the principle of the Sabbath, committed many acts of work on many Sabbaths, is liable only to one Sin-offering; but if, mindful of the principle of the Sabbath, he
5 yet committed many acts of work on many Sabbaths, he is liable for every Sabbath [which he profaned]. If he knew that it was the Sabbath and he yet committed many acts of work on many Sabbaths, he is liable for every main class of work [which he performed]; if he committed many acts of work of one main class, he
10 is liable only to one Sin-offering.

The main classes of work are forty save one: sowing, ploughing, reaping, binding sheaves, threshing, winnowing, cleansing crops, grinding, sifting, kneading, baking, shearing wool, washing or beating or dyeing it, spinning, weaving, making two loops, weav-
15 ing two threads, separating two threads, tying [a knot], loosening [a knot], sewing two stitches, tearing in order to sew two stitches, hunting a gazelle, slaughtering or flaying or salting it or curing its skin, scraping it or cutting it up, writing two letters, erasing in order to write two letters, building, pulling down, putting out a
20 fire, lighting a fire, striking with a hammer and taking out aught from one domain into another. These are the main classes of work: forty save one.

l. 2 *The principle of the Sabbath.* "Principle" translates עיקר ('*iqqar*), literally, "root". The point seems to be that he who is unaware of the fundamental principle of Sabbath observance incurs guilt only in respect of this one (fundamental) ignorance, or forgetfulness. The man who knows and remembers the Law, but forgets the Sabbath day and thus commits breaches of the Sabbath law is responsible for each act of forgetting and the consequent breach. The Law was a delight; but the Law had to be kept.

149 *Shabbath* 2. 7. Three things must a man say within his house when darkness is falling on the eve of Sabbath; Have ye tithed? Have ye prepared the *Erub*? and, Light the lamp. If it is in doubt whether darkness has already fallen or not, they may not set apart Tithes
5 from what is known to be untithed, or immerse utensils or light the lamps; but they may set aside Tithes from *demai*-produce and prepare the *Erub* and cover up what is to be kept hot.

l. 2 *Have ye tithed?* Food intended for use on the Sabbath had to be tithed before the Sabbath began.

l. 3 *Have ye prepared the Erub?* The Rabbis insisted upon the observance of the Sabbath, but all possible steps were taken to see that observance was reasonably possible. For example, the law against "going out" (based on Ex. 16. 29 and interpreted as referring to "going out" of one domain (e.g. one's own residence) into another; see above, **148**) was mitigated by means of the *'Erub* (עירוב). This word means literally "interweaving", "mixture", and was used to denote various means by which movement on the Sabbath might be liberated. The most important means are given by M. Jastrow (*A Dictionary of the Targumim, etc.* (1926), 1075*b*, 1076*a*) thus: " *'Erub,* a symbolical act by which the legal fiction of community or continuity is established, e.g. (*a*) with reference to Sabbath limits: a person deposits, before the Sabbath (or the Holy Day), certain eatables to remain in their place over the next day, by which act he transfers his abode to that place, and his movements on the Sabbath are measured from it as the centre; (*b*) with reference to buildings with a common court: the inmates contribute their share towards a dish which is deposited in one of the dwellings, by which act all the dwellings are considered as common to all, and the carrying of objects on the Sabbath from one to the other and across the court is permitted; (*c*) with reference to preparing meals for the Sabbath on a Holy Day occurring on a Friday: a person prepares a dish on Thursday and lets it lie over until the end of the Sabbath, by which fiction all the cooking for the Sabbath which he does on the Holy Day (Friday) is merely a continuation of the preparation begun on Thursday."

l. 3 *Light the lamp.* The practice of lighting a lamp on Sabbath eve is very ancient. It may have had its origin in the fact that it was forbidden to kindle a fire on the Sabbath itself, but it has long been interpreted in terms of the joy of Sabbath.

l. 6 *Demai-produce,* produce on which it is uncertain whether tithe has been paid, e.g. produce acquired from an *'am ha-'aretz* (see pp. 163f. (**165**)).

(2) *Passover.* The yearly feast of Passover brought multitudes of pilgrims to Jerusalem. The feast commemorated the deliverance of Israel from Egypt, a deliverance in which each participating Jew was bidden to feel that he had personally shared; and it pointed forward to a future act of deliverance by God, that is, it was eschatological as well as commemorative.

150 *Pesahim* 10. 1, 3ff. On the eve of Passover, from about the time of the Evening Offering, a man must eat naught until nightfall. Even the poorest in Israel must not eat unless he sits down to table, and they must not give them less than four cups of wine to drink, even
5 if it is from the [Paupers'] Dish. . . .
    When [food] is brought before him he eats it seasoned with lettuce, until he is come to the breaking of bread; they bring before him unleavened bread and lettuce and the *haroseth*, although *haroseth* is not a religious obligation. R. Eliezer b. R. Zadok [second

10 century A.D.] says: It is a religious obligation. And in the Holy City
they used to bring before him the body of the Passover-offering.
They then mix him the second cup. And here the son asks his
father (and if the son has not enough understanding his father instructs him [how to ask]), "Why is this night different from other
15 nights? For on other nights we eat seasoned food once, but this
night twice; on other nights we eat leavened or unleavened bread,
but this night all is unleavened; on other nights we eat flesh
roast, stewed, or cooked, but this night all is roast." And according
to the understanding of the son his father instructs him. He begins
20 with the disgrace and ends with the glory; and he expounds
from *A wandering Aramean was my father* . . . until he finishes
the whole section [Deut. 26. 5–9].

Rabban Gamaliel used to say: Whosoever has not said [the
verses concerning] these three things at Passover has not fulfilled his
25 obligation. And these are they: Passover, unleavened bread, and
bitter herbs: "Passover"—because God passed over the houses of
our fathers in Egypt; "unleavened bread"—because our fathers
were redeemed from Egypt; "bitter herbs"—because the Egyptians embittered the lives of our fathers in Egypt. In every genera-
30 tion a man must so regard himself as if he came forth himself out
of Egypt, for it is written. *And thou shalt tell thy son in that day
saying, It is because of that which the Lord did for me when I came forth
out of Egypt* (Ex. 13. 8). Therefore are we bound to give thanks, to
praise, to glorify, to honour, to exalt, to extol, and to bless him
35 who wrought all these wonders for our fathers and for us. He
brought us out from bondage to freedom, from sorrow to gladness,
and from mourning to a Festival-day, and from darkness to great
light, and from servitude to redemption; so let us say before him
the *Hallelujah.*

l. 3 *He sits down to table*, that is, in the manner of the *triclinium* (reclining rather
than sitting). The Passover was a feast of *freedom*; reclining was the attitude
of free men.

l. 5 *The [Paupers'] Dish*, the *tamḥuy*, or daily charitable distribution. All Israelites,
however poor, had a share in God's act of redemption.

l. 7 *The breaking of bread (parper 'eth ha-path)*; other texts read *parpereth*, the bread
condiment, or bitter herbs. The breaking of the bread would refer to the
distribution of the unleavened bread with which the Passover had to be
eaten, the *parpereth* to the sauce in which the unleavened bread was dipped.
The difference in meaning (with regard to the course of the meal) is therefore not great.

l. 8 *Ḥaroseth*, a sauce made of nuts, fruit, and vinegar.

l. 10 *In the Holy City*. After the destruction of the Temple in A.D. 70 the lamb (or
kid) could no longer be eaten.

l. 19 *He begins with the disgrace and ends with the glory;* as in the narrative of Deut. 26.5–9. This theme, which of course turns upon the salvation wrought by God, is the keynote of the Passover.

l. 39 *The Hallelujah:* The "*Hallel*", Pss. 113–18.

(3) *Pentecost.* This feast, held seven weeks (fifty days) after Passover, retained its primitive character as a harvest festival. Passover marked the beginning, Pentecost the end, of the ingathering. In the second century Pentecost was interpreted as the feast of the giving of the Law. In some traditions the Law was offered from Sinai to all nations in their own languages. If this legend could be traced to the first half of the first century it might be thought an important source of the narrative of Acts 2; but such an early origin is improbable.

151 *Pesahim* 68*b*. R. Eleazar [*c.* A.D. 270] said: Pentecost . . . the day on which the Law was given.

(4) *Booths.* When "the Feast" is mentioned without the addition of a name, the feast of Booths is generally referred to. Like Passover this feast attracted great multitudes to Jerusalem, but it could be kept anywhere by the devout Jew who was prepared to live in a *Sukkah*, or leafy booth (as prescribed in Lev. 23. 42), for eight days. There were, however, special celebrations in the Temple.

152 *Sukkah* 4. 1, 5ff.; 9. 5ff. [The rites of] the *Lulab* and the Willow-branch [continue] six days and sometimes seven days; the *Hallel* and the rejoicing, eight days; the *Sukkah* and the Water-libation, seven days; the Flute-playing, sometimes five and sometimes six 5 days. . . .

How was the rite of the Willow-branch fulfilled? There was a place below Jerusalem called Motza. Thither they went and cut themselves young willow-branches. They came and set these up at the sides of the Altar so that their tops were bent over the Altar.

10 They then blew [on the *shofar*] a sustained, a quavering and then another sustained blast. Each day they went in procession a single time around the Altar, saying, *Save now, we beseech thee, O Lord: We beseech thee, O Lord, send now prosperity!* (Ps. 118. 25). R. Judah says: "*Ani waho!* save us we pray! *Ani waho!* save us we pray!" But

15 on that day they went in procession seven times around the Altar. When they departed what did they say? "Homage to thee, O Altar! Homage to thee, O Altar!" R. Eliezer says: "To the Lord and to thee, O Altar! To the Lord and to thee, O Altar!"

As was the rite on a week-day so was the rite on a Sabbath, save

20　that they gathered [the willow-branches] on the eve of the Sabbath
and set them in gilded troughs that they might not wither. R.
Johanan b. Baroka says: They used to bring palm tufts and beat
them on the ground at the sides of the Altar, and that day was
called, "The day of beating the palm tufts".

25　Straightway the children used to cast away their *Lulabs* and eat
their citrons. . . .

"The Water-libation, seven days"—what was the manner of
this? They used to fill a golden flagon holding three *logs* with water
from Siloam. When they reached the Water Gate they blew [on the

30　*shofar*] a sustained, a quavering and another sustained blast. [The
priest whose turn of duty it was] went up the [Altar-] Ramp and
turned to the right where were two silver bowls. R. Judah says:
They were of plaster, but their appearance was darkened because
of the wine. They had each a hole like to a narrow snout, one wide

35　and the other narrow, so that both bowls emptied themselves together. The bowl to the west was for water and that to the east was
for wine. But if the flagon of water was emptied into the bowl for
wine, or the flagon of wine into the bowl for water, that sufficed.
R. Judah says: With one *log* they could perform the libations

40　throughout eight days. To the priest who performed the libation
they used to say, "Lift up thine hand!" for once a certain one
poured the libation over his feet, and all the people threw their
citrons at him. . . .

"The Flute-playing, sometimes five and sometimes six days"—

45　this is the flute-playing at the Beth ha-She'ubah, which overrides
neither a Sabbath nor a Festival-day. They have said: He that never
has seen the joy of the Beth ha-She'ubah has never in his life seen
joy.

At the close of the first Festival-day of the Feast they went down

50　to the Court of the Women where they had made a great amendment. There were golden candlesticks there with four golden
bowls on the top of them and four ladders to each candlestick, and
four youths of the priestly stock and in their hands jars of oil holding a hundred and twenty *logs* which they poured into all the bowls.

55　They made wicks from the worn out drawers and girdles of the
priests and with them they set the candlesticks alight, and there was
not a courtyard in Jerusalem that did not reflect the light of the
Beth ha-She'ubah.

l. 1　*The Lulab.* Properly a palm-branch; but the *lulab* carried and shaken in the
Temple at this feast was made of palm-, myrtle-, and willow-branches.

l. 14　*Ani waho.* "We beseech thee, O Lord" is in Hebrew יהוה אנא, *'ana'*
Y H W H. In order to avoid the use of the sacred name there was substituted

אני והו ('*ani waho*); other forms are given, including '*ani w*e*hu*, "I and he"
—an expression which has been given mystical interpretations.

l. 26 *Their citrons.* Citrons were used in fulfilment of Lev. 23. 40.

l. 28 *Three logs.* A *log* is rather less than a pint.

l. 42 *The people threw their citrons at him.* According to Josephus (*Ant.* xiii. 372)
the offending priest was Alexander Jannaeus (see pp. 115f. (**106**)), but he
was pelted for his general unpopularity.

l. 45 *Beth ha-She'ubah*, בית השאובה, sometimes written בית השואבה, *Beth
ha-Sho'ebah.* The root שאב (*sh-'-b*) means "to draw (water)", and the
expression in the text very probably means "house of water-drawing"
This rite has been thought to be connected with John 7. 37f.

l. 50 *A great amendment.* The women's gallery was refitted with rails.

l. 57 *The light of the Beth ha-She'ubah.* This has been thought to be connected
with the pronouncement of John 8. 12.

(5) *The Day of Atonement.* The Day of Atonement is not a feast but
a fast—the only one in the Jewish calendar. It is fully described in
the Mishnah tractate *Yoma*, from which the following quotations are
taken. The Mishnah only elaborates the Old Testament regulations
for the Temple ceremonies.

153 *Yoma* 3. 8. He came to his bullock and his bullock was standing between the Porch and the Altar, its head to the south and its face to
the west; and he set both his hands upon it and made confession.
And thus used he to say: "O God, I have committed iniquity,
5 transgressed, and sinned before thee, I and my house. O God, forgive the iniquities and transgressions and sins which I have committed and transgressed and sinned before thee, I and my house, as
it is written in the Law of thy servant Moses, *For on this day shall
atonement be made for you to cleanse you; from all your sins shall ye be
10 clean before the Lord* (Lev. 16. 30)". And they answered after him,
"Blessed be the name of the glory of his kingdom for ever and
ever!"

l. 1 *He came to his bullock.* The high priest was obliged first of all to offer sacrifice
on account of his own sins.

154 *Yoma* 5. 1ff. Before this passage opens the high priest has offered a
second bullock on account of the sins of the people.

They brought out to him the ladle and the fire-pan and he took
his two hands full [of incense] and put it in the ladle, which was
large according to his largeness [of hand], or small according to his
smallness [of hand]; and such [alone] was the prescribed measure of
5 the ladle. He took the fire-pan in his right hand and the ladle in his

left. He went through the Sanctuary until he came to the space
between the two curtains separating the Sanctuary from the Holy
of Holies. And there was a cubit's space between them. R. Jose
says: Only one curtain was there, for it is written, *And the veil shall*
10 *divide for you between the holy place and the most holy* (Ex. 26. 33).
The outer curtain was looped up on the south side and the inner
one on the north side. He went along between them until he
reached the north side; when he reached the north he turned round
to the south and went on with the curtain on his left hand until he
15 reached the Ark. When he reached the Ark he put the fire-pan
between the two bars. He heaped up the incense on the coals and
the whole place became filled with smoke. He came out by the way
he went in, and in the outer space he prayed a short prayer. But he
did not prolong his prayer lest he put Israel in terror.
20 After the Ark was taken away a stone remained there from the
time of the early prophets, and it was called "Shetiyah". It was
higher than the ground by three fingerbreadths. On this he used to
put [the fire-pan].
He took the blood from him that was stirring it and entered
25 [again] into the place where he had entered and stood [again] on
the place whereon he had stood, and sprinkled [the blood] once
upwards and seven times downwards, not as though he had intended to sprinkle upwards or downwards but as though he were
wielding a whip. And thus used he to count: One, one and one,
30 one and two, one and three, one and four, one and five, one and
six, one and seven. He came out and put it on the golden stand in
the Sanctuary.

l. 19 *Lest he put Israel in terror*—fearing lest evil should have befallen him in the
Holy of Holies.
l. 20 *The Ark was taken away*—at the Babylonian captivity.

155 *Yoma* 6. 1f. 5. 4–7 describes the sacrifice of one of the pair of goats.

The two he-goats of the Day of Atonement should be alike in
appearance, in size, and in value, and have been bought at the same
time. Yet even if they are not alike they are valid, and if one was
bought one day and the other on the morrow they are valid. If one
5 of them died before the lot was cast, a fellow may be bought for the
other; but if after the lot was cast, another pair must be brought
and the lots cast over them anew. And if that cast for the Lord
died, he [the high priest] should say, "Let this on which the lot 'For
the Lord' has fallen stand in its stead"; and if that cast for Azazel
10 died, he should say, "Let this on which the lot 'For Azazel' has

fallen stand in its stead." The other is left to pasture until it suffers
a blemish, when it must be sold and its value falls to the Temple
fund; for the Sin-offering of the congregation may not be left to
die. R. Judah says: It is left to die. Moreover R. Judah said: If the
15 blood was poured away the scapegoat is left to die; if the scapegoat
died the blood is poured away.

He then came to the scapegoat and laid his two hands upon it
and made confession. And thus used he to say: "O God, thy
people, the House of Israel, have committed iniquity, transgressed,
20 and sinned before thee. O God, forgive, I pray, the iniquities and
transgressions and sins which thy people, the House of Israel, have
committed and transgressed and sinned before thee; as it is
written in the Law of thy servant Moses, *For on this day shall atonement be made for you to cleanse you; from all your sins shall ye be clean
25 before the Lord* (Lev. 16. 30). And when the priests and the people
which stood in the Temple Court heard the Expressed Name come
forth from the mouth of the High Priest, they used to kneel and
bow themselves and fall down on their faces and say, "Blessed be
the name of the glory of his kingdom for ever and ever!"

l. 26 *The Expressed Name.* The sacred name of God, of which the consonants are
יהוה (Y H W H), was uttered with the proper vowels only by the high
priest on the Day of Atonement.

156 *Yoma* 7. 1. Then the High Priest came to read. If he was minded to
read in the linen garments he could do so; otherwise he would read
in his own white vestment. The minister of the synagogue used to
take a scroll of the Law and give it to the chief of the synagogue,
5 and the chief of the synagogue gave it to the Prefect, and the Prefect gave it to the High Priest, and the High Priest received it
standing and read it standing. And he read *After the death . . .* (Lev.
16) and *Howbeit on the tenth day . . .* (Lev. 23. 26–32). Then he used
to roll up the scroll of the Law and put it in his bosom and say,
10 "More is written here than I have read out before you." *And on the
tenth . . .* (Num. 29. 7–11) which is in the Book of Numbers, he
recited by heart. Thereupon he pronounced eight Benedictions:
for the Law, for the Temple-Service, for the Thanksgiving, for the
Forgiveness of Sin, and for the Temple separately, and for the
15 Israelites separately, and for the priests separately; and for the rest
a [general] prayer.

l. 5 *The Prefect,* הסגן (*ha-sagan*); the full title was סגן הכהנים (*sᵉgan ha-kohᵃnim*),
the prefect of the priests. He was a high dignitary set over the building and
services of the Temple.

157 *Yoma* 8. 1. On the Day of Atonement, eating, drinking, washing, anointing, putting on sandals, and marital intercourse are forbidden. A king or a bride may wash their faces and a woman after childbirth may put on sandals. So R. Eliezer. But the Sages
5 forbid it.

E. The Synagogue

The Temple and its services were, even at the great Festivals when Jerusalem was thronged with worshippers, for the few. The majority of Jews found corporate practice of their religion in the Synagogue, where the Law and the Prophets were read, and the community engaged in common prayer. There follow several selections from the Eighteen Benedictions (*Sh⁴moneh 'Esreh*), one of the oldest parts of the synagogue service. For another of these Benedictions see below **169**.

158 *Benediction* 1. Blessed art thou, O Lord our God and God of our fathers, God of Abraham, God of Isaac, and God of Jacob, the great, mighty and revered God, the most high God, who bestowest loving-kindnesses, and possessest all things; who rememberest the
5 pious deeds of the patriarchs, and in love wilt bring a redeemer to their children's children for thy name's sake.

O King, Helper, Saviour and Shield. Blessed art thou, O Lord, the Shield of Abraham.

159 *Benediction* 2. Thou, O Lord, art mighty for ever, thou quickenest the dead, thou art mighty to save.

Thou sustainest the living with loving-kindness, quickenest the dead with great mercy, supportest the falling, healest the sick,
5 loosest the bound, and keepest thy faith to them that sleep in the dust. Who is like unto thee, lord of mighty acts, and who resembleth thee, O King, who killest and quickenest, and causest salvation to spring forth?

Yea, faithful art thou to quicken the dead. Blessed art thou, O
10 Lord, who quickenest the dead.

160 *Benediction* 6. Forgive us, O our Father, for we have sinned; pardon us, O our King, for we have transgressed; for thou dost pardon and forgive. Blessed art thou, O Lord, who art gracious, and dost abundantly forgive.

161 *Benediction* 7. Look upon our affliction and plead our cause, and redeem us speedily for thy name's sake; for thou art a mighty redeemer. Blessed art thou, O Lord, the Redeemer of Israel.

162 *Benediction* 9. Bless this year unto us, O Lord our God, together with every kind of the produce thereof, for our welfare; give a blessing upon the face of the earth. O satisfy us with thy goodness, and bless our year like other good years. Blessed art thou, O Lord,
5 who blessest the years.

163 *Benediction* 10. Sound the great horn for our freedom; lift up the ensign to gather our exiles, and gather us from the four corners of the earth. Blessed art thou, O Lord, who gatherest the banished ones of thy people Israel.

164 *Benediction* 14. And to Jerusalem, thy city, return in mercy, and dwell therein as thou hast spoken; rebuild it soon in our days as an everlasting building, and speedily set up therein the throne of David.
5 Blessed art thou, O Lord, who rebuildest Jerusalem.

F. *Ḥaber and 'Am ha-'aretz*

The social and religious commandments by which the written and oral Law regulated Jewish life were so numerous and far-reaching as to produce marked social distinctions between the scrupulous and the careless. Those who were most punctilious in their observance of the laws of purity and tithing banded themselves together into groups of *ḥᵃberim* (חברים), or "associates". These associates met for religious and charitable purposes, but their main aim was to observe the levitical rules, and a man was admitted to their company only on his undertaking to do this. At the other extreme were the *amme ha-'aretz* (עמי הארץ) or "people of the land", those who were known to be lax in their obedience to the Law. Intercourse between the two groups was limited, but by no means impossible. The scrupulous desired the lax to join their number, and the famous R. Akiba, for example, was in early life an *'am ha-'aretz* (see above, pp. 142f. (**131**)). That ill-feeling between the extreme religious classes existed cannot be denied; but it probably varied much from place to place and time to time, and allowance must be made for the hyperbole of some Rabbinic sayings on the subject.

165 *Demai* 2. 2ff. The corresponding passage in the Tosephta contains more details about the relations between *ḥᵃberim* and *'amme ha-'aretz*.

He that undertakes to be trustworthy must give tithe from what he eats and from what he sells and from what he buys [to sell

again]; and he may not be the guest of an *'am ha-'aretz*. R. Judah
says: Even he that is the guest of an *'am ha-'aretz* may still be
5 reckoned trustworthy. They replied: He would not be trustworthy
in what concerns himself; how then could he be trustworthy in
what concerns others?

He that undertakes to be an Associate may not sell to an *'am ha-
'aretz* [foodstuff that is] wet or dry, or buy from him [foodstuff
10 that is] wet; and he may not be the guest of an *'am ha-'aretz* nor may
he receive him as a guest in his own raiment. R. Judah says: Nor
may he rear small cattle or be profuse in vows or levity or contract
uncleanness because of the dead, but he should minister in the
House of Study. They said to him: These things come not within
15 the scope of the subject [of the Associate].

If [they that undertake to be Associates are] bakers, the Sages
lay upon them only the duty of settling apart [from *demai*-produce]
enough for Heave-offering of Tithe and Dough-offering. If [they
are] shopkeepers, they may not sell *demai*-produce. All that deal in
20 large quantities may sell *demai*-produce. Who are they that deal
in large quantities? The like of wholesale merchants and dealers in
grain.

l. 1 *He that undertakes to be trustworthy*; not (it seems) a member of a society of
ḥaberim, but "one who can be relied upon in matters of tithes and *Tᵉrumah*"
(Jastrow, *s.v.* נאמן).

l. 9 *Wet*. Wetness predisposes foodstuffs to uncleanness.

l. 11 *R. Judah* by his additional requirements changes the character of associate-
ship; the majority however insist that it remains primarily levitical and
ceremonial.

l. 17 *Demai*. See pp. 154f. (**149**).

G. *Proselytes*

The missionary activity of Judaism is attested in the gospels (Matt.
23. 15), and in Acts we meet repeatedly not only full proselytes
(2. 10; 6. 5; 13. 43), but also those devout "God-fearers" (σεβόμενοι,
13. 43, 50; 16. 14; 17. 4, 17; 18. 7; cf. p. 136 (**125**)) who were attracted
by the worship, theology, and ethics of the synagogue but could not
bring themselves to take the final step of circumcision, by which they
would have cut themselves off from their own people and race. Non-
Jewish authors, and Roman laws against circumcision, also attest the
practice of proselytization.

In general (there are a few exceptions) the Rabbinic literature is
friendly to proselytes. See **128** above. Their courage and faith in joining
the ranks of Israel were esteemed.

166 *Numbers Rabbah* 8. 3. The Holy One loves the proselytes exceedingly. To what is the matter like? To a king who had a number of sheep and goats which went forth every morning to the pasture, and returned in the evening to the stable. One day a stag joined the flock
5   and grazed with the sheep, and returned with them. Then the shepherd said to the king, "There is a stag which goes out with the sheep and grazes with them, and comes home with them." And the king loved the stag exceedingly. And he commanded the shepherd, saying: "Give heed unto this stag, that no man beat it"; and when
10 the sheep returned in the evening, he would order that the stag should have food and drink. Then the shepherds said to him, "My Lord, thou hast many goats and sheep and kids, and thou givest us no directions about these, but about this stag thou givest us orders day by day." Then the king replied: "It is the custom of the sheep
15 to graze in the pasture, but the stags dwell in the wilderness, and it is not their custom to come among men in the cultivated land. But to this stag who has come to us and lives with us, should we not be grateful that he has left the great wilderness, where many stags and gazelles feed, and has come to live among us? It behoves us to be
20 grateful." So too spoke the Holy One: "I owe great thanks to the stranger, in that he has left his family and his father's house, and has come to dwell among us; therefore I order in the Law: 'Love ye the stranger' (Deut. 10. 19)".

167 *Yebamoth* 47a, *b*. For the admission of a male proselyte there were required circumcision, baptism, and (before the destruction of the Temple) sacrifice.

One who comes to be made a proselyte in the present time is to be asked: "Why dost thou come to be made a proselyte? Dost thou not know that at this time Israel is afflicted, buffeted, humiliated and harried, and that sufferings and sore trials come upon
5   them?" If he answer: "I know this, and am not worthy," they are to accept him immediately.
Then they are to instruct him in some of the lighter and some of the weightier commandments; and inform him as to the sins in regard to the corner of the field, the forgotten sheaf, the gleaning,
10 and the tithe for the poor. Then shall they teach him the penalties for transgression: "Know well that up until the time that thou hast come hither thou hast eaten the forbidden fat of cattle without incurring the sentence of excommunication; that thou hast profaned the Sabbath without incurring the penalty of lapidation. But
15 from now on if thou eat the forbidden fat of cattle thou wilt be

excommunicated; if thou profanest the Sabbath thou wilt be stoned." In the same way as they instruct him about the penalties of transgression shall they teach him the rewards for the observance of the commandments and shall say to him: "Know thou that the
20 world to come was made only for the righteous, but Israel at this present time may not experience very great good or very great afflictions." Yet one must not multiply words or go too much into detail.

If he accept, he is to be circumcised immediately and received.
25 In case of the discovery of any defect as to [a previous] circumcision, he is to be circumcised over again, and when healed brought to baptism immediately.

Two men learned in the Law shall stand near him and instruct him as to some of the lighter and some of the weightier command-
30 ments. He immerses himself and when he comes up he is in all respects an Israelite.

H. *Heretics*

A word commonly used to describe a heretic or sceptic is אפיקורוס ('*appiqoros*). The origin of the word is uncertain, but even if it was derived from a Hebrew root the coincidence of its sound with the name of the Greek thinker Epicurus must have played no small part in the development of its meaning.

168 *Sanhedrin* 10. 1. All Israelites have a share in the world to come, for it is written, *Thy people also shall be all righteous, they shall inherit the land for ever; the branch of my planting, the work of my hands that I may be glorified* (Isa. 60. 21). And these are they that have no
5 share in the world to come: he that says that there is no resurrection of the dead prescribed in the Law, and [he that says] that the Law is not from heaven, and an Epicurean. R. Akiba says: Also he that reads the heretical books, or that utters charms over a wound and says, *I will put none of the diseases upon thee which I have*
10 *put upon the Egyptians: for I am the Lord that healeth thee* (Ex. 15. 26). Abba Saul says: Also he that pronounces the Name with its proper letters.

l. 5 *He that says there is no resurrection* . . . Cf. the beliefs of the Sadducees, **115**.
l. 11 *The Name*. See above, p. 161 (**155**).

Of particular interest are the persons described as *Minim*. They at least include Jewish Christians, and the term may have been originally the name of that party, the corresponding abstract noun *Minuth* standing for their faith. There are many Rabbinic passages which refer to these sectaries; here we may quote only the twelfth of the *Eighteen Benedictions* (see above, pp. 162f. (158–64)). This was drawn up towards the close of the first century A.D. as a "test benediction"; it was one which no heretic could pronounce (like the anathemas at the end of a creed) and therefore had the effect of banning heretics from the synagogue. It has taken various forms under the activity of Christian censors of the Jewish Prayer Book. The following is probably very close to the original wording.

169 *Benediction* 12. For the renegades let there be no hope, and may the arrogant kingdom soon be rooted out in our days, and the Nazarenes and the *minim* perish as in a moment and be blotted out from the book of life and with the righteous may they not be in-
5 scribed. Blessed art thou, O Lord, who humblest the arrogant.

l. 2 *The arrogant kingdom.* Perhaps Rome.
l. 3 *And the Nazarenes,* והנוצרים, w*e*ha-notzrim. This may not have been part of the original text.

I. Theology

The theology and religion of Rabbinism cannot be sketched or illustrated within short compass. Fundamentally both were derived from the Old Testament, but they were developed on lines which, though paralleled elsewhere in Judaism, were characteristic. Pursuit of the details of this development is the task of a lifetime; here a few more characteristic quotations from the tractate Aboth are given. See also 127–32, 143ff.

170 *Aboth* 3. 1. Akabya b. Mahalaleel [first century A.D.] said: Consider three things and thou wilt not fall into the hands of transgression. Know whence thou art come and whither thou art going and before whom thou art about to give account and reckoning.
5 "Whence thou art come"—from a putrid drop; "and whither thou art going"—to the place of dust, worm, and maggot; "and before whom thou art about to give account and reckoning"—before the King of kings of kings, the Holy One, blessed is he.

171 *Aboth* 4. 2. Ben Azzai [first half of second century A.D.] said: Run to fulfil the lightest duty even as the weightiest, and flee from transgression; for one duty draws another duty in its train, and one

transgression draws another transgression in its train; for the
5 reward of a duty [done] is a duty [to be done], and the reward of
one transgression is [another] transgression.

172 *Aboth* 4. 16f. R. Jacob [perhaps the teacher of R. Judah the
Patriarch—see **129**] said: This world is like a vestibule before the
world to come: prepare thyself in the vestibule that thou
mayest enter into the banqueting hall.
5   He used to say: Better is one hour of repentance and good works
in this world than the whole life of the world to come; and better
is one hour of bliss in the world to come than the whole life of this
world.

173 *Aboth* 5. 10f. There are four types among men: he that says, "What
is mine is mine and what is thine is thine"—this is the common
type, and some say that this is the type of Sodom; [he that says,]
"What is mine is thine and what is thine is mine"—he is an
5 ignorant man ('*am ha-'aretz*); [he that says,] "What is mine is
thine and what is thine is thine own"—he is a saintly man; [and
he that says,] "What is thine is mine, and what is mine is mine
own"—he is a wicked man.
   There are four types of character: easy to provoke and easy to
10 appease—his loss is cancelled by his gain; hard to provoke and
hard to appease—his gain is cancelled by his loss; hard to provoke
and easy to appease—he is a saintly man; easy to provoke and hard
to appease—he is a wicked man.

174 *Aboth* 5. 16. If love depends on some [transitory] thing, and the
[transitory] thing passes away, the love passes away too; but if it
does not depend on some [transitory] thing it will never pass away.
Which love depended on some [transitory] thing? This was the
5 love of Amnon and Tamar. And which did not depend on some
[transitory] thing? This was the love of David and Jonathan.

175 *Aboth* 5. 20. Judah b. Tema [end of the second century A.D.] said:
Be strong as the leopard and swift as the eagle, fleet as the gazelle
and brave as the lion to do the will of thy Father which is in
heaven. He used to say: The shameless are for Gehenna and the
5 shamefast for the Garden of Eden. May it be thy will, O Lord our
God and the God of our fathers, that the Temple be built speedily
in our days, and grant us our portion in thy Law with them that do
thy will.

J. *Judicial Procedure*

Legislation regarding the constitution and conduct of courts, their procedure in civil and criminal cases, their competence, authority, and sentences, is detailed and large in bulk. Here only a few specimen regulations are given. It must be remembered that conditions and regulations were not static, and that occasionally the best-intentioned rules might be disregarded. New Testament interests suggest that some rules for capital trials, the law of blasphemy, and the method of execution by stoning should be quoted.

176 *Sanhedrin* 4. 1, 3–5a; 5. 1. Non-capital and capital cases are alike in examination and inquiry, for it is written, *Ye shall have one manner of law* (Lev. 24. 22). In what do non-capital cases differ from capital cases? Non-capital cases [are decided] by three and capital cases by
5 three and twenty [judges]. Non-capital cases may begin either with reasons for acquittal or for conviction, but capital cases must begin with reasons for acquittal and may not begin with reasons for conviction. In non-capital cases they may reach a verdict either of acquittal or of conviction by the decision of a majority of one;
10 but in capital cases they may reach a verdict of acquittal by the decision of a majority of one, but a verdict of conviction only by the decision of a majority of two. In non-capital cases they may reverse a verdict either [from conviction] to acquittal or [from acquittal] to conviction; but in capital cases they may reverse a
15 verdict [from conviction] to acquittal but not [from acquittal] to conviction. In non-capital cases all may argue either in favour of acquittal or of conviction; but in capital cases all may argue in favour of acquittal but not in favour of conviction. In non-capital cases he that had argued in favour of conviction may afterward
20 argue in favour of acquittal, or he that had argued in favour of acquittal may afterward argue in favour of conviction; in capital cases he that had argued in favour of conviction may afterward argue in favour of acquittal, but he that had argued in favour of acquittal cannot afterward change and argue in favour of convic-
25 tion. In non-capital cases they hold the trial during the daytime and the verdict may be reached during the night; in capital cases they hold the trial during the daytime and the verdict also must be reached during the daytime. In non-capital cases the verdict, whether of acquittal or of conviction, may be reached the same
30 day; in capital cases a verdict of acquittal may be reached on the same day, but a verdict of conviction not until the following day. Therefore trials may not be held on the eve of a Sabbath or on the eve of a Festival-day. . . .

The Sanhedrin was arranged like the half of a round threshing-
35 floor so that they all might see one another. Before them stood the
two scribes of the judges, one to the right and one to the left, and
they wrote down the words of them that favoured acquittal and
the words of them that favoured conviction. R. Judah says: There
were three: one wrote down the words of them that favoured
40 acquittal, and one wrote down the words of them that favoured
conviction, and the third wrote down the words both of them that
favoured acquittal and of them that favoured conviction.

Before them sat three rows of disciples of the Sages, and each
knew his proper place. If they needed to appoint [another as a
45 judge], they appointed him from the first row, and one from the
second row came into the first row, and one from the third row
came into the second; and they chose yet another from the congregation and set him in the third row. He did not sit in the place of
the former, but he sat in the place that was proper for him.

50 How did they admonish the witnesses in capital cases? They
brought them in and admonished them, [saying,] "Perchance ye
will say what is but supposition or hearsay or at secondhand, or [ye
may say in yourselves], We heard it from a man that was trustworthy. Or perchance ye do not know that we shall prove you by
55 examination and inquiry? Know ye, moreover, that capital cases
are not as non-capital cases: in non-capital cases a man may pay
money and so make atonement, but in capital cases the witness is
answerable for the blood of him [that is wrongfully condemned]
and the blood of his posterity [that should have been born to him]
60 to the end of the world. . . ."

They used to prove witnesses with seven inquiries: In what week
of years? In what year? In what month? On what date in the
month? On what day? In what hour? In what place? (R. Jose
says: [They asked only,] On what day? In what hour? In what
65 place?) [Moreover they asked:] Do ye recognize him? Did ye
warn him? If a man had committed idolatry [they asked the
witnesses], What did he worship? and, How did he worship it?

l. 1 *Non-capital cases.* "Literally 'cases concerning property'; it includes all charges
not entailing penalty by death" (Danby, ad loc.).

l. 16 *All may argue,* even those who are not judges. The general effect of these
regulations is to favour the man accused of a capital offence.

l. 32 *Trials may not be held . . . on the eve of a Festival-day.* Nevertheless there
were occasions when, for special reasons, Festivals were chosen for trials.
Cf. *Sanhedrin* 11. 4.

177 Sanhedrin 7. 5. "The blasphemer" is not culpable unless he pronounces the Name itself. R. Joshua b. Karha [*c.* A.D. 150] says: On

every day [of the trial] they examined the witnesses with a
substituted name, [such as] "May Jose smite Jose". When sentence
5 was to be given they did not declare him guilty of death [on the
grounds of evidence given] with the substituted name, but they
sent out all the people and asked the chief among the witnesses
and said to him, "Say expressly what thou heardest", and he
says it; and the judges stand up on their feet and rend their gar-
10 ments, and they may not mend them again. And the second witness says, "I also heard the like", and the third says, "I also heard
the like".

l. 2 *The Name.* See p. 161 (**155**).

178 *Sanhedrin* 6. 1–4. When sentence [of stoning] has been passed they
take him forth to stone him. The place of stoning was outside [far
away from] the court, as it is written, *Bring forth him that hath
cursed outside the camp* (Lev. 24. 14). One man stands at the door of
5 the court with a towel in his hand, and another, mounted on a
horse, far away from him [but near enough] to see him. If [in the
court] one said, "I have somewhat to argue in favour of his acquittal", that man waves the towel and the horse runs and stops him
[that was going forth to be stoned]. Even if he himself said, "I
10 have somewhat to argue in favour of my acquittal", they must
bring him back, be it four times or five, provided that there is
aught of substance in his words. If then they found him innocent
they set him free; otherwise he goes forth to be stoned. A herald
goes out before him [calling], "Such-a-one, the son of such-a-one,
15 is going forth to be stoned for that he committed such or such an
offence. Such-a-one and such-a-one are witnesses against him. If
any man knoweth aught in favour of his acquittal let him come and
plead it".
        When he was about ten cubits from the place of stoning they
20 used to say to him, "Make thy confession", for such is the way of
them that have been condemned to death to make confession, for
every one that makes his confession has a share in the world to
come. For so have we found it with Achan. Joshua said to him, *My
son, give, I pray thee, glory to the Lord, the God of Israel, and make con-*
25 *fession unto him, and tell me now what thou hast done; hide it not from
me. And Achan answered Joshua and said, Of a truth I have sinned
against the Lord, the God of Israel, and thus and thus have I done*
(Joshua 7. 19). Whence do we learn that his confession made
atonement for him? It is written, *And Joshua said, Why hast thou
30 troubled us? the Lord shall trouble thee this day* (Joshua 7. 25)—*this day*
thou shalt be troubled, but in the world to come thou shalt not be

troubled. If he knows not how to make his confession they say to him, "Say, May my death be an atonement for all my sins". R. Judah says: If he knew that he was condemned because of false
35 testimony he should say, "Let my death be an atonement for all my sins excepting this sin". They said to him: If so, every one would speak after this fashion to show his innocence.

When he was four cubits from the place of stoning they stripped off his clothes. A man is kept covered in front and a woman both in
40 front and behind. So R. Judah. But the Sages say: A man is stoned naked but a woman is not stoned naked.

The place of stoning was twice the height of a man. One of the witnesses knocked him down on his loins; if he turned over on his heart the witness turned him over again on his loins. If he straight-
45 way died that sufficed; but if not, the second [witness] took the stone and dropped it on his heart. If he straightway died, that sufficed; but if not, he was stoned by all Israel, for it is written, *The hand of the witnesses shall be first upon him to put him to death and afterward the hand of all the people* (Deut. 17. 7). All that have been
50 stoned must be hanged. So R. Eliezer. But the Sages say: None is hanged save the blasphemer and the idolator. A man is hanged with his face to the people and a woman with her face towards the gallows. So R. Eliezer. But the Sages say: A man is hanged but a woman is not hanged. R. Eliezer said to them: Did not Simeon b.
55 Shetah hang women in Ashkelon? They answered: He hanged eighty women, whereas two ought not to be judged in one day. How did they hang a man? They put a beam into the ground and a piece of wood jutted from it. The two hands [of the body] were brought together and [in this fashion] it was hanged. R. José says:
60 The beam was made to lean against a wall and one hanged the corpse thereon as the butchers do. And they let it down at once; if it remained there overnight a negative command is thereby transgressed, for it is written, *His body shall not remain all night upon the tree, but thou shalt surely bury him the same day; for he that is hanged is*
65 *a curse against God* (Deut. 21. 23); as if to say: Why was this one hanged? Because he blessed the Name, and the Name of Heaven was found profaned.

l. 12 *If then they found him innocent.* Bias in favour of the accused is again inculcated.
l. 54 *Did not Simeon b. Shetah ...?* Later tradition justified Simeon's departure from the Law by saying "The time demanded it". It would be wrong to suggest that such a device was often used to cover illegal action; but it is at least possible that on other occasions (for example, on some recorded in the New Testament) what was believed to be the spirit of the Law was obeyed rather than the safeguarding letter.
l. 66 *He blessed the Name*; a euphemism for "he cursed ...".

9

PHILO

PHILO is the only Jew contemporary with the origins of Christianity who is well known to us from his own writings. The dates of his birth and death cannot be given with precision, but his life must have covered approximately the period 20 B.C.–A.D. 45. During the greater part of this time he seems to have lived quietly in Alexandria. He was wealthy and belonged to one of the leading Jewish families in Alexandria; in his old age he was employed in an important mission on behalf of his fellow-countrymen; see pp. 44–7, 137f. (45, 126). The rest of his life was, so far as we know, uneventful; and it is certain that the production of his extensive philosophical works must have required a good deal of learned leisure. There is however no reason to doubt that Philo was sufficiently acquainted with at least the religious activities of his fellow-Jews in Alexandria.

It is in his writings, not his life, that the interest of Philo for the student of early Christianity lies. These fall roughly into two parts. One set of treatises is devoted to an allegorical and homiletical exposition, discursive but, within the limits of Philo's methods, systematic, of a considerable part of the Greek text of Genesis. In substance, Philo's ideas are often far removed from his biblical text, but formally he offers us here a solid piece of verse by verse exegesis. The other set of treatises is less homogeneous, and less closely bound to the text of Scripture. It contains biographies (for example, of Moses); books on particular Old Testament laws (for example, the Decalogue); more strictly philosophical writings, and two historical works.

A. *Philo's Faithfulness to the Law*

Philo, as a philosophical writer, made much use of non-Jewish material; yet, unlike some Hellenistic Jews, he never ceased to be a Jew, and to maintain the strict observance of the national laws.

179 *De Mig.* 89–93. There are some who, regarding laws in their literal sense in the light of symbols of matters belonging to the intellect,

are overpunctilious about the latter, while treating the former
with easy-going neglect. Such men I for my part should blame for
5 handling the matter in too easy and off-hand a manner: they ought
to have given careful attention to both aims, to a more full and
exact investigation of what is not seen and in what is seen to be
stewards without reproach. As it is, as though they were living
alone by themselves in a wilderness, or as though they had become
10 disembodied souls, and knew neither city nor village nor household
nor any company of human beings at all, overlooking all that the
mass of men regard, they explore reality in its naked absoluteness.
These men are taught by the sacred word to have thought for good
repute, and to let go nothing that is part of the customs fixed by
15 divinely empowered men greater than those of our time.

It is quite true that the Seventh Day is meant to teach the power
of the Unoriginate and the non-action of created beings. But let
us not for this reason abrogate the laws laid down for its observance, and light fires or till the ground or carry loads or institute
20 proceedings in court or act as jurors or demand the restoration
of deposits or recover loans, or do all else that we are permitted
to do as well on days that are not festival seasons. It is true also
that the Feast is a symbol of gladness of soul and of thankfulness to
God, but we should not for this reason turn our backs on the
25 general gatherings of the year's seasons. It is true that receiving
circumcision does indeed portray the excision of pleasure and all
passions, and the putting away of the impious conceit, under which
the mind supposed that it was capable of begetting by its own
power: but let us not on this account repeal the law laid down for
30 circumcising. Why, we shall be ignoring the sanctity of the
Temple and a thousand other things, if we are going to pay heed
to nothing except what is shown us by the inner meaning of
things. Nay, we should look on all these outward observances as
resembling the body, and their inner meanings as resembling the
35 soul. It follows that, exactly as we have to take thought for the
body, because it is the abode of the soul, so we must pay heed to
the letter of the laws. If we keep and observe these, we shall gain
a clearer conception of those things of which these are the symbols;
and besides that we shall not incur the censure of the many and
40 the charges they are sure to bring against us.

l. 1 *There are some* . . . Thus Philo was not alone in his allegorical treatment of the
Pentateuch; and some of his fellow-allegorists went further than he did,
and disregarded the literal sense of the laws.

l. 2 *Matters belonging to the intellect.* Philo is here using Platonic language; the
laws literally understood belong to the world of phenomena, while their

inward meaning belongs to the world of ideas. But Philo has no intention of belittling the phenomenal world.

l. 13 *The sacred word* (λόγος). The plain meaning of the laws must not be neglected because men live in society. The "sacred word" here means primarily the Scriptures, but it moves over to a wider meaning, and the "divinely empowered" men (primarily Moses) are spoken of in terms of the Stoic sage, who lives according to reason (λόγος).

l. 16 *The power of the Unoriginate.* The Sabbath is really a witness to the eternal activity of God (cf. John 5. 17 and contrast the notion that God himself keeps the Sabbath, e.g. Jubilees 2. 19).

l. 23 *The Feast.* Philo does not say which feast he means, and it is possible that the word should be translated "The keeping of feasts". In Rabbinic usage "the feast" commonly means Tabernacles. If the reference is not general, one of the "Pilgrim Feasts" (see pp. 155–9) is probably meant.

l. 26 *Circumcision.* In the somewhat later Judaism which is clearly known from the Rabbinic sources circumcision was demanded of all proselytes, but it is possible that earlier the demand was sometimes waived. In Josephus *Ant.* xx. 17ff. a conversion to Judaism is recorded in which circumcision was not required; in *Yebamoth* 46a there is a discussion (which may be dated at about A.D. 100) on the question whether baptism without circumcision, or circumcision without baptism availed to make a proselyte, but the almost universal view was that both were necessary.

l. 31 *Temple.* It is worth noting the provincial Jew's interest in the Temple which he so rarely saw.

l. 39 *The censure of the many.* It may be inferred that both the allegorists and those who resisted their treatment of Scripture were fairly numerous. Philo characteristically seeks to mediate between these two extreme positions.

B. *His Philosophical Eclecticism*

Perhaps more influential in Philo's day than any strongly marked philosophical system was the eclectic method which was fostered by the mixing of nations and the flux of ideas in the early Empire. Platonism, Stoicism, and Neo-Pythagoreanism contributed complementary elements to the general intellectual atmosphere of the time; they can hardly be regarded as rivals for the whole-hearted allegiance of thinking men. Philo, with no great discrimination, selects from his knowledge of pagan thought any argument that will serve his turn.

PLATONISM

180 *De Opif. M.* 15f. Philo is writing of the first day of creation.

We must recount as many as we can of the elements embraced in it. To recount them all would be impossible. Its pre-eminent element is the intelligible world, as is shown in the treatise dealing

with the "One". For God, being God, assumed that a beautiful
5 copy would never be produced apart from a beautiful pattern,
and that no object of perception would be faultless which was
not made in the likeness of an original discerned only by the
intellect. So when he willed to create this visible world he first
fully formed the intelligible world, in order that he might have
10 the use of a pattern wholly God-like and incorporeal in producing the material world, as a later creation, the very image of
an earlier, to embrace in itself objects of perception of as many
kinds as the other contained objects of intelligence.

l. 3 *The intelligible world.* The adjective is used by Plato, and the phrase signifies
the world of ideas, of which, according to Plato, the phenomenal world
(the objects of perception, l. 12) is but a copy. It is important to note that
Philo professes to find this world of ideas in Gen. 1.

l. 4 *The "One".* This treatise is not extant.

l. 10 *Incorporeal.* The Platonic doctrine which Philo is handling in this paragraph
led very quickly to an ethical dualism between matter and spirit. Philo's
firm adherence to an essentially realist Judaism shielded him to some extent
from this kind of dualism.

181 *Leg. Alleg.* i. 70–3. In this paragraph Philo describes the soul as
threefold, a division thoroughly Platonic; cf. Plato, *Timaeus* 69C,
Republic iv. 439D. He proceeds with a mythical picture of the chariot of
the soul which is taken directly from *Phaedrus* 246ff., while the location
of the various faculties in parts of the body is borrowed from *Timaeus*
69E, 90A, though it is not without parallels in the psychological
language of the Old Testament.

[Philo is allegorizing the rivers of Gen. 2. 10–14]. It is worth
inquiring why courage is mentioned in the second place, self-
mastery in the third, and prudence in the first, and why he has not
set forth a different order of the virtues. We must observe, then,
5 that our soul is threefold, and has one part that is the seat of
reason, another that is the seat of high spirit, and another that is
the seat of desire. And we discover that the head is the place and
abode of the reasonable part, the breast of the passionate part, the
abdomen of the lustful part; and that to each of the parts a virtue
10 proper to it has been attached; prudence to the reasonable part,
for it belongs to reason to have knowledge of the things we ought
to do and of the things we ought not; courage to the passionate
part; and self-mastery to the lustful part. For it is by self-mastery
that we heal and cure our desires. As, then, the head is the first and
15 highest part of the living creature, the breast of the second, and
the abdomen the third, and again of the soul the reasoning

faculty is first, the high-spirited second, the lustful third: so too of the virtues, first is prudence which has its sphere in the first part of the soul which is the domain of reason, and in the first part of
20 the body, namely the head; and second is courage, for it has its seat in high spirit, the second part of the soul, and in the breast, the corresponding part of the body; and third self-mastery, for its sphere of action is the abdomen, which is of course the third part of the body, and the lustful faculty, to which has been assigned the
25 third place in the soul.

"*The fourth river*", he says, "*is Euphrates*". "Euphrates" means "fruitfulness", and is a figurative name for the fourth virtue, justice, a virtue fruitful indeed and bringing gladness to the mind. When, then, does it appear? When the three parts of the soul are
30 in harmony. Harmony for them is the dominance of the more excellent; for instance, when the two, the high-spirited and the lustful, are guided by the reasoning faculty as horses by their driver, then justice emerges; for it is justice for the better to rule always and everywhere, and for the worse to be ruled: and the
35 reasoning faculty is better, the lustful and the high-spirited the inferior. Whenever, on the other hand, high spirit and desire turn restive and get out of hand, and by the violence of their impetus drag the driver, that is the reason, down from his seat and put him under the yoke, and each of these passions gets hold of the reins,
40 injustice prevails. For it cannot but be that owing to the badness and want of skill of the driver, the team is swept down precipices and gullies, just as by experience and skill it must needs be brought safely through.

ll. 2f. The virtues prudence, courage, and self-mastery are fancifully derived from the names of the rivers Pheison, Geon, and Tigris (which flows over against the Assyrians). These three (together with justice, l. 28) are the cardinal virtues of Platonism.

l. 26 "*Euphrates*" *means* "*fruitfulness*". See below (pp. 182f.) on Philo's use of etymological arguments. Here his etymology is almost certainly wrong.

STOICISM

Much of Philo's ethical teaching, and from time to time his anthropology also, shows clear traces of Stoic origins. The passages printed below are perhaps even more significant, for they show the interpretation of a fundamental element of Judaism—Law—in terms of a fundamental concept of Stoicism, Nature, the vital and regulative power of the universe.

182 *De Opif. M.* 3, 8f. His exordium is one that excites our admiration
in the highest degree. It consists of an account of the creation of
the world, implying that the world is in harmony with the Law,
and the Law with the world, and that the man who observes the
5 Law is constituted thereby a loyal citizen of the world, regulating
his doings by the purpose and will of Nature, in accordance with
which the entire world itself also is administered. . . .

Moses, both because he had attained the very summit of philosophy, and because he had been divinely instructed in the greater
10 and most essential part of Nature's lore, could not fail to recognize
that the universal must consist of two parts, one part active Cause
and the other passive object; and that the active Cause is the
perfectly pure and unsullied Mind of the universe, transcending
virtue, transcending knowledge, transcending the good itself and
15 the beautiful itself; while the passive part is in itself incapable of
life and motion, but, when set in motion and shaped and quickened
by Mind, changes into the most perfect masterpiece, namely this
world. Those who assert that this world is unoriginate uncon-
sciously eliminate that which of all incentives to piety is the most
20 beneficial and the most indispensable, namely providence.

l. 1 *His exordium.* The *de Opificio Mundi* is the first work in Philo's systematic
exposition of Genesis (see above), and in it he comments upon the seven
days of creation, adding notes on Gen. 2. 4–7. Unlike some lawgivers,
Moses (he says) begins his code with a cosmogony—a very significant fact,
according to Philo, for it shows that the detailed laws which follow are not
arbitrary but arise out of the fundamental Natural Law.

l. 5 *Citizen of the world*—a very characteristic Stoic term; see pp. 71f. (**76**).

l. 6 *Regulating his doings by the purpose and will of Nature.* This was the Stoic ideal
of the wise and virtuous life. Philo—always ready to identify Judaism with
the best wisdom of the Greeks—asserts that the man who practises the Law
of Moses achieves the ideal of the Stoic sage.

l. 8 *Moses.* The giver of the Law, obedience to which means living according to
Nature, is naturally presented as the greatest of philosophers.

l. 11 *Active Cause . . . passive object.* The distinction between cause and object
belongs to the Stoic view of the universe; it should be compared with the
use we have already seen Philo making of the Platonic framework of ideal
and phenomenal.

l. 13 *Mind* (νοῦς). One of Philo's most frequent terms for God; it allowed a
rapprochement between the Stoic and Platonic categories mentioned in the
last note, and also led to the doctrine of providence (πρόνοια) which was
equally important in Stoicism and Judaism.

NEO-PYTHAGOREANISM

Philo's indebtedness to this school of thought is perhaps less deep
than his relation to Platonism and Stoicism, which seem to have

affected the substance of his thinking. But from time to time at least the form of his writing has been moulded by Neo-Pythagorean methods; note especially his fantastic discussions of the significance of numbers.

183 *De Opif. M.* 99f. Philo is discussing the significance of the number 7.

So august is the dignity inherent by nature in the number 7, that it has a unique relation distinguishing it from all the other numbers within the decade: for of these some beget without being begotten, some are begotten but do not beget, some do both these,
5 both beget and are begotten: 7 alone is found in no such category. We must establish this assertion by giving proof of it. Well then, 1 begets all the subsequent numbers while it is begotten by none whatever: 8 is begotten by twice 4, but begets no number within the decade: 4 again holds the place of both, both of parents and of
10 offspring; for it begets 8 by being doubled, and is begotten by twice 2. It is the nature of 7 alone, as I have said, neither to beget nor to be begotten. For this reason other philosophers liken this number to the motherless and virgin Nike, who is said to have appeared out of the head of Zeus, while the Pythagoreans liken it
15 to the chief of all things: for that which neither begets nor is begotten remains motionless; for creation takes place in movement, since there is movement both in that which begets and in that which is begotten, in the one that it may beget, in the other that it may be begotten. There is only one thing that neither causes
20 motion nor experiences it, the original Ruler and Sovereign. Of him 7 may be fitly said to be a symbol. Evidence of what I say is supplied by Philolaus in these words: "There is, he says, a supreme Ruler of all things, God, ever One, abiding, without motion, himself [alone] like unto himself, different from all others."

l. 3 *Beget . . . begotten.* That is, they may be factorized; or (*or,* and) are themselves factors of numbers in the first decade.
l. 16 *Motionless.* The freedom of God from all motion, and thus from all experience or passibility, was a doctrine common to Platonism and Pythagoreanism.
l. 22 *Philolaus.* A Pythagorean philosopher of the fifth century B.C.

EPICUREANISM

On Philo's objection to the Epicurean philosophy see the next passage, **184.**

C. *The Allegorical Method*

It has already been pointed out that one of Philo's principal aims was to read the doctrines of Hellenistic religious philosophy out of the canonical documents of Judaism. This could hardly be the easiest of tasks, since the doctrines Philo wished to find were not contained in the sources in which he sought them. They existed in Philo's mind, and the means by which he transferred them from their place of origin to the place where he hoped to find them was Allegory.

Allegorical exegesis, which was by no means confined to Judaism, was widely practised in the Hellenistic age. It arose partly out of the undoubted fact that some of the earlier philosophers had written with intentional obscurity; partly out of the longing of somewhat enervated minds for the authority of the great ones of the past; and partly out of the conviction that philosophy was superior to narrative, and that the reputation of Homer and other poets must be salvaged by finding hidden meanings in their sometimes all too vulgar stories. When Philo wished to fashion the Old Testament into something its authors had not intended, the allegorical tool lay ready to hand; and it must be admitted that he used it with skill, and that sometimes the results are pleasing and effective, though quite unconvincing as exegesis.

184 *De Post. Caini* 1–11. "*And Cain went out from the face of God, and dwelt in the land of Naid, over against Eden*" (Gen. 4. 6). Let us here raise the question whether in the books in which Moses acts as God's interpreter we ought to take his statements figuratively,
5 since the impression made by the words in their literal sense is greatly at variance with truth. For if the Existent Being has a face, and he that wishes to quit its sight can with perfect ease remove elsewhere, what ground have we for rejecting the impious doctrines of Epicurus, or the atheism of the Egyptians, or the mythical
10 plots of play and poem of which the world is full? For a face is a piece of a living creature, and God is a whole not a part, so that we shall have to assign to him the other parts of the body as well, neck, breasts, hands, feet, to say nothing of the belly and genital organs, together with the innumerable inner and outer organs. And if
15 God has human forms and parts, he must needs also have human passions and experiences. For in the case of these organs, as in all other cases, Nature has not made idle superfluities, but aids to the weakness of those furnished with them. And she adjusts to them, according to their several needs, all that enables them to render

20 their own special services and ministries. But the Existent Being
is in need of nothing, and so, not needing the benefit that parts
bestow, can have no parts at all.

And whence does Cain "go out"? From the palace of the Lord
of all? But what dwelling apparent to the senses could God have,
25 save this world, for the quitting of which no power or device
avails? For all created things are enclosed and kept within itself by
the circle of the sky. Indeed the particles of the deceased break up
into their original elements and are again distributed to the various
forces of the universe out of which they were constituted, and the
30 loan which was lent to each man is repaid, after longer or shorter
terms, to Nature his creditor, at such time as she may choose to
recover what she herself had lent.

Again he that goes out from someone is in a different place from
him whom he leaves behind. [If, then, Cain goes out from God],
35 it follows that some portions of the universe are bereft of God. Yet
God has left nothing empty or destitute of himself, but has completely filled all things.

Well, if God has not a face, transcending as he does the
peculiarities that mark all created things; if he is to be found not
40 in some particular part only, seeing that he contains all and is not
himself contained by anything; if it is impossible for some part of
this world to remove from it as from a city, seeing that nothing has
been left over outside it; the only thing left for us to do is to make
up our minds that none of the propositions put forward is literally
45 intended and to take the path of figurative interpretation so dear to
philosophical souls. Our argument must start in this way. If it is a
difficult thing to remove out of sight of a mortal monarch, must it
not be a thousandfold more difficult to quit the vision of God and
be gone, resolved henceforth to shun the sight of him; in other
50 words to become incapable of receiving a mental picture of him
through having lost the sight of the soul's eye? Men who have
suffered this loss under compulsion, overwhelmed by the force of
an inexorable power, deserve pity rather than hatred. But those
who have of their own free choice turned away and departed from
55 the Existent Being, transcending the utmost limit of wickedness
itself—for no evil could be found equivalent to it—these must pay
no ordinary penalties, but such as are specially devised and far
beyond the ordinary. Now no effort of thought could hit upon a
penalty greater and more unheard of than to go forth into banish-
60 ment from the Ruler of the Universe.

Adam, then, is driven out by God; Cain goes out voluntarily.
Moses is showing us each form of moral failure, one of free choice,

the other not so. The involuntary act, not owing its existence to our deliberate judgement, is to obtain later on such healing as the
65 case admits of, *"for God shall raise up another seed in place of Abel whom Cain slew"* (Gen. 4. 25). This seed is a male offspring, Seth or "Watering", raised up to the soul whose fall did not originate in itself. The voluntary act, inasmuch as it was committed with forethought and of set purpose, must incur woes for ever beyond
70 healing. For even as right actions that spring from previous intention are of greater worth than those that are involuntary, so, too, among sins those which are involuntary are less weighty than those which are voluntary.

l. 4 *Figuratively* (τροπικώτερον). The word is a common one in Philo for his own method of treating the biblical text. He proceeds to give the principal ground for this treatment: the text as it stands is nonsense. God has not a face, and it is impossible to "go out from" him. Consequently, Moses, the inspired sage, must have meant something other than he appeared to have said. It was in precisely this way that the Hellenistic writers allegorized the anthropomorphisms of Homer.

l. 8 *The impious doctrines of Epicurus.* Philo means his anthropomorphism. It is doubtful whether he is fair in his judgement of Epicurus, but he always mentions him unfavourably. Cf. p. 166.

l. 9. *The atheism of the Egyptians.* The Egyptians were frequently blamed by philosophical writers for their worship of animals. But if we say, or imply, that God has a face how are we better than those who see him in a cat?

l. 20 *The Existent Being* (τὸ ὄν). This philosophical term for God is probably connected in Philo's mind with Ex. 3. 14 (see below, p. 209).

l. 45 *The path of figurative interpretation so dear to philosophical souls.* Philo certainly does not think of himself as a pioneer in allegorical work; he has predecessors and colleagues.

l. 61 *Adam, then, . . . Cain goes out voluntarily.* It is important to note that the use Philo makes of his allegorical method, once he has justified it, is ethical rather than metaphysical. This is often so; his allegorizing is akin to the Rabbinic Haggadah (see p. 145).

D. *Etymological Arguments*

These should perhaps be regarded as a special case of allegory. The question whether they reveal ignorance or knowledge of Hebrew is hardly capable of an answer. The etymologies are often very fanciful, and quite incorrect, but so sometimes are those of the Rabbis, who undoubtedly knew Hebrew.

185 *De Abrahamo* 81ff. What has been said is attested by the alteration and change in his name, for his original name was Abram, but

afterwards he was addressed as Abraham [*Greek*, Abraam]. To the
ear there was but the duplication of one letter, alpha, but in fact
5 and in the truth conveyed this duplication showed a change of
great importance. Abram is by interpretation "uplifted father";
Abraham, "elect father of sound". The former signifies one called
astrologer and meteorologist, one who takes care of the Chaldean
tenets as a father would of his children. The latter signifies the Sage,
10 for he uses "sound" as a figure for spoken thought and "father"
for the ruling mind, since the inward thought is by its nature
father of the uttered, being senior to it, the secret begetter of what
it has to say. "Elect" signifies the man of worth, for the worthless
character is random and confused, while the good is elect, chosen
15 out of all for his merits.

ll. 2f. *Abram . . . Abraham.* The reference is to Gen. 17. 5. An etymology is given
in the biblical text ("father of a multitude of nations"), but it is certainly
mistaken. It is probably wrong to seek any difference in meaning at all; the
longer name seems to be an orthographical variant of the shorter.

l. 6 *Uplifted father.* The true meaning of Abram seems to be "My father (a
divine title) is exalted", or "My father is the Exalted One" (both divine
titles).

l. 7 *Elect father of sound.* How Philo derived this meaning from Abraham is not
clear; possibly he was using traditional material.

l. 8. *Astrologer.* The Rabbinic literature also knows a tradition that Abraham
before he was called by God was an astrologer (see e.g. *Shabbath* 156a).

l. 10 *Spoken thought* (τὸν προφορικὸν λόγον). For Philo's conception of the Logos
see below. The relation of the outgoing word, or spoken thought, to the
inward word or reason (ἐνδιάθετος λόγος), or mind (νοῦς), is here made
very clear. In the present passage, mind, inward thought, and outward
word are all human. But if the νοῦς becomes the mind which creates and
upholds all things, then the προφορικὸς λόγος naturally undergoes a
corresponding transformation into the divine Word.

E. *Philo's Doctrine of the Logos and other intermediate Beings*

To speak of Philo's "doctrine" of the Logos is certainly misleading
if by doctrine is meant an articulated and thoroughly thought-out
system. The background of his thought, and therefore the thought
itself, is not simple. The Logos played a considerable part in the Stoic
account of the universe (see p. 61), and there can be no doubt that
Philo writes under the influence of Stoic ideas. Not that these can be
defined with precision: the Stoics speak of a λόγος σπερματικός
(seminal reason) which is the life-giving, constitutive factor in all
existence, through which alone plants, animals and men have the life

proper to them; they speak also of a λόγος ἐνδιάθετος (immanent reason; see above) and a λόγος προφορικός (expressed reason; see above). These last may belong to God (so far as the Stoic system may be said to have a God), or to men. Men themselves think, and may express their thought to others; and it is this very faculty that relates them to God (or the universe). This Stoic Logos, then, is a quasi-physical principle of life, which is capable of being crystallized into concrete expressions of life. There is also, however, a Platonic element in Philo's use of Logos, which comes to particularly clear expression in the account of creation at *de Opif. M.* 24f., where the thought is as follows. When man surveys the physical universe there rises to his mind the thought of an ideal universe, of which the phenomenal world is but a copy. This ideal universe is called the κόσμος νοητός (since it exists in the mind, νοῦς). But, Philo urges, this ideal universe has an existence prior to our thought of it; it is in fact the thought of the divine mind which was before the creation of the visible world and was the means by which the visible world was made. This "archetypal seal" (ἀρχέτυπος σφραγίς) may be called ὁ τοῦ θεοῦ λόγος, the Logos of God. In this identification Philo was no doubt influenced by the biblical cosmogony, in which creation is effected by the powerful word (or speech) of God. Here Philo's thought is in close contact with Jewish speculation about Wisdom; see pp. 216–21 (**208**).

The passage now to be quoted is one of very many; it is perhaps more biblical than most of Philo's references to the Logos.

186 *Quis R. d. Heres?* 205f. To his Word, his chief messenger, highest in age and honour, the Father of all has given the special prerogative, to stand on the border and separate the creature from the Creator. This same Word both pleads with the immortal as sup-
5 pliant for afflicted mortality and acts as ambassador of the ruler to the subject. He glories in this prerogative and proudly describes it in these words "*and I stood between the Lord and you*", that is neither uncreated as God, nor created as you, but midway between the two extremes, a surety to both sides; to the parent, pledging the
10 creature that it should never altogether rebel against the rein and choose disorder rather than order; to the child, warranting his hopes that the merciful God will never forget his own work. For "I am the harbinger of peace to creation from that God whose will is to bring wars to an end, who is ever the guardian of peace."

l. 1 *Chief messenger*, literally, *archangel*. The word seems to be of biblical origin; that is, Philo is identifying his Logos with the Old Testament "angel of the Lord".

l. 3 *To stand on the border*. The Logos is mediator; he mediates between creature and Creator both ontologically (since he is neither created nor creating) and epistemologically (since he brings to men knowledge of God, and of their relation to God).

l. 4 *Suppliant*. This description of the Logos recalls several New Testament statements about both Christ and the Holy Spirit, who make intercession for men. But it must be inferred from the following lines that the Logos is able to evoke God's mercy as being in himself a proof that men, who partake in him, are ultimately rational and will not altogether revolt from God.

l. 7. *I stood between the Lord and you* (Deut. 5. 5). Philo ignores the fact that these words were spoken by Moses. It is true that in the Targum of Onkelos the verse is paraphrased, "I stood between the Memra (word) of the Lord and you", but in this form the text is even further from what Philo wishes it to mean.

The Logos is not the only intermediate being in Philo's view of the universe. Subordinate to him there are also the Powers (δυνάμεις). If it is difficult to make precise statements about the personality and functions of the Logos it is impossible to make them about the Powers. They are partly personifications of divine attributes, partly emanations from God's being; but they derive substance, as it were, from the common belief of antiquity in angels and demons.

In the following passage Philo allegorizes the narrative (Gen. 18) of the three travellers entertained by Abraham.

187 *De Abrahamo* 119–22. Here we may leave the literal exposition and begin the allegorical. Spoken words contain symbols of things apprehended by the understanding only. When, then, as at noontide God shines around the soul, and the light of the mind fills it
5   through and through and the shadows are driven from it by the rays which pour all around it, the single object presents to it a triple vision, one representing the reality, the other two the shadows reflected from it. Our life in the light which our senses perceive gives us a somewhat similar experience, for objects
10 standing or moving often cast two shadows at once. No one, however, should think that the shadows can be properly spoken of as God. To call them so is loose speaking, serving merely to give a clearer view of the fact which we are explaining, since the real truth is otherwise. Rather, as anyone who has approached nearest
15 to the truth would say, the central place is held by the Father of the Universe, who in the sacred scriptures is called he that IS as his proper name, while on either side of him are the senior potencies, the nearest to him, the creative and the kingly. The title of the

former is God, since it made and ordered the All; the title of the
20 latter is Lord, since it is the fundamental right of the maker to rule
and control what he has brought into being. So the central Being
with each of his potencies as his squire presents to the mind which
has vision the appearance sometimes of one, sometimes of three:
of one, when that mind is highly purified and passing beyond not
25 merely the multiplicity of other numbers, but even the dyad which
is next to the unit, presses on to the ideal form which is free from
mixture and complexity, and being self-contained needs nothing
more; of three, when, as yet uninitiated into the highest mysteries,
it is still a votary of the minor rites and unable to apprehend the
30 Existent alone by itself and apart from all else, but only through its
actions, as either creative or ruling.

l. 2 *The allegorical.* The literal exposition drew out the example of Abraham's
hospitality. Philo now seeks the underlying truth.

l. 7 *A triple vision.* Philo's similitude is not happy; it has been made to fit his
exposition. Two of the travellers, he means, are but shadows of the third.
He goes on to point out that the shadows (which later he will call Powers)
are not to be spoken of as God.

l. 16 *He that IS.* See above, p. 181 (**184**, l. 20), where however the neuter, and
therefore less personal form is used, as it is below (l. 30, the Existent).

ll. 19f. *God . . . Lord* (θεός . . . κύριος). Philo of course knows well that these
two names are used in the Greek Old Testament; but while all names are
inadequate, ὁ ὤν (He that IS) is that which best expresses God in his absoluteness. "God" and "Lord" reveal him to men in his functions and attributes.
"God" describes God's creative and ordering power (ἡ ποιητικὴ δύναμις);
"Lord" suggests his sovereign power (ἡ βασιλικὴ δύναμις).

l. 28 *The highest mysteries.* For this metaphorical language see below, pp. 188f.
(**190**f.).

F. *Philo's own Religion and Ethics*

It is possible to criticise Philo's theology and philosophy, especially
on grounds of consistency; but it is impossible to mistake the sincere
piety without which none of his works would have been written.
Moral exhortation is thrown out on page after page of his works, and
it would be difficult to illustrate in short compass the Stoic-Jewish
ethics which were the guide of his life. It must be sufficient to quote two
passages which illustrate, first, the ideal of humble dependence upon
God which is certainly the noblest contribution Philo makes to the
history of religion, and, second, the moments of ecstatic illumination
which brought him into communion with God and inspired his
literary activity.

188 *Quis R. d. Heres?* 24–9. Philo is interpreting Gen. 15. 2.

He who says, "Master, what wilt thou give me?" virtually says no less than this, "I am not ignorant of thy transcendent sovereignty; I know the terrors of thy power; I come before thee in fear and trembling, and yet again I am confident. For thou hast vouchsafed
5 to bid me fear not; thou hast given me a tongue of instruction that I should know when I should speak (Isa. 50. 4), my mouth that was knitted up thou hast unsewn, and when thou hadst opened it, thou didst strengthen its nerves for speech; thou hast taught me to say what should be said, confirming the oracle "I will open
10 thy mouth and teach thee what thou shalt speak" (Ex. 4. 12). For who was I, that thou shouldst impart speech to me, that thou shouldst promise me something which stood higher in the scale of goods than "gift" or grace, even a "reward"? Am I not a wanderer from my country, an outcast from my kinsfolk, an alien from my
15 father's house? Do not all men call me excommunicate, exile, desolate, disfranchised? But thou, Master, art my country, my kinsfolk, my paternal hearth, my franchise, my free speech, my great and glorious and inalienable wealth. Why then shall I not take courage to say what I feel? Why shall I not inquire of thee and
20 claim to learn something more? Yet I, who proclaim my confidence, confess in turn my fear and consternation, and still the fear and confidence are not at war within me in separate camps, as one might suppose, but are blended in a harmony. I find then a feast which does not cloy in this blending, which has schooled
25 my speech to be neither bold without caution, nor cautious without boldness. For I have learnt to measure my own nothingness, and to gaze with wonder on the transcendent heights of thy loving-kindnesses. And when I perceive that I am earth or cinders or whatever is still more worthless, it is just then that
30 I have confidence to come before thee, when I am humbled, cast down to the clay, reduced to such an elemental state, as seems not even to exist.

189 *De Migr. Abr.* 34f. I feel no shame in recording my own experience, a thing I know from its having happened to me a thousand times. On some occasions, after making up my mind to follow the usual course of writing on philosophical tenets, and knowing definitely
5 the substance of what I was to set down, I have found my understanding incapable of giving birth to a single idea, and have given it up without accomplishing anything, reviling my understanding for its self-conceit, and filled with amazement at the might of him that IS to whom is due the opening and closing of the soul-wombs.

10 On other occasions, I have approached my work empty and suddenly become full, the ideas falling in a shower from above and
being sown invisibly, so that under the influence of the divine
possession I have been filled with corybantic frenzy and been un-
conscious of anything, place, persons present, myself, words
15 spoken, lines written. For I obtained language, ideas, an enjoyment
of light, keenest vision, pellucid distinctness of objects, such as
might be received through the eyes as the result of clearest
shewing.

Finally, an attempt may be made to show briefly some of the
evidence on which it has been held that Philo constructed out of
Judaism a sort of mystery religion (see Chapter 6). There are not a few
passages in which Philo makes wholesale use of language drawn from
the mystery cults. The following is representative.

190 *De Cherub.* 48f. These thoughts, ye initiated, whose ears are purified, receive into your souls as holy mysteries indeed and babble
not of them to any of the profane. Rather as stewards guard the
treasure in your own keeping, not where gold and silver, substances
5 corruptible, are stored, but where lies that most beautiful of all
possessions, the knowledge of the Cause and of virtue, and, besides
these two, of the fruit which is engendered by them both. But, if
ye meet with any of the initiated, press him closely, cling to him,
lest knowing of some still newer secret he hide it from you; stay
10 not till you have learnt its full lesson. I myself was initiated under
Moses the God-beloved into his greater mysteries, yet when I saw
the prophet Jeremiah and knew him to be not only himself enlightened, but a worthy minister of the holy secrets, I was not slow
to become his disciple.

l. 1 *Ye initiated* . . . Almost all the words in this sentence are technical.
l. 11 *Greater mysteries.* At Eleusis there were "greater" and "lesser" mysteries.
Here Philo distinguishes the greater mysteries of Moses from the lesser
mysteries of the prophets—an interesting comment upon the state of the
Old Testament canon in Philo's time.
l. 12 *I saw the prophet Jeremiah.* This kind of language is sufficient to show that
throughout the present passage Philo is speaking metaphorically; it is unnecessary therefore to assume that he is turning Judaism into a real mystery
cult.
Not only himself enlightened . . . holy secrets. Once more the language is
technical.

Philo's own view of the pagan mysteries was not likely to cause him
to produce a rival to them.

191 *De Spec. Leg.* i. 319f. He banishes from the sacred legislation the
lore of occult rites and mysteries and all such imposture and
buffoonery. He would not have those who were bred in such a
commonwealth as ours take part in mummeries and clinging on to
5 mystic fables despise the truth and pursue things which have taken
night and darkness for their province, discarding what is fit to bear
the light of day. Let none, therefore, of the followers and disciples
of Moses either confer or receive initiation to such rites. For both
in teacher and taught such action is gross sacrilege. For tell me, ye
10 mystics, if these things are good and profitable, why do you shut
yourselves up in profound darkness and reserve their benefits for
three or four alone, when by producing them in the midst of the
market-place you might extend them to every man and thus
enable all to share in security a better and happier life?

l. 1 *He banishes.* The subject is Moses, and the ground for Philo's statement is the
LXX text of Deut. 23. 17(18).

l. 9 *For tell me* . . . This argument is borrowed from contemporary philosophy,
where it appears frequently.

10

JOSEPHUS

JOSEPHUS the son of Matthias, a Jew of Palestine, was born shortly after the Crucifixion and lived till about the end of the first century. He lived through, and participated in, the great revolt and war of A.D. 66–70, and had the unusual privilege of seeing them from both the Jewish and the Roman side. He makes much (see below) of his distinguished ancestry and of his personal gifts; and the latter indeed were not small. He wrote the history of his people from the Creation to his own times, and, though it is not free from faults, his story is one of the most valuable ancient records extant. He defended his race and his religion against attack, and was in fact one of the first apologists. There is no doubt that in his literary compositions he received assistance, especially in the writing of Greek, which was not his native tongue; and it is equally certain that his actions were sometimes guided by the motives of self-preservation rather than by loyalty to his cause. But the historian of the first century before and the first century after Christ may well be grateful to Josephus both for his personal observation and for the, often important, sources he incorporates.

The extant works of Josephus are:

(1) *The Jewish War*. This work was originally written, immediately after the close of the war, in Aramaic, for the inhabitants of Upper Syria (*War* i. 3). Its aim was to urge upon these orientals the futility of further conflict with Rome, a piece of propaganda no doubt emanating from Josephus's Roman patrons (see below pp. 195f. (**195**)). Later an expanded version was drawn up in Greek, with the aid of literary assistants. On the Slavonic VS. of the *War* see below pp. 205ff. (**203ff.**).

(2) *The Antiquities of the Jews*. This much longer book, which begins with a paraphrase of the biblical narrative of creation, carries the history of the Jews from the earliest times up to the period of the *War*. It was published *c.* A.D. 93–4. It is possible to distinguish in it the work of several different assistants, who must have put Josephus's material into shape.

(3) *The Life*. This autobiography seems to have been added to a second edition of the *Antiquities* (see *Ant*. xx. 259, 266f.). It was written in reply to a rival history, drawn up by Justus of Tiberias, who not only claimed that his history was superior to all others, Josephus's included, but also made allegations against Josephus himself. Josephus replies by recapitulating his version of the story. It appears incidentally (*Life* 359f.) that Justus's history, and therefore also the *Life*, was not written till after A.D. 100.

(4) *Against Apion*. This book of Jewish apologetics was written because Josephus found that the *Antiquities* was discredited by reason of the calumnies which certain persons were spreading about the Jews. Josephus makes a reply to this anti-semitic propaganda, writing, probably, in the first years of the second century.

(5) There are indications that Josephus wrote, or intended to write, several other works, but not even fragments of them survive.

A. *Biographical Material*

It has already been indicated that we possess materials for a long and detailed life of Josephus. Here only the following essential points may be brought out.

192 *Life* 7–12. Distinguished as he was by his noble birth, my father Matthias was even more esteemed for his upright character, being among the most notable men in Jerusalem, our greatest city. Brought up with Matthias, my own brother by both parents, I
5 made great progress in my education, gaining a reputation for an excellent memory and understanding. While still a mere boy, about fourteen years old, I won universal applause for my love of letters; insomuch that the chief priests and leading men of the city used constantly to come to me for precise information on some particu-
10 lar of our ordinances. At about the age of sixteen I determined to gain personal experience of the several sects into which our nation is divided. These, as I have frequently mentioned, are three in number—the first that of the Pharisees, the second that of the Sadducees, and the third that of the Essenes. I thought that, after a
15 thorough investigation, I should be in a position to select the best. So I submitted myself to hard training and laborious exercises and passed through the three courses. Not content, however, with the experience thus gained, on hearing of one named Bannus, who dwelt in the wilderness, wearing only such clothing as trees
20 provided, feeding on such things as grew of themselves, and using frequent ablutions of cold water, by day and night, for purity's

sake, I became his devoted disciple. With him I lived for three years and, having accomplished my purpose, returned to the city. Being now in my nineteenth year I began to govern my life by the
25 rules of the Pharisees, a sect having points of resemblance to that which the Greeks call the Stoic school.

l. 1 *Noble birth.* Josephus has already (*Life* 2) claimed that his family was descended from the Hasmoneans; on whom see pp. 107–18.

l. 7 *Universal applause.* It was at about the age of fourteen that a Jewish boy entered fully upon the responsibilities of Judaism. Josephus may exaggerate his precocity, but there is no reason to doubt it altogether.

l. 11 *The several sects.* See the descriptions in *War* ii. 119; *Ant.* xiii. 171; xviii. 11; and pp. 124–7 (**115**). In trying to make the "sects" (αἱρέσεις) intelligible to his Greek and Roman readers Josephus has to some extent distorted them (see below), but his descriptions are of great value; he knew them all at first hand.

l. 18 *Bannus* was clearly an ascetic; not an Essene, because he was a solitary, yet similar to the Essenes in some of his practices, especially his repeated lustrations. His desert life also calls to mind John the Baptist, but the differences also must be remembered. Bannus baptized himself, not converts, and he did not (so far as Josephus tells us) preach either the practice of righteousness or the advent of judgement and the kingdom of God.

l. 26 *The Stoic school.* The similarity between Pharisees and Stoics is in fact slight. Both groups were earnest seekers after the virtuous life, and both believed in some kind of destiny which could override man's choice; but between them lay the difference between a personal predestinating God, and an impersonal fatalism.

When Josephus was not quite thirty his career was interrupted by the outbreak of the Jewish war, in A.D. 66. Both in the *War* and in the *Life* he gives a detailed account of the part he played—and according to his own narrative it was a prominent one—in the campaigns, first on the one side, then on the other. He was soon entrusted with an important mission to Galilee.

193 *Life* 28f. After the defeat of Cestius, already mentioned, the leading men in Jerusalem, observing that the brigands and revolutionaries were well provided with arms, feared that, being without weapons themselves, they might be at the mercy of their adversaries, as in
5 fact eventually happened. Being informed, moreover, that the whole of Galilee had not yet revolted from Rome, and that a portion of it was still tranquil, they dispatched me with two other priests, Joazar and Judas, men of excellent character, to induce the disaffected to lay down their arms and to impress upon them the
10 desirability of reserving these for the picked men of the nation. The latter, such was the policy determined on, were to have their

weapons constantly in readiness for future contingencies, but should wait and see what action the Romans would take.

l. 1 *Cestius Gallus* was governor of the Roman province of Syria. When the Jewish revolutionary movement first made head he marched with his forces to put down the disturbances, but, after preliminary successes, he was disastrously defeated at the pass of Bethhoron (*War* ii. 546; November 66), to the regret of Josephus and his friends, who had no desire for a struggle with Rome (though it is perhaps not unfair to suggest that had the war turned out differently they would have had no objection to taking advantage of a Jewish victory).

l. 2 *The brigands* (λῄστας) *and revolutionaries*. These were the nationalist group who were really enthusiastic in the prosecution of the war, and as Josephus says in this passage, ultimately gained control of Jewish policy and overcame the resistance of the moderates.

l. 7 *Two other priests*. Josephus was himself a priest. It has already been noted that Josephus was descended from the Hasmoneans, the priest-kings of the previous century. It is worth noting that unlike many of the priests he was a Pharisee (see above p. 192 (**192**)).

l. 13 *What action the Romans would take*. The official Jewish policy was opportunist. A greater measure of independence was desirable, but it was not worth while to take too many risks.

Josephus's activity as a Jewish general, though skilful and resourceful (as he tells us), did not last long. He was besieged in Jotapata (a town in Galilee); and in spite of his successful use of many stratagems, the town was captured by the Romans. Josephus and a few others escaped.

194 *War* iii. 392–408. Having thus survived both the war with the Romans and that with his own friends, Josephus was brought by Nicanor into Vespasian's presence. The Romans all flocked to see him, and from the multitude crowding around the general arose
5 a hubbub of discordant voices: some exulting at his capture, some threatening, some pushing forward to obtain a nearer view. The more distant spectators clamoured for the punishment of their enemy, but those close beside him recalled his exploits and marvelled at such a reversal of fortune. Of the officers there was not one who,
10 whatever his past resentment, did not then relent at the sight of him. Titus in particular was specially touched by the fortitude of Josephus under misfortunes and by pity for his youth. As he recalled the combatant of yesterday and saw him now a prisoner in his enemy's hands, he was led to reflect on the power of fortune, the
15 quick vicissitudes of war, and the general instability of human affairs. So he brought over many Romans at the time to share his compassion for Josephus, and his pleading with his father was the main influence in saving the prisoner's life. Vespasian, however,

ordered him to be guarded with every precaution, intending
20 shortly to send him to Nero.

On hearing this, Josephus expressed a desire for a private interview with him. Vespasian having ordered all to withdraw except
his son Titus and two of his friends, the prisoner thus addressed
him: "You imagine, Vespasian, that in the person of Josephus you
25 have taken a mere captive; but I come to you as a messenger of
greater destinies. Had I not been sent on this errand by God, I knew
the law of the Jews and how it becomes a general to die. To Nero
do you send me? Why then? Think you that [Nero and] those
who before your accession succeed him will continue? You will be
30 Caesar, Vespasian, you will be Emperor, you and your son here.
Bind me then yet more securely in chains and keep me for yourself; for you, Caesar, are master not of me only, but of land and
sea and the whole human race. For myself, I ask to be punished by
stricter custody, if I have dared to trifle with the words of God."
35 To this speech Vespasian, at the moment, seemed to attach little
credit, supposing it to be a trick of Josephus to save his life.
Gradually, however, he was led to believe it, for God was already
rousing in him thoughts of empire and by other tokens foreshadowing the throne. He found, moreover, that Josephus had
40 proved a veracious prophet in other matters. For one of the two
friends present at the private interview remarked: "If these words
are not a nonsensical invention of the prisoner to avert the storm
which he has raised, I am surprised that Josephus neither predicted
the fall of Jotapata to its inhabitants nor his own captivity." To
45 this Josephus replied that he had foretold to the people of Jotapata
that their city would be captured after forty-seven days and that he
himself would be taken alive by the Romans. Vespasian, having
privately questioned the prisoners on these statements and found
them true, then began to credit those concerning himself. While
50 he did not release Josephus from his custody or chains, he presented
him with raiment and other precious gifts, and continued to treat
him with kindness and solicitude, being warmly supported by
Titus in these courtesies.

l. 1 *Both the war with the Romans*, the Roman attack on Jotapata.
l. 2 *And that with his own friends*. A number of Jewish soldiers, including Josephus,
took refuge in a cave. His suggestion of surrender to the Romans so enraged
his compatriots that they were for killing him. From this course he cleverly
dissuaded them, and urged them instead to agree to kill one another, draw-
ing lots to determine who should be killed first. As the lot fell out ("should
one say by fortune or by the providence of God?" asks Josephus) he was in
the end left alive with one other man, whom he was able to persuade to
surrender with him.

l. 3 *Vespasian*, sent by Nero to undertake the Jewish war in A.D. 66/67, himself became emperor in A.D. 69. See pp. 18f. (**15**).

l. 11 *Titus*, Vespasian's son, who succeeded him in A.D. 79.

l. 12 *His youth*. It was now A.D. 67, and Josephus was thirty.

l. 20 *Nero*, the Emperor. See pp. 15ff. (**11–14**). Josephus evidently thought that if he were sent to Rome his prospects of safety would be small.

l. 29 *You will be Caesar*. The family name Caesar had already become a title of the reigning emperor. This prophecy is reported also by Suetonius, *Vesp.* 5, and by Dio Cassius (*Epit*. lxvi. 1).

l. 38 *By other tokens*. Cf. Tacitus, *Hist*. i. 10; ii. 1. A belief (for which see Tacitus, *Hist*. v. 13, and Suetonius, *Vesp*. 4) had become current that "persons proceeding from Judaea were to become masters of the world".

In due course Josephus's prediction was fulfilled, and he was now secure in the imperial favour. He lived at Rome under the protection first of Vespasian, then of Titus. For some further information about the subsequent activities of Josephus see the short account of his literary works above. The following description of his career in Rome is given in the *Life*.

195 *Life* 422–30. When Titus had quelled the disturbances in Judaea, conjecturing that the lands which I held at Jerusalem would be unprofitable to me, because a Roman garrison was to be quartered there, he gave me another parcel of ground in the plain. On his
5 departure for Rome, he took me with him on board, treating me with every mark of respect. On our arrival in Rome I met with great consideration from Vespasian. He gave me a lodging in the house which he had occupied before he became Emperor; he honoured me with the privilege of Roman citizenship; and he
10 assigned me a pension. He continued to honour me up to the time of his depature from this life, without any abatement in his kindness towards me.

My privileged position excited envy and thereby exposed me to danger. A certain Jew, named Jonathan, who had promoted an
15 insurrection in Cyrene, occasioning the destruction of two thousand of the natives, whom he had induced to join him, on being sent in chains by the governor of the district to the Emperor, asserted that I had provided him with arms and money. Undeceived by this mendacious statement, Vespasian condemned him
20 to death, and he was delivered over to execution. Subsequently, numerous accusations against me were fabricated by persons who envied me my good fortune; but, by the providence of God, I came safe through all. Vespasian also presented me with a considerable tract of land in Judaea.

25   At this period I divorced my wife, being displeased at her behaviour. She had borne me three children, of whom two died; one, whom I named Hyrcanus, is still alive. Afterwards I married a woman of Jewish extraction who had settled in Crete. She came of very distinguished parents, indeed the most notable people in that
30 country. In character she surpassed many of her sex, as her subsequent life showed. By her I had two sons, Justus the elder, and then Simonides, surnamed Agrippa. Such is my domestic history.

The treatment which I received from the Emperors continued unaltered. On Vespasian's decease Titus, who succeeded to the
35 empire, showed the same esteem for me as did his father, and never credited the accusations to which I was constantly subjected. Domitian succeeded Titus and added to my honours. He punished my Jewish accusers, and for a similar offence gave orders for the chastisement of a slave, a eunuch and my son's tutor. He also
40 exempted my property in Judaea from taxation—a mark of the highest honour to the privileged individual. Moreover, Domitia, Caesar's wife, never ceased conferring favours upon me.

Such are the events of my whole life; from them let others judge as they will of my character.
45   Having now, most excellent Epaphroditus, rendered you a complete account of our antiquities, I shall here for the present conclude my narrative.

l. 14 *Jonathan*. Another, and somewhat fuller, account of this man's plots is given in the *War* vii. 437–50. His revolt was part of the widespread activity of the Sicarii after A.D. 70. The revolt was put down by Catullus and Jonathan burnt alive.

l. 25 *I divorced my wife, being displeased at her behaviour*. This was Josephus's second wife. He had previously married at the order of Vespasian (*Life* 414f.), but his wife, one of the women taken captive by the Romans at Caesarea, soon left him. For the Jewish law of divorce see Deut. 24. 1–4, and for its interpretation by the School of Hillel and the School of Shammai see pp. 140f. Josephus does not tell us whether he was displeased with his wife on moral or other grounds.

l. 37 *Domitian*, emperor A.D. 81–96.

l. 38 *My Jewish accusers*. Josephus's unpopularity with his compatriots is plain, and understandable.

l. 45 *Epaphroditus*. The *Life*, the work *Against Apion*, and the *Antiquities* are all dedicated to Epaphroditus, who appears to have succeeded after the death of Domitian to the position of Josephus's imperial patrons. Josephus's Epaphroditus may have been the grammarian of that name, but this is quite uncertain.

B. *Josephus on John the Baptist, Jesus Christ, and James*

A small quantity of the valuable historical material given by Josephus appears in other parts of this book (see especially Chapter 7). It is unnecessary to give a further selection here, but it will be convenient to add his famous and important references to John the Baptist, Jesus, and James the Just.

196 *Ant.* xviii. 116–19. Josephus's reference to the Baptist arises almost casually out of his account of the affairs of Herod Antipas.

> Some of the Jews thought that Herod's army had been destroyed by God as a just punishment for his treatment of John called the Baptist. Herod killed him, though he was a good man and commanded the Jews to practise virtue, by exercising justice towards
> 5 one another and piety towards God, and to come together to baptism. For the baptism would be acceptable to God if they used it, not for the putting away of certain sins, but for the purification of the body, the soul having previously been cleansed by righteousness. Now when the rest crowded together to him (for they were
> 10 greatly moved by hearing his words) Herod was afraid lest John's great influence over the people might lead to a revolt; for they seemed ready to do anything he advised. He therefore thought it much the better course to anticipate any rebellion that might arise from him by destroying him, than be involved in difficulties
> 15 through an actual revolution and then regret it. So John, a victim to Herod's suspicion, was sent to Machaerus (the fortress mentioned above), and there killed.

l. 1 *Herod's army had been destroyed by God.* The Herod in question is Herod Antipas, a son of Herod the Great and tetrarch of Galilee (see e.g. Luke 3. 1). His army had been destroyed by Aretas, king of the Nabataean Arabs, who had been enraged by Herod's treatment of his (Aretas's) daughter, to whom he was married. Herod, who wished to marry Herodias, his brother's wife, planned to divorce the daughter of Aretas; she however heard of his plans and escaped to her father, who collected an army and destroyed Herod's forces. This narrative does not agree in all particulars with that of Mark 6. 14–29; there is also a difficulty regarding its date. The defeat of Herod by Aretas took place not long before the death of Tiberius in March A.D. 37, which is long after any date that can be reasonably deduced from the gospels for the death of John. Nevertheless, Aretas may have lacked an earlier opportunity and his anger may have continued to smoulder for seven years or more.

l. 2 *John called the Baptist.* It is possible that the title was interpolated from a Christian source; but Josephus has not a little to say about John's practice of baptizing and it is not impossible that his use of the name is independent. The general picture of John that he presents is different from that of the Christian sources; the eschatological and messianic element is lacking (but see note on l. 4).

l. 3 *Herod killed him.* Josephus does not relate the "bazaar story" of Mark 6. His interests and tastes were different from those of the primitive Christian communities.

l. 4 *To practise virtue.* The evangelists (Matt. 3. 7–10=Luke 3. 7ff.; Luke 3. 10–14) provide some account of John's moral teaching; but their primary interest was in his prediction of the Coming One. Josephus, writing in Rome, would no doubt find it convenient to avoid the discussion of such matters (a Christian interpolator would not have omitted them); but in point of fact his later references to Herod's fear of a revolutionary movement show that the Baptist was concerned in messianic activity which either was, or showed the possibility of becoming, political and military.

l. 6 *Baptism . . . baptism.* Josephus uses two words, one of which (βαπτισμός) is rare in the New Testament, while the other (βάπτισις) does not occur at all. This fact does not suggest Christian influence or interpolation.

l. 7 *Not for the putting away of certain sins, but for the purification of the body.* Josephus's account hardly makes sense. The multitudes who were baptized by John did not go to Jordan to wash. There may be anti-Christian propaganda here; but compare Josephus's remark on the baptisms of the Essenes and of Bannus; see pp. 125ff., 191f. (**192**).

l. 9 *The rest.* The expression is awkward, and emendations have been proposed. The Latin *perplurima multitudo*, a very numerous multitude, gives the sense. It does not seem to be correct to distinguish between a company of ascetics who before John's ministry had practised virtue and the "rest" who subsequently joined the movement.

l. 16 *Machaerus.* The gospels do not name the place where John was killed. It is sometimes said that Herod's birthday feast would not have been held in a gloomy fortress like Machaerus; but compare *War* vii. 175 ". . . a palace with magnificently spacious and beautiful apartments".

197 *Ant.* xviii. 63f. The authenticity of Josephus's reference to Jesus as it now stands is very questionable. The passage is found in all the MSS. of the *Antiquities* (but none of these is older than the eleventh century), and was known to Eusebius (fourth century); but Origen (first half of the third century) does not seem to have read it, at least in its present form, since he says plainly that Josephus did not believe Jesus to be the Christ. It does not however follow from this fact that the whole passage is spurious. It will be indicated in the notes that several clauses could not have been written by Josephus; but when these are removed there remains a notice of Jesus comparable with that of John the Baptist, a notice from which all messianic and eschatological claims have been suppressed. It is, moreover, possible that Christian omissions as well as Christian interpolations should be allowed for; Christian writers, adding material in praise of Jesus, may quite well have omitted what they thought derogatory to his person.

About this time arose Jesus, a wise man, if indeed it be lawful to call him a man. For he was a doer of wonderful deeds, and a teacher of men who gladly receive the truth. He drew to himself

many both of the Jews and of the Gentiles. He was the Christ; and
5 when Pilate, on the indictment of the principal men among us, had
condemned him to the cross, those who had loved him at the first
did not cease to do so, for he appeared to them again alive on the
third day, the divine prophets having foretold these and ten
thousand other wonderful things about him. And even to this day
10 the race of Christians, who are named from him, has not died out.

l. 1 *About this time.* Josephus has just described two disturbances made by the
Jews under the provocation of Pilate who had (*a*) brought into Jerusalem
military standards bearing images of the emperor, (*b*) diverted Temple
funds for the building of an aqueduct. The immediately preceding passage
ends, "And so the disturbance (στάσις, cf. Mark 15. 7, *et al.*) came to an
end." It is in such a context as this that Josephus might be expected to refer
to the messianic disturbances which accompanied the execution of Jesus.

A wise man. This does not seem to be a Christian description of Jesus. Josephus
is probably "civilizing" Jesus as he did John.

If indeed it be lawful to call him a man. This, on the other hand, is almost
certainly a Christian addition. One who was not a Christian would have no
hesitation in calling Jesus a man.

l. 4 *Many . . . of the Gentiles.* Either this is a Christian interpolation, or Josephus is
writing out of his knowledge of the composition of the Church of his day.

He was the Christ. This must be a Christian interpolation; it is quite impossible
to make Josephus's words mean, "He was believed to be the Christ."

l. 5 *On the indictment . . . condemned him to the cross.* This agrees sufficiently with
the narratives of the gospels, but it is not necessarily to be ruled out as an
interpolation, especially as "those who loved him at the first" is not a
specifically Christian phrase.

l. 7 *He appeared to them . . . about him.* These words must have been written by a
Christian.

l. 10 *The race of Christians.* The expression (φῦλον) is not found in the earliest
Christian literature, though in the second century Christians are spoken of
as a "new (i.e. neither Jewish nor Gentile) race (γένος)" (*Epistle to Diognetus* 1).

198 *Ant.* xx. 200. Like the reference to John the Baptist, Josephus's
allusion to James the brother of Jesus arises out of his account of the
political history of the time. It is repeated by Eusebius (*H.E* II, xxiii.
22), who also cites in the same passage another paragraph which he (in
company with Origen) attributes to Josephus but which is not in our
MSS., and Hegesippus's, somewhat divergent, narrative of James's
death.

Ananus, therefore, being of this character, and supposing that he
had a favourable opportunity on account of the fact that Festus
was dead, and Albinus was still on the way, called together the

Sanhedrin, and brought before them the brother of Jesus, the
5 so-called Christ, James by name, together with some others, and
accused them of violating the law, and condemned them to be
stoned.

l. 1 *Ananus, being of this character.* He was a son of the Annas mentioned in the
gospels as participating in the arraignment of Jesus; Josephus has in the
context described him as exceptionally bold and reckless.

ll. 2f. *Festus ... Albinus* were successive procurators of Judaea. The latter was
particularly rapacious and unscrupulous, and did much to provoke the
revolt of A.D. 66; he took office in A.D. 62, which accordingly will be the
date of this incident.

l. 5 *The so-called Christ.* This seems to be the best rendering of the phrase in the
MSS. of Josephus (τοῦ λεγομένου χριστοῦ). It is noteworthy that Eusebius
transposes the words so as to read τοῦ Χριστοῦ λεγομένου, perhaps with the
intention of giving the sense, "who was called Christ".

l. 7 *To be stoned.* This was the normal punishment for blasphemy and certain
other offences; see *Sanhedrin* 7. 4. Hegesippus has a different and more
circumstantial account which it is worth while to compare with *Sanhedrin*
9. 6.

C. *Josephus as Apologist*

The Jews were perhaps the most favoured and the most hated race in
the Roman Empire. Their peculiarities led to incessant friction with
other races, yet they also, unlike other nations, were constantly active in
commending their religious practices to others. Their self-defence and
their zeal for their faith led to a fairly considerable literary output, of
which little remains to us. Philo (see Chapter 9) may be regarded as a
propagandist at the higher level; he was a thinker concerned to show
the unity of his own faith with the best of Greek philosophy, and to set
it forth in terminology which the Greek mind could understand and
accept. Josephus works at a lower level; he rebuts slanders, demonstrates
the antiquity of his faith, and commends the piety and virtue which it
engenders. The whole of the *Antiquities* is a kind of apology; but the
work *against Apion* shows him most clearly as an apologist. The
following passages bring out characteristic arguments.

199 *Against Apion* i. 69–72. Josephus introduces his argument for the
antiquity of his race. The Egyptians reproached the Greeks as a youthful
race; Josephus would show that the Jews were younger than neither of
these peoples.

Suppose that we were to presume to dispute the antiquity of the
Greek nation and to base our contention on the absence of any

mention of them in our literature. Would they not undoubtedly laugh us to scorn? They would, I imagine, offer the very reasons 5 which I have just given for such silence, and produce the neighbouring nations as witnesses to their antiquity. Well, that is just what I shall endeavour to do. As my principal witnesses I shall cite the Egyptians and Phoenicians, whose evidence is quite unimpeachable; for the Egyptians, the whole race without exception, 10 and among the Phoenicians the Tyrians, are notoriously our bitterest enemies. Of the Chaldaeans I could not say the same, because they are the original ancestors of our race, and this blood-relationship accounts for the mention which is made of the Jews in their annals. After producing the evidence supplied by these nations, I 15 shall then bring forward those Greek historians who have spoken of the Jews, in order to deprive our jealous enemies of even this pretext for controversy.

l. 4 *Reasons which I have just given.* The principal reasons given by Josephus for the paucity of references to the Jews in Greek authors are that the cities of the Jews lay inland, and that as a people they gave themselves rather to the cultivation of their land and the education of their children than to such activities as piracy or military aggrandizement, which might have made them better known.

l. 8 *Egyptians.* Josephus draws his evidence from Manetho, an Egyptian priest of about 300 B.C. Josephus takes over from him the well known (though inaccurate) identification of the Israelites with the Hyksos, who lived in Egypt in the second millennium B.C.

l. 8 *Phoenicians.* Here Josephus's evidence is more varied. He draws it from the archives of Tyre; a certain Dius, "an accurate historian of Phoenicia", and Menander of Ephesus.

l. 11 *Chaldaeans.* Josephus cites Berosus, a priest of the temple of Bel at Babylon, about 300 B.C.

l. 15 *Greek historians.* Josephus mentions and quotes Pythagoras, Theophrastus, Herodotus, Choerilus, Aristotle (as quoted by Clearchus), Hecataeus, and Agatharcides; then lists a number more, whose briefer allusions he does not trouble to record.

We may next take examples of the way in which Josephus rebuts slanders made against his people and their religion.

200 *Against Apion* ii. 79–85. I am no less amazed at the proceedings of the authors who supplied him with his materials, I mean Posidonius and Apollonius Molon. On the one hand they charge us with not worshipping the same gods as other people; on the other, they 5 tell lies and invent absurd calumnies about our Temple, without showing any consciousness of impiety. Yet to high-minded men nothing is more disgraceful than a lie, of any description, but

above all on the subject of a Temple of world-wide fame and commanding sanctity.

10   Within this sanctuary Apion has the effrontery to assert that the Jews kept an ass's head, worshipping that animal and deeming it worthy of the deepest reverence; the fact was disclosed, he maintains, on the occasion of the spoliation of the Temple by Antiochus Epiphanes, when the head, made of gold and worth a high price,

15   was discovered. On this I will first remark that, even if we did possess any such object, an Egyptian should be the last person to reproach us; for an ass is no worse than the cats, he-goats, and other creatures which in his country rank as gods. Next, how did it escape him that the facts convict him of telling an incredible lie?

20   Throughout our history we have kept the same laws, to which we are eternally faithful. Yet, notwithstanding the various calamities which our city, like others, has undergone, when the Temple was occupied by successive conquerors, [Antiochus] the Pious, Pompey the Great, Licinius Crassus, and most recently Titus Caesar, they

25   found there nothing of the kind, but the purest type of religion, the secrets of which we may not reveal to aliens. That the raid of Antiochus Epiphanes on the Temple was iniquitous, and that it was impecuniosity which drove him to invade it, when he was not an open enemy, that he attacked us, his allies and friends, and that he

30   found there nothing to deserve ridicule; these facts are attested by many sober historians. Polybius of Megalopolis, Strabo the Cappadocian, Nicolas of Damascus, Timagenes, Castor the chronicler, and Apollodorus all assert that it was impecuniosity which induced Antiochus, in violation of his treaties with the Jews, to

35   plunder the Temple with its stores of gold and silver. There is the evidence which Apion should have considered, had he not himself been gifted with the mind of an ass and the impudence of the dog, which his countrymen are wont to worship. An outsider can make no sense of his lies.

l. 2 *Him*, that is Apion, Josephus's adversary.

Posidonius, the famous Stoic philosopher; see pp. 61, 65 (**66f.**).

l. 3 *Apollonius Molon*, a teacher of rhetoric in the first century B.C.; he seems to have made a point of attacking the Jews, and Josephus several times replies to his charges.

l. 13 *The spoliation of the temple by Antiochus Epiphanes.* For this, cf. *Ant.* xii. 248; *War* i. 32; 1 Macc. 1; 2 Macc. 5; and see pp. 106f. (**98f.**). It took place *c.* 168 B.C.

l. 23 *[Antiochus] the Pious.* The reference must be to Antiochus VII Eusebes (or Pious), who received his title from his behaviour at the siege of Jerusalem in 135 B.C. (*Ant.* xiii. 244). The MSS. of Josephus (in Latin only at this point) read Dius, probably by confusion with Antiochus VI Theos (in Latin, Diuus).

Pompey the Great captured Jerusalem in 63 B.C. See pp. 116ff. (**107**).

l. 24 *Licinius Crassus* took the city in 54–53 B.C.

Titus Caesar, the victor of A.D. 70. See pp. 132f. (**120**).

201 *Against Apion* ii. 91–6. Apion, who is here the spokesman of others, asserts that:

Antiochus found in the Temple a couch, on which a man was re-clining, with a table before him laden with a banquet of fish of the
5 sea, beasts of the earth, and birds of the air, at which the poor fellow was gazing in stupefaction. The king's entry was instantly hailed by him with adoration, as about to procure him profound relief; falling at the king's knees, he stretched out his right hand and implored him to set him free. The king reassured him and bade him
10 tell him who he was, why he was living there, what was the meaning of his abundant fare. Thereupon, with sighs and tears, the man, in a pitiful tone, told the tale of his distress. He said that he was a Greek and that, while travelling about the province for his liveli-hood, he was suddenly kidnapped by men of a foreign race and
15 conveyed to the Temple; there he was shut up and seen by nobody, but was fattened on feasts of the most lavish description. At first these unlooked for attentions deceived him and caused him pleasure; suspicion followed, then consternation. Finally, on consulting the attendants who waited upon him, he heard of the unutterable law
20 of the Jews, for the sake of which he was being fed. The practice was repeated annually at a fixed season. They would kidnap a Greek foreigner, fatten him up for a year, and then convey him to a wood, where they slew him, sacrificed his body with their customary ritual, partook of his flesh, and, while immolating the
25 Greek, swore an oath of hostility to the Greeks. The remains of their victim were then thrown into a pit. The man (Apion continues) stated that he had now but a few days left to live, and implored the king, out of respect for the gods of Greece, to defeat this Jewish plot upon his life-blood and to deliver him from his
30 miserable predicament.

l. 3 *Antiochus*, that is, Antiochus Epiphanes. See pp. 105ff. (**97ff.**).

l. 24 *Partook of his flesh . . . swore an oath of hostility to the Greeks.* How many intelligent non-Jews believed slanders of this kind it is difficult to estimate. Behind it lie, it appears, a perversion of the Passover ritual, and the un-doubted aloofness of the Jews from the whole range of pagan life. Socially and in religion the Jews refused the ordinary tolerant give and take of the cosmopolitan life of the Mediterranean world. Their motives were not understood, and it is not altogether surprising that such tales as these, ridiculous as they are, were disseminated.

l. 30 *His miserable predicament.* So far Josephus quotes Apion. His reply is interest-ing, but so long that it must be summarized rather than quoted. The story, he points out, is simply ridiculous. Why should only Greeks be murdered? For how few Jews would the body of one Greek suffice! Why did Antiochus never produce the man? But the strongest argument lies in a plain and positive account of the Temple and its management, which are such as to make the allegations quite impossible. Josephus's account of the Temple has considerable value apart from its apologetic purpose.

Lastly we may hear Josephus at his best, extolling the religion and virtue practised among his fellow-countrymen.

202 *Against Apion* ii. 164-71. There is endless variety in the details of the customs and laws which prevail in the world at large. To give but a summary enumeration: some peoples have entrusted the supreme political power to monarchs, others to oligarchies, yet
5 others to the masses. Our lawgiver, however, was attracted by none of these forms of polity, but gave to his constitution the form of what—if a forced expression be permitted—may be termed a "theocracy", placing all sovereignty and authority in the hands of God. To him he persuaded all to look, as the author of all blessings,
10 both those which are common to all mankind, and those which they had won for themselves by prayer in the crises of their history. He convinced them that no single action, no secret thought, could be hid from him. He represented him as one, uncreated and immutable to all eternity; in beauty surpassing all
15 mortal thought, made known to us by his power, although the nature of his real being passes knowledge.

That the wisest of the Greeks learnt to adopt these conceptions of God from principles with which Moses supplied them, I am not now concerned to urge; but they have borne abundant witness to
20 the excellence of these doctrines, and to their consonance with the nature and majesty of God. In fact, Pythagoras, Anaxagoras, Plato, the Stoics who succeeded him, and indeed nearly all the philosophers appear to have held similar views concerning the nature of God. These, however, addressed their philosophy to the few, and
25 did not venture to divulge their true beliefs to the masses who had their own preconceived opinions; whereas our lawgiver, by making practice square with precept, not only convinced his own contemporaries, but so firmly implanted this belief concerning God in their descendants to all future generations that it cannot be
30 moved. The cause of his success was that the very nature of his legislation made it [always] far more useful than any other; for he did not make religion a department of virtue, but the various virtues—I mean, justice, temperance, fortitude, and mutual harmony in all things between the members of the community—
35 departments of religion. Religion governs all our actions and

occupations and speech; none of these things did our lawgiver leave unexamined or indeterminate.

l. 8 *Theocracy* (θεοκρατία). Liddell and Scott quote no other use of the word, and it seems from Josephus's own language that he has coined it. The thought that God alone is the true ruler of Israel is, of course, common in the Old Testament.

l. 18 *Principles with which Moses supplied them.* The notion that the best of Greek philosophy was plagiarized from Moses was current long before Josephus (e.g. in the Jewish apologist Aristobulus, *apud* Eusebius, *Praep. Ev.* XIII, xii.), and was taken up by the Christians (e.g. Justin, *Apol.* i. 60). There is no evidence that the Greek writers were in any way familiar with the Pentateuch.

l. 33 *Justice, temperance, fortitude, and mutual harmony.* These are the four cardinal virtues of the Platonists, except that here mutual harmony takes the place of understanding.

l. 35 *Departments of religion.* If Josephus has above quite misrepresented the relation between Greek and Jewish thought (since Hellenistic Jewish thought at least was much indebted to the philosophers) he has here seized upon a profound truth of biblical theology.

D. *The Slavonic Josephus*

In the course of the present century translations have been published of the Old Slavonic version of Josephus's *Jewish War.* This version follows in general the plan which has long been known as that of the Greek text of the *War*, but differs from it in some notable features, not least important because several of them relate to John the Baptist, Jesus, and the origins of Christianity. The question of their historical value is under debate. By some (e.g. R. Eisler, *The Messiah Jesus and John the Baptist*) it has been maintained that the Slavonic text is a translation of the original Aramaic text of the *War* (see above, p. 190), and that it is therefore of great historical importance; others, however (e.g. J. M. Creed, *Harvard Theological Review*, xxv, pp. 277–319), have held that the special features of the Slavonic Josephus are medieval in origin and worthless as evidence for the history of the first century. It is very difficult to withstand the force of Creed's arguments, but some examples of the additions made in the Slavonic version may be given. The evidence of Christian editing is easy to see.

203 (*a*) Now at that time there walked among the Jews a man in wondrous garb. He had put the hair of beasts upon his body, wherever it was not covered with his own hair; and in countenance

he was like a wild man. He came to the Jews and enticed them
5 to liberty, saying: "God has sent me to show you the way of the
law, whereby ye may be freed from many masters. And there shall
be no mortal ruling over you, save only the Highest who has
sent me." And when the people heard this they were glad, and
there went·after him the whole of Judaea which is about Jerusalem.
10 And he did nothing else to them, save that he dipped them in the
river Jordan and let them go, admonishing them to cease from evil
works. And [he said that] there would be granted to them a king
who would set them free and subject all who were not obedient,
but himself would be subject to no one. Some mocked at his words;
15 but others put faith in him.

And when they had brought him to Archelaus and the teachers
of the law were gathered together, they asked him who he was and
where he had been until then. And he answered and said: "I am a
man, and hither the divine spirit has brought me; and I feed on
20 cane and roots and wood-shavings." But when they threatened to
torture him if he did not desist from these words and deeds, he
spake nevertheless: "It is meet rather for *you* to desist from your
shameful works and to submit to the Lord your God."

And Simon, an Essene by birth, a scribe, arose in wrath and
25 spake: "We read the divine books every day, but thou, but now
come forth from the wood like a wild man, dost thou dare to
teach us and to seduce the multitudes with thy cursed speeches?"
And he rushed upon him to rend his body. But he spake in reproach
to them: "I will not disclose to you the mystery which is among
30 you, because you would not have it [*or* him]. Therefore has unspeakable misfortune come upon you, and through your own
doing." And after he had thus spoken, he went forth to that region
of Jordan, and, since no man durst hinder him, he did what he had
done before.

204 (*b*) At that time there appeared a man, if indeed it is fitting to call
him a man. His nature and his form were those of a man, yet his
appearance was more than that of men. But his works were divine,
and he worked miracles wonderful and mighty. Again if I look at
5 his nature common [with that of men], I will not call him an angel.
And whatsoever he did, he did it by some invisible power through
word and command.

Some said of him that our first lawgiver had risen from the dead
and performed many healings and arts; others thought that he was
10 sent from God. Howbeit in many things he disobeyed the law and
kept not the Sabbath according to the custom of our fathers. Yet,
on the other hand, he did nothing shameful; nor [did he do any-

thing] with aid of hands, but by word alone did he provide everything.

15 And many of the multitude followed after him and hearkened to his teaching; and many souls were in commotion, thinking that thereby the Jewish tribes might free themselves from Roman hands.

Now it was his custom in general to sojourn before the city upon 20 the Mount of Olives; there also he bestowed his healings upon the people.

And there were gathered unto him servants, and a multitude of the people. When they saw his power, that whatever he would he wrought by a word, they urged him to enter the city, slay the 25 Roman army and Pilate, and reign over them. But he heeded it not.

And when afterwards news of it was brought to the Jewish leaders, they assembled together with the high priest and said: "We are weak, and unable to oppose the Romans, as if the bow were 30 bent; we will go and tell Pilate what we have heard, and we shall be clear of trouble, lest he hear it from others, and we be robbed of our substance and ourselves slaughtered and our children scattered." And they went and told Pilate. And he sent and slew many of the people, and had that wonder-worker brought up. And after 35 inquiring of him, he learnt that he was a benefactor, not a malefactor, and not seditious, nor yet desirous of kingship. And he let him go, for he had healed his dying wife.

And he went to his wonted place and did his wonted works. And when more people again assembled round him, and he was 40 glorified for his work before all, those who were learned in the law were smitten with envy, and gave thirty talents to Pilate that he might put him to death. And he took the money and gave them his consent that they should fulfil their wish. And they took him and crucified him contrary to the law of their fathers.

205 (c) And in it [the Temple] there stood equal pillars, and upon them titles in Greek and Latin and Jewish characters, giving warning of the law of purification, [to wit] that no foreigner should enter within. For this they called the sanctuary, being approached by 5 fourteen steps, and the upper area was built in quadrangular form.

And above these titles there hung a fourth title in these characters, announcing that Jesus the King did not reign, but was crucified by the Jews, because he prophesied the destruction of the city and the devastation of the Temple.

THE SEPTUAGINT

IT is not possible in this book to investigate the history of the Greek translation of the Old Testament which, made by Jews, was adopted by the first Christians and subsequently abandoned within the religion which first produced it. The date at which the translation was made is in dispute. The tradition that was already current in antiquity will be illustrated below; it is almost certainly false, although here and there it shows glimpses of what appears to be the truth. The Jewish community in Egypt, and particularly in Alexandria, was both numerous and influential (see pp. 44–7 (45); pp. 136ff. (125f.)); and it was Greek-speaking. Probably as early as the second century B.C. this community felt the need of a version of its sacred books in what was its every-day tongue, the dialect of vernacular Greek current in those parts. The translation was made, and the tradition, though false, clearly reveals the popularity of the new text and the veneration in which it was held. It is not probable that the whole of the Old Testament was translated at the same time; first came the Pentateuch, next the prophets, and last the books that were the latest to be received into the Jewish canon. More books were in fact translated into Greek than were ultimately received and authorized in Hebrew; the excess of material which the LXX contains in comparison with the Hebrew Bible constitutes what are known as the Old Testament apocrypha.

The importance of this book, which was the Bible of the apostolic Church, is beyond all exaggeration. In it the first Christians sought the prophecies which justified their interpretation of the life and death of Jesus, and sometimes the Greek text was more accommodating than the Hebrew. Thus Isa. 7. 14 in Greek spoke of a *virgin*, while in Hebrew it spoke of a *young woman* who might well be married and bearing a child in the course of nature. Again, at Acts 15. 16ff. James is represented as basing an argument upon a passage in Amos (9. 11f.) as read in the LXX but not in the Hebrew text. Justin's *Dialogue with Trypho* illustrates the textual disputes which inevitably arose between Church and Synagogue. Even more significant however than this use of the

LXX is the fact that the characteristic theological terminology of the New Testament can again and again be shown to rest, in great part, upon the usage of the LXX. That this should be so is not surprising, and is due not simply to the fact that the minds of many of the early Christian writers had been formed upon the LXX. They succeeded to a task in which the LXX translators had been pioneers. Jewish Christianity, like the parent religion, Judaism itself, was a Semitic faith maintaining and propagating itself in the Hellenistic world. Its basic thoughts, as well as their expression in language, had to be translated from one world into another, and the earliest Christian writers found their work in part done for them by those who had already adapted the Greek language to express the faith of the Old Testament.

In the LXX a double interaction of Greek and Hebrew thought took place. On the one hand, Greek words took on a new meaning under the influence of the Hebrew words they represented. Thus ἱλάσκεσθαι, which is normally used in Greek to describe man's act in propitiating God, is in the LXX used (as a rendering of כפר, kipper) of God's act in expiating sin. νόμος, whose earliest meaning, *custom*, hardened into the sense of *law*, came, as a rendering of תורה (*torah*), to mean *teaching*, *instruction*. This modification of the Greek language under the influence of Hebrew terminology and thought is of very great importance, but cannot be discussed here. On the other hand, Greek ideas were occasionally introduced into Old Testament passages which originally were innocent of them. The clearest example of this process is at Ex. 3. 14, where אהיה אשר אהיה (I am that I am; or, I will be that I will be) becomes ἐγώ εἰμι ὁ ὤν (I am the Self-Existent); in general it is confined to the removal of anthropomorphisms, e.g. Ex. 24. 10, They saw the place where the God of Israel stood, for They saw the God of Israel.

In the following paragraphs the linguistic importance of the LXX will not be treated. First, the tradition of the origin of the LXX will be illustrated and criticized; next, certain aspects of LXX thought and writing, not represented or only slightly represented in the canonical Old Testament, will be presented.

A. *The Traditional Origin of the Septuagint*

The tradition regarding the origin of the LXX is given in the simplest and briefest form by Philo; it is given at great length in the so-called *Epistle of Aristeas*, of which a fairly extensive paraphrase and summary is given by Josephus (*Ant.* xii. 11–118; cf. i. 10ff.; *Against Apion* ii.

45ff.), and alluded to by Aristobulus (*apud* Eusebius *Praep. Ev.* XIII, xii. 2). All these sources agree in ascribing the design of translating the Jewish scriptures to the Alexandrian king Ptolemy Philadelphus, who ruled 283–245 B.C. Philo and Josephus wrote, of course, in the first century A.D.; the *Epistle of Aristeas* claims to have been written by a contemporary of the events it records; in fact it is undoubtedly pseudonymous, and was probably written between 140 and 100 B.C. The passage in Philo runs as follows.

206 *Philo, de Vit. Mos.* ii. 26–42. In ancient times the laws were written in the Chaldean tongue, and remained in that form for many years, without any change of language, so long as they had not yet revealed their beauty to the rest of mankind. But, in course of
5 time, the daily, unbroken regularity of practice exercised by those who observed them brought them to the knowledge of others, and their fame began to spread on every side. For things excellent, even if they are beclouded for a short time through envy, shine out again under the benign operation of nature when their time comes.
10 Then it was that some people, thinking it a shame that the laws should be found in one half only of the human race, the barbarians, and denied altogether to the Greeks, took steps to have them translated. In view of the importance and public utility of the task, it was referred not to private persons or magistrates, who
15 were very numerous, but to kings, and amongst them to the king of highest repute. Ptolemy, surnamed Philadephus, was the third in succession to Alexander, the conqueror of Egypt. . . .

   This great man, having conceived an ardent affection for our laws, determined to have the Chaldean translated into Greek, and
20 at once dispatched envoys to the high priest and king of Judaea, both offices being held by the same person, explaining his wishes and urging him to choose by merit persons to make a full rendering of the Law into Greek. The high priest was naturally pleased, and, thinking that God's guiding care must have led the king to
25 busy himself in such an undertaking, sought out such Hebrews as he had of the highest reputation, who had received an education in Greek as well as in their native lore, and joyfully sent them to Ptolemy. When they arrived, they were offered hospitality, and, having been sumptuously entertained, requited their entertainer
30 with a feast of words full of wit and weight. For he tested the wisdom of each by propounding for discussion new instead of the ordinary questions, which problems they solved with happy and well-pointed answers in the form of apophthegms, as the occasion did not allow of lengthy speaking.

35 After standing this test, they at once began to fulfil the duties
    of their high errand. Reflecting how great an undertaking it was
    to make a full version of the laws given by the voice of God, where
    they could not add or take away or transfer anything, but must
    keep the original form and shape, they proceeded to look for the
40 most open and unoccupied spot in the neighbourhood outside the
    city. For, within the walls, it was full of every kind of living
    creatures, and consequently the prevalence of diseases and deaths,
    and the impure conduct of the healthy inhabitants, made them
    suspicious of it. In front of Alexandria lies the island of Pharos,
45 stretching with its narrow strip of land towards the city, and en-
    closed by a sea not deep but mostly consisting of shoals, so that the
    loud din and booming of the surging waves grows faint through
    the long distance before it reaches the land. Judging this to be the
    most suitable place in the district, where they might find peace
50 and tranquillity and the soul could commune with the laws with
    none to disturb its privacy, they fixed their abode there ; and, taking
    the sacred books, stretched them out towards heaven with the
    hands that held them, asking of God that they might not fail in
    their purpose. And he assented to their prayers, to the end that the
55 greater part, or even the whole, of the human race might be
    profited and led to a better life by continuing to observe such wise
    and truly admirable ordinances.

    Sitting here in seclusion with none present save the elements of
    nature, earth, water, air, heaven, the genesis of which was to
60 be the first theme of their sacred revelation, for the laws begin with
    the story of the world's creation, they became as it were possessed,
    and, under inspiration, wrote, not each several scribe something
    different, but the same word for word, as though dictated to each
    by an invisible prompter. Yet who does not know that every
65 language, and Greek especially, abounds in terms, and that the
    same thought can be put in many shapes by changing single words
    and whole phrases and suiting the expression to the occasion? This
    was not the case, we are told, with this law of ours, but the Greek
    words used corresponded literally with the Chaldean, exactly
70 suited to the things they indicated. . . . The clearest proof of this is
    that, if Chaldeans have learned Greek, or Greeks Chaldean, and
    read both versions, the Chaldean and the translation, they regard
    them with awe and reverence as sisters, or rather one and the same,
    both in matter and words, and speak of the authors not as trans-
75 lators but as prophets and priests of the mysteries, whose sincerity
    and singleness of thought has enabled them to go hand in hand
    with the purest of spirits, the spirit of Moses.

Therefore, even to the present day, there is held every year a
feast and general assembly in the island of Pharos, whither not only
80 Jews but multitudes of others cross the water, both to do honour to
the place in which the light of that version first shone out, and
also to thank God for the good gift so old yet ever young. But,
after the prayers and thanksgivings, some fixing tents on the seaside
and others reclining on the sandy beach in the open air feast with
85 their relations and friends, counting that shore for the time a more
magnificent lodging than the fine mansions in the royal precincts.

l. 18 *This great man.* Ptolemy Philadelphus, who succeeded Ptolemy Soter, who
himself was one of the successors of Alexander the Great. The omitted
passage represents him as the most distinguished of the Ptolemies. Aristeas
also ascribed to him the initiative in the translation of the Law, and the
tradition appears also in Rabbinic writings, e.g. *Megillah* 9*a* (see below, p.
213).

l. 21 *Both offices being held by the same person.* The high priest, according to Aristeas
(33), followed by Josephus, was Eleazar. On his place in the succession of
high priests see Josephus, *Ant.* xii. 43f., and Appendix B in Vol. VII of the
Loeb edition of Josephus (R. Marcus). At this period the high priest was
also the secular head of the Jewish state, but not a "king".

l. 25 *Sought out such Hebrews as he had of the highest reputation.* In Aristeas (46)
the high priest selects six elders from each of the twelve tribes; the seventy-
two names are given. By this means the Greek translation is given the full
sanction and approval of Palestinian Judaism; and indeed some such connection is not impossible.

l. 26 *Who had received an education in Greek.* That there were such persons need
not be doubted. It was much later that Judaism shut the door against Greek
learning and influence. Both the earlier attitude to Greek studies and the
later are well expressed in the Mishnah (*Sotah* 9. 14: During the war of
Titus (*v. l.* Quietus, governor of Judaea A.D. 117) they forbade . . . that a
man should teach his son Greek). For further evidence see below on l. 72.

l. 29 *Having been sumptuously entertained.* Aristeas gives further details, especially
of the "feast of words". In such passages it becomes very clear that the
Epistle of Aristeas is an apology for, and praise of, Judaism, put, for effect,
into the mouth of a Gentile.

l. 44 *The island of Pharos* was connected with the mainland by a sea-wall nearly
a mile in length (the "Heptastadion") which divided the harbour into two
parts. Neither Aristeas nor Josephus mentions the name Pharos, but it is
clear that they thought of this place as the scene of the translators' labours.

l. 63 *The same word for word.* It is evident that Philo believes that he is describing
a miracle. The translators wrote "under inspiration" (προεφήτευον). A
different view is given by Aristeas (followed by Josephus); no miraculous
agreement was involved, but the translators compared their work so as to
produce an agreed result. The development of the tradition in Philo well
illustrates the veneration felt in his day for the LXX. On this see the next
note.

l. 72 *They regard them with awe and reverence as sisters.* Note that Philo is able to think of Greeks who have learned Chaldean (Hebrew) and Hebrews who have learned Greek. In his day there were such bilingual Jews, though later the learning of Greek was frowned upon (see on l. 26). This changing attitude to Greek was reflected in a changing attitude to the LXX. In the early period it was allowed. Thus *Megillah* 1. 8: ... the Books may be written in any language ... Rabban Simeon b. Gamaliel [before A.D. 70] says: The Books, too, they have only permitted to be written in Greek [in addition to Hebrew]. Both a changing attitude and the old tradition appear in *Megillah* 9 *a*: R. Judah [*c.* A.D. 150] said: When our teachers permitted the Holy Scriptures to be written in Greek they permitted it only in respect of the book of the Law [i.e. the Pentateuch], and on account of the incident of King Ptolemy. For it is taught in a *baraita*: King Ptolemy brought together seventy-two elders, whom he led into seventy-two closets, without telling them for what purpose he had assembled them. Then he went into each and said to them, Write out for me the Law of Moses your teacher. God gave each one counsel in his heart, so that they all agreed in every point. This statement appears to agree with Philo's; but a difference in tone should be observed. Here the point is that translations are never desirable but that the Greek Pentateuch may be justified on account of a special miracle. The developed attitude which prevailed after the Church had appropriated the LXX is found in *Sepher Torah* 1, § 8: Seventy elders wrote the Law in Greek, writing for King Ptolemy, and that day was as bad for Israel as the day on which they made the calf, for the Law could not be translated in a way corresponding to all requirements. When the LXX fell out of favour (to a great extent because of its use by Christians) its place was taken among Greek-speaking Jews by more literal renderings, those of Aquila, Symmachus and Theodotion.

l. 79 *A feast and general assembly.* This festival Philo must have known himself, and there is no need to doubt its existence in his day, though no other evidence for its celebration is known. It does not of course prove a historical connexion between the island and the LXX.

Only a small part of the long *Epistle of Aristeas* can be quoted here.

207 *Epistle of Aristeas*, 301-16. Three days later Demetrius took the men and passing along the sea-wall, seven stadia long, to the island, crossed the bridge and made for the northern districts [of Pharos]. There he assembled them in a house, which had been built upon
  5 the sea-shore, of great beauty and in a secluded situation, and invited them to carry out the work of translation, since everything that they needed for the purpose was placed at their disposal. So they set to work comparing their several results and making them agree, and whatever they agreed upon was suitably copied out
 10 under the direction of Demetrius. And the session lasted until the ninth hour; after this they were set free to minister to their physical needs. Everything they wanted was furnished for them on

a lavish scale. In addition to this Dorotheus made the same preparations for them daily as were made for the king himself—for
15 thus he had been commanded by the king. In the early morning they appeared daily at the Court, and after saluting the king went back to their own place. And as is the custom of all the Jews, they washed their hands in the sea and prayed to God and then devoted themselves to reading and translating the particular passage [upon
20 which they were engaged], and I put the question to them, Why it was that they washed their hands before they prayed? And they explained that it was a token that they had done no evil (for every form of activity is wrought by means of the hands) since in their noble and holy way they regard everything as a symbol of
25 righteousness and truth.

As I have already said, they met together daily in the place which was delightful for its quiet and its brightness and applied themselves to their task. And it so chanced that the work of translation was completed in seventy-two days, just as if this had been arranged of
30 set purpose.

When the work was completed, Demetrius collected together the Jewish population in the place where the translation had been made, and read it over to all, in the presence of the translators, who met with a great reception also from the people, because of the
35 great benefits which they had conferred upon them. They bestowed warm praise upon Demetrius, too, and urged him to have the whole law transcribed and present a copy to their leaders.

After the books had been read, the priests and the elders of the translators and the Jewish community and the leaders of the people
40 stood up and said, that since so excellent and sacred and accurate a translation had been made, it was only right that it should remain as it was and no alteration should be made in it. And when the whole community expressed their approval, they bade them pronounce a curse in accordance with their custom upon any
45 one who should make any alteration either by adding anything or changing in any way whatever any of the words which had been written or making any omission. This was a very wise precaution to ensure that the book might be preserved for all the future time unchanged.

50 When the matter was reported to the king, he rejoiced greatly, for he felt that the design which he had formed had been safely carried out. The whole book was read over to him and he was greatly astonished at the spirit of the lawgiver. And he said to Demetrius, "How is it that none of the historians or the poets have
55 ever thought it worth their while to allude to such a wonderful

achievement?" And he replied, "Because the law is sacred and of divine origin. And some of those who formed the intention [of dealing with it] have been smitten by God and therefore desisted from their purpose." He said that he had heard from Theopompus
60 that he had been driven out of his mind for more than thirty days because he intended to insert in his history some of the incidents from the earlier and somewhat unreliable translations of the law. When he had recovered a little, he besought God to make it clear to him why the misfortune had befallen him. And it was
65 revealed to him in a dream, that from idle curiosity he was wishing to communicate sacred truths to common men, and that if he desisted he would recover his health. I have heard, too, from the lips of Theodectes, one of the tragic poets, that when he was about to adapt some of the incidents in the book for one of his plays, he
70 was affected with cataract in both his eyes. And when he perceived the reason why the misfortune had befallen him, he prayed to God for many days and was afterwards restored.

l. 1 *Three days later*, that is, after the banquet at which the king entertained the translators.

Demetrius, according to Aristeas (9), was at this time president of the king's library. This is almost certainly a mistake, and a proof that the Epistle was not written by a contemporary of Ptolemy II Philadephus. Demetrius of Phalerum was brought to Alexandria by Ptolemy I Soter to supervise his library. He fell into disfavour, however, towards the end of this king's reign because he supported the claim to succession of the elder son, Keraunos, against those of his brother Philadelphus. He was sent into exile and died *c.* 283 B.C.

l. 3 *The northern districts of Pharos*. Pharos is not named in the Greek text but is clearly intended.

l. 13 *Dorotheus* is mentioned at 182 as having charge of the entertainment of the Jewish translators.

l. 17 *As is the custom of all the Jews, they washed their hands . . .* Cf. Mark 7. 3; but it should be noted that this is not a washing before eating, but in the early morning and before prayer. This seems to be the earliest evidence for the custom of washing before morning prayer.

l. 22 *A token that they had done no evil.* This of course was not the true origin and meaning of Jewish ablutions; but it is quite possible that Alexandrian Jews so explained their practices to their heathen neighbours.

l. 29 *In seventy-two days*, as there were seventy-two translators.

l.32 *The Jewish population.* It is noteworthy that, though Aristeas represents the translation as due to the initiative of the king and his librarian, and as commissioned by them, yet when the work is completed it is presented not to the royal patron but to the Jewish people. It may be that Aristeas here unwittingly allows us to see a glimpse of the truth. In all probability it was the Jewish community in Alexandria which needed and produced the LXX.

l. 42 *It should remain as it was.* Probably a secondary purpose of the Epistle (which is to be regarded as primarily a piece of Jewish propaganda) was to commend and insist upon the authority of a standard LXX text.

l. 54 *How is it that none of the historians or the poets ...* ? This question implies what is expressly stated in l. 62 (and perhaps in Aristeas 30 also), namely, that earlier translations had been made, even though they had proved unsatisfactory. This supports the suggestion of the last note. The question itself is of some interest, since there is in fact little trace of the LXX in non-Jewish Greek authors (the most notable exception being certain tractates of the *Corpus Hermeticum*; see Chapter 5). The primary reasons for this neglect are to be found not, as Aristeas suggests, in the divine origin of the Law, but in the general dislike for the Jews and their religion, and in the extreme barbarity of LXX Greek.

B. *Selections from the Septuagint*

Peculiar difficulty accompanies the selection of passages from the LXX itself. No attempt is made in this book to describe the history and theology of the Old Testament, though they are both elements of fundamental importance in the background of the New Testament, and it has already been pointed out that a comparison of the Hebrew and Greek texts of the Old Testament is particularly instructive. Certain parts of the Greek Old Testament are quoted elsewhere (see 97–105, 211f., 215f., 218, 224) for special purposes; here three passages only will be given. They will be drawn from parts of the LXX which have no canonical Hebrew equivalent, and they will illustrate ideas which are important in the development of Hellenistic Judaism but are only scantily represented, or not represented at all, in the Hebrew Old Testament.

(1) *The Divine Wisdom.* Already in the later parts of the Hebrew Old Testament Wisdom (חכמה, *ḥokmah*) is recognized as one of the good gifts of God to men. The word means, at first, practical good sense; the ability to live life intelligently, virtuously, and successfully (e.g. Prov. 1. 2ff.). Whether this view of Wisdom was a native Jewish development or was borrowed from foreign sources is a question we need not here examine. Since however this Wisdom was naturally spoken of as the Wisdom *of God* (for from what other source could it spring?) it came to be thought of in a new way, once more, perhaps, under the pressure of foreign influence as well as inward development. Wisdom belonged to the stuff of the universe, and therefore, since God was the Creator of the universe, it stood in a double relationship to God and to the universe. Wisdom was not merely an attribute of wise

men, or even an attribute of God himself; it had a more or less independent, a more or less personal, existence. It is necessary here to use terms of considerable vagueness since precision is one of the least evident characteristics of the Wisdom literature, and it is probably not correct to describe Wisdom as portrayed there as, in any strict sense, a hypostasis. We are moving in the realm of poetical and imaginative description, not of metaphysics, and it is certainly not one single view of Wisdom that we find in the Wisdom books, or even within any one of them.

It is possible that the Jewish conception of Wisdom, and the literary form which it sometimes took, were influenced by the contemporary belief in the goddess Isis (on this see the notes below); and possible also that the figure of Wisdom is related to the Stoic conception of the Logos (see pp. 61f. (59ff.); pp. 183–6 (186f.)). Probably, however, the influence of these external factors was in general secondary; that is, the Jewish writers employed the language of Hellenistic religion or philosophy as a means of commending their own faith.

It seems very probable that the Wisdom of Solomon is to be regarded as a composite work. For the doctrine of Wisdom the most significant section (part of which is quoted below) is 7. 1 (or 6. 1)—9. 18. This discourse upon, and prayer for, Wisdom is put into the mouth of Solomon. It mav be dated before the time of Philo, probably in the first century B.C.

208 *Wisdom of Solomon 7. 1—8. 1.*

> I myself also am mortal, like to all,
> And am sprung from one born of the earth, the man first formed,
> And in the womb of a mother was I moulded into flesh in the time
> of ten months,
> Being compacted in blood of the seed of man and pleasure that
> came with sleep.
> 5 And I also, when I was born, drew in the common air,
> And fell upon the kindred earth,
> Uttering, like all, for my first voice, the self-same wail:
> In swaddling clothes was I nursed, and with watchful cares.
> For no king had any other first beginning;
> 10 But all men have one entrance into life, and a like departure.
> For this cause I prayed, and understanding was given me:
> I called upon God, and there came to me a spirit of wisdom
> I preferred her before sceptres and thrones,
> And riches I esteemed nothing in comparison of her.

15 Neither did I liken to her any priceless gem,
    Because all the gold of the earth in her sight is but a little sand,
    And silver shall be accounted as clay before her.
    Above health and comeliness I loved her,
    And I chose to have her rather than light,
20 Because her bright shining is never laid to sleep.
    But with her there came to me all good things together,
    And in her hands innumerable riches;
    And I rejoiced over them all because wisdom leadeth them;
    Though I knew not that she was the mother of them.
25 As I learned without guile, I impart without grudging;
    I do not hide her riches.
    For she is unto men a treasure that faileth not,
    And they that use it obtain friendship with God,
    Commended to him by the gifts which come through discipline.
30 But to me may God give to speak with judgement,
    And to conceive thoughts worthy of what hath been given me;
    Because himself is one that guideth even wisdom and correcteth
        the wise.
    For in his hand are both we and our words;
    All understanding, and all acquaintance with divers crafts.
35 For he hath given me an unerring knowledge of the things that
        are,
    To know the constitution of the world, and the operation of the
        elements;
    The beginning and end and middle of times,
    The alternations of the solstices and the changes of seasons,
    The circuits of years and the positions of stars;
40 The natures of living creatures and the ragings of wild beasts,
    The powers of spirits and the thoughts of men,
    The diversities of plants and the virtues of roots:
    All things that are either secret or manifest I learned,
    For she that is the artificer of all things taught me, even wisdom.
45 For there is in her a spirit quick of understanding, holy,
    Alone in kind, manifold,
    Subtil, freely moving,
    Clear in utterance, unpolluted,
    Distinct, that cannot be harmed,
50 Loving what is good, keen, unhindered,
    Beneficent, loving toward man,
    Steadfast, sure, free from care,
    All-powerful, all-surveying,
    And penetrating through all spirits

55 That are quick of understanding, pure, subtil:
 For wisdom is more mobile than any motion;
 Yea, she pervadeth and penetrateth all things by reason of her
 pureness.
 For she is a breath of the power of God,
 And a clear effluence of the glory of the Almighty;
60 Therefore can nothing defiled find entrance into her,
 For she is an effulgence from everlasting light
 And an unspotted mirror of the working of God,
 And an image of his goodness.
 And she, though but one, hath power to do all things;
65 And remaining in herself, reneweth all things:
 And from generation to generation passing into holy souls
 She maketh them friends of God and prophets.
 For nothing doth God love save him that dwelleth with wisdom.
 For she is fairer than the sun,
70 And above all the constellations of the stars:
 Being compared with light, she is found to be before it;
 For to the light of day succeedeth night,
 But against wisdom evil doth not prevail;
 But she reacheth from one end of the world to the other with full
 strength,
75 And ordereth all things well.

l. 1 *I myself also am mortal.* Solomon speaks. King though he is, he shares in the
 common descent of men from Adam, the man first formed of the dust of
 the earth. Wisdom is therefore for him no natural possession; he must pray
 for it, if he is to be the "understanding king" who is "tranquillity to his
 people" (6. 24).

l. 11 *I prayed.* The author recalls 1 Kings 3. 4-15; 2 Chron. 1. 7-13.

ll. 11f. *Understanding . . . spirit of wisdom* (φρόνησις . . . πνεῦμα σοφίας). The two
 expressions are used in parallelism without difference of meaning. The
 spirit of wisdom is wisdom itself (see l. 45, and cf. Isa. 11. 2), and wisdom is
 here meant in the sense of practical wisdom.

l. 13 *I preferred her before sceptres and thrones.* This preference, which is expanded in
 the following lines, rests primarily upon the choice of Solomon in his
 prayer (1 Kings 3. 9; 2 Chron. 1. 10), but it is one which occurs frequently,
 and is frequently elaborated, in the Wisdom books; see e.g. Prov. 3. 14f;
 8. 10f.; 16. 16; Job 28. 15-19; Eccles. 7. 11f.

l. 19 *Light.* Cf. ll. 61f., 69-72, and the note on l. 61.

l. 24 *The mother of them.* Once more the writer is dependent not so much on his
 own thought about wisdom and its value as on the Old Testament; see
 1 Kings 3. 13; 2 Chron. 1. 12.

l. 36 *The constitution of the world.* The writer proceeds in the next lines to parade
 his knowledge of astronomy, zoology, and medicine; but there is no reason
 to suppose that it was more than superficial, or that he knew more of Greek

science than the imposing phrases he uses. Cf. 1 Kings 4. 33, and the frequent allusions to the natural world in Proverbs.

l. 41 *The powers of spirits.* A possible translation would be "the forces of winds"; but in view of the widespread tradition that Solomon enjoyed unusual powers over spirits and demons the translation in the text is more probable.

l. 44 *The artificer of all things.* Wisdom is no longer mere pious common sense but, metaphorically at least, a person. The description of Wisdom as artificer (τεχνῖτις) of all things probably rests upon Prov. 8. 30 (LXX ἁρμόζουσα), though it is doubtful whether the corresponding Hebrew word (אָמוֹן) means "master workman" (EV). To suppose that this description of Wisdom means that our author was thinking in terms of either a Platonic pattern of the universe or a Stoic world-soul is to press his language a great deal too far; but he probably means to show that Judaism also is able to produce a mediator at once cosmological and revelatory. Cf. l. 61 and note.

l. 45 *There is in her a spirit.* See the note on ll. 11f. above. There follows a list of twenty-one adjectives, by which Wisdom is described. It may be recalled that Philo (*de Conf. Ling.* 146) speaks of the Logos as "many-named"; also that the multiplication of titles is not unusual in addresses to divine persons, not least in addresses to Isis. The author of Wisdom is probably following non-Jewish models; this is confirmed by the fact that some of his adjectives are certainly of non-Jewish background and origin.

Quick of understanding. This translation hardly succeeds in bringing out the sense of νοερόν, a Stoic word which means rather "pertaining to the intellect (νοῦς)". The κόσμος itself was described by Zeno[1] as ἔμψυχος, νοερός, and λογικός (living, rational, and spiritual).

l. 46 *Alone in kind, manifold.* Like the Stoic world-soul, Wisdom is one, yet expresses itself in many forms.

l. 54 *Penetrating through all spirits.* This is expanded and justified in l. 57, where Wisdom is said to pervade all things; *a fortiori* it will pervade all rational beings. The Stoic concept of the Logos is parallel to the thought here; Logos is everywhere, but is pre-eminently to be found in those wise and virtuous souls which live according to Logos.

l. 59 *Effluence,* or emanation. The thought is far from clear; but Wisdom seems here to be a distinct being, derived from God but differentiated from him. This definitely theistic conception is Platonic rather than Stoic, though it is not suggested that the author is himself consciously combining the two schools.

l. 61 *Effulgence.* This is the natural meaning of the word ἀπαύγασμα (cf. Heb. 1. 3); but in view of the next line some prefer to render "reflection". The frequent use of the imagery of light is noteworthy, but perhaps too natural to demand belief that it has been borrowed from Hellenistic sources. Yet, here and elsewhere, it is doubtless true that the author means to say to his readers, "All those properties which you ascribe to νοῦς [Mind] and λόγος [Reason], the divine Wisdom which I have to proclaim to you also possesses, and is indeed even more glorious" (Fichtner, *ad loc.*).

l. 67 *Friends of God and prophets.* Abraham was the friend of God (Isa. 41. 8;

---

[1] von Arnim, op. cit. i. 32.

2 Chron. 20. 7; James 2. 23; cf. John 15. 14); but it seems probable that the author is here dependent on the Hellenistic description of the wise man as the friend of God. Many references could be given: e.g. Xenophon, *Memorabilia* II, i. 33 where Virtue (ἀρετή) claims to make men friends of God; Plato, *Laws* iv. 716 D. Philo also took up the notion; e.g. *de Abra.* 273, of Abraham. Similarly the inspired prophet is a common enough figure in the Old Testament, but an attempt is made here to combine the Old Testament prophet with the Hellenistic wise man. Cf. Cicero, *de Divinatione* ii. 63 (129). There is a close approximation between Spirit, Wisdom, and Logos.

l. 75 *Ordereth all things well.* The word and thought are both Platonic and Stoic. Cf. Plato, *Phaedrus* 246 C; Diogenes Laertius 133: the Stoics said that the cosmos was ordered according to Mind and Providence; which need not be greatly different from the statement that all things are ordered by the Wisdom of God.

(2) *Ethical Paraenesis.* The conception of Wisdom, though in origin practical, may be regarded as an expression of the speculative activity of Judaism. A more characteristic feature of Judaism is however its deep-rooted interest in ethics, and this interest is reflected in the later LXX books, where moral paraenesis is a not uncommon literary form. The book of Tobit in particular may be described as an ethical romance designed to teach the practice of virtue and to demonstrate God's providential care for the righteous, especially for righteous Israelites. Its date is difficult to estimate since the story seems to have been known in a number of different forms; the earliest of these was probably not much later than 200 B.C. In the passage quoted here the aged Tobit gives parting advice (most of which needs no explanation) to his son Tobias.

209 *Tobit* 4. 3–19. And he called Tobias his son and he came unto him and he said unto him, Bury me well, and honour thy mother; and forsake her not all the days of her life, and do that which is pleasing before her, and grieve not her spirit in any matter.

5 Remember her, child, that she hath experienced many dangers for thee in her womb; and when she is dead, bury her by me in one grave. My child, be mindful of the Lord all thy days, and let not thy will be set to sin and to transgress his commandments: do acts of righteousness all the days of thy life, and walk not in the

10 ways of unrighteousness. For if thou doest the truth, success shall be in thy works, and so it shall be unto all that do righteousness. Give alms of thy substance: turn not away thy face from any poor man, and the face of God shall not be turned away from thee. As thy substance is, give alms of it according to thine abundance:

15 if thou have much, according to the abundance thereof, give

alms; if thou have little bestow it, and be not afraid to give alms
according to that little: for thou layest up a good treasure for
thyself against the day of necessity: because alms delivereth from
death, and suffereth not to come into darkness. Alms is a good
20 offering in the sight of the Most High for all that give it. Beware,
my child, of all whoredom, and take first a wife of the seed of
thy fathers, take not a strange wife, which is not of thy father's
tribe; for we are the sons of the prophets. Noah, Abraham, Isaac,
Jacob, our fathers of old time, remember, my child, that they all
25 took wives of their kinsmen, and were blessed in their children,
and their seed shall inherit the land. And now, my child, love thy
brethren, and scorn not in thy heart thy brethren and the sons
and the daughters of thy people so as not to take one of them; for
in scornfulness is destruction and much trouble, and in idleness is
30 decay and great want, for idleness is the mother of famine. Let not
the wages of any man, which shall work for thee, tarry with
thee, but render it unto him out of hand: and if thou serve God,
recompense shall be made unto thee. Take heed to thyself, my
child, in all thy works, and be discreet in all thy behaviour. And
35 what thou thyself hatest, do to no man. Drink not wine unto
drunkenness, and let not drunkenness go with thee on thy way.
Give of thy bread to the hungry, and of thy garments to them that
are naked: of all thine abundance give alms; and let not thine eye
be grudging when thou givest alms. Pour out thy bread and thy
40 wine on the tomb of the just, and give not to sinners. Ask counsel
of every man that is wise, and despise not any counsel that is
profitable. And bless the Lord thy God at all times, and ask of him
that thy ways may be made straight, and that all thy paths and thy
counsels may prosper: for every nation hath not good counsel;
45 but the Lord will give to them all good things; and whom he will
the Lord humbleth unto the nethermost Hades. And now, child,
remember these commandments, and let them not be blotted out
of thy heart.

l. 2 *Bury me well.* Care for the dead is a primary moral obligation in Judaism.
Tobit himself had made a practice of burying those whose bodies would
otherwise have been neglected (1. 17; cf. 2. 4–8), and was rewarded for
doing so (cf. 12. 12). Cf. Matt. 8. 21; Luke 9. 59; 16. 22; 1 Enoch 22. 10.
Honour thy mother. Cf. Ex. 20. 12. For examples of the honouring of parents
(and especially mothers) in late Judaism, see C. G. Montefiore and H.
Loewe, *A Rabbinic Anthology*, 500–4.

l. 10 *If thou doest the truth.* Cf. John 3. 21; 1 John 1. 6. Here it means "to act
faithfully", in obedience to the law.

ll. 12f. *Give alms.* Another primary obligation, for which many examples can
be given both in Jewish literature and the New Testament. *Turn not away thy*

face from any poor man: cf. Matt. 5. 42; Luke 6. 30. *Thou layest up a good treasure*: cf. Matt. 6. 19ff.; Luke 12. 33f.; Mark 10.21, *et al.*

l. 19 *Suffereth not to come into darkness.* Cf. 14. 10: See, child, what things Nadab did unto Ahikar that brought him up! Was he not brought down alive into the earth? and God recompensed the shame upon his face, and Ahikar came forth into the light, and Nadab went into the eternal darkness, because he had sought to slay Ahikar. Because I did alms, he came forth from the snare of death which Nadab had set for him, and Nadab fell into the snare of death, and it destroyed him. Tobit, certainly in ch. 14 and probably in ch. 4, refers to the legend of Ahikar and his enemy Nadab. See R. H. Charles, *Apocrypha and Pseudepigrapha*, ii. 724–84.

l. 22 *A strange wife.* It is not clear whether Tobit insists upon marriage within the tribe, or, more generally, within the race. The patriarchs (here called prophets) fall within the scope of the former regulation only if later traditions are taken into account (Jubilees 4. 33). The reference to "thy brethren" suggests the latter alternative.

l. 26 *Love thy brethren.* Cf. Lev. 19. 18. The fellow-Jew is meant; but hatred of the enemy, or non-Jew, is not implied; cf. Matt. 5. 43.

l. 31 *Let not the wages of any man . . . tarry with thee.* Cf. James 5. 4.

l. 35 *What thou thyself hatest, do to no man.* Cf. Matt. 7. 12; Luke 6. 31. Tobit states the Golden Rule in its negative form; this is how it usually appears, for example in the teaching of Hillel and Akiba.

l. 39 *Pour out thy bread and thy wine on the tomb of the just.* This seems to be the original text. The zeugma by which "pour" is applied to bread as well as wine is harsh, but readily comprehensible. Again we have a parallel with the Ahikar legend; see the Arabic text 2. 13 (Pour out thy wine on the tombs of the just, and drink not with ignorant, contemptible people), and the Syriac A text 2. 10 (Pour out thy wine on the graves of the righteous, rather than drink it with evil men; Charles, op. cit., ii. 730f.). The practice referred to may be of pagan origin, and the words taken from a non-Jewish literary source; but the fact that such a reference can be made throws a surprising light upon the fervent Jewish piety which produced the book of Tobit. Judaism was more open to foreign influences than is often supposed; more open, perhaps, than it supposed itself to be.

(3) *Martyrdom, and the Future Life.* The development of Judaism as a religion of obedience to the written Law, and the recurring misfortunes which befell the national life of the Jews, provoked new experiences and fresh thinking. The attack upon Judaism by Antiochus IV Epiphanes (see pp. 105–8 (**97–100**)), though it was directed against the nation and the national religion, fell in the first instance upon those who were, in their own consciences, confronted with the question whether they should or should not continue to be obedient to the Law. The question was not, as once it had been, whether the whole nation should remain in its own land or be carried away to Babylon, but whether a particular man should remain faithful to the religion in which

he had been reared, and receive death by torture as his reward, or should compromise, and live. In these circumstances martyrdoms took place, perhaps for the first time in religious history. But (men began to ask) what was to be the ultimate fate of the martyrs? Were their suffering and death to be the last word? This was an intolerable thought, and the notion of a blessed personal future life, to which doubtless other sources contributed, was fostered by the faith and the sufferings of those who gave their lives for the Law.

The Second Book of Maccabees is an epitome of a longer work; so much the book itself tells us (2. 23: . . . this [the things concerning Judas Maccabaeus and his brothers], recounted by Jason in five books, we will try to compress into a single volume). Who Jason was, when he lived, and who was his epitomist, are questions which cannot be precisely answered. Probably the origins of the book go back into the second century B.C., and they reveal both a Pharisaic kind of piety and the influence of Hellenistic Judaism. The seventh chapter (quoted below) is a vignette of the persecution which took place when Antiochus IV Epiphanes attempted to make the Jews surrender their religious rites and legal observances.

210 2 *Maccabees* 7. It also came to pass that seven brothers and their
  mother were arrested and shamefully lashed with whips and
  scourges, by the king's orders, that they might be forced to taste the
  abominable swine's flesh. But one of them spoke up for the others
 5 and said, Why question us? What wouldst thou learn from us? We
  are prepared to die sooner than transgress the laws of our fathers.
  Then the king, in his exasperation, ordered pans and cauldrons to
  be heated, and when they were heated immediately, ordered the
  tongue of the speaker to be torn out, had him scalped and muti-
 10 lated before the eyes of his brothers and mother, and then had him
  put on the fire, all maimed and crippled as he was, but still alive,
  and set to fry in the pan. And as the vapour from the pan spread
  abroad, they and their mother exhorted one another to die nobly,
  uttering these words: The Lord God beholdeth this, and truly hath
 15 compassion on us, even as Moses declared in his song which testi-
  fieth against them to their face, saying,
    And he shall have compassion on his servants.
  And when the first had died after this manner, they brought the
  second to the shameful torture, tearing off the skin of his head
 20 with the hair and asking him, Wilt thou eat, before we punish thy
  body limb by limb? But he answered in the language of his fathers
  and said to them, No. So he too underwent the rest of the torture,

as the first had done. And when he was at the last gasp, he said,
Thou cursed miscreant! Thou dost dispatch us from this life, but
25 the King of the world shall raise us up, who have died for his
laws, and revive us to life everlasting. And after him the third
was made a mocking-stock. And when he was told to put out his
tongue, he did so at once, stretching forth his hands courageously,
with the noble words, These I had from heaven; for his name's sake
30 I count them naught; from him I hope to get them back again. So
much so that the king himself and his company were astounded at
the spirit of the youth, for he thought nothing of his sufferings.
And when he too was dead, they tortured the fourth in the same
shameful fashion. And when he was near his end, he said: 'Tis meet
35 for those who perish at men's hands to cherish hope divine that
they shall be raised up by God again; but thou—thou shalt have
no resurrection to life. Next they brought the fifth and handled
him shamefully. But he looked at the king and said, Holding
authority among men, thou doest what thou wilt, poor mortal;
40 but dream not that God hath forsaken our race. Go on, and thou
shalt find how his sovereign power will torture thee and thy seed!
And after him they brought the sixth. And when he was at the
point of death he said, Deceive not thyself in vain! We are suffering
this on our own account, for sins against our own God. That is why
45 these awful horrors have befallen us. But think not thou shalt
go unpunished for daring to fight against God! The mother, however, was a perfect wonder; she deserves to be held in glorious
memory, for, thanks to her hope in God, she bravely bore the
sight of seven sons dying in a single day. Full of noble spirit and
50 nerving her weak woman's heart with the courage of a man, she
exhorted each of them in the language of their fathers, saying, How
you were ever conceived in my womb, I cannot tell! 'Twas not I
who gave you the breath of life or fashioned the elements of each!
'Twas the creator of the world who fashioneth men and deviseth the
55 generating of all things, and he it is who in mercy will restore to
you the breath of life even as you now count yourselves naught for
his laws' sake. Now Antiochus felt that he was being humiliated,
but, overlooking the taunt of her words, he made an appeal to the
youngest brother, who still survived, and even promised on oath
60 to make him rich and happy and a Friend and a trusted official of
State, if he would give up his fathers' laws. As the young man paid
no attention to him, he summoned his mother and exhorted her to
counsel the lad to save himself. So, after he had exhorted her at
length, she agreed to persuade her son. She leant over to him, and,
65 befooling the cruel tyrant, spoke thus in her fathers' tongue: My

son, have pity on me. Nine months I carried thee in my womb, three years I suckled thee; I reared thee and brought thee up to this age of thy life. Child, I beseech thee, lift thine eyes to heaven and earth, look at all that is therein, and know that God did not make
70 them out of the things that existed. So is the race of men created. Fear not this butcher, but show thyself worthy of thy brothers, and accept thy death, that by God's mercy I may receive thee again together with thy brothers. Ere she had finished, the young man cried, What are you waiting for? I will not obey the king's com-
75 mand, I will obey the command of the law given by Moses to our fathers. But thou, who hast devised all manner of evil against the Hebrews, thou shalt not escape the hands of God. We are suffering for our own sins, and though our living Lord is angry for a little, in order to rebuke and chasten us, he will again be reconciled to his
80 own servants. But thou, thou impious wretch, vilest of all men, be not vainly uplifted with thy proud, uncertain hopes, raising thy hand against the heavenly children; thou hast not yet escaped the judgement of the Almighty God who seeth all. These our brothers, after enduring a brief pain, have now drunk of everflowing life, in
85 terms of God's covenant, but thou shalt receive by God's judgement the just penalty of thine arrogance. I, like my brothers, give up body and soul for our fathers' laws, calling on God to show favour to our nation soon, and to make thee acknowledge, in torments and plagues, that he alone is God, and to let the Al-
90 mighty's wrath, justly fallen on the whole of our nation, end in me and in my brothers. Then the king fell into a passion and had him handled worse than the others, so exasperated was he at being mocked. Thus he also died unpolluted, trusting absolutely in the Lord. Finally after her sons the mother also perished.
95   Let this suffice for the enforced sacrifices and the excesses of barbarity.

l. 15 *Moses declared in his song.* Deut. 32. 36.
l. 25 *The King of the world shall raise us up, who have died for his laws, and revive us to life everlasting.* See the introductory note above and cf. Dan. 12. 2 (written at the time to which 2 Macc. 7 refers).
l. 30 *I hope to get them back again.* The resurrection will be a resurrection of the body.
l. 36 *Thou shalt have no resurrection to life.* The resurrection will be a resurrection of the righteous. The fate of the wicked is not clear. This passage might suggest annihilation; but l. 41 (His sovereign power will torture thee and thy seed) and l. 45 (Think not thou shalt go unpunished), punishment.
l. 60 *A Friend.* The title of a high official at court.
Passim: it seems almost certain that the author of Heb. 11 had this chapter in mind. See especially Heb. 11. 3, 34ff.: cf. 11. 26f.

APOCALYPTIC

THE roots of Jewish and Christian apocalyptic are in Old Testament prophecy, though not a few non-Jewish influences helped to shape its development. On the general question of the relation between prophecy and apocalyptic, see H. H. Rowley, *The Relevance of Apocalyptic*, Ch. 1. Here it may simply be emphasized that while both prophecy and apocalyptic were concerned with the future they conceived it in different ways. Prophets and apocalyptists alike believed that the future lay entirely within the prevision and control of God; but whereas the former saw the future developing continuously out of the present, good and evil bearing their own fruit and reaping their own reward, the latter saw the future as essentially discontinuous with the present. History would, as it were, take a leap to a new level, on which the judgements of God would be more plainly visible; or, better, God would, by entering history, either personally or through a representative, introduce into it a new factor which would revolutionize its course. A prophet might announce the captivity or restoration of his people; the apocalyptist announces the end of the age. The apocalyptists "foreshorten" history even more radically than the prophets, and for them the last days are always at hand. This is not simply because the apocalyptic writers believed they could see the signs of the times in the growing evil of their age and that God must surely act speedily if he was to act at all. "Apocalypse" means revealing, the disclosing of secrets; and the secrets were not only secrets of what was to be. They included also secrets of what already was, but was concealed in heaven. Out of their knowledge of these heavenly realities grew their awareness of what would in due course take place on earth; and since the heavenly beings stood ready for action their manifestation could not be long delayed.

The widespread influence of apocalyptic in the period of primitive Christianity hardly needs demonstration; not only can most of the apocalypses which are still extant be dated within that period, many other documents also, not primarily apocalyptic, bear clear traces of apocalyptic in their style and matter. This is true both of Jewish literature and of Christian, for though there is in the New Testament only one Apocalypse, apocalyptic material is to be found in almost every book.

A. *The Literary Forms of Apocalyptic*

Most of the apocalypses reveal almost stereotyped forms of construction and expression.

PSEUDONYMITY

The Christian Apocalypse is noteworthy in that it makes no claim to be the work of a famous hero of the past; in the Church, prophecy flourished again, and in the presence of direct inspiration there was no need to claim antiquity as a source of authority. Nearly every Jewish apocalypse however is attributed to some ancient worthy; and a corollary of this pseudonymity is the necessity of finding some means of explaining why the book had not become known before its actual date of publication.

211 *Daniel* 12. Daniel was written at the time of the attempt of Antiochus Ephiphanes to impose Hellenism upon the Jews (see pp. 106ff. (98ff.)), i.e., *c.* 167 B.C.

> And at that time shall Michael stand up, the great prince which standeth for the children of thy people: and there shall be a time of trouble, such as never was since there was a nation even to that same time: and at that time thy people shall be delivered, everyone
> 5 that shall be found written in the book. And many of them that sleep in the dust of the earth shall awake, some to everlasting life, and some to shame and everlasting contempt. And they that be wise shall shine as the brightness of the firmament; and they that turn many to righteousness as the stars for ever and ever. But thou, O
> 10 Daniel, shut up the words, and seal the book, even to the time of the end: many shall run to and fro, and knowledge shall be increased. Then I Daniel looked, and, behold, there stood other two, the one on the brink of the river on this side, and the other on the brink of the river on that side. And one said to the man clothed in
> 15 linen, which was above the waters of the river, How long shall it be to the end of these wonders? And I heard the man clothed in linen, which was above the waters of the river, when he held up his right hand and his left hand unto heaven, and sware by him

that liveth for ever that it shall be for a time, times, and a half; and
20 when they have made an end of breaking in pieces the power of the
holy people, all these things shall be finished. And I heard, but I
understood not: then said I, O my lord, what shall be the issue of
these things? And he said, Go thy way, Daniel: for the words are
shut up and sealed till the time of the end. Many shall purify them-
25 selves, and make themselves white, and be refined; but the wicked
shall do wickedly; and none of the wicked shall understand: but
they that be wise shall understand. And from the time that the
continual burnt-offering shall be taken away, and the abomination that maketh desolate set up, there shall be a thousand two
30 hundred and ninety days. Blessed is he that waiteth, and cometh
to the thousand three hundred and five and thirty days. But go thy
way till the end be: for thou shalt rest, and shalt stand in thy lot,
at the end of the days.

l. 5 *Many of them that sleep . . . shall awake.* The notion of a resurrection, not
found in the older parts of the Old Testament, is common in the apocalypses,
where supernatural occurrences are common.

l. 10 *Shut up the words, and seal the book.* Daniel seems to have been the name of a
legendary figure of famous wisdom and virtue (cf. Ezek. 14. 14, 20; 28. 3).
In the book of Daniel he is represented as having lived in the time of the
Exile and having received his visions then. To account for the fact that his
writings did not appear till the age of Antiochus Epiphanes the author uses
a literary device common in the apocalypses. Daniel had been bidden to
seal his writings; they were to be released only when the "end" was imminent—as the author of Daniel believed it to be. Cf. l. 24.

212 4 *Ezra* (otherwise 2 *Esdras*) 14. 1–17. 4 Ezra is a composite work,
but the greater part of it was written in the first century A.D. Christian
additions were made, and the whole edited, at a later time.

And it came to pass after the third day, while I sat under the oak,
lo! there came a voice out of a bush over against me; and it said,
Ezra, Ezra! And I said: Here am I, Lord. And I rose upon my feet.
Then said he unto me: I did manifestly reveal myself in the bush,
5 and talked with Moses when my people were in bondage in Egypt:
and I sent him, and led my people out of Egypt, and brought them
to Mount Sinai; and I held him by me for many days.
    I told him many wondrous things,
        showed him the secrets of the times,
10   declared to him the end of the seasons:
    Then I commanded him saying:
    These words shalt thou publish openly, but these keep secret.
And now I do say to thee:

The signs which I have shewed thee,
15   The dreams which thou hast seen,
        and the interpretations which thou hast heard—
lay them up in thy heart! For thou shalt be taken up from among
men, and henceforth thou shalt remain with my Son, and with
such as are like thee, until the times be ended.
20   For the world has lost its youth,
        The times begin to wax old.
For the world-age is divided into twelve parts; nine parts of it are
passed already, and the half of the tenth part; and there remain of
it two parts, besides the half of the tenth part.
25   Now, therefore, set in order thy house,
        and reprove thy people;
            Comfort the lowly among them,
            and instruct those that are wise.
        Now do thou renounce the life that is corruptible,
30   let go from thee the cares of mortality;
            cast from thee the burdens of man,
                put off now the weak nature;
            lay aside thy burdensome cares,
                and hasten to remove from these times!
35   For still worse evils than those which thou hast seen happen shall
yet take place. For the weaker the world grows through age, so
much more shall evils increase upon the dwellers on earth.
        Truth shall withdraw further off,
            and falsehood be nigh at hand:
40   for already the Eagle is hastening to come whom thou sawest in
vision.

l. 3 *Ezra, Ezra.* Ezra in Jewish tradition was the great continuator of the work of
Moses, the example and model of the scribes. To ascribe an apocalypse to
him was to claim the shelter not merely of a respectable antiquity but also
of the Law itself.

l. 12 *These words shalt thou publish openly,* that is, the Law.
These keep secret. This refers to the apocalyptic tradition, some at least of
which was ascribed to Moses. The oral Law (see p. 139 (**127**)) as well as
the written was ascribed to Moses; here his authority is claimed for the
apocalyptic material also. It had not been published earlier because Moses
had been forbidden to make it known.

l. 17 *Lay them up in thy heart.* These revelations are not for Ezra's own time.

l. 18 *With my Son.* The Messiah, who, as God's Son, is already pre-existent in
heaven.

l. 22 *The world-age is divided into twelve parts.* See below on the Two Ages.

l. 35 *Still worse evils.* Before the messianic age must come the messianic afflictions;
see pp. 245-50 (**222f.**).

l. 40 *The Eagle.* See 4 Ezra 11 (**215**).

213 1 *Enoch* 1. 1f. The words of the blessing of Enoch, wherewith he
blessed the elect and righteous, who will be living in the day of
tribulation, when all the wicked and godless are to be removed.
And he took up his parable and said—Enoch a righteous man, whose
5 eyes were opened by God, saw the vision of the Holy One in the
heavens, which the angels showed me, and from them I heard
everything, and from them I understood as I saw, but not for this
generation, but for a remote one which is for to come.

HISTORY IN ALLEGORICAL FORM

The apocalyptist very commonly conveys his meaning by portraying
contemporary history in symbolic form, and continuing the symbolic
narrative so as to include the supernatural events which he believes
to be close at hand. This method often permits the dating of apocalypses; the point at which the history loses precision and accuracy is
the moment of writing.

214 *Psalms of Solomon* 2. 1–6, 24–35. The Psalms of Solomon were
written about the middle of the first century B.C., and seem to have come
from the Pharisaic party within Judaism (see pp. 124–7 (**115**)). In this
Psalm the history is scarcely concealed, except that names are not
mentioned.

When the sinner waxed proud, with a battering-ram he cast down
fortified walls,
And thou didst not restrain him.
Alien nations ascended thine altar,
5   They trampled it proudly with their sandals;
Because the sons of Jerusalem had defiled the holy things of the
Lord,
Had profaned with iniquities the offerings of God.
Therefore he said: Cast them far from me;
10 It was set at naught before God,
It was utterly dishonoured;
The sons and the daughters were in grievous captivity,
Sealed was their neck, branded was it among the nations.
. . . .
15 And I saw and entreated the Lord and said,
Long enough, O Lord, has thine hand been heavy on Israel, in
bringing the nations upon them.
For they have made sport unsparingly in wrath and fierce anger;
And they will make an utter end, unless thou, O Lord, rebuke
20   them in thy wrath.

For they have done it not in zeal, but in lust of soul,
    Pouring out their wrath upon us with a view to rapine.
Delay not, O God, to recompense them on their heads,
    To turn the pride of the dragon into dishonour.
25 And I had not long to wait before God showed me the insolent one
    Slain on the mountains of Egypt,
    Esteemed of less account than the least, on land and sea;
His body, too, borne hither and thither on the billows with much
    insolence,
30 With none to bury him, because he had rejected him with dis-
    honour.
He reflected not that he was man,
    And reflected not on the latter end;
He said: I will be lord of land and sea;
35 And he recognized not that it is God who is great,
    Mighty in his great strength.
He is king over the heavens,
    And judgeth kings and kingdoms.
It is he who setteth me up in glory,
40 And bringeth down the proud to eternal destruction in dis-
    honour,
Because they knew him not.

l. 1 *With a battering-ram.* This, and other details in the passage, correspond closely to the siege of Jerusalem by Pompey in 63 B.C. Cf. Josephus, *War* i. 147 (Pompey . . . brought up the battering engines which had been conveyed from Tyre), 150 (Many of the priests, seeing the enemy advancing sword in hand, calmly continued their sacred ministrations, and were butchered in the act of pouring libations and burning incense).

l. 21 *Not in zeal.* It was indeed God's purpose to punish Israel, but the Roman soldiers were not acting with this in mind.

l. 24 *The dragon.* Probably the "insolent one" of the next line; that is, Pompey.

l. 26 *The mountains of Egypt.* After the battle of Pharsalia (48 B.C.) Pompey escaped, but when he landed in Egypt he was at once killed. The word "mountains" does not seem apt in reference to Egypt and may be an error for "rivers" or "borders".

l. 35 *It is God who is great.* This is probably an allusion to Pompey's name Magnus, the Great.

215 4 *Ezra* 11. The vision of this chapter, the well known Eagle Vision, is based on Daniel 7. The eagle represents the fourth kingdom seen by Daniel in the vision of ch. 7; but here it stands for the Roman Empire, whereas in Daniel it stands for the Greek.

And it came to pass the second night that I saw a dream: and lo! there came up from the sea an eagle which had twelve feathered wings, and three heads. And I beheld, and lo! he spread his wings

over the whole earth, and all the winds of heaven blew on him, and
5 the clouds were gathered together unto him. And I beheld, and lo!
out of his wings there grew anti-wings; and they became wings
petty and small. But his heads were at rest; the middle head was
greater than the other heads, yet it rested with them. And I beheld,
and lo! the eagle flew with his wings to reign over the earth and
10 over them that dwell therein. And I beheld how all things under
heaven were subject unto him, and no one spake against him—not
even one of the creatures upon earth. And I beheld, and lo! the
eagle rose upon his talons, and uttered his voice to his wings,
saying, Watch not all at once: sleep every one in his place, and
15 watch by course: but let the heads be preserved for the last. And I
beheld, and lo! the voice proceeded not from his heads, but from
the midst of his body. And I numbered his anti-wings, and lo!
there were eight.

And I beheld, and lo! [on the right side] there arose one wing,
20 and reigned over the whole earth. And it came to pass that, after it
had reigned, it came to its end and disappeared, so that the place of
it was not visible. Then arose the second and reigned, and this bare
rule for a long time. And it came to pass that, after it had reigned,
it also came to its end, so that it disappeared even as the first. And
25 lo! a voice sounded which said to it: Hear, thou that hast borne rule
over the earth so long a time; this I proclaim unto thee before
thou shalt disappear—After thee shall none bear rule the length of
thy time, nay not even the half of it! Then the third lifted itself up
and held the rule even as the former, and it also disappeared.
30 And so it fell to all the wings [in turn] to rule and then disappear.
And I beheld, and lo! in process of time the little wings also were
set up [upon the right side] that they also might hold the rule;
and some of them bare rule but disappeared suddenly: and some of
them were set up but did not hold the rule. After this I beheld, and
35 lo! the twelve wings disappeared, and two little wings; and nothing
was left in the eagle's body save only the three heads that were at
rest, and six little wings. And I beheld, and lo! from the six little
wings two detached themselves, and remained under the head that
was upon the right side: but four remained in their place. And I
40 beheld, and lo! one was set up, but immediately disappeared; a
second also, and this disappeared more quickly than the first. And I
beheld, and lo! the two that remained thought also in themselves
to reign; and while they were thinking thus, lo! one of the heads
that were at rest—it, namely, that was in the midst—awoke; for
45 this one was greater than the two [other] heads. And I beheld how
it allied itself with the two other heads; and lo! the head was

turned with them that were with it, and did eat up the two under-wings that thought to have reigned. This head bare rule over the whole earth, and exercised lordship over the dwellers
50 therein with much oppression; [and it wielded more power over the inhabited world than all the wings that had been.] And after this I beheld, and lo! the middle head suddenly disappeared, even as the wings. But there remained the two heads which also reigned over the earth, and over the inhabitants therein. And I
55 beheld, and lo! the head upon the right side devoured that which was upon the left. Then I heard a voice, which said unto me: Look before thee, and consider what thou seest. And I beheld, and lo! as it were a lion, roused out of the wood, roaring; and I heard how he uttered a man's voice against the eagle; and he spake, saying: Hear,
60 thou Eagle—I will talk with thee; the Most High saith to thee: Art thou not it that remainest of the four beasts which I made to reign in my world, that the end of my times might come through them? Thou, however, the fourth, who art come, hast overcome all the beasts that are past;

65 Thou hast wielded power over the world with great terror,
        and over all the inhabited earth with grievous oppression;
      Thou hast dwelt so long in the civilized world with fraud,
        and hast judged the earth, but not with faithfulness:
      For thou hast afflicted the meek,
70   and oppressed the peaceable;
      Thou hast hated the upright,
        and loved liars;
      Thou hast destroyed the strongholds of the fruitful,
        and laid low the walls of such as did thee no harm—
75 And so thine insolence hath ascended to the Most High,
        and thy pride to the Mighty One.
      Then the Most High regarded his times—
        And lo! they were ended:
      And his ages—
80   and they were fulfilled.
      Therefore shalt thou disappear, O thou Eagle,
        and thy horrible wings,
        and thy little wings most evil,
        thy harm-dealing heads,
85   thy hurtful talons,
          and all thy worthless body!
And so the whole earth, freed from thy violence, shall be refreshed again, and hope for the judgement and mercy of him that made her.

l. 2 *An eagle which had twelve feathered wings, and three heads.* For a similar por-
trayal of an empire and its rulers cf. Rev. 13. 1. The twelve wings are the
Emperors up to Vitellius, with Julius Caesar, Vindex, Nymphidius and
Piso; the three heads Vespasian, Titus and Domitian.

l. 6 *Anti-wings.* This obscure expression probably means rivals to the Emperors.
They are eight in number (see l. 18).

l. 22 *This bare rule for a long time.* This refers to Augustus, who ruled (from the
battle of Actium, 31 B.C.) forty-five years; Tiberius ruled twenty-three, no
other Emperor so long.

l. 35 *Two little wings.* Perhaps Mucianus, proconsul of Syria, and Tiberius
Alexander, prefect of Egypt.

l. 50 *And it wielded more power . . .* This may be an addition by a later editor who
thought that the middle head represented Trajan; its original meaning was
Vespasian.

l. 55 *The head upon the right side devoured . . .* Domitian was believed to have
compassed the death of his brother and predecessor Titus.

l. 58 *A lion.* In the time of Domitian the Messiah arises, and the eagle is destroyed.
It is noteworthy that though Ezra is manifestly dependent upon Dan. 7 he
does not (at this point) identify the "one like unto a son of man" (Dan. 7.
13) with the Messiah; a fresh figure is introduced. From this point the
apocalyptist has no more exact information; naturally, since he is now
writing about the future.

l. 87 *The . . . earth . . . shall be refreshed again.* A very brief and bare description of
the messianic age.

VISION AND PARABLE

It is impossible to carry through a rigid distinction of these two
forms, and they have already been illustrated incidentally (see especially
4 Ezra 11). The visions described by the apocalyptists were undoubtedly
influenced in form by a literary tradition. It is impossible to think
that the whole of the last passage, for example, was seen and remembered in a dream. On the other hand, it is quite unnecessary to suppose that, because the apocalyptists edited their visions and gave them
literary order, they never received real visionary experiences. It is very
probable that they did receive such visions, reflected upon them, and
produced thereby the parables and allegories which we now read.

216 4 *Ezra* 13. 1–13. This is the sixth vision of this book. A long
interpretation follows, from which some notes are taken here. Almost
every detail is interpreted allegorically.

And it came to pass after seven days that I dreamed a dream by
night: [and I beheld,] and lo! there arose a violent wind from the
sea, and stirred all its waves. And I beheld, and lo! [The wind

caused to come up out of the heart of the seas as it were the form of
5 a man. And I beheld, and lo!] this Man flew with the clouds of
heaven. And wherever he turned his countenance to look everything seen by him trembled; and whithersoever the voice went
out of his mouth, all that heard his voice melted away, as the wax
melts when it feels the fire. And after this I beheld, and lo! there
10 was gathered together from the four winds of heaven an innumerable multitude of men to make war against the Man that came up
out of the sea. And I beheld, and lo! he cut out for himself a great
mountain and flew up upon it. But I sought to see the region or
place from whence the mountain had been cut out; and I could
15 not. And after this I beheld, and lo! all who were gathered together
against him were seized with great fear; yet they dared to fight.
And lo! when he saw the assault of the multitude as they came he
neither lifted his hand, nor held spear nor any warlike weapon; but
I saw only how he sent out of his mouth as it were a fiery stream,
20 and out of his lips a flaming breath, and out of his tongue he shot
forth a stream of sparks. And these were all mingled together—the
fiery stream, the flaming breath, and the . . . storm, and fell upon
the assault of the multitude which was prepared to fight, and
burned them all up, so that suddenly nothing more was to be seen
25 of the innumerable multitude save only dust of ashes and smell of
smoke. When I saw this I was amazed. Afterwards I beheld the
same Man come down from the mountain, and call unto him
another multitude which was peaceable. Then he drew nigh unto
him the faces of many men, some of whom were glad, some
30 sorrowful; while some were in bonds, some brought others who
should be offered.

l. 1 *After seven days*, from the Eagle vision of chs. 11f.; see **215**.
  I dreamed. Cf. 11. 1 and many other passages. The dream is a regular form of
  revelation, going back to Daniel, and beyond.

l. 4 *The form of a man . . . this Man flew with the clouds of heaven.* The passage "the
  wind . . . and lo!" is not in the Latin VS. from which the translation in
  the English Apocrypha was made; it is in the Syriac and was omitted
  probably by error. The description of the Man flying with the clouds, and
  the phrase "the form of a man", recall the vision of Dan. 7. 13 ("one like
  unto a son of man"), and it is very probable that Ezra is dependent upon the
  earlier work. But the strange expression "son of man" has disappeared, and
  it is now said that the Man rises from a storm-tossed sea. In the interpretation it is explained that the Man represents God's son, the Messiah, whom
  God has kept in readiness through many ages; he is a pre-existent Messiah.
  The sea may be merely a picturesque detail; more probably it is drawn from
  some earlier speculation regarding the primal Man, or Saviour, or from a
  recollection of the agitated deep of Gen. 1. 2, out of which came the first
  creation.

l. 11 *To make war against the Man.* Cf. the description in Dan. 7 of the four beasts who persecute the people of God (represented by the human figure of the one like a son of man). Ezra elsewhere attests the common belief that the bliss of the messianic age would be ushered in by a period of conflict and woe. See pp. 245–50 (**222f.**).

l. 12 *A great mountain.* The picture may be derived from Dan. 2. 45, but the use made of it is fresh.

l. 18 *Nor held spear nor any warlike weapon.* The victory of the Messiah is supernatural. In the interpretation the fire by which the Man slays his enemies is said to be the Law.

l. 28 *Another multitude.* After the destruction of his adversaries the Messiah assembles his holy people (note that the Man is now wholly distinguished from the people; whether this is so in Dan. 7 is disputed). The description of the peaceable multitude is not in all respects clear. Jews are being brought together from the dispersion; and some of them, it seems, have passed through great tribulation.

217 1 *Enoch* 90. 28–42. 1 Enoch 85–90 is a long allegorical account of the history of Israel from the Creation to the messianic age. There is some mixing of metaphor, but in general men, Israelites and others, are represented by various kinds of animals. The present passage is the close of the allegory, which was written probably in or not long after the time of the Maccabees (see the notes and pp. 105–13 (**97–104**)).

And I stood up to see till they folded up that old house; and carried off all the pillars, and all the beams and ornaments of the house were at the same time folded up with it, and they carried it off and laid it in a place in the south of the land. And I saw till the
5 Lord of the sheep brought a new house greater and loftier than that first, and set it up in the place of the first which had been folded up: all its pillars were new, and its ornaments were new and larger than those of the first, the old one which he had taken away, and all the sheep were within it.
10 And I saw all the sheep which had been left, and all the beasts on the earth, and all the birds of the heaven, falling down and doing homage to those sheep and making petition to and obeying them in every thing. And thereafter those three who were clothed in white and had seized me by my hand [who had taken me up before], and
15 the hand of that ram also seizing hold of me, they took me up and set me down in the midst of those sheep before the judgement took place. And those sheep were all white, and their wool was abundant and clean. And all that had been destroyed and dispersed, and all the beasts of the field, and all the birds of the heaven, assembled in that
20 house, and the Lord of the sheep rejoiced with great joy because they were all good and had returned to his house. And I saw till

they laid down that sword, which had been given to the sheep, and they brought it back into the house, and it was sealed before the presence of the Lord, and all the sheep were invited into that house,
25 but it held them not. And the eyes of them all were opened, and they saw the good, and there was not one among them that did not see. And I saw that that house was large and broad and very full.

And I saw that a white bull was born, with large horns, and all
30 the beasts of the field and all the birds of the air feared him and made petition to him all the time. And I saw till all their generations were transformed, and they all became white bulls; and the first among them became a lamb, and that lamb became a great animal and had great black horns on its head; and the Lord of the
35 sheep rejoiced over it and over all the oxen. And I slept in their midst: and I awoke and saw everything. This is the vision which I saw while I slept, and I awoke and blessed the Lord of righteousness and gave him glory. Then I wept with a great weeping and my tears stayed not till I could no longer endure it: when I saw,
40 they flowed on account of what I had seen; for everything shall come and be fulfilled, and all the deeds of men in their order were shown to me. On that night I remembered the first dream, and because of it I wept and was troubled—because I had seen that vision.

l. 1 *That old house.* The old Jerusalem is to be replaced by a new one which God himself will establish. The idea of a new Jerusalem, or new Temple, is fairly common in apocalyptic writings; cf. Rev. 21. 2.

l. 5 *The Lord of the sheep.* The faithful of Israel are described as sheep; cf. Ezek. 34, a chapter to which the author of this vision is much indebted.

l. 9 *All the sheep were within it.* A variant reading, giving what is a frequent description of the Temple in the last days, runs, "the Lord of the sheep was within it."

l. 10 *The sheep which had been left.* The preceding section of the allegory or vision (90. 20–7) has described a judgement and destruction of apostate "sheep". *All the beasts . . . all the birds,* that is, the Gentiles. Cf. Dan. 4. 12, 21f.; Ezek. 31. 6, 13. The Gentiles will be converted and become servants of Israel. The apocalypses differ widely regarding the fate of the Gentiles.

l. 13 *Those three who were clothed in white.* Cf. 1 Enoch 87. 3; they are three archangels.

l. 15 *That ram,* probably Elijah; cf. 1 Enoch 89. 52, where, however, he is not called a ram. In 89. 42ff. the ram is first Saul, then those who succeed him as kings.

l. 22 *That sword, which had been given to the sheep.* 1 Enoch 90. 19. The reference is to the fierce and successful resistance made by Israel under the Maccabees, which the author seems to regard as foreshadowing, or even ushering in, the messianic age.

l. 29 *A white bull was born.* The Messiah. It is to be noted that he is born after the Judgement, the establishment of faithful Israel in the new Jerusalem and the conversion of the Gentiles. He is therefore a somewhat otiose figure, for whom the author's evident admiration for Judas Maccabaeus left little room. Adam was represented by a white bull at 85. 3.

l. 33 *The first among them became a lamb, and that lamb became* . . . This is a possible restoration of a corrupt text, which runs: The first among them became (*or*, became among them) a word, and the word became . . . But even with the emendation the text is too corrupt to yield a satisfactory sense.

l. 35 *I slept.* The author speaks in the person of Enoch. This long and highly wrought allegory cannot possibly be regarded as a real dream.

B. *The Essential Notions of Apocalyptic*

Some of these have already been brought out, directly in the general introduction to the chapter and indirectly in the passages quoted for the sake of their literary form. In speaking of these essential notions it would be quite misleading to suggest that all the writers of apocalypses looked forward to precisely the same programme of events in the imminent end of the world. The expectations which may rather loosely be labelled messianic were in the period under consideration entirely fluid; indeed there never was, and never could be, an apocalyptic orthodoxy. In the following pages no attempt is made to give a complete account of the different forms taken by the apocalyptic hope in the age of the New Testament; various aspects of this hope, all of them in their way important, are illustrated from the documents.

THE TWO AGES

The apocalyptists inherited the feeling for history which was characteristic of the prophets, and accordingly their thought was cast in a chronological mould. The line drawn between the secret and the manifest activity of God was a line in time, which separated the Present Age from the Age to Come. The present age witnessed the usurpation of God's authority by evil powers; in the Age to Come God alone would be the supreme ruler, and his perfect will would be perfectly seen and done. This distinction between two ages is no peculiarity of the apocalypses; it was current also among the Rabbis; see **132**.

218 4 *Ezra* 7. 45–61. And I answered and said: O Lord, I said even then and say now: Blessed are they who come into the world and keep thy commandments.

But concerning those for whom my prayer was offered: who is
5 there of those who have come into the world that has not sinned?

Or who of the earth-born is there that has not transgressed thy covenant? And now I see that the coming Age shall bring delight to few, but torment unto many. For the evil heart has grown up in us which has estranged us from God,

10   and brought us into destruction;
And has made known to us the ways of death,
    And showed us the paths of perdition,
    and removed us far from life;
and that not a few only, but well nigh all that have been created!

15   And he answered me and said:
    Hear me, and I will instruct thee,
      and a second time will admonish thee:
For this cause the Most High has made not one Age but two. And whereas thou hast said that the righteous are not many but

20 few, while the ungodly abound—hear the answer to this: Suppose thou have choice stones, in number exceeding few; wilt thou set [place] with them lead and clay?
And I said: Lord, how should it be possible?
And he said unto me: Not only so, but

25   Ask the earth, and she shall tell thee;
    Speak to her, and she shall declare it unto thee.
Say to her: Thou bringest forth gold and silver and brass—and also iron and lead and clay: but silver is more abundant than gold, and brass than silver, and iron than brass, lead than iron, and clay

30 than lead. Do thou, then, consider which things are precious and to be desired: that which is abundant or that which is rare?
And I said: O Lord my Lord, that which is plentiful is of less worth, but that which is more rare is precious.
And he answered me and said: Weigh within thyself what thou

35 hast thought! For he that has what is rare rejoices beyond him that has what is plentiful.
So also shall be my promised judgement; I will rejoice over the few that shall be saved, inasmuch as they it is that make my glory prevail now already and through them my name is now already

40 named [with praise].
And I will not grieve over the multitude of them that perish: for they it is who now
    are made like vapour,
    counted as smoke,

45   are comparable unto the flame:
They are fired, burn hotly, are extinguished!

l. 2 *Blessed are they who come (into the world) and keep thy commandments.* The words in brackets are added because the phrase "those who come into the world" is a common one for "the human race". Ezra is appalled by a problem which appears also in the New Testament. The Law is given as a condition, or means, of salvation. Few or none observe the Law perfectly; what of the remainder of mankind? Ezra's evident distress at the fewness of those who should be saved is illuminating, but he cannot give so hopeful an answer as Paul.

l. 7 *The coming Age.* See below, where the two Ages are contrasted.

l. 8 *The evil heart,* that is, the evil inclination. See p. 144 (**132**).

l. 18 *For this cause the Most High has made not one Age but two,* that is, in order to redress the wickedness and ill of the present Age. Evil men cannot be allowed for ever to dominate over the good; there is a just reward for the godly.

l. 37 *So also shall be my promised judgement.* The coming Age will be inaugurated by the judgement, the separation of good from evil. It may be noted that though God is said to save the righteous few, it is from their misfortunes, not from their sins, that he saves them. The apocalyptists in general take the somewhat naïve view that there *are* righteous and there *are* wicked, white and black; we do not hear of the reclamation and conversion of the wicked.

l. 46 *They are fired, burn hotly, are extinguished!* A period of torment followed by annihilation seems to be intended.

219 2 *Baruch* 83. 4–9. Let none therefore of these present things ascend into your hearts, but above all let us be expectant, because that which is promised to us shall come. And let us not now look unto the delights of the Gentiles in the present, but let us remember
5 what has been promised to us in the end. For the ends of the times and of the seasons and whatsoever is with them shall assuredly pass by together. The consummation, moreover, of the age shall then show the great might of its ruler, when all things come to judgement. Do ye therefore prepare your hearts for that which before ye
10 believed, lest ye come to be in bondage in both worlds, so that ye be led away captive here and be tormented there. For that which exists now, or which has passed away, or which is to come, in all these things, neither is the evil fully evil, nor again the good fully good.

l. 2 *Let us be expectant.* Baruch (another pseudonym, of course) is dealing with the religious attitude proper to those who are looking for the speedy arrival of a new age. They must not be preoccupied with things belonging to the present world, but "look for the kingdom of God" (cf. Mark 15. 43; Luke 2. 25; Col. 3. 1f.).

l. 7 *The consummation . . . of the age.* The end of the present order and the beginning of the new. As frequently, between the two Ages stands the judgement.

l. 10 *In bondage in both worlds.* To endure bondage now would be a price worth paying for bliss in the world to come. But to apostatize now would lead to the worst results in both worlds.

l. 13 *Neither is the evil fully evil, nor again the good fully good.* In contrast with the age to come, in which felicity and torment are unmixed. Baruch is apparently referring to the doctrine that in this Age the good receive full punishment for their few sins, that their bliss may be perfect in the Age to come, and that the wicked, for a similar reason, receive compensation for their few virtues.

JUDGEMENT AND THE KINGDOM OF GOD

Reference to a final judgement has appeared in many of the passages already quoted; it is a constant theme of apocalyptic, and a necessary event before present wrongs could be righted under the rule of God.

220 *Assumption of Moses* 10. This book was probably written during the lifetime of Jesus.

And then his kingdom shall appear throughout all his creation,
And then Satan shall be no more,
And sorrow shall depart with him.
Then the hands of the angel shall be filled
5   Who has been appointed chief,
And he shall forthwith avenge them of their enemies.
For the Heavenly One will arise from his royal throne,
And he will go forth from his holy habitation
With indignation and wrath on account of his sons.
10   And the earth shall tremble: to its confines shall it be shaken:
And the high mountains shall be made low
And the hills shall be shaken and fall.
And the horns of the sun shall be broken and he shall be turned
into darkness;
15   And the moon shall not give her light, and be turned wholly into
blood.
And the circle of the stars shall be disturbed.
And the sea shall retire into the abyss,
And the fountains of waters shall fail,
20   And the rivers shall dry up.
For the Most High will arise, the Eternal God alone,
And he will appear to punish the Gentiles,
And he will destroy all their idols.
Then thou, O Israel, shalt be happy,
25   And thou shalt mount upon the necks and wings of the eagle,
And they shall be ended.
And God will exalt thee,

And he will cause thee to approach to the heaven of the stars,
In the place of their habitation.

30   And thou shalt look from on high and shalt see thy enemies in
Gehenna,
And thou shalt recognize them and rejoice,
And thou shalt give thanks and confess thy Creator.

And do thou, Joshua the son of Nun, keep these words and this

35 book: for from my death [assumption] until his advent there shall
be CCL times. And this is the course of the times which they shall
pursue till they are consummated. And I shall go to sleep with my
fathers. Wherefore, Joshua thou son of Nun, [be strong and] be of
good courage; [for] God hath chosen [thee] to be minister in the

40 same covenant.

l. 1 *Then his kingdom shall appear.* There has probably been some dislocation in the
text of this apocalypse; but it is clear that "Moses" means that the coming
of the kingdom will be preceded by a period of special affliction and distress
for the people of God. This period was often called the "travail-pains of the
Messiah"; but it should be observed that in the Assumption of Moses there
is no Messiah.

l. 2 *Satan shall be no more.* The establishment of God's rule necessarily means the
removal of Satan who has usurped God's authority.

l. 7 *The Heavenly One will arise from his royal throne.* It becomes very clear that
the "coming of the Kingdom" is a way of expressing God's royal authority,
now at length put into action.

l. 10 *The earth shall tremble.* Physical portents are particularly characteristic of
apocalyptic over against prophecy; see above, p. 227.

l. 21 *The Eternal God alone.* The emphasis on the fact that God works alone
excludes the notion of a Messiah, and may be intended to combat such a
notion.

l. 22 *To punish the Gentiles.* "Moses" takes a nationalist view of the kingdom of
God. For a different view of the fate of the Gentiles see the next passage, **221.**

l. 25 *Mount upon . . . be ended.* The text seems to be corrupt. Charles emends to:
Thou shalt go up against the eagle
And its necks and wings shall be destroyed.

l. 29 *In the place of their habitation.* Another corrupt passage; Charles's emendation
is:
And he will establish thy habitation among them.

l. 34 *Joshua (the son of) Nun.* This part of the apocalypse is cast in the form of an
address made by Moses to Joshua. For this use of pseudonymity see above,
pp. 228–31.

l. 35 *There shall be CCL times.* By "times" are meant weeks of years, that is 1750
years altogether. This is the period between the death of Moses and the
coming of the kingdom of God. We do not know the date the author would
have ascribed to the death of Moses, but there can be little doubt that he
thought that, in his day, the 250 times had almost elapsed. Apocalypses were
written under the conviction that the end was near.

221 *Sibylline Oracles* iii. 767–808. In antiquity, considerable weight was attached to utterances attributed to the various Sibyls. Their oracles conveyed, for those who could understand them, divine judgements on human affairs. The production of such oracles was easy to anyone capable of writing Greek hexameter verses (their traditional medium), and Jewish writers (later, Christian also) were not slow to adopt this valuable means of propaganda. The Sibylline books as they have come down to us are not a unity, but there can be no doubt of the Jewish origin of the following verses.

> And then indeed he will raise up his kingdom for all ages over men, he who once gave a holy law to godly men, to all of whom he promised to open out the earth and the world, and the portals of the blessed, and all joys, and everlasting sense and eternal gladness.
> 5 And from every land they shall bring frankincense and gifts to the house of the great God: and there shall be no other house for men even in future generations to know but only that which he has given to faithful men to honour. For mortals call that alone the house of the great God. And all the paths of the plain and the sheer
> 10 banks, and the lofty mountains and the wild sea waves shall become easy to travel over by foot or sail in those days. For nought but peace shall come upon the land of the good: and the prophets of the Mighty God shall take away the sword. For they are the judges of mortal men and just kings. Even wealth shall be righteous
> 15 among men: for this is the judgement and the rule of the Mighty God.
> Rejoice, O virgin, and exult: for to thee the Creator of heaven and earth has given everlasting joy. And in thee shall he dwell, and thou shalt have eternal light.
> 20 And wolves and lambs together shall crop grass upon the mountains, and leopards shall feed with kids. Prowling bears shall lie with calves, and the carnivorous lion shall eat in the manger like the ox, and the tiniest infants shall lead them in bonds, for he shall make the beasts upon the earth incapable of harm. Serpents
> 25 and asps shall sleep with babes, and shall not harm them: for God's hand shall be stretched over them.
> Now I will tell thee a very evident sign, that thou mayest understand when the end of all things is coming on the earth. When swords in the star-lit heaven appear by night towards dusk
> 30 and towards dawn, and straightway dust is carried from heaven to earth, and all the brightness of the sun fails at midday from the heavens, and the moon's rays shine forth and come back to earth, and a sign comes from the rocks with dripping streams of blood:

and in a cloud ye shall see a battle of foot and horse, as a hunt of
35 wild beasts, like unto misty clouds. This is the consummation of
war which God, whose dwelling is in heaven, is bringing to pass.
But all must sacrifice to the Mighty King.

l. 2 *Who once gave a holy law to godly men.* The Jewish propagandist is too subtle to
declare himself, though his meaning is apparent to the initiated.

l. 5 *From every land . . . of the great God.* The "Sibyl" is a Jewish universalist, who
believes not in the destruction but in the conversion of the Gentiles. The
Temple in Jerusalem will become the centre of a worldwide faith and cultus.

l. 17 *O virgin.* Presumably Jerusalem. The Old Testament language (e.g. 2 Kings
19. 21) would be evident to Jews, cryptic to others.

l. 20 *Wolves and lambs* . . . Probably a reference to Isa. 11. 6.

l. 27 *A very evident sign.* This interest in signs brings the author of the present
passage into the field of apocalyptic.

l. 31 *To earth* . . . "The line is defective and emendations can only be conjectural" (H. C. O. Lanchester in Charles, op. cit., ii. 392).

l. 35 *The consummation of war.* It is possible that the text is again corrupt; some
would read "the end of all things".

THE MESSIANIC WOES AND THE MESSIAH

The notion that the good Age would be preceded by a period of
affliction and trial has its roots in Old Testament prophecy and other
religious movements of the ancient East. It appears in many apocalyptic documents, and in the New Testament, but in several different
forms. Sometimes the distress is political and military; sometimes it
arises from supernatural portents; often from a combination of both.
Similarly there is no consistency of thought about the Messiah.

222 2 *Baruch* 25–30. And he answered and said unto me: Thou too shalt
be preserved till that time, till that sign which the Most High will
work for the inhabitants of the earth in the end of days. This therefore shall be the sign. When a stupor shall seize the inhabitants of
5 the earth, and they shall fall into many tribulations, and again when
they shall fall into great torments. And it will come to pass when
they say in their thoughts by reason of their much tribulation: The
Mighty One doth no longer remember the earth—yea, it will come
to pass when they abandon hope, that the time will then awake.
10 And I answered and said: Will that tribulation which is to be
continue a long time, and will that necessity embrace many years?
And he answered and said unto me: Into twelve parts is that time
divided, and each one of them is reserved for that which is appointed for it. In the first part there shall be the beginning of
15 commotions. And in the second part there shall be slayings of the

great ones. And in the third part the fall of many by death. And in
the fourth part the sending of the sword. And in the fifth part
famine and the withholding of rain. And in the sixth part earth-
quakes and terrors. [Wanting]. And in the eighth part a multitude
20 of spectres and attacks of the Shedim. And in the ninth part the fall
of fire. And in the tenth part rapine and much oppression. And in
the eleventh part wickedness and unchastity. And in the twelfth
part confusion from the mingling together of all those things aforesaid. For these parts of that time are reserved, and shall be mingled
25 one with another and minister one to another. For some shall
leave out some of their own, and receive in its stead from others,
and some complete their own and that of others, so that those may
not understand who are upon the earth in those days that this is the
consummation of the times.

30   Nevertheless, whosoever understandeth shall then be wise. For
the measure and reckoning of that time are two parts a week of
seven weeks. And I answered and said: It is good for a man to come
and behold, but it is better that he should not come lest he fall. [But
I will say this also: Will he who is incorruptible despise those things
35 which are corruptible, and whatever befalls in the case of those
things which are corruptible, so that he might look only to those
things which are not corruptible?] But if, O Lord, those things shall
assuredly come to pass which thou hast foretold to me, so do thou
show this also unto me if indeed I have found grace in thy sight. Is it
40 in one place or in one of the parts of the earth that those things are
come to pass, or will the whole earth experience them?

And he answered and said unto me: Whatever will then befall
will befall the whole earth; therefore all who live will experience
them. For at that time I will protect only those who are found in
45 those selfsame days in this land. And it shall come to pass when all
is accomplished that was to come to pass in those parts, that the
Messiah shall then begin to be revealed. And Behemoth shall be revealed from his place and Leviathan shall ascend from the sea, those
two great monsters which I created on the fifth day of creation, and
50 shall have kept until that time; and then they shall be for food for
all that are left. The earth also shall yield its fruit tenthousandfold
and on each [?] vine there shall be a thousand branches, and each
branch shall produce a thousand clusters, and each cluster produce
a thousand grapes, and each grape produce a cor of wine. And those
55 who have hungered shall rejoice: moreover, also, they shall behold
marvels every day. For winds shall go forth from before me to
bring every morning the fragrance of aromatic fruits, and at the
close of the day clouds distilling the dew of health. And it shall

come to pass at that selfsame time that the treasury of manna shall
60 again descend from on high, and they will eat of it in those years,
because these are they who have come to the consummation of
time.

And it shall come to pass after these things, when the time of the
advent of the Messiah is fulfilled, that he shall return in glory.
65 Then all who have fallen asleep in hope of him shall rise again.
And it shall come to pass at that time that the treasuries will be
opened in which is preserved the number of the souls of the
righteous, and they shall come forth, and a multitude of souls shall
be seen together in one assemblage of one thought, and the first
70 shall rejoice and the last shall not be grieved. For they know that
the time is come of which it is said, that it is the consummation of
the times. But the souls of the wicked, when they behold all these
things, shall then waste away the more. For they shall know that
their torment is come and their perdition has arrived.

l. 1 *Thou too.* That is, Baruch, who is supposed to receive the apocalypse.

l. 12 *Into twelve parts is that time divided.* This kind of cryptic chronology was
popular among those who "calculated the end". See for example the passage
from Ass. Mos. 10 quoted above (220).

l. 19 *Terrors.* Reference to the seventh part of the time has fallen out of the text.

ll. 27–30 *So that those may not understand . . . shall then be wise.* The author distinguishes between himself and his friends, who can discern the signs of the
times, and those who either make no calculations at all or differ from him
in their conclusions. If there are those who hold a different (and, to his
mind, incorrect) view, it is because their misapprehension has been willed
by God.

l. 31 *Two parts a week of seven weeks.* This seems unintelligible. There may have
been corruption in the text. If it is to be emended the simplest guess is that
Baruch wrote not "two" but "twelve parts", and meant that the whole
time of the tribulation would last a week of seven weeks (perhaps, forty-nine
years). But this is no more than a guess.

l. 33–7 *But I will say . . . not corruptible.* This sentence seems to interrupt the
thought and to be out of place here. It may have been displaced from a point
later in the book (see 43. 2).

l. 45 *In this land.* Palestine will be an island of safety. The thought is not uncommon.

l. 47 *The Messiah shall then begin to be revealed*, that is, after the tribulation. In this
apocalypse the Messiah is revealed, but is not said to do anything. He is
really an unnecessary figure.

ll. 47f. *Behemoth . . . and Leviathan.* These two monsters appear in the Old Testament (e.g. Job 40. 15, 25); as the context shows they belong to the creation
myth. There is other evidence for the belief that they would provide food
for the messianic banquet.

l. 51 *Tenthousandfold.* For this opinion also there is other evidence. The prediction
was apparently ascribed to Jesus by Papias (*apud* Irenaeus, *Haer.* v. 33).

l. 59 *The treasury of manna.* This belief also is widely attested in Jewish sources, and appears in the New Testament (see Rev. 2. 17, with Charles's note for parallels).

l. 64 *He shall return in glory.* This has been taken to mean, He will, after residence on earth, return to heaven; this is however improbable. It is more likely that the resurrection would be heralded by the coming of the Messiah than by his departure. This statement may simply be parallel to "the Messiah shall then begin to be revealed" (l. 47). But the use of the word "return" suggests that we may be dealing here with a Christian interpolation.

223 *Psalms of Solomon* 17. 23–51. In the earlier part of the Psalm (which is to be dated soon after Pompey's capture of Jerusalem, 63 B.C.; see pp. 116ff. **(107)**) the writer laments the calamities that have befallen his people by reason of foreign invaders, and sinful Jews.

> Behold, O Lord, and raise up unto them their king, the son of David,
>   At the time in the which thou seest, O God, that he may reign over Israel thy servant.
> And gird him with strength, that he may shatter unrighteous rulers,
> 5   And that he may purge Jerusalem from nations that trample her down to destruction.
> Wisely, righteously he shall thrust out sinners from the inheritance,
>   He shall destroy the pride of the sinner as a potter's vessel.
> With a rod of iron he shall break in pieces all their substance,
> 10   He shall destroy the godless nations with the word of his mouth;
> At his rebuke nations shall flee before him,
>   And he shall reprove sinners for the thoughts of their heart.
> And he shall gather together a holy people, whom he shall lead in righteousness,
> 15   And he shall judge the tribes of the people that has been sanctified by the Lord his God.
> And he shall not suffer unrighteousness to lodge any more in their midst,
>   Nor shall there dwell with them any man that knoweth wicked-
> 20   ness,
>   For he shall know them, that they are all sons of their God.
> And he shall divide them according to their tribes upon the land,
>   And neither sojourner nor alien shall sojourn with them any more.
> 25 He shall judge peoples and nations in the wisdom of his righteousness. *Selah.*
> And he shall have the heathen nations to serve him under his yoke;
>   And he shall glorify the Lord in a place to be seen of [?] all the earth;

30   And he shall purge Jerusalem, making it holy as of old:
       So that nations shall come from the ends of the earth to see his glory,
           Bringing as gifts her sons who had fainted,
           And to see the glory of the Lord, wherewith God hath glorified
               her.
35 And he shall be a righteous king, taught of God, over them,
       And there shall be no unrighteousness in his days in their midst,
           For all shall be holy and their king the anointed of the Lord.
       For he shall not put his trust in horse and rider and bow,
           Nor shall he multiply for himself gold and silver for war,
40   Nor shall he gather confidence from [?] a multitude [?] for the
           day of battle.
       The Lord himself is his king, the hope of him that is mighty
           through his hope in God.
       [?] All nations shall be in fear before him,
45   For he will smite the earth with the word of his mouth for ever.
       He will bless the people of the Lord with wisdom and gladness,
           And he himself will be pure from sin, so that he may rule a great
               people.
       He will rebuke rulers, and remove sinners by the might of his word;
50   And relying upon his God, throughout his days he will not
           stumble;
       For God will make him mighty by means of his holy spirit,
           And wise by means of the spirit of understanding, with strength
               and righteousness.
55 And the blessing of the Lord will be with him: he will be strong
           and stumble not;
       His hope will be in the Lord: who then can prevail against him?
       He will be mighty in his works, and strong in the fear of God,
       He will be shepherding the flock of the Lord faithfully and
60   righteously,
       And he will suffer none among them to stumble in their pasture,
       He will lead them all aright,
           And there will be no pride among them that any among them
               should be oppressed.
65 This will be the majesty of the king of Israel whom God knoweth;
       He will raise him up over the house of Israel to correct him.
       His words shall be more refined than costly gold, the choicest;
           In the assemblies he will judge the peoples, the tribes of the
               sanctified.
70 His words shall be like the words of the holy ones in the midst of
           sanctified peoples.
       Blessed be they that shall be in those days,

In that they shall see the good fortune of Israel which God shall
bring to pass in the gathering together of the tribes.

75 May the Lord hasten his mercy upon Israel!

May he deliver us from the uncleanness of unholy enemies!

The Lord himself is our king for ever and ever.

l. 1 *The son of David.* In 17. 5 the promise to David's family is recalled. The
Messiah of this Psalm is a warrior, who will triumph over Israel's foes.

l. 23 *Neither sojourner nor alien* . . . Palestine will be evacuated of all non-Jewish
residents. The Gentiles will be spared but will be governed by the Messiah.

l. 37 *Their king the anointed of the Lord.* A literal rendering of the Greek text is, the
Lord Messiah (Messiah = Anointed One). It is however very probable that
the Psalms were originally written in Hebrew, though they are no longer
extant in that language, and the Hebrew which "Lord Messiah" represents
could, if unpointed, equally well be read as "the Lord's Anointed". It is
probable that the Greek translator is here in error, since in a similar passage
(18. 6) we have "his (*sc.* the Lord's) anointed". The Lord's Christ is a common phrase, and though "King Messiah" also is common in Rabbinic
literature this hardly supplies precedent for "Lord Messiah". It may be that
the erring translator was a Christian (cf. Luke 2. 11), but this is by no means
necessary.

l. 38 *He shall not put his trust* . . . Cf. Deut. 17. 16f. The new king will not fall into
the errors of David's son Solomon.

l. 42 *The Lord himself is his king,* and thus the Messiah represents to his people the
kingship of God.

l. 52 *Holy Spirit.* Better, spirit of holiness. There is no reference to the Holy
Spirit. Cf. Isa. 11. 1.

l. 59 *Shepherding the flock of the Lord.* Cf. Micah 5. 4; Ezek. 34. 23.

ll. 67, 70 *His words.* The king will have some of the properties of a Pharisaic
scribe; he will be a teacher as well as a ruler.

THE SON OF MAN

No attempt will be made here to give an account of the problems
raised by the use of this title in the gospels, much less to answer them.
There are indeed few New Testament problems which require a more
extensive knowledge of Jewish and kindred literature. The following
are among the most important apocalyptic passages in which the expression "Son of man" occurs, and may on no account be neglected in
any consideration of the title. The reader should also note 4 Ezra 13
(quoted above, **216**) where "the Man" is almost certainly related in
some way to "the Son of man".

224 *Daniel* 7. 1-14. On the date and origin of Daniel see above, p.
228.

In the first year of Belshazzar king of Babylon Daniel had a
dream and visions of his head upon his bed: then he wrote the

dream and told the sum of the matters. Daniel spake and said, I
saw in my vision by night, and, behold, the four winds of the
5 heaven brake forth upon the great sea. And four great beasts came
up from the sea, diverse one from another. The first was like a lion,
and had eagle's wings: I beheld till the wings thereof were plucked,
and it was lifted up from the earth, and made to stand upon two
feet as a man, and a man's heart was given to it. And behold an-
10 other beast, a second, like to a bear, and it was raised up on one
side, and three ribs were in his mouth between his teeth: and they
said unto it, Arise, devour much flesh. After this I beheld, and lo
another, like a leopard, which had upon the back of it four wings
of a fowl; the beast had also four heads; and dominion was given
15 to it. After this I saw in the night visions, and behold a fourth
beast, terrible and powerful, and strong exceedingly; and it had
great iron teeth: it devoured and brake in pieces, and stamped the
residue with his feet: and it was diverse from all the beasts that were
before it; and it had ten horns. I considered the horns, and,
20 behold, there came up among them another horn, a little one,
before which three of the first horns were plucked up by the roots:
and, behold, in this horn were eyes like the eyes of a man, and a
mouth speaking great things. I beheld till thrones were placed, and
one that was ancient of days did sit: his raiment was white as snow,
25 and the hair of his head like pure wool; his throne was fiery flames,
and the wheels thereof burning fire. A fiery stream issued and came
forth from before him; thousand thousands ministered unto him,
and ten thousand times ten thousand stood before him; the judgement was set, and the books were opened. I beheld at that time
30 because of the voice of the great words which the horn spake; I
beheld even till the beast was slain, and his body destroyed, and he
was given to be burned with fire. And as for the rest of the beasts
their dominion was taken away: yet their lives were prolonged for
a season and a time. I saw in the night visions, and, behold, there
35 came with the clouds of heaven one like unto a son of man, and he
came even to the ancient of days, and they brought him near before
him. And there was given him dominion, and glory, and a kingdom, that all the peoples, nations, and languages should serve
him: his dominion is an everlasting dominion, which shall not
40 pass away, and his kingdom that which shall not be destroyed.

l. 5 *The great sea.* Cf. the reference to the sea out of which the "Man" rises in
4 Ezra 13. 3. This is a strong indication that in this human figure we are
dealing with an ancient myth, probably a cosmological myth. It may be
that ultimately the "Son of man" became simply a feature of the Jewish
messianic hope, but his origin may well lie elsewhere, in speculations
concerning a primal, or heavenly, man.

Four great beasts. The beasts are explained in the second part of the chapter as "four kings"; "four kingdoms" would have been a plainer statement. It seems that the first beast represents the Babylonian Empire, the second the Median, the third the Persian, and the fourth the Greek Empire of Alexander and his successors. The little horn represents Antiochus IV Epiphanes, whose assaults upon Judaism provoked the writing of Daniel.

l. 23   *Thrones were placed.* If this means that the Son of man is to sit on a throne beside God, it squares ill with the view (see next note) that he is no more than a personification of Israel.

l. 35   *One like unto a son of man,* that is to say, a human figure. Like the four beasts the human figure is explained in the second part of the chapter: The kingdom and the dominion, and the greatness of the kingdoms under the whole heaven, shall be given to the people of the saints of the Most High (7. 27). Thus the human figure represents Israel; his glory is the glory of the people. It must not be inferred from this that he is a mere personification; see the preceding note, and the fact that elsewhere in Daniel nations are represented by angels, real personal heavenly beings. It seems probable that the "Man" was originally a figure in an ancient myth, was taken over by the author of Daniel for the present purpose, and by reason of his function as representing the people of God came ultimately to have messianic status.

225 1 *Enoch* (*a*) 48 (*b*) 69. 26–9 (*c*) 71. 14–17. The central section (37–71) of 1 Enoch, generally known as the Similitudes of Enoch, contains frequent reference to a person described as the (or that) Son of man. The date of the Similitudes is disputed, but it is almost certainly earlier than the earliest books of the New Testament, and some would say nearly 200 years earlier. The Similitudes (and, still more, the mode of thought they represent) may therefore quite possibly have influenced the thought and language of Jesus.

(*a*)   And in that place I saw the fountain of righteousness
    Which was inexhaustible:
    And around it were many fountains of wisdom:
    And all the thirsty drank of them,
  5   And were filled with wisdom,
    And their dwellings were with the righteous and holy and elect.
    And at that hour that Son of man was named
.   In the presence of the Lord of Spirits,
    And his name before the Head of Days.
 10   Yea, before the sun and the signs were created,
    Before the stars of the heaven were made,
    His name was named before the Lord of Spirits.
    He shall be a staff to the righteous whereon to stay themselves and
      not fall,
 15   And he shall be the light of the Gentiles,

And the hope of those who are troubled of heart.
All who dwell on earth shall fall down and worship him,
And will praise and bless and celebrate with song the Lord of Spirits.
And for this reason hath he been chosen and hidden before him,
20 Before the creation of the world and for evermore.
And the wisdom of the Lord of Spirits hath revealed him to the
holy and righteous;
For he hath preserved the lot of the righteous,
Because they have hated and despised this world of unrighteousness,
25 And have hated all its works and ways in the name of the Lord of
Spirits:
For in his name they are saved,
And according to his good pleasure hath it been in regard to their
life.
30 In these days downcast in countenance shall the kings of the earth
have become,
And the strong who possess the land because of the works of their
hands,
For on the day of their anguish and affliction they shall not be able
35 to save themselves.
And I will give them over into the hands of mine elect:
As straw in the fire so shall they burn before the face of the righteous,
And no trace of them shall any more be found.
And on the day of their affliction there shall be rest on the earth,
40 And before them they shall fall and not rise again:
And there shall be no one to take them with his hands and raise
them:
For they have denied the Lord of Spirits and his Anointed.
The name of the Lord of Spirits be blessed.

45 (b) And there was great joy amongst them,
And they blessed and glorified and extolled
Because the name of that Son of man had been revealed unto them.
And he sat on the throne of his glory,
And the sum of judgement was given unto the Son of man,
50 And he caused the sinners to pass away and be destroyed from off
the face of the earth,
And those who have led the world astray.
With chains shall they be bound,
And in their assemblage-place of destruction shall they be im-
55 prisoned,
And all their works vanish from the face of the earth.
And from henceforth there shall be nothing corruptible;
For that Son of man has appeared,

And has seated himself on the throne of his glory,
60 And all evil shall pass away before his face,
And the word of that Son of man shall go forth
And be strong before the Lord of Spirits.
This is the third Parable of Enoch.

(c) And he came to me and greeted me with his voice, and said unto
65   me:
This is the Son of man who is born unto righteousness,
And righteousness abides over him,
And the righteousness of the Head of Days forsakes him not.
And he said unto me:
70 He proclaims unto thee peace in the name of the world to come;
For from hence has proceeded peace since the creation of the world,
And so shall it be unto thee for ever and for ever and ever.
And all shall walk in his ways since righteousness never forsaketh
     him:
75 With him will be their dwelling-places, and with him their heritage,
And they shall not be separated from him for ever and ever and
     ever.
And so there shall be length of days with that Son of man,
And the righteous shall have peace and an upright way
80 In the name of the Lord of Spirits for ever and ever.

l. 1 *In that place.* Enoch sees heaven, and even God himself (described as the Lord
of Spirits, and the Head of Days). It will be remembered that the secrets
disclosed in apocalyptic are not exclusively secrets of the future.

l. 10 *Before the sun and the signs were created . . . his name was named.* Cf. 1. 20. The
Son of man is represented as having a real pre-existence as a heavenly being.

l. 19 *Hath he been chosen and hidden before him.* The Son of man holds his office in
dependence on the will of God; but his existence is at the time of writing an
apocalyptic secret, known only to the apocalyptist and the circle to which he
discloses his visions.

l. 21 *The wisdom of the Lord of Spirits hath revealed him to the holy and righteous,* that
is, by means of Enoch and his visions. In face of sayings such as this it is
difficult to think that (in 1 Enoch) the Son of man is identified with the
righteous as a group.

l. 27 *In his name they are saved.* The righteous are saved by the Son of man from
their affliction. There is no suggestion in 1 Enoch that the Son of man came
to seek and save that which was lost (Luke 19. 10) or to save men from their
sins.

l. 38 *No trace of them shall any more be found.* The wicked are annihilated.

l. 43 *His Anointed,* or, if we take the word as a technical term, his Messiah. The
question whether the Son of man in 1 Enoch is thought of as Messiah is a
difficult and disputed one.

l. 47 *The name of that Son of man had been revealed unto them.* The name of the Son of man is made generally known in the last days.

l. 49 *The sum of judgement was given unto the Son of man.* The Son of man acts as the judge of sinners. The "sum of judgement" means "all judgement"; cf. John 5. 22, 27.

l. 66 *This is the Son of man who is born unto righteousness.* This translation (of R. H. Charles) does not represent the text of the MSS., which give the second person, not the third: Thou art the Son of man . . . (and similarly in the following verses). The scene is the final exaltation of Enoch to heaven (these are the last verses of the Similitudes); according to Charles he is shown the Son of man, about whom he has already received revelations; according to the MSS. it is revealed to Enoch, as the last secret of all, that he himself is the Son of man. Charles abandoned the MSS. because they did not seem to him intelligible; and indeed the thought they convey is very difficult. The Son of man (according to the Similitudes) has existed from eternity in heaven. Enoch, the man, came to exist on earth and after a long life is translated to heaven. We now learn that the one of these distinct characters *is* the other. This identification cannot be rationally conceived; but rationality is perhaps the last quality we should expect in an apocalypse, and the wisest course may be to suppose that there were circles in Judaism in which this strange belief was held. There are several other pieces of evidence which attest the belief that Enoch was translated to heaven to become a celestial being. If there were, in the first century A.D., Jews who believed that it was possible for a man to be exalted to heaven so as to be identified with a supernatural being who was called Son of man and was to come in glory as judge and saviour, their existence and their belief can hardly fail to be relevant to the study of the gospels.

APPENDIX

JEWISH SECTARIAN DOCUMENTS

IN 1910 S. Schechter published under the title *Fragments of a Zadokite Work* a MS. which had been acquired not many years previously by the Cambridge University Library. It had been found in the *genizah* (or cupboard used for storing disused copies of the Scriptures and other works which it was thought undesirable to destroy) of a synagogue in Cairo. The document appeared to have been written in or about the tenth century A.D., and to emanate from a Jewish sect, whose history, constitution, and hopes it described.

In and since 1947 a number of MSS. have been discovered in the desert to the west of the Dead Sea. Among them are Biblical MSS., and other documents of a religious kind, which appear to have been the products of a sect in some respects at least akin to that which produced the *genizah* MS. mentioned above. There are also more purely historical documents, including what seems to be an autograph letter of the Bar Cocheba whose career is briefly described on pp. 133–6 above. The most considerable non-biblical MSS. hitherto investigated (not all have been published in full) are:

(1) A commentary on part of the book of Habakkuk.
(2) The Manual of Discipline (which gives an account of the rules of the sect).
(3) The Book of Lamech (?).
(4) The War of the Sons of Light against the Sons of Darkness.
(5) Hymns of Thanksgiving.

The origin, date, and significance of all these MSS. (including the *genizah* MS.), and of the original documents of which they are, perhaps, copies, are vigorously disputed. The best introductions to the facts and to the debate are given by H. H. Rowley, *The Zadokite Fragments and the Dead Sea Scrolls* (Oxford, 1952), and Millar Burrows, *The Dead Sea Scrolls* (London, 1956). Many scholars are prepared to date the documents to a period which makes them relevant to New Testament

studies, and their view seems to justify the inclusion of a few passages
here; but no attempt will be made to deal with the very complicated
questions which they raise. All such questions are *sub judice*, and this
is not the place to discuss them.

226 Zadokite Fragments 2.

And now, hearken unto me all ye who have entered into the
    covenant,
And I will disclose to you the ways of the wicked.
God loveth wisdom:
And counsel he hath set before him:
5 Prudence and knowledge minister unto him.
Longsuffering is with him
And plenteousness of forgivenesses
To pardon those who repent of transgression.
And power and might and great fury and flames of fire
10 For them who turned aside out of the way,
And abhorred the statute,
So that there should be no remnant,
Nor any escape of them.
For God chose them not from the beginning of the world,
15 And ere they were formed he knew their works.
And he abhorred their generations from of old,
And hid his face from their land till they were consumed.

And he knew the years of their office and the number and exact
statement of their periods for all the things that belong to the
20 ages and have been, moreover whatsoever shall come to pass in
their periods for all the years of eternity.

Yet in all of them he raised him up men called by name,
In order to leave a remnant to the earth,
And to fill the face of the earth with their seed.
25 And through his Messiah he shall make them know his holy spirit,
And he is true, and in the true interpretation of his name are their
    names:
But them he hated he made to go astray.

l. 3 Omitting "knowledge" as an interpolation.
l. 9 Omitting as an interpolation "Therein are all the angels of destruction".
ll. 18–21 These lines are regarded by Charles as an interpolation.

227 Zadokite Fragments 6. 1–8.
The priests are the penitents of Israel
who went forth out of the land of Judah: and [the Levites are]
they who joined them. And the sons of Zadok are the elect of

Israel called by the name, that are holding office in the end of
5 the days. Behold the statement of their names according to
their generations, and the period of their office, and the number
of their afflictions, and the years of their sojournings, and the
statement of their works.

The first saints whom God pardoned,
10 Both justified the righteous,
And condemned the wicked.
And all they who come after them must do according to the
interpretation of the Law,
In which the forefathers were instructed
Until the consummation of the period of these years.
15 In accordance with the covenant which God established with the
forefathers
In order to pardon their sins,
So shall God pardon them.
And on the consummation of the period of these years
They shall no more join themselves to the house of Judah,
20 But shall every one stand up against his net.
The wall shall have been built,
The boundary been far removed.

l. 1 *Penitents* might be rendered "captivity".
l. 18 Omitting as a gloss, "of the number".

228 *Zadokite Fragments* 8. 1–10. And during the period of the destruction of the land there arose those who removed the landmark
and led Israel astray. And the land became desolate because
they spake rebellion against the commandments of God through
5 Moses and also through his holy anointed one, and they prophesied a lie to turn away Israel from God.
But God remembered the covenant with the forefathers:
And he raised up from Aaron men of understanding,
and from Israel wise men:
10 And he made them to hearken,
And they digged the well.
"A well the princes digged,
The nobles of the people delved it
By the order of the Lawgiver."
15 The well is the Law, and they who digged it are the penitents of
Israel who went forth out of the land of Judah and sojourned in
the land of Damascus, all of whom God called princes. For they
sought him and his glory was not turned back in the mouth of
one of them. And the Lawgiver is he who studies the Law, in

20 regard to whom Isaiah said, "He bringeth forth an instrument for
his work." And the nobles of the people are those who came to dig
the well by the precepts in the which the Lawgiver ordained that
they should walk throughout the full period of the wickedness.
And save them they shall get nothing until there arises the Teacher
25 of Righteousness in the end of the days.

ll. 12ff. Num. 21. 8.
l. 20 Isa. 54. 16.

229 *Zadokite Fragments* 8. 11–21. And none who have entered into the
covenant shall enter into the Sanctuary to kindle his altar but they
shall shut the doors concerning whom God said,
"O that there was one among you to shut the doors,
5 So that ye might not vainly kindle the fire upon my altar,"
Unless they observe to do according to the true meaning of the
Law until the period of the wickedness, and to sever themselves
from the children of the pit, and to hold aloof from the polluted
wealth of wickedness under a vow and a curse, and from the
10 wealth of the sanctuary:
And in respect to robbing the poor of his people,
So that widows may be their spoil,
And they may murder the fatherless:
And to make a difference between the clean and the unclean and
15 to make men discern between the holy and the profane: And to
observe the Sabbath according to its true meaning and the feasts
and the day of the Fast according to the utterances of them who
entered into the New Covenant in the land of Damascus:
To contribute their holy things according to the true interpretation:
20 To love every one his brother as himself, and to strengthen the
hand of the poor and the needy and the stranger, and to seek every
one the peace of his brother: To hold aloof from harlots according
to the Law: and that no man should commit a trespass against his
next of kin: To rebuke every one his brother according to the
25 commandment, and not to bear a grudge from day to day, and to
separate from all the pollutions according to their judgements.
And no man shall make abominable with these his holy spirit,
according as God separated these from them. As for all those who
walk in these things in the perfection of holiness according to all
30 the ordinances, the covenant of God standeth fast unto them to
preserve them to a thousand generations.

ll. 4f. Mal. 1. 10.
l. 31 *Generations*. A parallel passage adds, "As it is written, Who keepeth
covenant and mercy with them that love him and keep his commandments
to a thousand generations (Deut. 7. 9)."

230 *Zadokite Fragments* 10. 2-6. As for that which he hath said: "Thou shalt not take vengeance nor bear a grudge against the children of thy people", every man of those who have entered into the covenant, who brings a charge against his neighbour
5 whom he had not rebuked before witnesses, and yet brings it in his fierce wrath or recounts it to his elders in order to bring him into contempt, is taking vengeance and bearing a grudge. But naught is written save that, "He taketh vengeance on his adversaries, and he beareth a grudge against his enemies." If he held his
10 peace with regard to him from day to day, but in his fierce wrath spake against him in a matter of death, he hath testified against himself because he did not give effect to the commandment of God, who said to him, "Thou shalt surely rebuke thy neighbour and not bear sin because of him." As
15 regards the oath, touching that which he said "Thou shalt not avenge thee with thine own hand", the man who makes another man swear in the open field—that is, not in the presence of the judges, or owing to their commands—hath avenged himself with his own hand.

ll. 1f. Lev. 19. 18.
ll. 8f. Nahum 1. 2.
ll. 13f. Lev. 19. 17.
ll. 15f. Cf. 1 Sam. 25. 26, 31.

231 *Zadokite Fragments* 13. As to the Sabbath, to observe it according to its law, no man shall do work on the sixth day from the time when the sun's orb in its fullness is still without the gate, for it is he who has said, "Observe the Sabbath day to keep it holy."
5 And on the Sabbath day no man shall utter a word of folly and vanity. No man shall lend aught to his neighbour. None shall dispute on matters of wealth and gain. None shall speak on matters of work and labour to be done on the following morning. No man shall walk in the field to do the work of his business. On the
10 Sabbath none shall walk outside his city more than a thousand cubits. No man shall eat on the Sabbath day aught save that which is prepared or perishing in the field. Nor shall one eat or drink unless in the camp. If he was on the way and went down to wash he may drink where he stands, but he shall not draw into any
15 vessel. No man shall send the son of a stranger to do his business on the Sabbath day.
No man shall put on garments that are filthy or were brought by a Gentile unless they were washed with water or rubbed with frankincense.
20 No man shall fast of his own will on the Sabbath. No man shall

walk after the animal to pasture it outside his city more than two thousand cubits. None shall lift his hand to smite it with his fist. If it be stubborn he shall not remove it out of his house. No man shall carry anything from the house to the outside or from the outside
25 into the house, and if he be in the vestibule he shall not carry anything out of it or bring in anything into it. None shall open the cover of a vessel that is pasted on the Sabbath. No man shall carry on him spices to go out or come in on the Sabbath. None shall lift up in his dwelling house róck or earth. Let not the nursing father
30 take the sucking child to go out or to come in on the Sabbath. No man shall provoke his manservant or his maidservant or his hireling on the Sabbath. No man shall help an animal in its delivery on the Sabbath day. And if it falls into a pit or ditch, he shall not raise it on the Sabbath. No man shall rest in a place near to the
35 Gentiles on the Sabbath. No man shall suffer himself to be polluted for the sake of wealth or gain on the Sabbath. And if any person falls into a place of water or into a place of . . . he shall not bring him up by a ladder or a cord or instrument. No man shall offer anything on the altar on the Sabbath, save the burnt-offering of
40 the Sabbath, for so it is written, "Excepting your Sabbaths".

l. 4 Deut. 5. 12.
l. 40 Cf. Lev. 23. 38.

232 *Zadokite Fragments* 16. And this is the regulation of the Censor· of the camp. He shall instruct the many in the works of God, and shall make them understand his wondrous mighty acts, and shall narrate before them the things of the world since its creation.
5 And he shall have mercy upon them as a father upon his children, and shall forgive all that have incurred guilt. As a shepherd with his flock he shall loose all the bonds of their knots . . . oppressed and crushed in his congregation. And every one who joins his congregation, he shall reckon him according to his works, his
10 understanding, his might, his strength, and his wealth. And they shall record him in his place in accordance with his position in a lot of the camp. No man of the children of the camp shall have power to bring a man into the congregation [without] the word of the Censor of the camp. Nor shall any man of them
15 who have entered into the covenant of God do business with the children of the pit unless hand to hand. No man shall do a thing as buying and selling unless he has spoken to the Censor of the camp, and he shall do it in the camp and not . . . and so to him who casts forth . . . they, and he who is not connected with
20 . . . And this is the settlement of the camps. All . . . shall not succeed

to settle in the land . . . that have not come from the day that
Ephraim departed from Judah. And as for all who walk in these
the covenant of God standeth fast unto them to save them from all
the snares of the pit, for suddenly . . .

l. 1   *The Censor*; in Hebrew, מבקר, m^e*baqqer*; equivalent to the Greek ἐπίσκοπος.
Some have seen in the Censor the original of the Christian bishop.

233 *Manual of Discipline* 6. 24–8. 19. Now these are the laws by
which they shall judge in the communal investigation, according to the following provisions: If there be found among
them a man who lies in the matter of wealth, and it become
5 known, they shall exclude him from the Purity of the Many
for one year, and he shall be fined one fourth of his food
allowance; and he who answers his fellow with a stiff neck,
or speaks with a quick temper so as to reject the instruction
of his comrade, by disobeying his fellow who is enrolled before
10 him, has taken the law into his own hands, so he shall be fined for
one year [and be excluded; and he] who mentions anything in
the Honoured Name against any [must be put to death]. And
if he who reads aloud from the Book or blesses has blasphemed,
either through being frightened by persecution, or through any
15 reason he may have, he shall be excluded so as to return no more
to the Council of the Community; and if it is against any of the
priests written in the Book that he has spoken in wrath, he shall
be fined for one year and be set apart by himself from the Purity
of the Many; but if he has spoken through inadvertence, he shall
20 be fined for six months; and whoever denies his knowledge of
having so spoken shall be fined for six more months. And the man
who vilifies unjustly his fellow, when it is known, shall be fined
for one year and be excluded; and whoever speaks haughtily [?]
with his fellow, or practises deceit knowingly, he shall be fined for
25 six months; but should he have done so inadvertently against his
fellow, he shall be fined for three months; and should he have
committed an inadvertence against the property of the Community so as to destroy it, he shall repay it in full; but should he
be unable to pay it, he shall be fined for sixty days. Whoever bears
30 a grudge against his fellow who has not been convicted shall be
fined for one year [and/or?] six months; and the same applies
to him who takes vengeance for himself in any way. And whoever
utters with his mouth a word of folly, for three months; and as
to him who interrupts his fellow, for ten days; and whoever lies
35 down and sleeps during a session of the Many, for thirty days.
Likewise the man who departs during a session of the Many

without permission and without good reason for as many as three times at a single session shall be fined for ten days; but should he leave again, he shall be fined for thirty days. And whoever

40 walks naked before his fellow and was not so compelled shall be fined for six months; and anyone who spits into the midst of the session of the Many shall be fined for thirty days; and whoever brings out his hand from under his garment when he is scantily clad, so that his nakedness is seen, shall be fined for thirty days.

45 Whoever laughs foolishly with audible voice shall be fined for thirty days; but he who brings forth his left hand to muffle [?] with it shall be fined for ten days. The man who slanders his fellow shall be excluded for one year from the Purity of the Many, and he shall be fined; but anyone who slanders the Many shall be

50 banished from them to return no more. They shall also banish never to return that man who murmurs against the institution of the Community; but if his murmuring be against his fellow who has not been convicted, he shall be fined for six months. And the man whose spirit is alienated from the institution of the Com-

55 munity so as to be a traitor to the truth and to walk in the stubbornness of his own heart, if he repents [and returns], he shall be fined for two years. In the first he shall not touch the Purity of the Many; and in the second he shall not touch the drink of the Many; and he shall sit after all the men of the Community. But upon his

60 completion of two years' time, the Many shall be asked concerning his affairs; and if they admit him, he shall be enrolled in his assigned order, and after that he shall be consulted in judgement. And any man who has been in the Council of the Community until the completion of ten years, should his spirit turn away and

65 become disloyal to the Community so that he goes forth from before the Many to walk in the stubbornness of his own heart, he shall never return to the Council of the Community; and any man of the men of the Community who shares with him in his Purity or in his property which he had pooled with the property

70 of the Many, his judgement shall be the same as his who is to be banished.

In the Council of the Community there shall be twelve laymen and three priests who are perfect in all that is revealed of the whole Torah, through practising truth and righteousness and justice

75 and loving devotion and walking humbly each with his fellow in order to maintain faithfulness in the land with a steadfast intent and with a broken spirit, and to expiate iniquity through practising justice and through the anguish of the refining furnace, and to walk with all in the measure of truth and in the proper reckoning

80 of the time. When these things come to pass in Israel, the Council
of the Community will have been established in truth:

> As an eternal planting, a holy house for Israel,
> A most holy institution for Aaron,
> Witnesses of truth concerning judgement,
85 And the chosen of grace to atone for the earth,
> And to render to the wicked their desert.
> That is the tried wall, the costly corner bulwark,
> Whose foundations shall not be shaken asunder,
> Nor be dislodged from their place!

90 A most holy abode belongs to Aaron with eternal knowledge to
enact laws, and to offer up an agreeable odour; and a house of
perfection and of truth is in Israel to establish a covenant with
eternal ordinances. These will serve the purpose of grace to make
atonement for the earth and to decree the condemnation of
95 wickedness that there may be no wrong-doing. When these men
have become established in the institution of the Community for
two years' time in perfection of way, they shall separate themselves as holy [or, as a sanctuary] within the Council of the men
of the Community; and every matter which was hidden from
100 Israel and is found by a man who seeks, let him not hide it from
these out of fear of an apostate spirit. Now when these things
come to pass in Israel to the Community, according to these
rules, they will separate themselves from the midst of the session
[or, habitation] of perverse men to go to the wilderness to clear
105 there the way of HUHA, as it is written:
> In the wilderness clear the way of . . . . ;
> Level in the desert a highway for our God:
That means studying the Torah which he commanded through
Moses, so as to do according to all that which the prophets revealed
110 through his Holy Spirit. As for anyone of the men of the Community, in the covenant of the Community, who wilfully removes
a word from all that he commanded, he shall not touch the
Purity of the holy men; nor shall he have any knowledge of any
of their counsel, until his deeds are purified from every kind of
115 perversity that he may walk in perfection of way. Then he shall
be admitted to the Council according to the judgement of the
Many; and afterward he shall be enrolled in his assigned position;
and according to this law shall it be for every one who joins the
Community.

. l. 58 *Drink*. The scribe wrote at first "assembly", but corrected it.
ll. 73ff. An allusion to Micah 6. 8.

l. 93 *With eternal ordinances.* The scribe wrote at first "to be an eternal wall", but corrected it.

ll. 93ff. *These will serve . . . wrong-doing.* In the MS. these words stand between "Israel" and "to establish" (l. 92).

l. 105 *HUHA*: evidently a substitute for the divine name.

l. 106 Four dots stand in place of the Tetragrammaton.

234 *Manual of Discipline* 9. 3–11. When these things come to pass in Israel according to all these rules for an institution of the Holy Spirit, for eternal truth, for making atonement for the guilt of transgression and sinful infidelity, and for divine favour
5 of the land more than flesh of whole burnt-offerings and than fats of sacrifice, while an offering of the lips is accounted as a fragrant offering of righteousness, and perfection of way as an acceptable freewill oblation—at that time the men of the Community shall be set apart as a house of holiness for Aaron,
10 being united so as to constitute a holy of holies and a house of Community for the Israelites who walk in perfection. Only the sons of Aaron shall have authority in matters of law and property; and according to their judgement the decision shall be reached in regard to every rule of the men of the Community and
15 in regard to all the property of the holy men who walk in perfection. Their property shall not be intermingled with the property of the men of deceit who have not cleansed their way by separating themselves from perversity and by walking in perfection of way; and they shall not depart from the whole counsel of the Torah to
20 walk in all their hardness of heart, but they shall be ruled by the first laws with which the men of the Community began to be disciplined until the coming of a Prophet and the anointed ones of Aaron and Israel.

235 *Manual of Discipline* 11. 15–22. This concluding psalm may be compared with the "Hymns of Thanksgiving" (see p. 256).

Blessed art thou, O my God!
Who openest the heart of thy servant unto knowledge,
Directing in righteousness all his deeds,
And causing the son of thy handmaid to stand,
5 Just as thou wert pleased that the elect of mankind
Should stand before thee for ever.
For without thee a way cannot be perfect,
And apart from thy will naught can be accomplished!
Thou hast taught all knowledge;
10 And everything that has come to pass has been by thy will.

For there is none other beside thee
To reply to thy counsel,
And to understand all thy holy purpose,
And to gaze into the depth of thy mysteries,
15 And to comprehend all thy marvels,
As well as the strength of thy might;
And who is able to bear thy glory?
For what, indeed, is he,
The son of man among thy miraculous works?
20 And what is that born of woman, in thy estimation?
For, as for him, from the dust is his kneading;
And the bread of worms is his final dwelling;
For he is something shaped, only fashioned clay
Whose longing is for the dust.
25 What will clay reply, or that which is shaped by hand?
And what counsel does he understand?

INDEX OF REFERENCES[1]

1. OLD TESTAMENT

[1] This Index does not include references to passages quoted as part of the text and listed in the Table of Contents.

2. NEW TESTAMENT

3. APOCRYPHA AND PSEUDEPIGRAPHA [1]

[1] As in R. H. Charles, *The Apocrypha and Pseudepigrapha of the Old Testament* (1913).

4. JOSEPHUS AND PHILO

5. RABBINIC LITERATURE

6. GREEK AND LATIN AUTHORS

7. PATRISTIC WRITINGS

INDEX OF NAMES AND SUBJECTS

71 72 73   12 11 10

Revised January, 1970

haRpeR ✦ cORChbOOKs

American Studies: General

HENRY ADAMS Degradation of the Democratic Dogma. ‡ *Introduction by Charles Hirschfeld.*   TB/1450
LOUIS D. BRANDEIS: Other People's Money, *and How the Bankers Use It. Ed. with Intro, by Richard M. Abrams*   TB/3081
HENRY STEELE COMMAGER, Ed.: The Struggle for Racial Equality   TB/1300
CARL N. DEGLER: Out of Our Past: *The Forces that Shaped Modern America*   CN/2
CARL N. DEGLER, Ed.: Pivotal Interpretations of American History
        Vol. I TB/1240;   Vol. II TB/1241
A. S. EISENSTADT, Ed.: The Craft of American History: *Selected Essays*
        Vol. I TB/1255;   Vol. II TB/1256
LAWRENCE H. FUCHS, Ed.: American Ethnic Politics   TB/1368
MARCUS LEE HANSEN: The Atlantic Migration: 1607-1860. *Edited by Arthur M. Schlesinger. Introduction by Oscar Handlin*   TB/1052
MARCUS LEE HANSEN: The Immigrant in American History. *Edited with a Foreword by Arthur M. Schlesinger*   TB/1120
ROBERT L. HEILBRONER: The Limits of American Capitalism   TB/1305
JOHN HIGHAM, Ed.: The Reconstruction of American History   TB/1068
ROBERT H. JACKSON: The Supreme Court in the American System of Government   TB/1106
JOHN F. KENNEDY: A Nation of Immigrants. *Illus. Revised and Enlarged. Introduction by Robert F. Kennedy*   TB/1118
LEONARD W. LEVY, Ed.: American Constitutional Law: *Historical Essays*   TB/1285
LEONARD W. LEVY, Ed.: Judicial Review and the Supreme Court   TB/1296
LEONARD W. LEVY: The Law of the Commonwealth and Chief Justice Shaw: *The Evolution of American Law, 1830-1860*   TB/1309
GORDON K. LEWIS: Puerto Rico: *Freedom and Power in the Caribbean. Abridged edition*   TB/1371
HENRY F. MAY: Protestant Churches and Industrial America   TB/1334
RICHARD B. MORRIS: Fair Trial: *Fourteen Who Stood Accused, from Anne Hutchinson to Alger Hiss*   TB/1335

GUNNAR MYRDAL: An American Dilemma: *The Negro Problem and Modern Democracy. Introduction by the Author.*
        Vol. I TB/1443;   Vol. II TB/1444
GILBERT OSOFSKY, Ed.: The Burden of Race: *A Documentary History of Negro-White Relations in America*   TB/1405
CONYERS READ, Ed.: The Constitution Reconsidered. *Revised Edition. Preface by Richard B. Morris*   TB/1384
ARNOLD ROSE: The Negro in America: *The Condensed Version of Gunnar Myrdal's* An American Dilemma. *Second Edition* TB/3048
JOHN E. SMITH: Themes in American Philosophy: *Purpose, Experience and Community*   TB/1466
WILLIAM R. TAYLOR: Cavalier and Yankee: *The Old South and American National Character*   TB/1474

American Studies: Colonial

BERNARD BAILYN: The New England Merchants in the Seventeenth Century   TB/1149
ROBERT E. BROWN: Middle-Class Democracy and Revolution in Massachusetts, 1691-1780. *New Introduction by Author*   TB/1413
JOSEPH CHARLES: The Origins of the American Party System   TB/1049
HENRY STEELE COMMAGER & ELMO GIORDANETTI, Eds.: Was America a Mistake? *An Eighteenth Century Controversy*   TB/1329
WESLEY FRANK CRAVEN: The Colonies in Transition: 1660-1712†   TB/3084
CHARLES GIBSON: Spain in America † TB/3077
CHARLES GIBSON, Ed.: The Spanish Tradition in America +   HR/1351
LAWRENCE HENRY GIPSON: The Coming of the Revolution: 1763-1775. † *Illus.*   TB/3007
JACK P. GREENE, Ed.: Great Britain and the American Colonies: 1606-1763. + *Introduction by the Author*   HR/1477
AUBREY C. LAND, Ed.: Bases of the Plantation Society +   HR/1429
JOHN LANKFORD, Ed.: Captain John Smith's America: *Selections from his Writings* ‡   TB/3078
LEONARD W. LEVY: Freedom of Speech and Press in Early American History: *Legacy of Suppression*   TB/1109

---

† The New American Nation Series, edited by Henry Steele Commager and Richard B. Morris.
‡ American Perspectives series, edited by Bernard Wishy and William E. Leuchtenburg.
a History of Europe series, edited by J. H. Plumb.
§ The Library of Religion and Culture, edited by Benjamin Nelson.
‖ Researches in the Social, Cultural, and Behavioral Sciences, edited by Benjamin Nelson.
Σ Harper Modern Science Series, edited by James A. Newman.
° Not for sale in Canada.
+ Documentary History of the United States series, edited by Richard B. Morris.
# Documentary History of Western Civilization series, edited by Eugene C. Black and Leonard W. Levy.
Λ The Economic History of the United States series, edited by Henry David et al.
¶ European Perspectives series, edited by Eugene C. Black.
** Contemporary Essays series, edited by Leonard W. Levy.
* The Stratum Series, edited by John Hale.

PERRY MILLER: Errand Into the Wilderness
TB/1139
PERRY MILLER & T. H. JOHNSON, Eds.: The Puritans: *A Sourcebook of Their Writings*
Vol. I TB/1093; Vol. II TB/1094
EDMUND S. MORGAN: The Puritan Family: *Religion and Domestic Relations in Seventeenth Century New England*
TB/1227
RICHARD B. MORRIS: Government and Labor in Early America
TB/1244
WALLACE NOTESTEIN: The English People on the Eve of Colonization: 1603-1630. † *Illus.*
TB/3006
FRANCIS PARKMAN: The Seven Years War: *A Narrative Taken from Montcalm and Wolfe, The Conspiracy of Pontiac, and A Half-Century of Conflict. Edited by John H. McCallum*
TB/3083
LOUIS B. WRIGHT: The Cultural Life of the American Colonies: 1607-1763. † *Illus.*
TB/3005
YVES F. ZOLTVANY, Ed.: The French Tradition in America +
HR/1425

American Studies: The Revolution to 1860

JOHN R. ALDEN: The American Revolution: 1775-1783. † *Illus.*
TB/3011
MAX BELOFF, Ed.: The Debate on the American Revolution, 1761-1783: *A Sourcebook*
TB/1225
RAY A. BILLINGTON: The Far Western Frontier: 1830-1860. † *Illus.*
TB/3012
STUART BRUCHEY: The Roots of American Economic Growth, 1607-1861: *An Essay in Social Causation. New Introduction by the Author.*
TB/1350
WHITNEY R. CROSS: The Burned-Over District: *The Social and Intellectual History of Enthusiastic Religion in Western New York, 1800-1850*
TB/1242
NOBLE E. CUNNINGHAM, JR., Ed.: The Early Republic, 1789-1828 +
HR/1394
GEORGE DANGERFIELD: The Awakening of American Nationalism, 1815-1828. † *Illus.*
TB/3061
CLEMENT EATON: The Freedom-of-Thought Struggle in the Old South. *Revised and Enlarged. Illus.*
TB/1150
CLEMENT EATON: The Growth of Southern Civilization, 1790-1860. † *Illus.*
TB/3040
ROBERT H. FERRELL, Ed.: Foundations of American Diplomacy, 1775-1872 +
HR/1393
LOUIS FILLER: The Crusade against Slavery: 1830-1860. † *Illus.*
TB/3029
DAVID H. FISCHER: The Revolution of American Conservatism: *The Federalist Party in the Era of Jeffersonian Democracy*
TB/1449
WILLIAM W. FREEHLING, Ed.: The Nullification Era: *A Documentary Record* ‡
TB/3079
WILLIM W. FREEHLING: Prelude to Civil War: *The Nullification Controversy in South Carolina, 1816-1836*
TB/1359
PAUL W. GATES: The Farmer's Age: *Agriculture, 1815-1860* △
TB/1398
FELIX GILBERT: The Beginnings of American Foreign Policy: *To the Farewell Address*
TB/1200
ALEXANDER HAMILTON: The Reports of Alexander Hamilton. ‡ *Edited by Jacob E. Cooke*
TB/3060
THOMAS JEFFERSON: Notes on the State of Virginia. ‡ *Edited by Thomas P. Abernethy*
TB/3052
FORREST MCDONALD, Ed.: Confederation and Constitution, 1781-1789 +
HR/1396

BERNARD MAYO: Myths and Men: *Patrick Henry, George Washington, Thomas Jefferson*
TB/1108
JOHN C. MILLER: Alexander Hamilton and the Growth of the New Nation
TB/3057
JOHN C. MILLER: The Federalist Era: 1789-1801. † *Illus.*
TB/3027
RICHARD B. MORRIS, Ed.: Alexander Hamilton and the Founding of the Nation. *New Introduction by the Editor*
TB/1448
RICHARD B. MORRIS: The American Revolution Reconsidered
TB/1363
CURTIS P. NETTELS: The Emergence of a National Economy, 1775-1815 △
TB/1438
DOUGLASS C. NORTH & ROBERT PAUL THOMAS, Eds.: *The Growth of the American Economy to 1860* +
HR/1352
R. B. NYE: The Cultural Life of the New Nation: 1776-1830. † *Illus.*
TB/3026
GILBERT OSOFSKY, Ed.: Puttin' On Ole Massa: *The Slave Narratives of Henry Bibb, William Wells Brown, and Solomon Northup* ‡
TB/1432
JAMES PARTON: The Presidency of Andrew Jackson. *From Volume III of the* Life of Andrew Jackson. *Ed. with Intro. by Robert V. Remini*
TB/3080
FRANCIS S. PHILBRICK: The Rise of the West, 1754-1830. † *Illus.*
TB/3067
MARSHALL SMELSER: The Democratic Republic, 1801-1815 †
TB/1406
TIMOTHY L. SMITH: Revivalism and Social Reform: *American Protestantism on the Eve of the Civil War*
TB/1229
JACK M. SOSIN, Ed.: The Opening of the West +
HR/1424
GEORGE ROGERS TAYLOR: The Transportation Revolution, 1815-1860 △
TB/1347
A. F. TYLER: Freedom's Ferment: *Phases of American Social History from the Revolution to the Outbreak of the Civil War. Illus.*
TB/1074
GLYNDON G. VAN DEUSEN: The Jacksonian Era: 1828-1848. † *Illus.*
TB/3028
LOUIS B. WRIGHT: Culture on the Moving Frontier
TB/1053

American Studies: The Civil War to 1900

W. R. BROCK: An American Crisis: *Congress and Reconstruction, 1865-67* °
TB/1283
T. C. COCHRAN & WILLIAM MILLER: The Age of Enterprise: *A Social History of Industrial America*
TB/1054
W. A. DUNNING: Reconstruction, Political and Economic: 1865-1877
TB/1073
HAROLD U. FAULKNER: Politics, Reform and Expansion: 1890-1900. † *Illus.*
TB/3020
GEORGE M. FREDRICKSON: The Inner Civil War: *Northern Intellectuals and the Crisis of the Union*
TB/1358
JOHN A. GARRATY: The New Commonwealth, 1877-1890 †
TB/1410
JOHN A. GARRATY, Ed.: The Transformation of American Society, 1870-1890 +
HR/1395
WILLIAM R. HUTCHISON, Ed.: American Protestant Thought: *The Liberal Era* ‡
TB/1385
HELEN HUNT JACKSON: A Century of Dishonor: *The Early Crusade for Indian Reform.* †
Edited by Andrew F. Rolle
TB/3063
ALBERT D. KIRWAN: Revolt of the Rednecks: *Mississippi Politics, 1876-1925*
TB/1199
WILLIAM G. MCLOUGHLIN, Ed.: The American Evangelicals, 1800-1900: An Anthology ‡
TB/1382
ARTHUR MANN: Yankee Reforms in the Urban Age: *Social Reform in Boston, 1800-1900*
TB/1247

ARNOLD M. PAUL: Conservative Crisis and the Rule of Law: *Attitudes of Bar and Bench, 1887-1895. New Introduction by Author*
TB/1415

JAMES S. PIKE: The Prostrate State: *South Carolina under Negro Government.* ‡ *Intro. by Robert F. Durden*
TB/3085

WHITELAW REID: After the War: *A Tour of the Southern States, 1865-1866.* ‡ *Edited by C. Vann Woodward*
TB/3066

FRED A. SHANNON: The Farmer's Last Frontier: *....Agriculture, 1860-1897*
TB/1348

VERNON LANE WHARTON: The Negro in Mississippi, 1865-1890
TB/1178

American Studies: The Twentieth Century

RICHARD M. ABRAMS, Ed.: The Issues of the Populist and Progressive Eras, 1892-1912 +
HR/1428

RAY STANNARD BAKER: Following the Color Line: *American Negro Citizenship in Progressive Era.* ‡ *Edited by Dewey W. Grantham, Jr. Illus.*
TB/3053

RANDOLPH S. BOURNE: War and the Intellectuals: *Collected Essays, 1915-1919.* ‡ *Edited by Carl Resek*
TB/3043

A. RUSSELL BUCHANAN: The United States and World War II. † *Illus.*
Vol. I TB/3044; Vol. II TB/3045

THOMAS C. COCHRAN: The American Business System: *A Historical Perspective, 1900-1955*
TB/1080

FOSTER RHEA DULLES: America's Rise to World Power: 1898-1954. † *Illus.*
TB/3021

JEAN-BAPTISTE DUROSELLE: From Wilson to Roosevelt: *Foreign Policy of the United States, 1913-1945. Trans. by Nancy Lyman Roelker*
TB/1370

HAROLD U. FAULKNER: The Decline of Laissez Faire, 1897-1917
TB/1397

JOHN D. HICKS: Republican Ascendancy: 1921-1933. † *Illus.*
TB/3041

ROBERT HUNTER: Poverty: *Social Conscience in the Progressive Era.* ‡ *Edited by Peter d'A. Jones*
TB/3065

WILLIAM E. LEUCHTENBURG: Franklin D. Roosevelt and the New Deal: 1932-1940. † *Illus.*
TB/3025

WILLIAM E. LEUCHTENBURG, Ed.: The New Deal: *A Documentary History* +
HR/1354

ARTHUR S. LINK: Woodrow Wilson and the Progressive Era: 1910-1917. † *Illus.*
TB/3023

BROADUS MITCHELL: Depression Decade: *From New Era through New Deal, 1929-1941* ∧
TB/1439

GEORGE E. MOWRY: The Era of Theodore Roosevelt and the Birth of Modern America: 1900-1912. † *Illus.*
TB/3022

WILLIAM PRESTON, JR.: Aliens and Dissenters: *Federal Suppression of Radicals, 1903-1933*
TB/1287

WALTER RAUSCHENBUSCH: Christianity and the Social Crisis. ‡ *Edited by Robert D. Cross*
TB/3059

GEORGE SOULE: Prosperity Decade: *From War to Depression, 1917-1929* ∧
TB/1349

GEORGE B. TINDALL, Ed.: A Populist Reader: *Selections from the Works of American Populist Leaders*
TB/3069

TWELVE SOUTHERNERS: I'll Take My Stand: *The South and the Agrarian Tradition. Intro. by Louis D. Rubin, Jr.; Biographical Essays by Virginia Rock*
TB/1072

Art, Art History, Aesthetics

CREIGHTON GILBERT, Ed.: Renaissance Art ** *Illus.*
TB/1465

EMILE MALE: The Gothic Image: *Religious Art in France of the Thirteenth Century.* § *190 illus.*
TB/344

MILLARD MEISS: Painting in Florence and Siena After the Black Death: *The Arts, Religion and Society in the Mid-Fourteenth Century. 169 illus.*
TB/1148

ERWIN PANOFSKY: Renaissance and Renascences in Western Art. *Illus.*
TB/1447

ERWIN PANOFSKY: Studies in Iconology: *Humanistic Themes in the Art of the Renaissance. 180 illus.*
TB/1077

JEAN SEZNEC: The Survival of the Pagan Gods: *The Mythological Tradition and Its Place in Renaissance Humanism and Art. 108 illus.*
TB/2004

OTTO VON SIMSON: The Gothic Cathedral: *Origins of Gothic Architecture and the Medieval Concept of Order. 58 illus.*
TB/2018

HEINRICH ZIMMER: Myths and Symbols in Indian Art and Civilization. *70 illus.*
TB/2005

Asian Studies

WOLFGANG FRANKE: China and the West: *The Cultural Encounter, 13th to 20th Centuries. Trans. by R. A. Wilson*
TB/1326

L. CARRINGTON GOODRICH: A Short History of the Chinese People. *Illus.*
TB/3015

DAN N. JACOBS, Ed.: The New Communist Manifesto and Related Documents. *3rd revised edn.*
TB/1078

DAN N. JACOBS & HANS H. BAERWALD, Eds.: Chinese Communism: *Selected Documents*
TB/3031

BENJAMIN I. SCHWARTZ: Chinese Communism and the Rise of Mao
TB/1308

BENJAMIN I. SCHWARTZ: In Search of Wealth and Power: *Yen Fu and the West*
TB/1422

Economics & Economic History

C. E. BLACK: The Dynamics of Modernization: *A Study in Comparative History*
TB/1321

STUART BRUCHEY: The Roots of American Economic Growth, 1607-1861: *An Essay in Social Causation. New Introduction by the Author.*
TB/1350

GILBERT BURCK & EDITORS OF *Fortune*: The Computer Age: *And its Potential for Management*
TB/1179

JOHN ELLIOTT CAIRNES: The Slave Power. ‡ *Edited with Introduction by Harold D. Woodman*
TB/1433

SHEPARD B. CLOUGH, THOMAS MOODIE & CAROL MOODIE, Eds.: Economic History of Europe: *Twentieth Century* #
HR/1388

THOMAS C.COCHRAN: The American Business System: *A Historical Perspective, 1900-1955*
TB/1180

ROBERT A. DAHL & CHARLES E. LINDBLOM: Politics, Economics, and Welfare: *Planning and Politico-Economic Systems Resolved into Basic Social Processes*
TB/3037

PETER F. DRUCKER: The New Society: *The Anatomy of Industrial Order*
TB/1082

HAROLD U. FAULKNER: The Decline of Laissez Faire, 1897-1917 ∧
TB/1397

PAUL W. GATES: The Farmer's Age: *Agriculture, 1815-1860* ∧
TB/1398

WILLIAM GREENLEAF, Ed.: American Economic Development Since 1860 +
HR/1353

J. L. & BARBARA HAMMOND: The Rise of Modern Industry. || *Introduction by R. M. Hartwell*
TB/1417

ROBERT L. HEILBRONER: The Future as History: *The Historic Currents of Our Time and the Direction in Which They Are Taking America* TB/1386

ROBERT L. HEILBRONER: The Great Ascent: *The Struggle for Economic Development in Our Time* TB/3030

FRANK H. KNIGHT: The Economic Organization TB/1214

DAVID S. LANDES: Bankers and Pashas: *International Finance and Economic Imperialism in Egypt. New Preface by the Author* TB/1412

ROBERT LATOUCHE: The Birth of Western Economy: *Economic Aspects of the Dark Ages* TB/1290

ABBA P. LERNER: Everbody's Business: *A Re-examination of Current Assumptions in Economics and Public Policy* TB/3051

W. ARTHUR LEWIS: Economic Survey, 1919-1939 TB/1446

W. ARTHUR LEWIS: The Principles of Economic Planning. *New Introduction by the Author*° TB/1436

ROBERT GREEN MC CLOSKEY: American Conservatism in the Age of Enterprise TB/1137

PAUL MANTOUX: The Industrial Revolution in the Eighteenth Century: *An Outline of the Beginnings of the Modern Factory System in England*° TB/1079

WILLIAM MILLER, Ed.: Men in Business: *Essays on the Historical Role of the Entrepreneur* TB/1081

GUNNAR MYRDAL: An International Economy. *New Introduction by the Author* TB/1445

HERBERT A. SIMON: The Shape of Automation: *For Men and Management* TB/1245

PERRIN STRYER: The Character of the Executive: *Eleven Studies in Managerial Qualities* TB/1041

RICHARD S. WECKSTEIN, Ed.: Expansion of World Trade and the Growth of National Economies ** TB/1373

Education

JACQUES BARZUN: The House of Intellect TB/1051

RICHARD M. JONES, Ed.: Contemporary Educational Psychology: *Selected Readings* ** TB/1292

CLARK KERR: The Uses of the University TB/1264

Historiography and History of Ideas

HERSCHEL BAKER: The Image of Man: *A Study of the Idea of Human Dignity in Classical Antiquity, the Middle Ages, and the Renaissance* TB/1047

J. BRONOWSKI & BRUCE MAZLISH: The Western Intellectual Tradition: *From Leonardo to Hegel* TB/3001

EDMUND BURKE: On Revolution. Ed. by Robert A. Smith TB/1401

WILHELM DILTHEY: Pattern and Meaning in History: *Thoughts on History and Society.*° *Edited with an Intro. by H. P. Rickman* TB/1075

ALEXANDER GRAY: The Socialist Tradition: *Moses to Lenin* ° TB/1375

J. H. HEXTER: More's Utopia: *The Biography of an Idea. Epilogue by the Author* TB/1195

H. STUART HUGHES: History as Art and as Science: *Twin Vistas on the Past* TB/1207

ARTHUR O. LOVEJOY: The Great Chain of Being: *A Study of the History of an Idea* TB/1009

JOSE ORTEGA Y GASSET: The Modern Theme. *Introduction by Jose Ferrater Mora* TB/1038

RICHARD H. POPKIN: The History of Scepticism from Erasmus to Descartes. *Revised Edition* TB/1391

G. J. RENIER: History: *Its Purpose and Method* TB/1209

MASSIMO SALVADORI, Ed.: Modern Socialism # HR/1374

GEORG SIMMEL et al.: Essays on Sociology, Philosophy and Aesthetics. *Edited by Kurt H. Wolff* TB/1234

BRUNO SNELL: The Discovery of the Mind: *The Greek Origins of European Thought* TB/1018

W. WARREN WAGER, ed.: European Intellectual History Since Darwin and Marx TB/1297

W. H. WALSH: Philosophy of History: In Introduction TB/1020

History: General

HANS KOHN: The Age of Nationalism: *The First Era of Global History* TB/1380

BERNARD LEWIS: The Arabs in History TB/1029

BERNARD LEWIS: The Middle East and the West ° TB/1274

History: Ancient

A. ANDREWS: The Greek Tyrants TB/1103

ERNST LUDWIG EHRLICH: A Concise History of Israel: *From the Earliest Times to the Destruction of the Temple in A.D. 70* ° TB/128

ADOLF ERMAN, Ed.: The Ancient Egyptians: *A Sourcebook of their Writings. New Introduction by William Kelly Simpson* TB/1233

THEODOR H. GASTER: Thespis: *Ritual Myth and Drama in the Ancient Near East* TB/1281

MICHAEL GRANT: Ancient History ° TB/1190

A. H. M. JONES, Ed.: A History of Rome through the Fifgth Century # *Vol. I: The Republic* HR/1364

Vol. II The Empire: HR/1460

SAMUEL NOAH KRAMER: Sumerian Mythology TB/1055

NAPHTALI LEWIS & MEYER REINHOLD, Eds.: Roman Civilization *Vol. I: The Republic* TB/1231

Vol. II: The Empire TB/1232

History: Medieval

MARSHALL W. BALDWIN, Ed.: Christianity Through the 13th Century # HR/1468

MARC BLOCH: Land and Work in Medieval Europe. *Translated by J. E. Anderson* TB/1452

HELEN CAM: England Before Elizabeth TB/1026

NORMAN COHN: The Pursuit of the Millennium: *Revolutionary Messianism in Medieval and Reformation Europe* TB/1037

G. G. COULTON: Medieval Village, Manor, and Monastery HR/1022

HEINRICH FICHTENAU: The Carolingian Empire: *The Age of Charlemagne. Translated with an Introduction by Peter Munz* TB/1142

GALBERT OF BRUGES: The Murder of Charles the Good: *A Contemporary Record of Revolutionary Change in 12th Century Flanders. Translated with an Introduction by James Bruce Ross* TB/1311

F. L. GANSHOF: Feudalism TB/1058

F. L. GANSHOF: The Middle Ages: *A History of International Relations. Translated by Rémy Hall* TB/1411

W. O. HASSALL, Ed.: Medieval England: *As Viewed by Contemporaries* TB/1205

DENYS HAY: The Medieval Centuries ° TB/1192

DAVID HERLIHY, Ed.: Medieval Culture and Socicety # HR/1340

4

J. M. HUSSEY: The Byzantine World   TB/1057
ROBERT LATOUCHE: The Birth of Western Economy: *Economic Aspects of the Dark Ages* °
TB/1290
HENRY CHARLES LEA: The Inquisition of the Middle Ages. || *Introduction by Walter Ullmann*   TB/1456
FERDINAND LOT: The End of the Ancient World and the Beginnings of the Middle Ages. *Introduction by Glanville Downey*   TB/1044
H. R. LOYN: The Norman Conquest   TB/1457
ACHILLE LUCHAIRE: Social France at the time of Philip Augustus. *Intro. by John W. Baldwin*
TB/1314
GUIBERT DE NOGENT: Self and Society in Medieval France: *The Memoirs of Guibert de Nogent.* || Edited by John F. Benton TB/1471
MARSILIUS OF PADUA: The Defender of Peace. *The Defensor Pacis. Translated with an Introduction by Alan Gewirth*   TB/1310
CHARLES PETET-DUTAILLIS: The Feudal Monarchy in France and England: *From the Tenth to the Thirteenth Century* °   TB/1165
STEVEN RUNCIMAN: A History of the Crusades Vol. I: *The First Crusade and the Foundation of the Kingdom of Jerusalem. Illus.*
TB/1143
Vol. II: *The Kingdom of Jerusalem and the Frankish East 1100-1187. Illus.*   TB/1243
Vol. III: *The Kingdom of Acre and the Later Crusades. Illus.*   TB/1298
J. M. WALLACE-HADRILL: The Barbarian West: *The Early Middle Ages, A.D. 400-1000*
TB/1061

History: Renaissance & Reformation

JACOB BURCKHARDT: The Civilization of the Renaissance in Italy. *Introduction by Benjamin Nelson and Charles Trinkaus. Illus.*
Vol. I TB/40; Vol. II TB/41
JOHN CALVIN & JACOPO SADOLETO: A Reformation Debate. *Edited by John C. Olin*   TB/1239
FEDERICO CHABOD: Machiavelli and the Renaissance   TB/1193
THOMAS CROMWELL: Thomas Cromwell on Church and Commonwealth,: *Selected Letters 1523-1540.* ¶ *Ed. with an Intro. by Arthur J. Slavin*   TB/1462
R. TREVOR DAVIES: The Golden Century of Spain, 1501-1621 °   TB/1194
J. H. ELLIOTT: Europe Divided, 1559-1598 α °
TB/1414
G. R. ELTON: Reformation Europe, 1517-1559 ° α
TB/1270
DESIDERIUS ERASMUS: Christian Humanism and the Reformation: *Selected Writings. Edited and Translated by John C. Olin*   TB/1166
DESIDERIUS ERASMUS: Erasmus and His Age: *Selected Letters. Edited with an Introduction by Hans J. Hillerbrand. Translated by Marcus A. Haworth*   TB/1461
WALLACE K. FERGUSON et al.: Facets of the Renaissance. *Illus.*   TB/1098
WALLACE K. FERGUSON et al.: The Renaissance: *Six Essays. Illus.*   TB/1084
FRANCESCO GUICCIARDINI: History of Florence. *Translated with an Introduction and Notes by Mario Domandi*   TB/1470
WERNER L. GUNDERSHEIMER, Ed.: French Humanism, 1470-1600. * *Illus.*   TB/1473
MARIE BOAS HALL, Ed.: Nature and Nature's Laws: *Documents of the Scientific Revolution* #   HR/1420
HANS J. HILLERBRAND, Ed., The Protestant Reformation #   HR/1342
JOHAN HUIZINGA: Erasmus and the Age of Reformation. *Illus.*   TB/19

JOEL HURSTFIELD: The Elizabethan Nation
TB/1312
JOEL HURSTFIELD, Ed.: The Reformation Crisis
TB/1267
PAUL OSKAR KRISTELLER: Renaissance Thought: *The Classic, Scholastic, and Humanist Strains*
TB/1048
PAUL OSKAR KRISTELLER: Renaissance Thought II: *Papers on Humanism and the Arts*
TB/1163
PAUL O. KRISTELLER & PHILIP P. WIENER, Eds.: Renaissance Essays   TB/1392
DAVID LITTLE: Religion, Order and Law: *A Study in Pre-Revolutionary England.* § *Preface by R. Bellah*   TB/1418
NICCOLO MACHIAVELLI: History of Florence and of the Affairs of Italy: *From the Earliest Times to the Death of Lorenzo the Magnificent. Introduction by Felix Gilbert*   TB/1027
ALFRED VON MARTIN: Sociology of the Renaissance. ° *Introduction by W. K. Ferguson*
TB/1099
GARRETT MATTINGLY et al.: Renaissance Profiles. *Edited by J. H. Plumb*   TB/1162
J. E. NEALE: The Age of Catherine de Medici °
TB/1085
J. H. PARRY: The Establishment of the European Hegemony: 1415-1715: *Trade and Exploration in the Age of the Renaissance* TB/1045
J. H. PARRY, Ed.: The European Reconnaissance: *Selected Documents* #   HR/1345
BUONACCORSO PITTI & GREGORIO DATI: Two Memoirs of Renaissance Florence: *The Diaries of Buonaccorso Pitti and Gregorio Dati. Edited with Intro. by Gene Brucker. Trans. by Julia Martines*   TB/1333
J. H. PLUMB: The Italian Renaissance: *A Concise Survey of Its History and Culture*
TB/1161
A. F. POLLARD: Henry VIII. *Introduction by A. G. Dickens.* °   TB/1249
RICHARD H. POPKIN: The History of Scepticism from Erasmus to Descartes   TB/139
PAOLO ROSSI: Philosophy, Technology, and the Arts, in the Early Modern Era 1400-1700. || *Edited by Benjamin Nelson. Translated by Salvator Attanasio*   TB/1458
FERDINAND SCHEVILL: The Medici. *Illus.* TB/1010
FERDINAND SCHEVILL: Medieval and Renaissance Florence. *Illus.* Vol. I: *Medieval Florence*
TB/1090
Vol. II: *The Coming of Humanism and the Age of the Medici*   TB/1091
R. H. TAWNEY: The Agrarian Problem in the Sixteenth Century. *Intro. by Lawrence Stone*
TB/1315
H. R. TREVOR-ROPER: The European Witch-craze of the Sixteenth and Seventeenth Centuries and Other Essays °   TB/1416
VESPASIANO: Rennaissance Princes, Popes, and XVth Century: *The Vespasiano Memoirs. Introduction by Myron P. Gilmore. Illus.*
TB/1111

History: Modern European

RENE ALBRECHT-CARRIE, Ed.: The Concert of Europe #   HR/1341
MAX BELOFF: The Age of Absolutism, 1660-1815
TB/1062
OTTO VON BISMARCK: Reflections and Reminiscences. *Ed. with Intro. by Theodore S. Hamerow* ¶   TB/1357
EUGENE C. BLACK, Ed.: British Politics in the Nineteenth Century #   HR/1427

5

EUGENE C. BLACK, Ed.: European Political History, 1815-1870: *Aspects of Liberalism* ¶ TB/1331
ASA BRIGGS: The Making of Modern England, 1783-1867: *The Age of Improvement* ° TB/1203
D. W. BROGAN: The Development of Modern France ° Vol. I: *From the Fall of the Empire to the Dreyfus Affair* TB/1184 Vol. II: *The Shadow of War, World War I, Between the Two Wars* TB/1185
ALAN BULLOCK: Hitler, A Study in Tyranny. ° *Revised Edition. Illus.* TB/1123
EDMUND BURKE: On Revolution. *Ed. by Robert A. Smith* TB/1401
E. R. CARR: International Relations Between the Two World Wars. 1919-1939 ° TB/1279
E. H. CARR: The Twenty Years' Crisis, 1919-1939: *An Introduction to the Study of International Relations* ° TB/1122
GORDON A. CRAIG: From Bismarck to Adenauer: *Aspects of German Statecraft. Revised Edition* TB/1171
LESTER G. CROCKER, Ed.: The Age of Enlightenment # HR/1423
DENIS DIDEROT: The Encyclopedia: *Selections. Edited and Translated with Introduction by Stephen Gendzier* TB/1299
JACQUES DROZ: Europe between Revolutions, 1815-1848. ° *a Trans. by Robert Baldick* TB/1346
JOHANN GOTTLIEB FICHTE: Addresses to the German Nation. *Ed. with Intro. by George A. Kelly* ¶ TB/1366
FRANKLIN L. FORD: Robe and Sword: *The Re-Louis XIV* TB/1217
ROBERT & ELBORG FORSTER, Eds.: European Society in the Eighteenth Century # HR/1404
C. C. GILLISPIE: Genesis and Geology: *The Decades before Darwin* § TB/51
ALBERT GOODWIN, Ed.: The European Nobility in the Enghteenth Century TB/1313
ALBERT GOODWIN: The French Revolution TB/1064
ALBERT GUERARD: France in the Classical Age: *The Life and Death of an Ideal* TB/1183
JOHN B. HALSTED, Ed.: Romanticism # HR/1387
J. H. HEXTER: Reappraisals in History: *New Views on History and Society in Early Modern Europe* ° TB/1100
STANLEY HOFFMANN et al.: In Search of France: *The Economy, Society and Political System In the Twentieth Century* TB/1219
H. STUART HUGHES: The Obstructed Path: *French Social Thought in the Years of Desperation* TB/1451
JOHAN HUIZINGA: Dutch Civilisation in the 17th Century and Other Essays TB/1453
LIONAL KOCHAN: The Struggle for Germany: 1914-45 TB/1304
HANS KOHN: The Mind of Germany: *The Education of a Nation* TB/1204
HANS KOHN, Ed.: The Mind of Modern Russia: *Historical and Political Thought of Russia's Great Age* TB/1065
WALTER LAQUEUR & GEORGE L. MOSSE, Eds.: Education and Social Structure in the 20th·Century. ° *Volume 6 of the Journal of Contemporary History* TB/1339
WALTER LAQUEUR & GEORGE L. MOSSE, Eds.: International Fascism, 1920-1945. ° *Volume 1 of the Journal of Contemporary History* TB/1276
WALTER LAQUEUR & GEORGE L. MOSSE, Eds.: Literature and Politics in the 20th Century. ° *Volume 5 of the Journal of Contemporary History.* TB/1328

WALTER LAQUEUR & GEORGE L. MOSSE, Eds.: The New History: *Trends in Historical Research and Writing Since World War II.* ° *Volume 4 of the Journal of Contemporary History* TB/1327
WALTER LAQUEUR & GEORGE L. MOSSE, Eds.: 1914: *The Coming of the First World War.* ° *Volume3 of the Journal of Contemporary History* TB/1306
C. A. MACARTNEY, Ed.: The Habsburg and Hohenzollern Dynasties in the Seventeenth and Eighteenth Centuries # HR/1400
JOHN MCMANNERS: European History, 1789-1914: *Men, Machines and Freedom* TB/1419
PAUL MANTOUX: The Industrial Revolution in the Eighteenth Century: *An Outline of the Beginnings of the Modern Factory System in England* TB/1079
FRANK E. MANUEL: The Prophets of Paris: *Turgot, Condorcet, Saint-Simon, Fourier, and Comte* TB/1218
KINGSLEY MARTIN: French Liberal Thought in the Eighteenth Century: *A Study of Political Ideas from Bayle to Condorcet* TB/1114
NAPOLEON III: Napoleonic Ideas: *Des Idées Napoléoniennes, par le Prince Napoléon-Louis Bonaparte. Ed. by Brison D. Gooch* ¶ TB/1336
FRANZ NEUMANN: Behemoth: *The Structure and Practice of National Socialism, 1933-1944* TB/1289
DAVID OGG: Europe of the Ancien Régime, 1715-1783 ° *a* TB/1271
GEORGE RUDE: Revolutionary Europe, 1783-1815 ° *a* TB/1272
MASSIMO SALVADORI, Ed.: Modern Socialism # TB/1374
HUGH SETON-WATSON: Eastern Europe Between the Wars, 1918-1941 TB/1330
DENIS MACK SMITH, Ed.: The Making of Italy, 1796-1870 # HR/1356
ALBERT SOREL: Europe Under the Old Regime. *Translated by Francis H. Herrick* TB/1121
ROLAND N. STROMBERG, Ed.: Realism, Naturalism, and Symbolism: *Modes of Thought and Expression in Europe, 1848-1914 # HR/1355
A. J. P. TAYLOR: From Napoleon to Lenin: *Historical Essays* ° TB/1268
A. J. P. TAYLOR: The Habsburg Monarchy, 1809-1918: *A History of the Austrian Empire and Austria-Hungary* ° TB/1187
J. M. THOMPSON: European History, 1494-1789 TB/1431
DAVID THOMSON, Ed.: France: Empire and Republic, 1850-1940 # HR/1387
ALEXIS DE TOCQUEVILLE & GUSTAVE DE BEAUMONT: Tocqueville and Beaumont on Social Reform. *Ed. and trans. with Intro. by Seymour Drescher* TB/1343
G. M. TREVELYAN: British History in the Nineteenth Century and After: 1792-1919 ° TB/1251
H. R. TREVOR-ROPER: Historical Essays TB/1269
W. WARREN WAGAR, Ed.: Science, Faith, and MAN: *European Thought Since 1914 #* HR/1362
MACK WALKER, Ed.: Metternich's Europe, 1813-1848 # HR/1361
ELIZABETH WISKEMANN: Europe of the Dictators, 1919-1945 ° *a* TB/1273
JOHN B. WOLF: France: 1814-1919: *The Rise of a Liberal-Democratic Society* TB/3019

Literature & Literary Criticism

JACQUES BARZUN: The House of Intellect TB/1051

W. J. BATE: From Classic to Romantic: *Premises of Taste in Eighteenth Century England* TB/1036
VAN WYCK BROOKS: Van Wyck Brooks: The Early Years: *A Selection from his Works, 1908-1921* Ed. with Intro. by Claire Sprague TB/3082
ERNST R. CURTIUS: European Literature and the Latin Middle Ages. *Trans. by Willard Trask* TB/2015
RICHMOND LATTIMORE, Translator: The Odyssey of Homer TB/1389
JOHN STUART MILL: On Bentham and Coleridge. *Introduction by F. R. Leavis* TB/1070
SAMUEL PEPYS: The Diary of Samual Pepys. ° *Edited by O. F. Morshead. 60 illus. by Ernest Shepard* TB/1007
ROBERT PREYER, Ed.: Victorian Literature ** TB/1302
ALBION W. TOURGEE: A Fool's Errand: *A Novel of the South during Reconstruction. Intro. by George Fredrickson* TB/3074
BASIL WILEY: Nineteenth Century Studies: *Coleridge to Matthew Arnold* ° TB/1261
RAYMOND WILLIAMS: Culture and Society, 1780-1950 ° TB/1252

Philosophy

HENRI BERGSON: Time and Free Will: *An Essay on the Immediate Data of Consciousness* ° TB/1021
LUDWIG BINSWANGER: Being-in-the-World: *Selected Papers. Trans. with Intro. by Jacob Needleman* TB/1365
H. J. BLACKHAM: Six Existentialist Thinkers: *Kierkegaard, Nietzsche, Jaspers, Marcel, Heidegger, Sartre* ° TB/1002
J. M. BOCHENSKI: The Methods of Contemporary Thought. *Trans. by Peter Caws* ° TB/1377
CRANE BRINTON: Nietzsche. *Preface, Bibliography, and Epilogue by the Author* TB/1197
ERNST CASSIRER: Rousseau, Kant and Goethe. *Intro. by Peter Gay* TB/1092
FREDERICK COPLESTON, S. J.: Medieval Philosophy TB/376
F. M. CORNFORD: From Religion to Philosophy: *A Study in the Origins of Western Speculation* § TB/20
WILFRID DESAN: The Tragic Finale: *An Essay on the Philosophy of Jean-Paul Sartre* TB/1030
MARVIN FARBER: The Aims of Phenomenology: *The Motives, Methods, and Impact of Husserl's Thought* TB/1291
MARVIN FARBER: Basic Issues of Philosophy: *Experience, Reality, and Human Values* TB/1344
MARVIN FARBER: Phenomenology and Existence: *Towards a Philosophy within Nature* TB/1295
PAUL FRIEDLANDER: Plato: *An Introduction* TB/2017
MICHAEL GELVEN: A Commentary on Heidegger's "Being and Time" TB/1464
J. GLENN GRAY: Hegel and Greek Thought TB/1409
W. K. C. GUTHRIE: The Greek Philosophers: *From Thales to Aristotle* ° TB/1008
G. W. F. HEGEL: On Art, Religion Philosophy: *Introductory Lectures to the Realm of Absolute Spirit.* || *Edited with an Introduction by J. Glenn Gray* TB/1463
G. W. F. HEGEL: Phenomenology of Mind. ° || *Introduction by George Lichtheim* TB/1303
MARTIN HEIDEGGER: Discourse on Thinking. *Translated with a Preface by John M. Anderson and E. Hans Freund. Introduction by John M. Anderson* TB/1459

F. H. HEINEMANN: Existentialism and the Modern Predicament TB/28
WERER HEISENBERG: Physics and Philosophy: *The Revolution in Modern Science. Intro. by F. S. C. Northrop* TB/549
EDMUND HUSSERL: Phenomenology and the Crisis of Philosophy. § *Translated with an Introduction by Quentin Lauer* TB/1170
IMMANUEL KANT: Groundwork of the Metaphysic of Morals. *Translated and Analyzed by H. J. Paton* TB/1159
IMMANUEL KANT: Lectures on Ethics. § *Introduction by Lewis White Beck* TB/105
WALTER KAUFMANN, Ed.: Religion From Tolstoy to Camus: *Basic Writings on Religious Truth and Morals* TB/123
QUENTIN LAUER: Phenomenology: *Its Genesis and Prospect. Preface by Aron Gurwitsch* TB/1169
MAURICE MANDELBAUM: The Problem of Historical Knowledge: *An Answer to Relativism* TB/1338
GEORGE A. MORGAN: What Nietzsche Means TB/1198
H. J. PATON: The Categorical Imperative: *A Study in Kant's Moral Philosophy* TB/1325
MICHAEL POLANYI: Personal Knowledge: *Towards a Post-Critical Philosophy* TB/1158
KARL R. POPPER: Conjectures and Refutations: *The Growth of Scientific Knowledge* TB/1376
WILLARD VAN ORMAN QUINE: Elementary Logic *Revised Edition* TB/577
WILLARD VAN ORMAN QUINE: From a Logical Point of View: *Logico-Philosophical Essays* TB/566
JOHN E. SMITH: Themes in American Philosophy: *Purpose, Experience and Community* TB/1466
MORTON WHITE: Foundations of Historical Knowledge TB/1440
WILHELM WINDELBAND: A History of Philosophy *Vol. I: Greek, Roman, Medieval* TB/38
Vol. II: Renaissance, Enlightenment, Modern TB/39
LUDWIG WITTGENSTEIN: The Blue and Brown Books ° TB/1211
LUDWIG WITTGENSTEIN: Notebooks, 1914-1916 TB/1441

Political Science & Government

C. E. BLACK: The Dynamics of Modernization: *A Study in Comparative History* TB/1321
KENNETH E. BOULDING: Conflict and Defense: *A General Theory of Action* TB/3024
DENIS W. BROGAN: Politics in America. *New Introduction by the Author* TB/1469
CRANE BRINTON: English Political Thought in the Nineteenth Century TB/1071
ROBERT CONQUEST: Power and Policy in the USSR: *The Study of Soviet Dynastics* ° TB/1307
ROBERT A. DAHL & CHARLES E. LINDBLOM: Politics, Economics, and Welfare: *Planning and Politico-Economic Systems Resolved into Basic Social Processes* TB/1277
HANS KOHN: Political Ideologies of the 20th Century TB/1277
ROY C. MACRIDIS, Ed.: Political Parties: *Contemporary Trends and Ideas* ** TB/1322
ROBERT GREEN MC CLOSKEY: American Conservatism in the Age of Enterprise, 1865-1910 TB/1137
MARSILIUS OF PADUA: The Defender of Peace. *The Defensor Pacis. Translated with an Introduction by Alan Gewirth* TB/1310
KINGSLEY MARTIN: French Liberal Thought in the Eighteenth Century: *A Study of Political Ideas from Bayle to Condorcet* TB/1114

7

Religion: Early Christianity Through Reformation

ANSELM OF CANTERBURY: Truth, Freedom, and Evil: *Three Philosophical Dialogues.* Edited and Translated by Jasper Hopkins and Herbert Richardson TB/317

MARSHALL W. BALDWIN, Ed.: Christianity through the 13th Century # HR/1468

W. D. DAVIES: Paul and Rabbinic Judaism: *Some Rabbinic Elements in Pauline Theology. Revised Edition* ° TB/146

ADOLF DEISSMAN: Paul: *A Study in Social and Religious History* TB/15

JOHANNES ECKHART: Meister Eckhart: *A Modern Translation by R. Blakney* TB/8

EDGAR J. GOODSPEED: A Life of Jesus TB/1

ROBERT M. GRANT: Gnosticism and Early Christianity TB/136

WILLIAM HALLER: The Rise of Puritanism TB/22

GERHART B. LADNER: The Idea of Reform: *Its Impact on the Christian Thought and Action in the Age of the Fathers* TB/149

ARTHUR DARBY NOCK: Early Gentile Christianity and Its Hellenistic Background TB/111

ARTHUR DARBY NOCK: St. Paul ° TR/104

ORIGEN: On First Principles. *Edited by G. W. Butterworth. Introduction by Henri de Lubac* TB/311

GORDON RUPP: Luther's Progress to the Diet of Worms ° TB/120

Religion: The Protestant Tradition

KARL BARTH: Church Dogmatics: *A Selection. Intro. by H. Gollwitzer. Ed. by G. W. Bromiley* TB/95

KARL BARTH: Dogmatics in Outline TB/56

KARL BARTH: The Word of God and the Word of Man TB/13

HERBERT BRAUN, et al.: God and Christ: *Existence and Province. Volume 5 of Journal for Theology and the Church, edited by Robert W. Funk and Gerhard Ebeling* TB/255

WHITNEY R. CROSS: The Burned-Over District: *The Social and Intellectual History of Enthusiastic Religion in Western New York, 1800-1850* TB/1242

NELS F. S. FERRE: Swedish Contributions to Modern Theology. *New Chapter by William A. Johnson* TB/147

WILLIAM R. HUTCHISON, Ed.: American Protestant Thought: *The Liberal Era* ‡ TB/1385

ERNST KASEMANN, et al.: Distinctive Protestant and Catholic Themes Reconsidered. *Volume 3 of Journal for Theology and the Church, edited by Robert W. Funk and Gerhard Ebeling* TB/253

SOREN KIERKEGAARD: On Authority and Revelation: *The Book on Adler, or a Cycle of Ethico-Religious Essays. Introduction by F. Sontag* TB/139

SOREN KIERKEGAARD: Crisis in the Life of an Actress, *and Other Essays on Drama. Translated with an Introduction by Stephen Crites* TB/145

SOREN KIERKEGAARD: Edifying Discourses. *Edited with an Intro. by Paul Holmer* TB/32

SOREN KIERKEGAARD: The Journals of Kierkegaard. ° *Edited with an Intro. by Alexander Dru* TB/52

SOREN KIERKEGAARD: The Point of View for My Work as an Author: *A Report to History.* § *Preface by Benjamin Nelson* TB/88

SOREN KIERKEGAARD: The Present Age. § *Translated and edited by Alexander Dru. Introduction by Walter Kaufmann* TB/94

SOREN KIERKEGAARD: Purity of Heart. *Trans. by Douglas Steere* TB/4

SOREN KIERKEGAARD: Repetition: *An Essay in Experimental Psychology* § TB/117

SOREN KIERKEGAARD: Works of Love: *Some Christian Reflections in the Form of Discourses* TB/122

WILLIAM G. MCLOUGHLIN, Ed.: The American Evangelicals: 1800-1900: *An Anthology* TB/1382

WOLFHART PANNENBERG, et al.: History and Hermeneutic. *Volume 4 of Journal for Theology and the Church, edited by Robert W. Funk and Gerhard Ebeling* TB/254

JAMES M. ROBINSON, et al.: The Bultmann School of Biblical Interpretation: New Directions? *Volume 1 of Journal for Theology and the Church, edited by Robert W. Funk and Gerhard Ebeling* TB/251

F. SCHLEIERMACHER: The Christian Faith. *Introduction by Richard R. Niebuhr.* Vol. I TB/108; Vol. II TB/109

F. SCHLEIERMACHER: On Religion: *Speeches to Its Cultured Despisers. Intro. by Rudolf Otto* TB/36

TIMOTHY L. SMITH: Revivalism and Social Reform: *American Protestantism on the Eve of the Civil War* TB/1229

PAUL TILLICH: Dynamics of Faith TB/42

PAUL TILLICH: Morality and Beyond TB/142

EVELYN UNDERHILL: Worship TB/10

Religion: The Roman & Eastern Christian Traditions

A. ROBERT CAPONIGRI, Ed.: Modern Catholic Thinkers II: *The Church and the Political Order* TB/307

G. P. FEDOTOV: The Russian Religious Mind: *Kievan Christianity, the tenth to the thirteenth Centuries* TB/370

GABRIEL MARCEL: Being and Having: *An Existential Diary. Introduction by James Collins* TB/310

GABRIEL MARCEL: Homo Viator: *Introduction to a Metaphysic of Hope* TB/397

Religion: Oriental Religions

TOR ANDRAE: Mohammed: *The Man and His Faith* § TB/62

EDWARD CONZE: Buddhism: *Its Essence and Development.* ° *Foreword by Arthur Waley* TB/58

EDWARD CONZE: Buddhist Meditation TB/1442

EDWARD CONZE et al, Editors: Buddhist Texts through the Ages TB/113

ANANDA COOMARASWAMY: Buddha and the Gospel of Buddhism TB/119

H. G. CREEL: Confucius and the Chinese Way TB/63

FRANKLIN EDGERTON, Trans. & Ed.: The Bhagavad Gita TB/115

SWAMI NIKHILANANDA, Trans. & Ed.: The Upanishads TB/114

D. T. SUZUKI: On Indian Mahayana Buddhism. ° *Ed. with Intro. by Edward Conze.* TB/1403

Religion: Philosophy, Culture, and Society

NICOLAS BERDYAEV: The Destiny of Man TB/61

RUDOLF BULTMANN: History and Eschatology: *The Presence of Eternity* ° TB/91

RUDOLF BULTMANN AND FIVE CRITICS: Kerygma and Myth: *A Theological Debate* TB/80

RUDOLF BULTMANN and KARL KUNDSIN: Form Criticism: *Two Essays on New Testament Research. Trans. by F. C. Grant* TB/96

WILLIAM A. CLEBSCH & CHARLES R. JAEKLE: Pastoral Care in Historical Perspective: *An Essay with Exhibits* TB/148

FREDERICK FERRE: Language, Logic and God. *New Preface by the Author* TB/1407

LUDWIG FEUERBACH: The Essence of Christianity. § *Introduction by Karl Barth. Foreword by H. Richard Niebuhr* TB/11

C. C. GILLISPIE: Genesis and Geology: *The Decades before Darwin* § TB/51

ADOLF HARNACK: What Is Christianity? § *Introduction by Rudolf Bultmann* TB/17

KYLE HASELDEN: The Racial Problem in Christian Perspective TB/116

MARTIN HEIDEGGER: Discourse on Thinking. *Translated with a Preface by John M. Anderson and E. Hans Freund. Introduction by John M. Anderson* TB/1459

IMMANUEL KANT: Religion Within the Limits of Reason Alone. § *Introduction by Theodore M. Greene and John Silber* TB/FG

WALTER KAUFMANN, Ed.: Religion from Tolstoy to Camus: *Basic Writings on Religious Truth and Morals. Enlarged Edition* TB/123

JOHN MACQUARRIE: An Existentialist Theology: *A Comparison of Heidegger and Bultmann. ° Foreword by Rudolf Bultmann* TB/125

H. RICHARD NIERUHR: Christ and Culture TB/3

H. RICHARD NIEBUHR: The Kingdom of God in America TB/49

ANDERS NYGREN: Agape and Eros. *Translated by Philip S. Watson* ° TB/1430

JOHN H. RANDALL, JR.: The Meaning of Religion for Man. *Revised with New Intro. by the Author* TB/1379

WALTER RAUSCHENBUSCHS Christianity and the Social Crisis. ‡ *Edited by Robert D. Cross* TB/3059

JOACHIM WACH: Understanding and Believing. *Ed. with Intro. by Joseph M. Kitagawa* TB/1399

Science and Mathematics

JOHN TYLER BONNER: The Ideas of Biology. Σ *Illus.* TB/570

W. E. LE GROS CLARK: The Antecedents of Man: *An Introduction to the Evolution of the Primates. ° Illus.* TB/559

ROBERT E. COKER: Streams, Lakes, Ponds. *Illus.* TB/586

ROBERT E. COKER: This Great and Wide Sea: *An Introduction to Oceanography and Marine Biology. Illus.* TB/551

W. H. DOWDESWELL: Animal Ecology. 61 *illus.* TB/543

C. V. DURELL: Readable Relativity. *Foreword by Freeman J. Dyson* TB/530

GEORGE GAMOW: Biography of Physics. Σ *Illus.* TB/567

F. K. HARE: The Restless Atmosphere TB/560

S. KORNER: The Philosophy of Mathematics: *An Introduction* TB/547

J. R. PIERCE: Symbols, Signals and Noise: *The Nature and Process of Communication* Σ TB/574

WILLARD VAN ORMAN QUINE: Mathematical Logic TB/558

Science: History

MARIE BOAS: The Scientific Renaissance, 1450-1630 ° TB/583

W. DAMPIER, Ed.: Readings in the Literature of Science. *Illus.* TB/512

STEPHEN TOULMIN & JUNE GOODFIELD: The Architecture of Matter: *The Physics, Chemistry and Physiology of Matter, Both Animate and Inanimate, as it has Evolved since the Beginnings of Science* TB/584

STEPHEN TOULMIN & JUNE GOODFIELD: The Discovery of Time TB/585

STEPHEN TOULMIN & JUNE GOODFIELD: The Fabric of the Heavens: *The Development of Astronomy and Dynamics* TB/579

Science: Philosophy

J. M. BOCHENSKI: The Methods of Contemporary Thought. *Tr. by Peter Caws* TB/1377

J. BRONOWSKI: Science and Human Values. *Revised and Enlarged. Illus.* TB/505

WERNER HEISENBERG: Physics and Philosophy: *The Revolution in Modern Science. Introduction by F. S. C. Northrop* TB/549

KARL R. POPPER: Conjectures and Refutations: *The Growth of Scientific Knowledge* TB/1376

KARL R. POPPER: The Logic of Scientific Discovery TB/576

STEPHEN TOULMIN: Foresight and Understanding: *An Enquiry into the Aims of Science. Foreword by Jacques Barzun* TB/564

STEPHEN TOULMIN: The Philosophy of Science: *An Introduction* TB/513

Sociology and Anthropology

REINHARD BENDIX: Work and Authority in Industry: *Ideologies of Management in the Course of Industrialization* TB/3035

BERNARD BERELSON, Ed., The Behavioral Sciences Today TB/1127

JOSEPH B. CASAGRANDE, Ed.: In the Company of Man: *Twenty Portraits of Anthropological Informants. Illus.* TB/3047

KENNETH B. CLARK: Dark Ghetto: *Dilemmas of Social Power. Foreword by Gunnar Myrdal* TB/1317

KENNETH CLARK & JEANNETTE HOPKINS: A Relevant War Against Poverty: *A Study of Community Action Programs and Observable Social Change* TB/1480

W. E. LE GROS CLARK: The Antecedents of Man: *An Introduction to the Evolution of the Primates. ° Illus.* TB/559

LEWIS COSER, Ed.: Political Sociology TB/1293

ROSE L. COSER, Ed.: Life Cycle and Achievement in America ** TB/1434

ALLISON DAVIS & JOHN DOLLARD: Children of Bondage: *The Personality Development of Negro Youth in the Urban South* ‖ TB/3049

ST. CLAIR DRAKE & HORACE R. CAYTON: Black Metropolis: *A Study of Negro Life in a Northern City. Introduction by Everett C. Hughes. Tables, maps, charts, and graphs* Vol. I TB/1086; Vol. II TB/1087

PETER E. DRUCKER: The New Society: *The Anatomy of Industrial Order* TB/1082

CORA DU BOIS: The People of Alor. *With a Preface by the Author* Vol. I *Illus.* TB/1042; Vol. II TB/1043

EMILE DURKHEIM et al.: Essays on Sociology and Philosophy: *with Appraisals of Durkheim's Life and Thought.* ‖ *Edited by Kurt H. Wolff* TB/1151

LEON FESTINGER, HENRY W. RIECKEN, STANLEY SCHACHTER: When Prophecy Fails: *A Social and Psychological Study of a Modern Group that Predicted the Destruction of the World* ‖ TB/1132

is bo